STATE-OWNED ENTITIES AND HUMAN RIGHTS

This monograph focuses on the human rights challenges that are associated with the involvement of States in economic activities and on the role that international law has to play in addressing and understanding some of those challenges. State-owned entities are looked at through the lens of several topics of international law that have been found to hold particular relevance in this context, such as the concept of legal personality in international law, the process of normativity in international law, State immunity and State responsibility. The monograph shows how State-owned entities have had a significant role in shaping the evolution of international law and how, in turn, international law is currently shaping the evolution of State-owned entities. By focusing on State-owned or State-controlled business entities, rather than private corporations, the monograph aims to offer an alternative perspective on the challenges associated with corporations and human rights.

Mihaela Maria Barnes earned her PhD in International Law from the Graduate Institute of International and Development Studies, Geneva. She also holds an LLM in International and European Law (specializing in International Trade and Investment Law) from the University of Amsterdam as well as undergraduate degrees, legal qualifications and experience in both common law and civil law. Dr Barnes is currently a visiting fellow at the Lauterpacht Centre for International Law, University of Cambridge, and a member of the Coordinating Committee of the European Society of International Law Interest Group on Business and Human Rights. She has published extensively in peer-reviewed journals on various topics of international law.

State-Owned Entities and Human Rights

THE ROLE OF INTERNATIONAL LAW

MIHAELA MARIA BARNES
Lauterpacht Centre for International Law

CAMBRIDGE
UNIVERSITY PRESS

CAMBRIDGE
UNIVERSITY PRESS

University Printing House, Cambridge CB2 8BS, United Kingdom

One Liberty Plaza, 20th Floor, New York, NY 10006, USA

477 Williamstown Road, Port Melbourne, VIC 3207, Australia

314–321, 3rd Floor, Plot 3, Splendor Forum, Jasola District Centre, New Delhi – 110025, India

103 Penang Road, #05–06/07, Visioncrest Commercial, Singapore 238467

Cambridge University Press is part of the University of Cambridge.

It furthers the University's mission by disseminating knowledge in the pursuit of
education, learning, and research at the highest international levels of excellence.

www.cambridge.org
Information on this title: www.cambridge.org/9781108832878
DOI: 10.1017/9781108966245

© Mihaela Maria Barnes 2022

First published 2022

A catalogue record for this publication is available from the British Library.

Library of Congress Cataloging-in-Publication Data
NAMES: Barnes, Mihaela Maria, 1981- author.
TITLE: State-owned entities and human rights : the role of international law / Mihaela Maria
    Barnes, Lauterpacht Centre for International Law.
DESCRIPTION: Cambridge, United Kingdom ; New York, NY : Cambridge University Press, 2021. |
    Based on author's thesis (doctoral - Graduate Institute of International and Development
    Studies (Geneva, Switzerland), 2014) issued under title: State-owned entities in international
    law. | Includes bibliographical references and index.
IDENTIFIERS: LCCN 2021027028 (print) | LCCN 2021027029 (ebook) | ISBN 9781108832878
    (Hardback) | ISBN 9781108965859 (paperback) | ISBN 9781108966245 (epub)
SUBJECTS: LCSH: Government business enterprises–Law and legislation. | Liability for human
    rights violations. | Government liability (International law) | International law and human rights.
CLASSIFICATION: LCC K1366 .B37 2021 (print) | LCC K1366 (ebook) | DDC 346/.067–dc23
LC record available at https://lccn.loc.gov/2021027028
LC ebook record available at https://lccn.loc.gov/2021027029

ISBN 978-1-108-83287-8 Hardback

To my family

Contents

Figures

Foreword

The role of corporations and their status has received much attention in international law in recent years. The focus has been on transnational private corporations and on ways of holding them accountable for human rights abuses. By contrast, Dr Mihaela Barnes' book examines the role of *state-owned* entities (SOEs) in international law and, in particular, whether international law provides any safeguards against human rights abuses that SOEs commit. Her book successfully investigates how international law regulates State ownership and addresses the limitations and opportunities inherent in existing systems of regulation. It is published at a time when the role of SOEs in international affairs is growing. As the activities of States have internationalised, SOEs have become a vehicle to further State objectives abroad. As Dr Barnes points out, such activities of SOEs abroad go hand in hand with serious human rights challenges that have largely remained unaddressed thus far.

Dr Barnes argues that SOEs constitute sui generis participants in international law and addresses corporations from a different perspective than most existing scholarship. Treating SOEs as their own category in international law would enable stakeholders to more directly address the accountability of SOEs for human rights violations and to close the accountability gap. Dr Barnes convincingly argues that international law does not pose any obstacles to such accountability. Her approach could lead to the acceptance that SOEs bear a duty rather than a mere responsibility to respect human rights. Given their status as sui generis participants in international law, Dr Barnes contends that states have more onerous obligations under the 'protect, respect, fulfill' human rights framework in respect of SOEs, compared to privately owned enterprises. Given these obligations, and because of the close connection between a State and their SOEs (a connection that does not usually exist for *privately owned* enterprises [POEs]), the approach to regulating SOEs should differ from that used for POEs.

According to Dr Barnes, 'soft law' regimes, such as the United Nations Guiding Principles on Business and Human Rights, provide opportunities for the effective regulation of SOEs from a human rights perspective. These 'soft law' regulatory frameworks could influence State practice and, in some cases, have already done so. In turn, this could lead to the emergence of new customary norms that could become applicable to States and/or SOEs.

Dr Barnes also carefully analyses existing, legally binding provisions in international law, which may, at first sight, pose significant obstacles to holding SOEs accountable for human rights abuses. She examines the rules on State immunity and State responsibility. With regard to State immunity, Dr Barnes argues that the engagement of SOEs in commercial activities at the international level has led to significant changes in the applicability of State immunity and that State practice can develop to include a human rights exception to immunity. Concerning State responsibility, Dr Barnes acknowledges that the high thresholds for attribution may make a large proportion of the conduct of SOEs unattributable to States. However, this does not rule out that a *lex specialis* might emerge to better regulate the conduct of SOEs. A more relaxed approach with respect to the attribution rules may also facilitate attribution. Nevertheless, Dr Barnes also sees due diligence as a viable alternative to attribution of SOE conduct to the State. The concept of due diligence may enable State accountability if States have done too little to ensure that the entities they own or control do not violate human rights.

Overall, Dr Barnes' book is a highly relevant and important addition to the literature on corporations and human rights, given the growing participation of SOEs in international affairs. By focusing on SOEs, Dr Barnes not only manages to provide the reader with a thorough and detailed analysis of the relevance of international law to the conduct of SOEs; she also offers valuable solutions for how existing international law can be applied to address major human rights abuses by SOEs, as well as for how 'soft law' may develop into an important tool to address these challenges. Her book provides an optimistic outlook on the regulation of SOEs through international law, as well as a much-needed assessment of how existing rules can help address human rights abuses by SOEs.

Michael Waibel
University of Vienna

Acknowledgements

This book is a revised and updated version of a doctoral dissertation that I submitted at the Graduate Institute of International and Development Studies in October 2018. I would like to thank my doctoral supervisor, Professor Zachary Douglas QC, for his guidance and support on this journey. I am also extremely grateful for the support of my second supervisor, Professor Thomas Schultz, who provided encouragement and pointed me to new directions. I owe a debt of gratitude to my external examiner Professor Michael Waibel, whose many suggestions for improvement can now be found throughout the book and who kindly agreed to write the foreword to this book.

I would also like to thank the two anonymous reviewers at Cambridge University Press, whose helpful comments and suggestions have significantly improved the final version of this book. Over time, I have benefitted from discussions and collaboration with many institutions and colleagues, but I would like to particularly thank Professor Surya Deva and Dr Mara Tignino for their encouragement. I thank both Dr Jim Thomson and Patrick Thaung for taking an interest in the development of my career and for their guidance over the years. I also thank my colleagues at the Graduate Institute for their friendship. I am also thankful to Xuexia Liao and Gor Movsisyan, my colleagues at the Graduate Institute, for their friendship. At the Lauterpacht Centre for International Law, University of Cambridge, where I was a visiting fellow when I finished this book, I am thankful to the director of the Centre, Professor Eyal Benvenisti for providing an enriching academic environment during my stay. Anita Rutherford, Vanessa Bystry and Karen Fachechi made sure that everything ran smoothly during my stay in Cambridge. Professor Nick Gay offered my family hospitality on many occasions and made our stay in Cambridge memorable. At Cambridge University Press, Tom Randall, Laura Blake and Neena Maheen have been a pleasure to work with and have provided much needed guidance at every step.

My family has also been supportive throughout and I am particularly grateful to my mother, Armiana, for all her help. Last but not least, this book would have never come into being without the support provided by my husband Julian. Over the past six years, life has brought, as it does, many ups and downs, but the happiest and most memorable occasion has been the birth of our daughter in 2019. Cecilia's arrival has not only put it all into perspective but has also provided us with some of the happiest moments of our lives so far.

The book reflects developments to December 2020. Any errors and omissions remain my responsibility.

Table of Cases

Table of Treaties

Table of Statutes and Statutory Instruments

Abbreviations

BIT	bilateral investment treaty
BHR	business and human rights
CSR	corporate social responsibility
ECA	export credit agency
ECHR	European Court of Human Rights
ECJ	European Court of Justice
EConHR	European Convention on Human Rights
EITI	Extractive Industries Transparency Initiative
EU	European Union
FDI	foreign direct investment
IACHR	Inter-American Court on Human Rights
ICCPR	International Covenant on Civil and Political Rights
ICESCR	International Covenant on Economic, Social and Cultural Rights
ICJ	International Court of Justice
ILO	International Labour Organisation
MNC	multinational corporation
MNE	multinational enterprise
NAP	National Action Plan on Business and Human Rights
NGO	non-governmental organisation
NOC	national oil company
OECD	Organisation for Economic Co-operation and Development
POE	privately owned entity
SASAC	State-owned Assets Supervision and Administration Commission of the State Council, the People's Republic of China
SO-MNE	State-owned multinational enterprise
SOE	State-owned entity

SWF	sovereign wealth fund
TNC	transnational corporation
UDHR	Universal Declaration of Human Rights
UK	United Kingdom of Great Britain and Northern Ireland
UN	United Nations
UNCTAD	United Nations Conference on Trade and Development
UNGPs	United Nations Guiding Principles on Business and Human Rights
US	United States of America
WTO	World Trade Organisation

1

Introduction to the Human Rights Dimension of State Corporate Ownership

1.1 INTRODUCTION AND CHAPTER OUTLINE

International law has provided frameworks for the development of the legal architecture of corporations since the late-nineteenth century.[1] International law has also equipped scholars with the vocabulary and concepts necessary to ask questions such as the following: Are corporations similar to States, individuals or to other types of institutions?[2] What kind of rights, privileges and responsibilities do those entities have?[3] Can corporations be 'subjects' of international law?[4] During the past two decades, the focus in the literature has been on providing answers to some of these questions.[5] While the Bhopal,

[1] Doreen Lustig, *Veiled Power: International Law and the Private Corporation, 1886–1981* (Oxford University Press 2020) 3. (Lustig argues that while corporations 'began to feature as a human rights concern and potential subjects of international legal responsibility only towards the end of the twentieth century', the reality is that it was 'international legal doctrines, practices, and institutions that were central to international law-making' and which ultimately 'constituted a facilitative legal order that was pivotal to the operation and flourishing of private business corporations'.).

[2] Fleur Johns, 'Theorizing the Corporation in International Law' in Anne Orford and Florian Hoffmann (eds), *The Oxford Handbook of the Theory of International Law* (Oxford University Press 2016).

[3] James Gathii and Sergio Puig, 'Introduction to the Symposium on Investor Responsibility: The Next Frontier in International Investment Law' (2019) 113 AJIL Unbound 1; Steven R Ratner, 'Corporations and Human Rights: A Theory of Legal Responsibility' (2001) 111 Yale L.J. 443; Jennifer A Zerk, *Multinationals and Corporate Social Responsibility: Limitations and Opportunities in International Law* (1st pbk. edn, Cambridge University Press 2011).

[4] José E Alvarez, 'Are Corporations "Subjects" of International Law?' (2011) 9 Santa Clara J. Int'l L. 1.

[5] Zerk (n 3); Surya Deva and David Bilchitz (eds), *Human Rights Obligations of Business: Beyond the Corporate Responsibility to Respect?* (Cambridge University Press 2013); Nadia Bernaz, *Business and Human Rights: History, Law and Policy: Bridging the Accountability Gap* (Routlege 2017); Andrew Clapham, *Human Rights Obligations of Non-State Actors* (Oxford University Press 2006) 195–266; Lee McConnell, *Extracting Accountability from Non-State*

Niger Delta and Rana Plaza disasters are recent and well-known examples of human rights tragedies that directly involved corporations, the development of ideologies, which sought to make business act in a responsible manner, can be traced back to the abolitionist movement of the Atlantic slave trade, which was later followed by numerous attempts to develop international labour law and also by the criminal prosecution of the German industrialists that supported the Nazis during World War II.[6] Most of the literature in this area, however, has largely focused on the private corporation, to the extent that business entities that are owned or controlled by States are largely absent from this narrative.[7] This may be due to the fact that the private corporation has been the main vehicle that has made globalisation possible,[8] with State-owned or controlled entities (SOEs) joining in the current episode of globalisation only relatively recently. Although the past twenty years or so is not the first time when SOEs have conducted economic activities outside of the borders of their home State – since it was ultimately their activities on the international plane in the 1950s and 1960s that led to fundamental changes in international law, as evidenced by the shift from the absolute to the restrictive doctrine of

---

Actors in International Law: Assessing the Scope for Direct Regulation (Taylor & Francis 2016); Adam McBeth, *International Economic Actors and Human Rights* (Routledge 2009); Lene Bomann-Larsen and Oddny Wiggen, *Responsibility in World Business: Managing Harmful Side-Effects of Corporate Activity* (United Nations University Press 2004); Peter T Muchlinski, *Multinational Enterprises and the Law* (2nd edn, Oxford University Press 2007); Philip Alston (ed), *Non-State Actors and Human Rights* (Oxford University Press 2005).

6   Lustig (n 1); Bernaz (n 5) 17–79.

7   By way of exception, see Larry Catá Backer, 'The Human Rights Obligations of State-Owned Enterprises (SOEs): Emerging Conceptual Structures and Principles in National and International Law and Policy' (2017) 50 Vand. J. Transnat'l L. 827; Mikko Rajavuori, 'State Ownership and the United Nations Business and Human Rights Agenda: Three Instruments, Three Narratives' (2016) 23 Indiana J. Glob. Leg. Stud. 665; M Rajavuori, 'How Should States Own? Heinisch v. Germany and the Emergence of Human Rights-Sensitive State Ownership Function' (2015) 26 Eur. J. Int. Law 727; Mikko Rajavuori, 'Governing the Good State Shareholder: The Case of the OECD Guidelines on Corporate Governance of State-Owned Enterprises' (2018) 29 Eur. Bus. Law Rev. 103; Mihaela M Barnes, 'The United Nations Guiding Principles on Business and Human Rights, the State Duty to Protect Human Rights and the State-Business Nexus' (2018) 15 Brazilian J. Int. Law 42; Ma Xili, 'Advancing Direct Corporate Accountability in International Human Rights Law: The Role of State-Owned Enterprises' (2019) 14 Frontiers of Law in China 43.

8   Grazia Ietto-Gillies, 'The Role of Transnational Corporations in the Globalisation Process' in Jonathan Michie (ed), *The Handbook of Globalisation, Second Edition* (Edward Elgar 2011) 173; Deepak Nayyar, 'Globalisation, History and Development: A Tale of Two Centuries' (2006) 30 Camb. J. Econ. 137; Giovanni Federico and Antonio Tena-Junguito, 'A Tale of Two Globalizations: Gains from Trade and Openness 1800–2010' (2017) 153 Rev. World Econ. 601.

immunity[9] – it is unlikely that SOEs have held more power and influence than they do now, having recently become some of the largest and most important players in the world economy.[10] As such, this monograph focuses on the human rights challenges that are associated with the involvement of States in economic activities and on the role that international law has to play in understanding and addressing some of those challenges. By focusing on a different type of actor, the State-owned or State-controlled business entity, as opposed to the private corporation, the monograph aims to offer not only an alternative perspective on the issue of corporations and human rights, but it also demonstrates that as a result of the link that exists between States and the entities that they own or control, international law has a fundamental role to play in this context. To this end, SOEs are looked at through the lens of several topics of international law that have been found to hold particular relevance in this context such as legal personality, the process of normativity in international law, State immunity and State responsibility. Consequently, at its broadest, the monograph shows how SOEs have significantly shaped the evolution of international law in certain cases and how, in turn, international law is currently shaping the evolution of SOEs, since the direction of influence goes both ways. Inasmuch as this monograph seeks to provide answers to some of the challenging questions associated with State corporate ownership and human rights, it is hoped that it will prompt further interest, debate and research in this area.

For the purposes of carrying on economic activities, States create entities that are specifically designed for this end. Some of those entities are designed to carry on economic activities directly, as is the case with State-owned enterprises, others are designed solely for the purposes of investing as sovereign wealth funds do and yet others offer financial assistance to private business in the form of export insurance. The ultimate type, legal form, structure and purpose of those entities vary from State to State, but their common feature is that they are owned by a State. Consequently, 'State corporate ownership' or

---

[9] Wolfgang Friedmann, 'Changing Social Arrangements in State-Trading States and Their Effect on International Law' (1959) 24 Law & Contemp. Probs. 350; W Friedmann, 'Some Impacts of Social Organization on International Law' (1956) 50 Am. J. Int. Law 475; Wolfgang Gaston Friedmann, *The Changing Structure of International Law* (Columbia University Press 1966).

[10] International Monetary Fund, Fiscal Affairs Dept, *Fiscal Monitor, April 2020 Policies to Support People during the COVID-19 Pandemic* (International Monetary Fund 2020) 49; Mihaela Maria Barnes, 'International Investment Law and State-Owned Entities: Recurrent Key Issues and Future Directions' in Lisa E Sachs and others (eds), *2018 Yearbook of International Investment Law and Policy* (Oxford University Press 2019) 432–433.

'State ownership' is understood to mean the *public* or *government* ownership of a corporation or of any other asset. For instance, on the one hand, State-owned enterprises and national oil companies exemplify the State ownership of corporations whereby a State owns, controls and actively manages an entity which has separate legal personality and is separate from the government. On the other hand, portfolio investing, or the financing activities of sovereign wealth funds or export credit agencies show that States can also be the owners of any other assets, such as an equity share in a given corporation or in an investment fund, without the requirement for active management of that entity. Detailed definitions and further analysis of the main vehicles through which States exercise their ownership function are provided in Sections 1.3.2.1–1.3.2.5. Throughout this monograph terms such as 'soft law' and 'hard law' are used in accordance with international law legal terminology.[11] Soft law relates to international non-binding norms,[12] while hard law relates to binding norms, backed by a legal instrument anchored in either an international treaty or a municipal law. Other key terms that will be used are 'transnational corporation' (TNC), 'multinational enterprise' (MNE), 'multinational corporations' (MNC) and 'State-owned multinational enterprise' (SO-MNE). TNCs are defined as 'incorporated or unincorporated enterprises comprising parent enterprises and their foreign affiliates'.[13] A parent enterprise is defined as 'an enterprise that controls assets of other entities in countries other than its home country, usually by owning a certain equity capital stake'.[14] The terms 'multinational enterprise' (MNE) or 'multinational corporation' (MNC) are also encountered in literature where such entities are defined as 'economic agents of their home States, with no particular allegiances to the States in which they choose to invest'.[15] Acknowledging the ultimate definitional difficulties that arise in this area,[16] the terms TNC, MNE and MNC will be used interchangeably. SO-MNEs are defined as 'separate legal entities established or acquired by governments to engage in commercial

---

[11] Gregory C Shaffer and Mark A Pollack, 'Hard vs. Soft Law: Alternatives, Complements, and Antagonists in International Governance' (2010) 94 Minn. L. Rev. 706.

[12] Malcolm N Shaw, *International Law* (7th edn, Cambridge University Press 2014) 83–84. ('Soft law' is not law, that needs to be emphasised, but a document, for example, does not need to constitute a binding treaty before it can exercise an influence in international politics.').

[13] UNCTAD, 'World Investment Report 2007: Transnational Corporations, Extractive Industries and Development' (United Nations 2007) 245.

[14] UNCTAD, 'World Investment Report 2017: Investment and the Digital Economy (Methodological Note)' (2017) 3.

[15] Zerk (n 3) 9; Muchlinski (n 5) 3–7.

[16] Surya Deva, *Regulating Corporate Human Rights Violations: Humanizing Business* (1st pbk. edn, Routledge 2014) 21.

activities, including foreign direct investment operations, by way of having affiliates abroad or engaging in non-equity modes'.[17]

The monograph is composed of five chapters. Chapter 1, 'Introduction to the Human Rights Dimension of State Corporate Ownership', provides an introduction to SOEs and frames the remainder of the monograph. Given that the terminology surrounding SOEs that engage in commercial activities varies from State to State, this chapter also provides the necessary definitions and carves out the monograph's sphere of application to entities such as State-owned multinational enterprises, national oil companies, sovereign wealth funds, export credit agencies and several other types of entities that are State-owned. A short history of the State as an economic actor follows next, then the focus is turned to some of the concerns associated with State ownership (Section 1.3.1). After an analysis of the traditional concerns associated with SOEs (unfair competition, national security and resource security) (Section 1.4.1) the discussion moves on to address the human rights dimension of State corporate ownership (Section 1.4.2). Several case studies demonstrate concretely how SOEs become involved in human rights violations (Section 1.4.2.2). Section 1.5 provides an overview of human rights in international law, the most fundamental human rights instruments, a general introduction to the 'respect, protect and fulfill' framework, the nature of States' obligations to 'respect, protect and fulfill' human rights and the relationship between international law, human rights and State ownership. While the focus of the discussion in this chapter is on the human rights obligations of States, in Chapter 2 the focus shifts onto SOEs.

Chapter 2, 'State-Owned Entities as a Sui Generis 'Participant' in International Law', looks at SOEs though the lens of the concept of legal personality in international law and argues that SOEs are a sui generis type of 'participant' in international law (Section 2.2). The chapter commences with a brief introduction to the concept of legal personality in international law and the long-standing debates and remaining challenges related to the recognition of corporations as subjects of international law (Section 2.3). It further argues that SOEs are a sui generis participant in international law (Section 2.4) by virtue of the following distinguishing characteristics: first, SOEs belong to the public domain, while privately owned entities belong to the private domain (Section 2.4.2.1); second, State ownership has a different role and rationale compared to private ownership (for example, the main rationale for private

---

[17] UNCTAD, 'World Investment Report 2017: Investment and the Digital Economy' (United Nations 2017) 30.

ownership is profit maximisation, while State ownership can be justified by other non-commercial considerations such as national security, resource security, the supply of public goods, etc.) (Section 2.4.2.2); third, the public nature of SOEs can also be ascertained by looking at the nature of the property rights that are inherent in State ownership (Section 2.4.2.3); fourth, often in international *and* municipal law separate regulatory regimes are created to deal with State corporate ownership (Section 2.4.2.4). The existence of separate regulatory regimes for State ownership can be observed at both the municipal and international levels. At the municipal level, many States have laws that create special regimes for the admission of sovereign investment based on national security concerns. At the international level, there are a multitude of soft law instruments that have either been entirely designed for SOEs or have specific provisions in this regard. The various regulatory frameworks present under international economic law also underline the different nature of SOEs. Section 2.5 asks whether international law places any obstacles on the recognition of SOEs as a sui generis participant. Having answered this question in the negative, Section 2.6.2 argues that the recognition of SOEs as sui generis has two main consequences: It demonstrates the increasing heterogeneity and complexity of the notion of participation on the international plane. Furthermore, the recognition of SOEs as sui generis participants shows that international law has an inherent capacity to expand on certain well-entrenched conceptual frameworks and to adapt to current circumstances, in order to address some of the pressing challenges of the international community. By delving deeper into the close connection between the State and its SOEs, it is further argued that from the perspective of the SOE, the widely accepted responsibility to respect human rights is elevated to the level of a duty in the case of SOEs (Section 2.6.2). The overall conclusion is that that in international law one may encounter certain corporate entities, such as SOEs, which may have obligations to respect human rights rather than a mere 'responsibility' to do so. Overall, this chapter demonstrates how a change of focus – from private corporations in general to SOEs in particular – can offer new perspectives and insights into some of the long-standing debates in international law.

Chapter 3, 'State-Owned Entities and Norm Development in International Law: International, Regional and Domestic Approaches to Regulation', examines various instruments created to regulate SOEs and seeks to determine their effect on international law. To this end, selected instruments that concern the regulation of SOEs are analysed on three levels: international, regional and domestic. At the international level, the chapter analyses the United Nations Guiding Principles on Business and Human Rights (UNGPs) (Section 3.3.1), the OECD Guidelines for Multinational Enterprises (Section 3.3.2.1), the OECD Guidelines on the Corporate Governance of State-Owned Enterprises (Section 3.2.2.2), the OECD Common Approaches for Officially Supported Export Credits and Environmental and Social Due Diligence (Section 3.3.2.3), the ILO Tripartite Declaration concerning Multinational Enterprises (Section 3.3.3), the Extractive Industries Transparency Initiative (Section 3.3.5), the Sovereign Wealth Funds Generally Accepted Principles and Practices (Section 3.3.4) and the Global Compact (Section 3.3.6). It will be observed that some of those instruments are specifically designed for SOEs (the OECD Guidelines on the Corporate Governance of State-Owned Enterprises and the OECD Common Approaches for Officially Supported Export Credits), while others only have specific provisions that apply to SOEs (the UNGPs and the Extractive Industries Transparency Initiative). Some instruments do not have any specific provisions that apply to SOEs, but it has been further elaborated that they apply to SOEs in equal measure (e.g., the OECD Guidelines for Multinational Enterprises and the ILO Tripartite Declaration concerning Multinational Enterprises). At the regional level, the chapter examines what might prove to be a key regulatory opportunity for the human rights dimension of State ownership: public procurement, which is analysed mainly through the prism of the EU Public Procurement Directives (Section 3.4). The section on domestic approaches to SOE regulation briefly examines measures that have been taken by several states that address the human rights dimension of State corporate ownership (Section 3.5). Overall, the ultimate aims of this chapter are to demonstrate how State corporate ownership is regulated on several levels through a complex web of regulatory instruments and to determine the effect that the emergence of those regimes could have on international law in general (Section 3.6).

Chapter 4, 'Fundamental Change in International Law: Sovereign Immunity and State-owned Entities', addresses the unique challenges posed by the doctrine of sovereign immunity to the regulation of SOEs. Sovereign immunity is a unique challenge, because if an SOE pleads immunity, a domestic court could be barred from either adjudicating the dispute in question or from enforcing a judgment that has been obtained against an SOE. A plea of immunity could thus leave victims without a method to access justice or without an effective remedy if the judgment that has been obtained cannot be enforced. The chapter begins by outlining a short history of the concept of sovereign immunity, the types of sovereign immunity (immunity from adjudication and immunity from execution) and the evolution of this concept from absolute immunity to restricted sovereign immunity (Section 4.2). With a focus on immunity from adjudication, the chapter addresses a key issue: the differences between *acta jure gestionis* and *acta jure imperii*, as it is only for acts *jure imperii* that immunity can be claimed (Section 4.4). As such, the analysis starts by asking when and how can SOEs be deemed to form an integral part of the State (Section 4.3)? For example, on the one hand, SOEs that are created by special law or that perform public functions may be in a position to claim sovereign immunity more easily. On the other hand, SOEs that are created under general corporate law would be regarded as private entities, even when they are 100 per cent owned by the State and even when the State in question sets out their strategy for operation. In such cases, immunity would only be granted for acts *jure imperii*. Section 4.5 addresses exceptions to immunity commences by looking at some of the 'established' exceptions to immunity such as the commercial transactions exception (Section 4.5.1), the non-commercial tort exception (Section 4.5.2) and their relevance to SOEs, then continues by asking if there is a human rights exception to State immunity (Section 4.5.3). The overall purpose of this chapter is to demonstrate how the increased participation of States in economic activities, through their SOEs, has fundamentally changed the fabric of international law through a redefinition of the functions of the State and ultimately that of the concept of sovereignty itself.

Chapter 5, 'The Continued Relevance of International Law: State Responsibility and State-Owned Entities', addresses the responsibility of States for the acts and omissions of their SOEs. The starting point is an introduction to the nature and scope of State responsibility (Section 5.1.1) and to the three elements that must be satisfied for State responsibility to exist: (a) the existence of a breach (Section 5.1.2), (b) which is attributable (Section 5.2) and (c) the absence of any valid justification for non-performance. Particular emphasis will be placed on the role and process of attribution and why a State should be allowed to shield themselves from liability for the acts and omissions of an entity that it owns or controls (Section 5.2.1). The analysis starts by examining the current status of the rules of attribution in general international law as codified in Articles 4, 5 and 8 of the International Law Commission Articles on the Responsibility of States for Internationally Wrongful Acts (ILC Articles) (Sections 5.2.2–5.2.4). It will be revealed that the rules of attribution found in general international law have high thresholds for attribution, meaning that a large proportion of the conduct of SOEs could be unattributable, which could ultimately lead to an accountability void. Several solutions will be offered to address those challenges. For example, a lower threshold for attribution (such as that expressed by the concept of 'overall control' rather than 'effective control') may be required to address this challenge. The analysis looks next into how the general rules of attribution have been applied by judicial bodies, such as the ECHR in cases dealing with SOEs (Section 5.2.5). The overall conclusion is that the general rules of State responsibility have been applied by judicial bodies such as the ECHR and that at this point in time one cannot speak about a *lex specialis* regime of attribution having developed which would depart from the general rules. That is not to say that such a regime could not develop in the future. Nevertheless, even if such regimes were to develop in the future, judicial and non-judicial bodies should still have as a point of departure for their analysis the customary rules for attribution found in the ILC Articles. This approach would not only be logical, but it could also lead to increased coherence between the various fields of international law. Section 5.2 analyses the concept of due diligence, which becomes relevant when certain acts and omissions cannot be attributed to the State, because, for instance, those acts are not perpetrated by State organs, by actors that are exercising governmental authority or by those that are not under the 'effective control' of the State. In such cases, States can, nevertheless, be held responsible for a failure to act diligently, to take all the necessary measures available to prevent or punish the occurrence of a specific act. Overall, this chapter demonstrates the continued importance and relevance of the general rules of international law in addressing some of the challenges encountered when dealing with State corporate ownership and human rights. Chapter 6 concludes.

1.2 RELEVANCE

If the 1970s and 1980s witnessed the retreat of the State from the economy in much of the Western world,[18] the 1990s brought about the same trend in Eastern Europe.[19] This trend lasted until the beginning of the 2007 financial crisis, when several 'too big to fail' Western banks needed bailing out.[20] As a result of the financial crisis, the viability of capitalism as an economic system was seriously questioned,[21] and since then, State-owned entities have played a

---

[18] David Parker, *The Official History of Privatisation Vol. I: The Formative Years 1970–1987* (1st edn, Routledge 2009) 52–89, 166–189.

[19] Thomas J Hyclak and Arthur E King, 'The Privatisation Experience in Eastern Europe' (1994) 17 World Econ. 529.

[20] Larry Catá Backer, 'Sovereign Investing in Times of Crisis: Global Regulation of Sovereign Wealth Funds, State-Owned Enterprises, and the Chinese Experience' (2010) 19 Transnat'l L. & Contemp. Probs. 3; Jason Kotter and Ugur Lel, 'Friends or Foes? Target Selection Decisions of Sovereign Wealth Funds and Their Consequences' (2011) 101 J. Financ. Econ. 360.

[21] Ian Bremmer, *The End of the Free Market: Who Wins the War between States and Corporations?* (Penguin 2010).

key role in the economy of many States.[22] Sovereign wealth funds have been regarded as lenders of last resort, who, among others, played a stabilising role in the financial system.[23] SOEs have also become critical actors during the COVID-19 pandemic, being called upon to produce and provide emergency goods and services such as medical equipment or the provision of loans to small businesses.[24] SOEs are key participants in many sectors of the economy, not only nationally, but also internationally, by providing necessary funds for the development of many States' key infrastructure. Chinese investment in African infrastructure, in exchange for access to mineral resources, is another case in point,[25] while national oil companies own and control the great majority of the world energy supply.[26] Consequently, the influence that State-owned entities have from a social, political and economic point of view is unquestionable. For example, the fully State-owned Petróleos de Venezuela (PDVSA) has played a critical role in the economy of Venezuela ever since the first wave of nationalisations that took place in the oil industry starting in 1976.[27] To a certain extent, PDVSA's critical role continues to this day, since oil is Venezuela's main export and means of generating revenue. Although initially PDVSA was given a high degree of autonomy in its day-to-day operations, this practice ceased when the oil prices started to decrease; and in 1982, the central Venezuelan government removed PDVSA's corporate autonomy with regard to all production decisions in order to address concerns relating to Venezuela's overall increasing fiscal deficit.[28] The recent developments concerning the restructuring of Venezuela's sovereign debt, whereby it has been suggested that a transfer of PDVSA's assets back to the Venezuelan

---

[22] UNCTAD, 'World Investment Report 2017: Investment and the Digital Economy' (n 17) 31.
[23] Hélène Raymond, 'Sovereign Wealth Funds as Domestic Investors of Last Resort during Crises' (2010) 123 J. Int. Econ. 121.
[24] IMFBlog, 'State-Owned Enterprises in the Time of COVID-19' (IMF Blog) <https://blogs.imf .org/2020/05/07/state-owned-enterprises-in-the-time-of-covid-19/> accessed 9 December 2020; 'The COVID-19 Crisis and State Ownership in the Economy: Issues and Policy Considerations' (OECD) <https://www.oecd.org/coronavirus/policy-responses/the-covid-19-crisis-and-state-ownership-in-the-economy-issues-and-policy-considerations-ce417c46/> accessed 10 December 2020.
[25] Uche Ewelukwa Ofodile, 'Trade, Empires, and Subjects-China-Africa Trade: A New Fair Trade Arrangement, or the Third Scramble for Africa' (2008) 41 Vand. J. Transnat'l L. 505.
[26] David R Hults, Mark C Thurber and David G Victor (eds), *Oil and Governance: State-Owned Enterprises and the World Energy Supply* (Cambridge University Press 2012) 3.
[27] G Philip, 'When Oil Prices Were Low: Petroleos de Venezuela (PdVSA) and Economic Policy-Making in Venezuela since 1989' (1999) 18 Bull. Lat. Am. Res. 361; An Xun, Bao Hanrui and Zhu Xiaoyang, 'A DEA Approach to Evaluate Economical and Social Roles of NOCs' (2011) 5 Energy Procedia 763.
[28] Philip (n 27) 366.

government could be an avenue to bypass a potential government default, further show the overall importance of PDVSA in Venezuela's affairs.[29] Nevertheless, it must be emphasised that the size, role and importance of State-owned entities varies from State to State, as a recent report from the International Monetary Fund (IMF) explains:

> SOEs operate in virtually every country in the world. In some, they number in the thousands (China, Germany, Italy, Russia, Sweden, Ukraine) and are owned by national or subnational governments. SOEs owned by subnational governments, such as local bus, sewer, and water services, often outnumber SOEs owned by the central government. SOEs are among the largest corporations in some advanced economies (France, Italy, Norway) and comprise one-third or more of the largest firms in several emerging markets (China, India, Indonesia, Malaysia, Russia, Saudi Arabia, United Arab Emirates). SOEs provide goods and services in almost all sectors of the economy but are especially prevalent in the key network sectors – banking, utilities, and transportation. They also manufacture everything from shoes to locomotive engines, manage real estate, and provide phone services. In Africa and Asia, SOEs dominate power generation. SOEs accounted for more than half of all infrastructure project commitments in emerging market economies and low-income developing countries in 2017. Moreover, banking sector SOEs account for 40 percent or more of banking system assets in the BRIC economies (Brazil, Russia, India, China) and some low-income developing countries, and one-third or more in Germany and Portugal among advanced economies.[30]

1.3 THE MONOGRAPH IN CONTEXT: THE UNIVERSE OF STATE-OWNED ENTITIES

1.3.1 *A Very Short History of the State as Economic Actor*

The Middle Ages has been pinpointed as the time when State trading was born. For example, it has been said that the Venetian city State was nothing more than a 'company of merchants of whom the Doge was chief'.[31] For the following centuries, trade was kept mainly in private hands, and merchants organised themselves into bodies like the Hanseatic League and joint stock

---

[29] Adam Lerrick, 'Venezuela's Debt: Untying the PDVSA Knot' (2018) 13 Cap. Mark. Law J. 131.
[30] International Monetary Fund, Fiscal Affairs Dept (n 10) 48. (Footnotes and figures omitted).
[31] Huntly McDonald Sinclair, *The Principles of International Trade* (The Macmillan Company 1932) 13.

companies.[32] The trade conducted by the chartered companies (such as the Muscovy Company, the East and West India Companies, Dutch East and West India Companies) was, however, in reality, a partnership between government and merchants, with the result of this partnership being called a 'strange absurdity', that is, 'a Company-State and a merchant empire',[33] and it is worthy of note that some of the great trading companies, such as the East India Company, were even endowed with treaty-making powers.[34] Wilhelm Grewe argues that the intermediate position of the great trading companies as 'semi-State'/'semi-private'

> made it possible to avoid a complete transfer of the overseas colonial sphere of the European concept of State, with all of its far-reaching legal consequences and associated concepts of sovereignty, nation-State, State territory and State borders. The intermediate position of the trading companies was the main reason that the legal ambiguity 'beyond the line' was not transformed directly into a situation where the strict rules of a law of nations applied, which was in conformity with the limited geographic extension and narrow political circumstances of Europe. Since it was not the States themselves which were confronting each other, but rather corporations, which were regarded as or at least pretended to be more or less self-reliant, a separate, flexible system of colonial law of nations developed.[35]

Later on, as the industrial revolution advanced, socialism became an entrenched ideology in some parts of the world; and by the end of the nineteenth century and the beginning of the twentieth century, the idea that trade could be conducted by the State as a producer, buyer and seller gained traction.[36] State interference in the economy, as we know it today, was born and the engagement in business was determined to a large extent by political ideology.[37] At the risk of overgeneralisation, the best way of explaining the

---

[32] John N Hazard, 'State Trading in History and Theory' (1959) 24 Law & Contemp. Probs. 243, 244.

[33] Philip J Stern, *The Company-State: Corporate Sovereignty and the Early Modern Foundations of the British Empire in India* (Oxford University Press 2012) 3.

[34] Michael Mulligan, 'East India Company: Non-State Actor as Treaty-Maker' in James Summers and Alex Gough (eds), *Non-State Actors and International Obligations* (Brill Nijhoff 2018) 51; Antony Anghie, *Imperialism, Sovereignty, and the Making of International Law* (1st pbk. edn, Cambridge University Press 2007) 84–85; *Nabob of The Carnatic v East India Company* (England and Wales, [1793] EngR 1368).

[35] Wilhelm G Grewe, *The Epochs of International Law* (Walter de Gruyter 2013) 298.

[36] Hazard (n 32) 244; Pier Angelo Toninelli, 'The Rise and Fall of Public Enterprise: The Framework' in Pier Angelo Toninelli (ed), *The Rise and Fall of State-Owned Enterprise in the Western World* (Cambridge University Press 2000) 11–12.

[37] David S Caudill, 'Breaking Out of the Capitalist Paradigm: The Significance of Ideology in Determining the Sovereign Immunity of Soviet and Eastern-Bloc Commercial Entities' (1979) 2 Houst. J. Int. Law 425; Friedmann, 'Changing Social Arrangements in State-Trading States

fundamental role of ideology[38] in this area is to compare the role of the State in economic systems that are capitalist with those that are considered socialist or communist. For instance, in Western styles of democracy and in capitalist societies, companies, ultimately answerable to their shareholders, conduct business through the private sector. Those business decisions are not directed or scrutinised by the State. Examples are countries such as the United States of America, the United Kingdom, Australia, etc. The business agenda in capitalist economies is first and foremost dictated by profit maximisation. In communist and socialist economies, the most important businesses are owned and controlled principally *by* the State *for the benefit* of the State. This is still the case in certain economies, principally in sectors of the economy that are considered 'sensitive', such as natural resources, defence and the technology sector. In China, the 'socialist market economy' and State-owned entities are given constitutional protection,[39] while other countries with a communist past make it extremely difficult for foreign investors to invest in certain sectors. The recent changes made by Russia to its Strategic Investment Law in 2017 is another example in this context. According to the latest changes in this law, States, international organisations, 'offshore companies', the companies controlled through 'offshore companies' and Russian citizens with dual nationality are banned from owning 'strategic companies', which include, among others, all companies related to natural resources, defence, media or other government monopolies.[40] Inasmuch as ideology has an important role to play in this area, it is important to recall that major changes in political and institutional environments as well as technological advances and changes in

and Their Effect on International Law' (n 9); Alvaro Cuervo-Cazurra, 'State-Owned Multinationals: An Introduction' in Cuervo-Cazurra (ed), *State-Owned Multinationals: Governments in Global Business* (Palgrave Macmillan 2018) 4; Yair Aharoni, 'The Evolution of State-Owned Multinational Enterprise Theory' in Alvaro Cuervo-Cazurra (ed), *State-Owned Multinationals: Governments in Global Business* (Palgrave Macmillan 2018) 15, 17, 24; Klaus E Meyer, Yuan Ding and Hua Zhang, 'Overcoming Distrust: How State-Owned Enterprises Adapt Their Foreign Entries to Institutional Pressures Abroad' in Alvaro Cuervo-Cazurra (ed), *State-Owned Multinationals: Governments in Global Business* (Palgrave Macmillan 2018) 219, 236; Aldo Musacchio and Sergio G Lazzarini, 'State-Owned Enterprises as Multinationals: Theory and Research Directions' in Alvaro Cuervo-Cazurra (ed), *State-Owned Multinationals: Governments in Global Business* (Palgrave Macmillan 2018) 259, 266, 270.

[38] Muchlinski (n 5) 90–104.
[39] Constitution of the People's Republic of China 1982. Articles 6 and 7.
[40] Russian Federation, Federal Law on Amendments to Article 5 of the Federal Law on Privatisation of State and Municipal Property and to the Federal Law on Procedures for Foreign Investment in Business Entities of Strategic Importance for National Defence and State Security 2017.

the economic development of States in general have also all had a 'profound effect on the policies of governments' and 'on the strategies and behaviors' of SOEs.[41] As Aharoni points out, 'it is very dangerous to be held captive by theories that were true in different times, different cultures, or different political regimes',[42] so it must be emphasised that SOEs are present in one form or another in virtually all States, even in capitalist systems,[43] the only thing that differs from State to State is the preponderance and size of SOEs in the economy of that particular State.

Out of necessity, during the two World Wars and in the aftermath of the 1929 depression, in Europe in particular, the role of the State was further entrenched as a dominant economic player, including in those countries that have adopted market liberalism as an economic ideology.[44] For example, in the United Kingdom, in order to cope with the 'war effort', strategic industries such as electricity, gas and parts of the transportation system, coal mining and iron and steel production were nationalised during the war period.[45] After the Second World War, significant privatisation programmes took place in Europe in the 1950s, 1980s and early 1990s, and in formerly communist countries, after the fall of the Berlin Wall in 1989.[46] Winston Churchill, who privatised British Steel, initially started this process in the United

---

[41] Aharoni (n 37) 9.

[42] ibid.

[43] Louis Galambos, 'State-Owned Enterprises in a Hostile Environment: The U.S. Experience' in Pier Angelo Toninelli (ed), *The Rise and Fall of State-Owned Enterprise in the Western World* (Cambridge University Press 2000).

[44] Hazard (n 31) 244–255; Pier Angelo Toninelli, 'The Rise and Fall of Public Enterprise: The Framework' in Pier Angelo Toninelli (ed), The Rise and Fall of State-Owned Enterprise in the Western World (Cambridge University Press 2000) 3. ('A comprehensive survey of SOE history has to take into consideration changes in the social, economic, and political environments that have profoundly influenced the course of the twentieth century. The move to autarkic and state-controlled policies in many Southern and Central European countries, the diffusion of collectivism and socialism in Eastern European countries, and the progressive growth of mixed economies in Western European countries all should be considered reactions – albeit profoundly different ones – to the same issue: the deep crisis that struck liberal capitalism in the period between the two world wars.').

[45] Parker (n 18) 5–6; Robert Millward and Pier Angelo Toninelli, 'State Enterprise in Britain in the Twentieth Century', in Pier Angelo Toninelli (ed), *The Rise and Fall of State-Owned Enterprise in the Western World* (Cambridge University Press 2000).

[46] Kalman Mizsei, 'Privatisation in Eastern Europe: A Comparative Study of Poland and Hungary' (1992) 44 Sov. Stud. 283; Nicola Bellini, 'The Decline of State-Owned Enterprise and the New Foundations of the State – Industry Relationship' in Pier Angelo Toninelli (ed), *The Rise and Fall of State-Owned Enterprise in the Western World* (Cambridge University Press 2000).

Kingdom[47] and Margaret Thatcher continued this process in the 1980s up until 1990.[48] In West Germany, the sale of the majority stake in Volkswagen to the general public was another important step,[49] and Latin America also followed this trend in the 1980s and 1990s.[50] Thus, in some States, such as, among others, Spain,[51] France,[52] Italy,[53] Austria[54] and the Netherlands,[55] SOEs went through a period of decline, which was largely due to 'increasing economic, financial and managerial difficulties' faced by States in the administration of their businesses.[56] Nevertheless, despite the decline of public enterprises in the West, in some other parts of the world, State-owned enterprises and State ownership continued to flourish. For instance, in India and Africa, State ownership was one of the main forms of economic organisation, through which development policies such as the doctrine of 'import-substitution industrialisation'[57] were implemented. However, the creation of the World Trade Organisation (WTO) in 1995, which resulted in the imposition of severe restrictions on subsidisation, and the privatisations that followed in ex-communist countries after the fall of the Berlin Wall, further diminished the importance of public enterprises across the world. During this period, the management and corporate governance of surviving State-owned entities was

---

[47] Martin Chick, 'Review of the First Privatisation: The Politicians, the City, and the Denationalisation of Steel' (1989) 63 Bus. Hist. Rev. 986.

[48] Aharoni (n 37) 17.

[49] Ulrich Wegenroth, 'The Rise and Fall of State-Owned Enterprise in Germany' in Pier Angelo Toninelli (ed), *The Rise and Fall of State-Owned Enterprise in the Western World* (Cambridge University Press 2000).

[50] Gérard Roland, *Privatization: Successes and Failures* (Columbia University Press 2013).

[51] Albert Carreras, Xavier Tafunell and Eugenio Torres, 'The Rise and Decline of Spanish State-Owned Firms' in Pier Angelo Toninelli (ed), *The Rise and Fall of State-Owned Enterprise in the Western World* (Cambridge University Press 2000).

[52] Emmanuel Chadeau, 'The Rise and Decline of State-Owned Industry in Twentieth-Century France' in Pier Angelo Toninelli (ed), *The Rise and Fall of State-Owned Enterprise in the Western World* (Cambridge University Press 2000).

[53] Franco Amatori, 'Beyond State and Market: Italy's Futile Search for a Third Way' in Pier Angelo Toninelli (ed), *The Rise and Fall of State-Owned Enterprise in the Western World* (Cambridge University Press 2000).

[54] Dieter Stiefel, 'Fifty Years of State-Owned Industry in Austria, 1946–1996' in Pier Angelo Toninelli (ed), *The Rise and Fall of State-Owned Enterprise in the Western World* (Cambridge University Press 2000).

[55] M Davids and Jan L Van Zanden, 'A Reluctant State and Its Enterprises: State-Owned Enterprises in the Netherlands in the "Long" Twentieth Century' in Pier Angelo Toninelli (ed), *The Rise and Fall of State-Owned Enterprise in the Western World* (Cambridge University Press 2000).

[56] Toninelli, 'The Rise and Fall of Public Enterprise: The Framework' (n 36) 3.

[57] The 'import-substitution industrialisation' doctrine purported the need to create trade barriers, which allowed the protection of infant industrial enterprises that were mainly State-owned.

also fundamentally transformed in order to increase transparency and competitivity. In some other parts of the world, such as China, State ownership has continued to remain of fundamental importance during this period, although this form of economic organisation witnessed transformation there as well. An example of particular importance in the evolution of State ownership, is the official 'Going Out Policy' adopted by the Chinese government in 1999.[58] According to this policy, all Chinese firms, regardless of their ownership, are encouraged to invest overseas and to become more competitive, and it has been estimated that around 80 per cent of all Chinese outbound direct investment has been funded through State-owned entities.[59] Consequently, State-owned firms were not only vehicles that were usually encountered inside a country, they started to become international actors again, in a similar fashion to privately owned transnational corporations. The rise of sovereign wealth funds during the 1990s and 2000s further shows that in other parts of the world, such as the Gulf States, for instance, State capitalism was not only surviving, but its importance was steadily increasing. The increasing importance of sovereign wealth funds has been attributed to two forces: the massive accumulation, in many States, of foreign official reserves as a precautionary measure that was taken in the follow-up of the East Asian financial crisis and the increase in oil prices from $10 per barrel in 1998 to $148 per barrel in 2008.[60] As a result of the increase in foreign official reserves and the additional currency generated through the sale of oil, States created special purpose vehicles to manage this additional wealth, which became known as sovereign wealth funds. Consequently, what can be observed from the historical narrative of State ownership is that, for a period of time, this form of economic organisation was in decline in certain parts of the world, such as Europe, Eastern Europe and Latin America, while in other parts of the world, State corporate ownership not only survived but also flourished. The advent of the 2007 financial crisis stopped the decline of State corporate ownership and, ironically, raised serious questions about the viability of capitalism as an economic system.[61]

According to the 2014 World Investment Report, State investment accounted for over 11 per cent of the global foreign direct investment (FDI),

---

[58] Ming Du, 'China's State Capitalism and World Trade Law' (2014) 63 Int. Comp. Law Q. 409, 412.

[59] ibid.

[60] Bernardo Bortolotti and Veljko Fotak, 'The Rise of Sovereign Wealth Funds: Definition, Organisation and Governance' [2014] BAFFI Center Research Paper Series No. 2014-163 26, 4.

[61] Bremmer (n 21) 1–7.

with State-owned multinational enterprises as 'heavyweights' of this FDI.[62] UNCTAD estimated the number of State-owned multinational enterprises at 550 as of 2014, which is a relatively small number. However, the number of their foreign affiliates (15,000) and the scale of their *foreign assets* are very significant ($2 trillion).[63] The internationalisation of SOEs increased in the following years; and in 2017, UNCTAD identified approximately 1,500 State-owned multinational enterprises that operated outside their home State and which had a network of more than 86,000 foreign affiliates operating around the globe.[64] In early 2020, the International Monetary Fund (IMF) estimated that

> over the past decade, the share of SOE assets among the world's 2,000 largest firms has doubled to 20 percent. At $45 trillion in 2018, these assets are equivalent to 50 percent of global GDP. An important factor has been the relatively high economic growth rate of emerging market economies and especially of China, where SOEs still play a large role in the domestic economy. However, the balance sheet expansion also reflects international activities, for example SOEs have accounted for 5–15 percent of annual cross-border acquisitions since 2008.[65]

Some State-owned multinational enterprises are some of the largest companies in the world, such as Volkswagen, Statoil SA, Vattenfall, Cosco, Deutsche Telekom AG, Orange, Airbus Group, Gazprom, Petrobras, Abu Dhabi National Energy and Saudi Aramco, to name a few.[66] As far as the location of their foreign affiliates is concerned, there seems to be a preference for developed countries, especially the EU, which hosts close to 33,000 foreign affiliates.[67] Figure 1.1 shows the 'Global reach of state-owned enterprises (number of SOEs per region)', while Figure 1.2 shows the 'Share of SOEs among the world's 2,000 largest firms'.[68] It should be noted, however, that the figures do not include sovereign wealth funds or export credit agencies.

---

[62] This number does not include the investments made by sovereign wealth funds, whose assets under management, in 2020, crossed the $8 trillion mark.

[63] UNCTAD, 'World Investment Report 2014: Investing in the SDGs: An Action Plan' (United Nations 2014) ix.

[64] UNCTAD, 'World Investment Report 2017: Investment and the Digital Economy' (n 17) 30.

[65] International Monetary Fund, Fiscal Affairs Dept (n 10) 49.

[66] Alvaro Cuervo-Cazurra and others, 'Governments as Owners: State-Owned Multinational Companies' (2014) 45 J. Int. Bus. Stud. 919, 926–927; UNCTAD, 'Investing in the SDGs' (n 3) 21; UNCTAD, 'World Investment Report 2017: Investment and the Digital Economy' (n 17) 33.

[67] UNCTAD, 'World Investment Report 2017: Investment and the Digital Economy' (n 17) 31–32.

[68] ibid 31, 35.

Global reach

Some state-owned enterprises are multinational companies operating around the world. The biggest ones account for 20 percent of the world's 2000 largest firms.

(Number of SOEs per region)

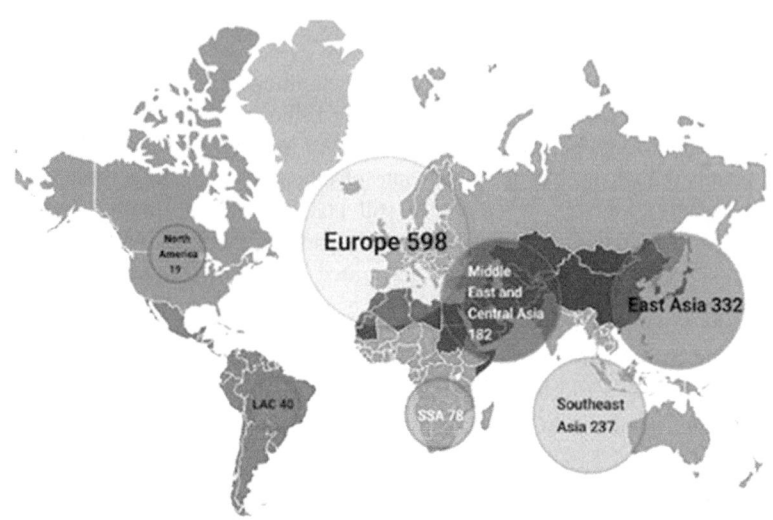

Source: UNCTAD; and IMF staff calculations.

FIGURE 1.1 Global reach of state-owned enterprises
(IMF)[69]

The growing influence of the State in the global economy is often examined under the terminology 'State capitalism', which, broadly speaking, is a political system in which the State has control of production and the use of capital.[70] This classic definition of State capitalism has been recently revised, to take into account developments that have occurred over the past decade, in particular increased minority ownership by the State in various public and

[69]   IMFBlog (n 24). The author would like to thank the IMF for permission to reproduce this figure.
[70]   Aldo Musacchio and Sérgio G Lazzarini, *Reinventing State Capitalism* (Harvard University Press 2014) 2.

Emerging giants
State-owned enterprises have grown in size and number in recent years, driven by emerging markets, and their assets are worth $45 trillion, about half of global GDP.

(Percent of assets of largest firms)

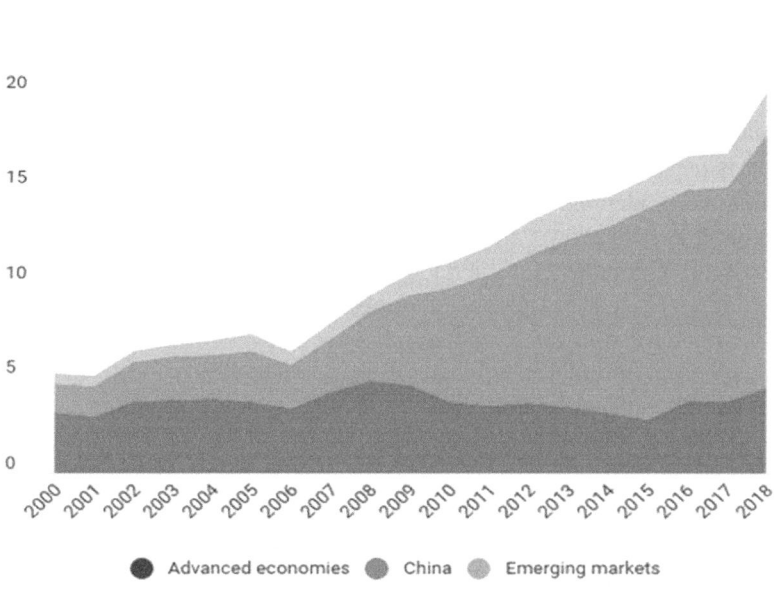

● Advanced economies ● China ● Emerging markets

Source: S&P Capital IQ; UNCTAD; S&P Global UDI World Electric Power Plant database; and IMF staff estimates.

FIGURE 1.2 Share of SOEs among the world's 2,000 largest firms
(IMF)[71]

private companies. As such, State capitalism has been redefined as 'the widespread influence of the government in the economy, either by owning majority or minority equity positions in companies, or by providing subsidised credit and/or other privileges to private companies'.[72] There are now many

[71] IMFBlog (n 24). The author would like to thank the IMF for permission to reproduce this figure.
[72] Aldo Musacchio and Sérgio G Lazzarini, Reinventing State Capitalism (Harvard University Press 2014) 2.

varieties of State capitalism, which may include the State as a *full owner* of an entity, and other various levels of ownership from *majority* and *minority* to *golden shares* and public–private partnerships.[73] It must also be emphasised that governments 'can also indirectly control or influence the behaviour of firms that are nominally private via other means such as convertible loans from state-owned banks, ownership by State-owned pension funds or ownership by sovereign wealth funds'.[74]

As can be observed, State capitalism is a complex concept that ultimately varies from State to State and can even be encountered in States that have been traditionally considered as adopting a capitalist system of economic organisation.[75] For example, in the United States, companies such as Fannie Mae, Freddie Mac and the Federal Home Loan Banks are backed by the government.[76] Another complex issue is the level at which SOEs are created and managed. This is usually dependent on the way that a particular State is organised internally, with three different levels of public enterprise having been identified: the federal level (in the case of States that are organised as federations), the state level and a local/municipal level.[77] For instance, in Germany, SOEs at the federal level are found in the railway and postal services, at state level in infrastructure and industrial activities, while local municipal companies are created as saving banks or for the purpose of managing public utilities.[78] As far as management is concerned, there are considerable differences from State to State as well, so an entity might be State-owned but its management could be in the hands of professional managers who are completely independent from the State. The ultimate economic performance of those entities varies as well, there often being not much difference in terms of performance between private entities and SOEs that have a professional and independent management.[79]

---

[73] Cuervo-Cazurra (n 37) 1; Ming Hua Li, Lin Cui and Jiangyong Lu, 'Varieties in State Capitalism: Outward FDI Strategies of Central and Local State-Owned Enterprises from Emerging Economy Countries' in Alvaro Cuervo-Cazurra (ed), *State-Owned Multinationals: Governments in Global Business* (Palgrave Macmillan 2018); Aldo Musacchio and Sergio G Lazzarini, 'Leviathan in Business: Varieties of State Capitalism and Their Implications for Economic Performance' [2012] Harvard Business School Working Paper, No. 12–108, June 2012.

[74] Cuervo-Cazurra (n 37) 1.

[75] Julien Chaisse, 'State Capitalism on the Ascent: Stress, Shock, and Adaptation of the International Law on Foreign Investment' (2018) 27 Minn. J. Int'l L. 339, 346–361.

[76] ibid 354–359.

[77] Pier Angelo Toninelli, 'Preface' in Pier Angelo Toninelli (ed), *The Rise and Fall of State-Owned Enterprise in the Western World* (Cambridge University Press 2000) 4.

[78] ibid.

[79] ibid 5.

This section has shown that, while State corporate ownership has a long and complex history, it has also recently undergone significant changes. The periods in history when State corporate ownership was popular have been followed with times when State ownership fell out of favour. This continuous ebb and flow in the popularity of State ownership has prompted scholars to wonder 'whether our societies are in some way predisposed toward [these types of] oscillations'[80] and have suggested that we might be 'currently living through either a recurrent cycle or a permanent secular trend in society's employment of SOEs'.[81] If, at one stage, States concentrated on their role as economic actors *within* their own borders, over the last two decades there has been a significant change in that model, with more and more States choosing to *internationalise* their 'national champions'. Larry Catá Backer summarises this recent development in the following manner:

> The 21st Century is witnessing a dramatic rise in the willingness of states to project economic power both at home and in host countries …. The facilitating cause of this change in approach is the creation of the very system that frees economic actors from the constraints of territory and more closely binds public actors thereto. Just as private economic entities may now cross borders to affect transactions that maximize their wealth, so states are now discovering that they might do the same thing …. Just as private actors are subject to the regulation and control of the sovereign in whose territories they act, states acting outside their borders as participants in local economic activity assume a similar character. Consequently, some states seem to have become, to some extent, pools of national economic wealth, the power of which matches or exceeds their traditional sovereign power.[82]

1.3.2 *Definitions*[83]

The terminology that surrounds State-owned entities that engage in economic activities is complex. Some of the terms encountered so far are: 'State company', 'national oil company', 'government company', 'government-owned

---

[80] ibid x. Quoting AO Hirschman, *Shifting involvements: Private Interest and Public Action* (Princeton, 1982).

[81] ibid; Louis Galambos and William Baumol, 'Conclusion' in Pier Angelo Toninelli (ed), *The Rise and Fall of State-Owned Enterprise in the Western World* (Cambridge University Press 2000).

[82] Backer, 'Sovereign Investing in Times of Crisis: Global Regulation of Sovereign Wealth Funds, State-Owned Enterprises, and the Chinese Experience' (n 20) 11.

[83] Barnes, 'The United Nations Guiding Principles on Business and Human Rights, the State Duty to Protect Human Rights and the State-Business Nexus' (n 7) 46–47. The ideas presented

company', 'State trading company', 'State-owned enterprise', 'sovereign wealth fund', 'State agency', 'State entity', 'foreign-government-owned corporations', 'State trading boards', 'export marketing boards', 'regulatory marketing boards', 'canalizing agencies', 'export credit agencies', etc. Even the term 'State-owned enterprise' has been acknowledged as providing only an 'approximate description of the complexity of forms and organisations that State companies may assume' and which appear to have reached an 'apogee of fantasy and ingenuity in terminology and legal forms', where it seems that 'State companies', 'State shareholding companies' and 'State concerns' exist alongside one another.[84] Despite this varied terminology, there are, however, two characteristics that all the entities above share: a State owns them and they engage in an economic activity as operators of a business or as investors in companies. Consequently, in this monograph the net is cast wide in terms of coverage. While recognising that there are inherent differences in terms of legal structure, purpose and governance between a sovereign wealth fund or an export credit agency and a State-owned multinational enterprise, this monograph focuses on State corporate ownership generally, regardless of the legal *form* chosen by a State. This approach thus seeks to avoid the 'mania for compartmentalisation' which has plagued most of the regulatory approaches concerning State-owned entities so far and aims to bypass the 'strongly held consensus that the focus of regulatory governance must be grounded in and through a formally constituted enterprise, the SOE, rather than focusing regulation on economic activity irrespective of the form in which it is undertaken'.[85] Consequently, for the purposes of this monograph, the term that will be used to encapsulate State ownership generally is that of 'State-owned entity' (SOE), while bearing in mind that this broad approach and all-encompassing terminology could be open to criticism from multiple perspectives. For example, would a minority shareholding by a State-owned enterprise in another company or portfolio investments by a

---

in this section, particularly those concerning the terminology surrounding State-owned entities have been previously published by the author in the cited journal article. The author would like to thank the Brazilian Journal of International Law for permission to reproduce those paragraphs.

[84] Toninelli, 'The Rise and Fall of Public Enterprise: The Framework' (n 36) 4–5.

[85] Backer, 'The Human Rights Obligations of State-Owned Enterprises (SOEs): Emerging Conceptual Structures and Principles in National and International Law and Policy' (n 7) 828, 848; Larry Catá Backer, 'Human Rights Responsibilities of State-Owned Enterprises' in Surya Deva and David Birchall (eds), *Research Handbook on Human Rights and Business* (Edward Elgar 2020) 230–232, 244. ('[T]he compartmentalisation of state-based economic activities among SOEs, SWFs investment instruments will produce a tendency towards policy incoherence. Conceptually these distinctions are without difference with respect to the duty of states.').

sovereign wealth fund automatically turn the investee company into an SOE? This issue is prone to confusion and could be subjected to further debate, as can be witnessed by the somewhat different approaches taken on this issue by UNCTAD and the OECD. In the definition adopted by UNCTAD for an entity to be classified as a State-owned multinational enterprise, the State must own at least 10 per cent of the capital, or the State has to own a 'golden share' in that entity.[86] In this circumstance, the focus is not necessarily solely on *control* but also on a given *ownership* stake. In the UNCTAD approach, 9 per cent capital ownership by the State in a given entity would not make it a State-owned multinational enterprise, unless of course we are dealing with a golden share. On the other hand, in the approach by the OECD – which is also adopted in this monograph – the focus is primarily on *control* over the entity and a State-owned enterprise can be 'any entity that is recognised by national law in which the State exercises ownership' and that engages in an activity that is economic in nature.[87] In this case, a 9 per cent or less capital ownership by the State would still make a given entity a State-owned enterprise if 'an equivalent degree of control' is exercised by the State over that particular entity.[88] Furthermore, support for this approach can also be found in jurisprudence. For example, for the purposes of sovereign immunity, the minority ownership interests of more than one foreign government may be combined to reach the majority ownership required by legislation such as the United States Foreign Sovereign Immunities Act section 1603(b)(2)[89] as shown in *Mangattu v M/V Ibn Hayyan*, where the plaintiffs/appellants worked as merchant seamen on *M/V Ibn Hayyan*, a vessel that was owned by six foreign sovereigns: Saudi Arabia, Kuwait, Qatar, United Arab Emirates, Iraq (each owning a 19.3 per cent share) and Bahrain (owning a 3.335 per cent share).[90] Another issue to bear in mind is that focusing on ownership percentages alone could lead to situations where the investing activities of sovereign wealth funds or export credit agencies would be excluded, given the often passive role that those entities usually employ. Since sovereign wealth funds manage in excess

---

[86] UNCTAD, 'World Investment Report 2017: Investment and the Digital Economy' (n 17) 30.

[87] OECD, *OECD Guidelines on Corporate Governance of State-Owned Enterprises* (OECD 2015) 14.

[88] ibid. (An 'equivalent degree of control' deals with those situations where 'legal stipulations or corporate articles of association ensure continued state control over an enterprise or its board of directors in which it holds a minority stake'.).

[89] Foreign Sovereign Immunities Act 1976 (United States).

[90] *Mangattu v M/V Ibn Hayyan* (United States, Court of Appeals, Fifth Circuit 35 F3d 205 (5th Cir 1994)).

of $8 trillion in assets,[91] it would be a missed opportunity not to extend coverage to those entities too. Furthermore, export credit agencies and other similar entities are expressly covered by the UNGPs along with State-owned enterprises under the State-business nexus, as will be further discussed in Chapter 2.[92] Sections 1.3.2.1–1.3.2.4 will briefly define the four main building blocks, which compose SOEs in this monograph: State-owned multinational enterprises, State-owned enterprises, national oil companies, sovereign wealth funds and export credit agencies.

1.3.2.1 State-Owned Multinational Enterprises and State-Owned Enterprises

UNCTAD defines State-owned multinational enterprises (SO-MNEs) as

> separate legal entities established or acquired by governments to engage in commercial activities, including FDI [foreign direct investment] operations, by way of having affiliates abroad or engaging in non-equity modes. An additional criterion is that a government entity should either own at least 10 per cent of the capital, be the largest shareholder or benefit from a 'golden share' – a type of share that gives special voting rights and the ability to block key strategic decisions, especially takeovers by other shareholders. Subnational entities in federal countries with significant State functions (e.g. German Laender, or Republics as federal subjects in the Russian federation, or States in the United States) and municipalities are considered State owners.[93]

The key element that distinguishes SO-MNEs from other State-owned entities, such as sovereign wealth funds, which are mostly passive investors, is the fact that they actively engage in commercial activities internationally.[94] SO-MNEs operate across the economic spectrum, but the largest are to be found in major sectors such as utilities, electricity, telecommunications, construction, natural resources, transportation, chemical industry, etc.[95] The

---

[91] 'Top 91 Largest Sovereign Wealth Fund Rankings by Total Assets – SWFI' <https://www.swfinstitute.org/fund-rankings/sovereign-wealth-fund> accessed 26 July 2020.

[92] John Ruggie, 'Guiding Principles on Business and Human Rights: Implementing the United Nations "Protect, Respect and Remedy" Framework (Report of the Special Representative of the Secretary-General on the Issue of Human Rights and Transnational Corporations and Other Business Enterprises)' (2011) A/HRC/17/31 9–10.

[93] UNCTAD, 'World Investment Report 2017: Investment and the Digital Economy' (n 17) 30.

[94] Raymond Vernon, 'The International Aspects of State-Owned Enterprises' in Alvaro Cuervo-Cazurra (ed), *State-Owned Multinationals: Governments in Global Business* (Palgrave Macmillan 2018).

[95] Cuervo-Cazurra and others (n 66) 926–927; Prithwiraj Choudhury and Tarun Khanna, 'Toward Resource Independence – Why State-Owned Entities Become Multinationals: An

growth of SO-MNEs has doubled over the past ten years and they now account for 20 per cent of the world's 2,000 largest firms.[96] Chinese State-owned companies are prolific in this area, particularly in the mining industry in Africa and Australia.[97] Some of the 'national champions', such as 'flag-carrier' airlines, airports, national railways, post offices, ports, banks, are also part of this category.[98] SOEs' process of internationalisation has puzzled scholars who have asked why those actors choose to internationalise and to become SO-MNEs. For a while it was even believed that SOEs were less likely than POEs to seek opportunities abroad.[99] Some alternative hypotheses have been advanced, but none fully explain this phenomenon. For example, if it was to be assumed that one of the reasons for the existence of SOEs is to solve market imperfections, then why would State A choose to solve market imperfections in State B, via its own SOEs?[100] Another hypothesis that has been advanced is that some SOEs 'are created as the result of the ideology of some governments who prefer to maintain control over the economy or over particular relationships'.[101] While it may be the case that governments 'may steer' some SO-MNEs to 'undertake activities in particular countries that may not have a direct business benefit, but may instead have an important political benefit',[102] it is unlikely that this is the case for each and every SO-MNE, given that being State-owned is often perceived as a liability.[103] Some commentators have suggested that SOEs may internationalise in order to achieve resource independence from other State actors.[104] It may ultimately be the case that just as the origin of a public enterprise cannot always be explained in terms of deliberate choice, it is the same with the internationalisation process of some SOEs.[105]

Empirical Study of India's Public R&D Laboratories' in Alvaro Cuervo-Cazurra (ed), *State-Owned Multinationals: Governments in Global Business* (Palgrave Macmillan 2018).

[96] International Monetary Fund, Fiscal Affairs Dept (n 10) 49.

[97] Andrew Szamosszegi and Kyle Cole, 'An Analysis of State-Owned Enterprises and State Capitalism in China' (US-China Economic and Security Review Commission 2011) 87; Li-Wen Lin and Curtis J Milhaupt, 'We Are the (National) Champions: Understanding the Mechanisms of State Capitalism in China' (2013) 65 Stan. L. Rev. 697; Li Xing, *The Rise of China and the Capitalist World Order* (Ashgate 2013).

[98] Szamosszegi and Cole (n 97).

[99] Renato Mazzolini, 'European Government-Controlled Enterprises: Explaining International Strategic and Policy Decisions' in Alvaro Cuervo-Cazurra (ed), *State-Owned Multinationals: Governments in Global Business* (Palgrave Macmillan 2018) 71.

[100] Cuervo-Cazurra (n 37) 3.

[101] ibid.

[102] ibid.

[103] Meyer, Ding and Zhang (n 37); Cuervo-Cazurra (n 37) 5.

[104] Mazzolini (n 99).

[105] Toninelli, 'The Rise and Fall of Public Enterprise: The Framework' (n 36) 5.

State-owned enterprises are defined as

any corporate entity recognised by national law as an enterprise, and in which the state exercises ownership, should be considered as a state-owned enterprise. This includes joint stock companies, limited liability companies and partnerships limited by shares. Moreover statutory corporations, with their legal personality established through specific legislation, should be considered as state-owned enterprises if their purpose and activities, or parts of their activities, are of a largely economic nature.[106]

Overall, the definition of State-owned enterprises covers many types of entities that are State-owned. One of the main differences between SO-MNEs and State-owned enterprises is their territorial sphere of activity. SO-MNEs operate internationally, while State-owned enterprises are those that operate largely domestically.

1.3.2.2 National Oil Companies

National oil companies (NOCs) own and control most of the world's energy supply.[107] They are companies that are *fully*, or in the *majority*, owned by the State.[108] Some 73 per cent of the world's oil reserves and 61 per cent of production are State-owned.[109] Dominance in gas is similar, with 68 per cent of reserves and 52 per cent of production.[110] Saudi Aramco, is the largest national oil company – and also the largest company – in the world, while Gazprom, Statoil, Sinopec and Petrobras are other well-known names.

---

[106] OECD, *OECD Guidelines on Corporate Governance of State-Owned Enterprises* (n 87) 14; Human Rights Council, 'Report of the Working Group on the Issue of Human Rights and Transnational Corporations and Other Business Enterprises' (Human Rights Council, Seventeenth Session, Agenda Item 3 2016) A/HRC/32/45 4.

[107] Hults, Thurber and Victor (n 26) 3; Silvana Tordo, *National Oil Companies and Value Creation* (The World Bank 2011).

[108] Rod Morrison, *The Principles of Project Finance* (Routledge 2016) 291; Nicolò Sartori, 'The European Commission's Policy towards the Southern Gas Corridor: Between National Interests and Economic Fundamentals' IAI Working Papers 12/01 January 2012 4; Patrick RP Heller, Paasha Mahdavi and Johannes Schreuder, 'Reforming National Oil Companies: Nine Recommendations' 24. (The term national oil company is taken to include companies that are *fully* or *majority* State owned. However, this does not mean that national oil companies that have private ownership are excluded from this definition. For example, Petrobras is a company that is 54 per cent directly owned by Brazil, while the Brazilian Development Bank and the Brazilian sovereign wealth fund own an additional 10 per cent between them. The remaining 34 per cent is privately owned. However, Petrobras is still classified as a national oil company [see Heller et all. at page 12]).

[109] Hults, Thurber and Victor (n 26) 3.

[110] ibid.

It should be noted that the term 'national oil company' is, however, not strictly correct, because some of those companies do not operate exclusively within a State's borders, so those entities could easily classify as SO-MNEs. Furthermore, sometimes NOCs are organised in other forms than classic corporate entities.

1.3.2.3 Sovereign Wealth Funds

Sovereign wealth funds (SWFs) are defined as

> funds established, owned and controlled by local or central governments, whose investment strategies include the acquisition of equity interests in companies listed in international markets operating in sectors considered strategic by their countries of incorporation.[111]

SWFs concentrate mainly on investing activities, rather than in actively managing an economic activity, and have been in existence since the mid-twentieth century. Their growth, however, is a recent phenomenon.[112] Today, the size of the SWFs market has surpassed $8 trillion[113] and they have played a key role in the stabilisation of markets during the financial crisis.[114]

1.3.2.4 Export Credit Agencies

Export Credit Agencies (ECAs) are

> (1) a highly specialised bank, insurance company, finance corporation, or dependency of the government, (2) offering loans and/or guarantees, insurance, technical assistance etc. to support exporters, (3) covering both commercial and political risks related to export sales, (4) with the backing or approval of the national government, and (5) dedicated to supporting the nation's exports.[115]

ECAs have a fundamental role to play in international trade and investment flows and they have been called the 'unsung giants' of international finance where, 'one out of every eight dollars of the world trade' being financed by

---

[111] Fabio Bassan, *The Law of Sovereign Wealth Funds* (Edward Elgar 2011) 32.
[112] ibid 7.
[113] 'Top 91 Largest Sovereign Wealth Fund Rankings by Total Assets – SWFI' (n 91).
[114] Backer, 'Sovereign Investing in Times of Crisis: Global Regulation of Sovereign Wealth Funds, State-Owned Enterprises, and the Chinese Experience' (n 20) 4, 15.
[115] Delio E Gianturco, *Export Credit Agencies: The Unsung Giants of International Trade and Finance* (Greenwood Publishing Group 2001) 2.

ECAs and 'much of the remaining seven dollars is influenced by what ECAs do', and their activity 'far exceeds' that of multilateral development banks.[116] ECAs have been signalled as potentially having a key role in ensuring respect for human rights by business entities.[117]

1.3.2.5 Other

Apart from SO-MNEs, State-owned enterprises, NOCs, SWFs and ECAs there are other types of vehicles through which states engage in economic activities, such as export marketing boards, regulatory market boards, etc. As such, it is impossible to define them all separately and they are covered in this section under 'other'. This section has shown that the presence of the State as an economic actor can take many forms. Among those are the more traditional forms such as State-owned enterprises, NOCs, ECAs, or SO-MNEs. There are, however, also newer actors on this scene, such as SWFs. A taxonomic representation thus makes, State-owned enterprises, SO-MNES, NOCs, SWFs, ECAs and other such entities a *species* which is part of a larger *family*, that of State-owned entities (SOEs). A schematic representation of SOEs is displayed in Figure 1.3.

1.4 WHAT IS THE CONCERN WITH STATE-OWNED ENTITIES?

1.4.1 *Traditional Concerns about State-Owned Entities: Unfair Competition, National Security and Resource Security*

State-owned entities are often viewed with suspicion because of their close relationship with the State that owns them.[118] By virtue of this close relationship, State-owned companies are in a position to enjoy certain privileges and immunities that are not generally available to the private sector.[119] That is, the State can use its power as a regulator to bestow certain privileges such as favourable taxation treatment, preferential access to finance, exemption from

---

[116] ibid 1.
[117] 'Remarks by SRSG John Ruggie "Engaging Export Credit Agencies in Respecting Human Rights" OECD Export Credit Group's "Common Approaches" Meeting'; Robert McCorquodale and Penelope Simons, 'Responsibility Beyond Borders: State Responsibility for Extraterritorial Violations by Corporations of International Human Rights Law' (2007) 70 Mod. L. Rev. 607.
[118] Karl P Sauvant, Lisa E Sachs and Wouter PF Schmit Jongbloed (eds), *Sovereign Investment: Concerns and Policy Reactions* (Oxford University Press 2012); Meyer, Ding and Zhang (n 37).
[119] Antonio Capobianco and Hans Christiansen, 'Competitive Neutrality and State-Owned Enterprises' (2011) OECD Corporate Governance Working Papers 1 5.

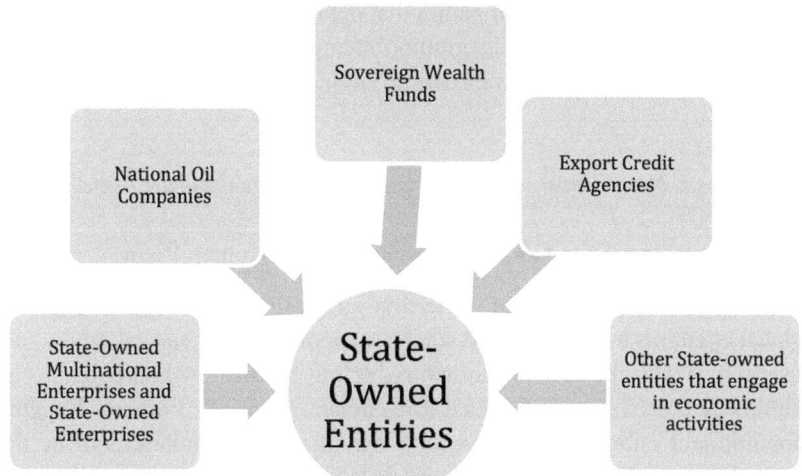

FIGURE 1.3 The universe of state-owned entities

bankruptcy rules and the outright subsidisation of State-owned companies.[120] Some of the concerns pertaining to SOEs may also stem from a clash of ideologies, between countries that adopt free market principles and those in which the State still has a significant role to play in the economic sphere. For example, countries that adopt free market principles view increased State ownership in their own economies as a potential threat to free markets. Additionally, the power plays between existing and potential new hegemons that do not share the same political ideology contributes to this debate.[121] Nevertheless, most of the traditional concerns that stand out relate to unfair competition, national security and resource security. SOEs may enjoy certain competitive advantages over privately owned entities, such as subsidies or access to capital at below market rates. SOEs are also considered opaque organisations, by Western standards, which may have a role to play in political power consolidation.[122] The national security argument relates mainly to access to sensitive market sectors, in particular the technology sector and other sectors deemed strategic. For example, many countries specifically prohibit, or they make it very difficult for foreign government-controlled investors to

---

[120] For a detailed analysis of the power of the State to regulate and a further examination of the concerns associated with State ownership, see Chapter 2.

[121] Xing (n 97).

[122] Bremmer (n 21); Aharoni (n 37); Lin Cui and Fuming Jiang, 'State Ownership Effect on Firms' FDI Ownership Decisions under Institutional Pressure: A Study of Chinese Outward-Investing Firms' in Alvaro Cuervo-Cazurra (ed), *State-Owned Multinationals: Governments in Global Business* (Palgrave Macmillan 2018).

acquire, shareholdings in companies that operate in those sectors. The limits imposed by Australia on the acquisition of any assets by foreign government-controlled entities is a relevant example among many others.[123]

1.4.2 *New Concerns: Human Rights and State-Owned Entities*

1.4.2.1 State Corporate Ownership and Human Rights

The topic of State corporate ownership and human rights was brought to global attention by John Ruggie, after his appointment as special representative to deal with the issue of human rights and transnational corporations by United Nations Secretary General Kofi Annan, in 2005.[124] Professor Ruggie's appointment culminated in 2011 with the unanimous endorsement by the United Nations Human Rights Council (UN Human Rights Council) of the United Nations Guiding Principles on Business and Human Rights (UNGPs).[125] As far as State corporate ownership is concerned, a year after his appointment as special representative, John Ruggie stated that

> ways must be found to engage State-owned enterprises in addressing human rights challenges in their spheres of operation. They are becoming increasingly important players in some of the most troubling industry sectors yet appear to operate beyond many of the external sources of scrutiny to which commercial firms are subject.[126]

The year 2006 was thus the point when State corporate ownership entered into the narrative of what were to become later the UNGPs, and as the mandate of the special representative progressed on this topic, so did the coverage of State corporate ownership.[127] Later on, other reports of the special representative continued to make references about the challenges associated

---

[123] 'Policy Documents | Foreign Investment Review Board' <https://firb.gov.au/guidance-resources/policy-documents> accessed 26 July 2020; 'Foreign Government Investors [GN23] | Foreign Investment Review Board' <https://firb.gov.au/resources/guidance/gn23> accessed 26 July 2020.

[124] Human Rights Commission, Human Rights and Transnational Corporations and Other Business Enterprises SRSG mandate 2005 (E/CN4/RES/2005/69).

[125] Human Rights Council, Resolution 17/4 Human Rights and Transnational Corporations and other Business Enterprises 2011 (A/HRC/RES/17/4).

[126] John Ruggie, 'Promotion and Protection of Human Rights (Interim Report of the Special Representative of the Secretary-General on the Issue of Human Rights and Transnational Corporations and Other Business Enterprises)' (2006) E/CN.4/2006/97 20.

[127] Barnes, 'The United Nations Guiding Principles on Business and Human Rights, the State Duty to Protect Human Rights and the State-Business Nexus' (n 7) 43–45.

with State corporate ownership and human rights and suggested ways in which this issue might be tackled.[128]

This monograph takes a broad approach to human rights and includes within the scope of analysis all substantive rights that can be found in the core human rights treaties,[129] the core conventions of the International Labour

---

[128] John Ruggie, 'State Responsibilities to Regulate and Adjudicate Corporate Activities under the United Nations Core Human Rights Treaties: An Overview of Treaty Body Commentaries (Report of the Special Representative of the Secretary-General on the Issue of Human Rights and Transnational Corporations and Other Business Enterprises)' (2007) A/HRC/4/35/Add.1 10, 32–33; John Ruggie, 'State Responsibilities to Regulate and Adjudicate Corporate Activities under the United Nations' Core Human Rights Treaties (Report of the Special Representative of the Secretary-General on the Issue of Human Rights and Transnational Corporations and Other Business Enterprises)' (John F Kennedy School of Government 2007) paras 10, 78–80; John Ruggie, 'Corporations and Human Rights: A Survey of the Scope and Patterns of Alleged Corporate-Related Human Rights Abuse (Report of the Special Representative of the Secretary-General on the Issue of Human Rights and Transnational Corporations and Other Business Enterprises)' (2008) A/HRC/8/5/Add.2 9; John Ruggie, 'Protect, Respect and Remedy: A Framework for Business and Human Rights (Report of the Special Representative of the Secretary-General on the Issue of Human Rights and Transnational Corporations and Other Business Enterprises, John Ruggie)' (2008) A/HRC/8/5 10, 11, 25; John Ruggie, 'Summary of Five Multi-Stakeholder Consultations (Report of the Special Representative of the Secretary-General on the Issue of Human Rights and Transnational Corporations and Other Business Enterprises)' (2008) A/HRC/8/5/Add.1 23; John Ruggie, 'State Obligations to Provide Access to Remedy for Human Rights Abuses by Third Parties, Including Business: An Overview of International and Regional Provisions, Commentary and Decisions (Report of the Special Representative of the Secretary-General on the Issue of Human Rights and Transnational Corporations and Other Business Enterprises, John Ruggie)' (2009) A/HRC/11/13/Add.1 33; John Ruggie, 'Business and Human Rights: Further Steps toward the Operationalization of the "Protect, Respect and Remedy" Framework (Report of the Special Representative of the Secretary-General on the Issue of Human Rights and Transnational Corporations and Other Business Enterprises, John Ruggie' (2010) A/HRC/14/27 7–8; John Ruggie, 'Guiding Principles on Business and Human Rights: Implementing the United Nations "Protect, Respect and Remedy" Framework (Report of the Special Representative of the Secretary-General on the Issue of Human Rights and Transnational Corporations and Other Business Enterprises)' (n 92) 9–10; John Ruggie, 'Human Rights and Corporate Law: Trends and Observations from a Crossnational Study Conducted by the Special Representative (Report of the Special Representative of the Secretary- General on the Issue of Human Rights and Transnational Corporations and Other Business Enterprises, John Ruggie)' (2011) A/HRC/17/31/Add.2 26, 30, 33, 40, 41. The bibliography in this footnote has been published previously by the author in Mihaela Maria Barnes, 'The United Nations Guiding Principles on Business and Human Rights, the State Duty to Protect Human Rights and the State-Business Nexus' (2018) 15 Brazilian J. Int. Law 42, 44–45. The author would like to thank the Brazilian Journal of International Law for permission to reproduce this content.

[129] Universal Declaration of Human Rights 1948; International Covenant on Civil and Political Rights 1966; International Covenant on Economic, Social and Cultural Rights 1966; International Convention for the Protection of All Persons from Enforced Disappearance 2006; Convention on the Rights of Persons with Disabilities 2006; International Convention on the Protection of the Rights of All Migrant Workers and Members of Their Families 1990;

Organisation[130] as well as those found in the United Nations Convention against Corruption and the Rio Declaration on the Environment and Development. This approach is thus broader than that taken by the UNGPs, which cover only the substantive rights that are found in the Universal Declaration of Human Rights, the International Covenant on Civil and Political Rights, the International Covenant on Economic, Social and Cultural Rights, and the International Labour Organisation Declaration on Fundamental Principles and Rights at Work. Nevertheless, a broader approach is indeed justified in the present circumstances due to the particular characteristics of SOEs. For instance, the inclusion of the United Nations Convention against Corruption[131] is justified because corruption has been proved to have a negative impact on human rights generally[132] and certain corporate governance weaknesses make SOEs specifically prone to corruption. The addition of matters pertaining to the environment is also justified in light of the emerging human right to a clean environment.[133]

International Convention on the Elimination of All Forms of Racial Discrimination 1965; Convention on the Rights of the Child 1989; International Convention on the Elimination of All Forms of Racial Discrimination 1965; Convention on the Elimination of All Forms of Discrimination against Women 1979; Convention against Torture and Other Cruel, Inhuman or Degrading Treatment or Punishment 1987.

[130] Convention C182 – Convention concerning the Prohibition and Immediate Action for the Elimination of the Worst Forms of Child Labour 1999; Convention C138 – Convention concerning Minimum Age for Admission to Employment 1973; Convention C111 – Convention Concerning Discrimination in Respect of Employment and Occupation 1958; Convention C105 – Convention concerning Forced or Compulsory Labour 1957; Convention C100 – Equal Remuneration Convention 1951; Convention C098 – Convention concerning the Right to Organise and Collective Bargaining 1949; Convention C029 – Convention concerning Forced or Compulsory Labour 1930; Convention C087 – Convention concerning Freedom of Association and Protection of the Right to Organise 1948.

[131] United Nations Convention against Corruption 2003.

[132] Thomas W Pogge, *World Poverty and Human Rights* (Polity 2008) 8–9, 27–29, 116–118, 243.

[133] *Obligaciones estatales en relación con el medio ambiente en el marco de la protección y garantia de los derechos a la vida y la integridad personal – interpretación y alcance de los artículos 41 y 51, en recion con los artículos 11 y 2 de la convención Americana sobre derechos humanos* 102 (Inter-American Court of Human Rights, Advisory Opinion OC 23/17, 15 November 2017); *Portillo Cáceres v Paraguay* (Human Rights Committee, 9 August 2019, Comm No 2751/2016, CCPR/C/126/D/ 2751/2016); *Teitiota v New Zealand* (Human Rights Committee, 24 October 2019, Comm No 2728/2016, CCPR/C/127/D/ 2728/2016); Ginevra Le Moli, 'The Human Rights Committee, Environmental Protection and the Right to Life' (2020) 69 Int. Comp. Law Q. 735; UN Human Rights Committee (HRC), General comment no. 36, Article 6 (Right to Life), 3 September 2019, CCPR/C/GC/35 paras 26; 62.

1.4.2.2 Case Studies: How Do State-Owned Entities Become Involved in Human Rights Violations?

SOEs can violate human rights in similar ways to privately owned companies. Lately, there has been an increased focus in literature on the human rights impact of Chinese SOEs;[134] however, all SOEs can violate human rights, regardless of their country of origin or sector of operation, as the jurisprudence of the European Court of Human Rights (ECHR) on this topic demonstrates. For further illustration, the cases of *Dubetska & ors v Ukraine*,[135] and *Heinisch v Germany*[136] will be used as examples. In *Dubetska & ors v Ukraine*, the applicants complained that their health and living environment deteriorated as a consequence of the operation of a State-owed coal mine. The application to the ECHR was based on Article 8 of the European Convention on Human Rights (EConHR) (the right to respect for private and family life). The applicants argued that Ukraine had done nothing to address this situation, although they had known about the situation for an extended period of time.[137] The fact that the entity in question was State-owned had a substantial role to play in the Court's ultimate decision that a violation did occur in those circumstances:

> [T]he Court reiterates that the present case concerns pollution emanating from the daily operation of the State-owned Vizeyska coal mine and the Chervonogradska coal-processing factory, which was State-owned at least until 2007; its spoil heap has remained in State ownership to the present day. The State should have been, and in fact was, well aware of the environmental effects of the operation of these facilities, as these were the only large industries in the vicinity of the applicant families' households.[138]

---

[134] Michael Kelly, 'Ending Corporate Impunity for Genocide: The Case against China's State-Owned Petroleum Company in Sudan' (2011) 90 Or. L. Rev. 413; Craig Forcese, '"Militarized Commerce" in Sudan's Oilfields: Lessons for Canadian Foreign Policy' (2001) 8 Can. Foreign Policy J. 37; John Harker, 'Human Security in Sudan: The Report of a Canadian Assessment Mission (The Harker Report)' (Department of Foreign Affairs and International Trade 2000); Michael J Kelly, *Prosecuting Corporations for Genocide* (Oxford University Press 2016).

[135] *Case of Dubetska & ors v Ukraine* (European Court of Human Rights, Fifth Section, Application No 30499/03).

[136] *Case of Heinisch v Germany* (European Court of Human Rights, Fifth Section, Application No 28274/08).

[137] *Case of Dubetska & ors v Ukraine* (n 135) paras 13–30.

[138] ibid para 120.

In *Heinisch v Germany*,[139] which is a 'whistle-blowing' case concerning the ill-treatment of the residents of a geriatric nursing home, the ECHR had to decide an application made under Article 34 of the EConHR for breach of freedom of expression pertinent to Article 10 of the EConHR. The applicant was working as a nurse in a geriatric nursing home called Vivantes. Vivantes was established as a limited liability company, but it was ultimately fully owned by the Land of Berlin. Over an extended period of time, the applicant and her colleagues informed the management that due to staff shortages, they were overburdened in their duties and had serious difficulties caring for the elderly in an appropriate manner. A series of official inspections of the nursing home confirmed the complaints of the applicant, but no meaningful improvements were made. The applicant logged a new internal complaint to the management, indicating that due to staff shortages, he could no longer guarantee the patients' basic hygienic care and sought to know how the care home was going to avoid criminal responsibility for its staff and how it was going to look after the patients in its care. Following a series of events, the applicant lodged a criminal complaint against Vivantes for aggravated fraud relating to the alleged falsification of records concerning the patients' care. After this incident, the applicant was soon dismissed without due notice. The ECHR ultimately held that the domestic courts had 'failed to strike a fair balance between the need to protect the employer's reputation and rights on the one hand, and the need to protect the applicant's right to freedom of expression on the other'.[140] On the issue of State ownership the ECHR noted:

> Turning to the circumstances of the present case, the Court notes that the information disclosed by the applicant was undeniably of public interest. In societies with an ever growing part of their elderly population being subject to institutional care, and taking into account the particular vulnerability of the patients concerned, who often may not be in a position to draw attention to shortcomings in the provision of care on their own initiative, the dissemination of information about the quality or deficiencies of such care is of vital importance with a view to preventing abuse. This is even more evident when institutional care is provided by a State-owned company, where the confidence of the public in an adequate provision of vital care services by the State is at stake.[141]

---

[139] *Case of Heinisch v Germany* (n 137).
[140] ibid 94.
[141] ibid 71.

The Court also accepted that while State-owned companies may be interested in their own commercial viability it also pointed out that

> the protection of public confidence in the quality of the provision of vital public service by State-owned or administered companies is decisive for the functioning and economic good of the entire sector. For this reason the public shareholder itself has an interest in investigating and clarifying alleged deficiencies in this respect within the scope of an open public debate.[142]

As the geographic distribution of cases above indicates, the important task at hand is to identify where and what the regulatory gaps are and to develop effective solutions that will close them. The UN Global Compact has also considered State-ownership under the 'Human Rights and Business Dilemmas', where many additional examples of case studies involving SOEs are considered.[143]

1.5 INTERNATIONAL LAW, HUMAN RIGHTS AND THE RELATIONSHIP WITH STATE OWNERSHIP

This section provides an overview of the place of human rights in international law, the most fundamental human rights instruments, a general introduction to the 'respect, protect and fulfill' framework, the nature of States' obligations to 'respect, protect and fulfill' human rights and the relationship between international law, human rights and State corporate ownership.

1.5.1 *Human Rights in International Law*

1.5.1.1 General Remarks on the Place of Human Rights in International Law

The fundamental principles of human rights are grounded in general international law and they form an integral part of customary international law and the general principles of law.[144] Grounding human rights in general

---

[142] ibid 89.
[143] 'Human Rights and Business Dilemmas Forum – Dilemmas' <https://hrbdf.org/dilemmas/working-soe/> accessed 27 July 2020.
[144] James Crawford, *Brownlie's Principles of Public International Law* (Oxford University Press 2012) 642–643; Olivier De Schutter, *International Human Rights Law: Cases, Materials, Commentary* (2nd edn, Cambridge University Press 2014) 62–68; *Legality of the Threat or Use of Nuclear Weapons* (International Court of Justice, Advisory Opinion, ICJ Reports 1996, p 226) [79].

international law – rather than just treaties – means that their sphere of application is wider, as Olivier de Schutter notes:

> First, we are far from having achieved universal ratification for all human rights. Second, ratifications by States may be accompanied by reservations about specific rights or about the scope of the application of the treaty: grounding the guarantees of the treaty in customary international law or in other sources of general international law may serve to overcome such restrictions. Third, it is increasingly acknowledged that States are not the only addressees of human rights law. As subjects of international law, international organisations are bound by general international law ... and some authors believe this could be extended to international corporations: in order to impose human rights obligations on such non-State actors, these obligations must have their source elsewhere than in treaties, which as a rule only States may ratify.[145]

The United Nations Charter (the Charter) states in Article 1(3) that, among others, the purposes of the UN is to 'achieve international cooperation in solving international problems of an economic, social, or humanitarian character, and in promoting and encouraging respect for human rights and for fundamental freedoms for all without distinction as to race, sex, language, or religion'.[146] The UN must also aim for higher standards of living, full employment and conditions of economic and social progress and development, as well as solutions relating to economic, social, health and related problems.[147] Furthermore, in accordance with Article 56 of the Charter, all Member States 'pledge themselves to take joint and separate action in co-operation with the Organisation' for the achievement of those purposes. While the Charter mentions human rights several times, it neither defines them, nor does it set their content. It is the Universal Declaration of Human Rights (UDHR)[148] that outlines some of the fundamental human rights that deserve to be universally protected and to which all human beings are inherently entitled. The UDHR has the status of customary international law.[149] While not a legally enforceable instrument as such, the UDHR has achieved the status of customary international law by virtue of its 'marked influence upon the constitutions of many states and upon the formulation of subsequent human rights treaties and resolutions', as well as it subsequent use in judicial

---

[145] Schutter (n 146) 68.
[146] Charter of the United Nations 1945.
[147] ibid Article 55.
[148] Universal Declaration of Human Rights 1948.
[149] Schutter (n 146) 63.

practice.[150] The UDHR does not impose direct obligations on States, instead, as declared in the Preamble, it 'reinforces the collective, society-wide nature of human rights and of the corresponding obligations by addressing responsibility for fulfillment of the Declaration to "every individual and *every organ* of society", rather than exclusively on States or the United Nations'.[151] For example, Article 4 states that 'no one shall be held in servitude'; under Article 16 everybody has the right to marry and found a family; Article 17 provides that everybody has the right to own property alone as well as in association with others, and that 'no one shall be arbitrarily deprived of his property'; Articles 19 and 20 provide for freedom of opinion and association; Article 21 provides for the right to take part in government affairs; Article 22 states that 'everyone, as a member of society has the right to social security'; Articles 23 and 24 deal with the right to work and some broad conditions under which such right should be exercised such as equal pay, the right to join trade unions, the right to rest and leisure and the protection against unemployment. Article 25 provides for the right to an adequate standard of living and the right to social security in the event of unemployment, sickness, disability, widowhood or old age. Motherhood and childhood are entitled to special care and assistance.[152] Article 27 states that everybody has the right to 'freely participate in the life of the community' to which he or she belongs.

Two further clarifications must be made in the context of the general remarks on the place of human rights in international law and which concern norms *jus cogens* and obligations *erga omnes*. In international law, there are certain peremptory norms (also known as norms *jus cogens*) from which no derogation is allowed. According to Article 53 of the Vienna Convention on the Law of the Treaties (VCLT), 'a treaty is void if, at the time of its conclusion, it conflicts with a peremptory norm of general international law'. Peremptory norms can only be modified by a subsequent norm of general international law having the same character. There has been a substantial amount of debate about what norms can be classified as having a peremptory character, but the general agreement is that they are limited in scope and of fundamental character and include the prohibition of aggression, slavery, genocide, racial discrimination, apartheid, torture, the application of the basic rules of humanitarian law applicable in armed conflict and the right

---

[150] Malcolm N Shaw, *International Law* (Cambridge University Press 2008) 279.
[151] McBeth (n 5) 14.
[152] Universal Declaration of Human Rights 1948 Article 25(2).

to self-determination.[153] Since the respect of human rights is of interest to the international community as a whole, any State can 'pursue remedies against the State alleged to have violated its obligations under the human rights recognised under customary international law or as general principles of law'.[154] It is in this sense that human rights are considered to be opposable *erga omnes* or 'towards everyone'.[155] For example, Article 48 of the International Law Commission Articles on the Responsibility of States for Internationally Wrongful Acts (ILC Articles) states that 'any State other than the injured State is entitled to invoke the responsibility of another State if the obligation breached is owed to the international community as a whole'. The International Court of Justice (ICJ) has also made similar statements.[156] What remains unsettled, however, is whether it is only norms *jus cogens* that impose obligations *erga omnes*, or whether the scope of this category extends to all recognised human rights.[157]

1.5.1.2 Fundamental Human Rights Treaties

In contrast to the UDHR, the International Covenant on Economic, Social and Cultural Rights (ICESCR)[158] and the International Covenant on Civil and Political Rights (ICCPR)[159] are binding and impose direct obligations on States.[160] Both the ICESCR and the ICCPR mention the provisions of the UN Charter and the UDHR and further expand on the rights contained in the

---

[153] Crawford, *Brownlie's Principles of Public International Law* (n 146) 594–598; A Bianchi, 'Human Rights and the Magic of Jus Cogens' (2008) 19 Eur. J. Int. Law 491.

[154] Schutter (n 146) 112.

[155] Clapham (n 5) 96–99.

[156] *Case Concerning Barcelona Traction, Light and Power Company, Limited (Belgium v Spain)* (International Court of Justice, Judgment, ICJ Reports 1970, p 3) [33–34]; *Legal Consequences of the Construction of a Wall in the Occupied Palestinian Territory* (International Court of Justice, Advisory Opinion, ICJ Reports 2004, p 136) [155–157]. (In the *Legal Consequences of the Construction of a Wall in the Occupied Palestinian Territory* the ICJ stated: 'The Court would observe that the obligations violated by Israel include certain obligations *erga omnes*. As the Court indicated in the Barcelona Traction case, such obligations are by their very nature "the concern of all States" and, "in view of the importance of the rights involved, all States can be held to have a legal interest in their protection" The obligations *erga omnes* violated by Israel are the obligation to respect the right of the Palestinian people to self-determination, and certain of its obligations under international humanitarian law.') (References omitted).

[157] Schutter (n 146) 114.

[158] International Covenant on Economic, Social and Cultural Rights 1966.

[159] International Covenant on Civil and Political Rights 1966.

[160] Office of the United Nations Commissioner for Human Rights, 'Status of Ratification of the 18 International Human Rights Treaties' <http://indicators.ohchr.org/> accessed 10 December 2020.

UDHR. Article 1 of the ICESCR (and the ICCPR) provides for the right to self-determination; Article 7 recognises the right to work and remuneration that is fair and equal for men and women, as well as safe and healthy working conditions and the right to rest and leisure. In similar fashion to the UDHR, Article 8 provides for the right of everyone to form trade unions and to strike (Article 22 of the ICCPR); Article 9 deals with the right to social security; Article 11 addresses the right of everyone to an adequate standard of living; Article 15 outlines the right to take part in cultural life. Article 8 of the ICCPR states that 'no one shall be held in slavery'. Article 24 of the ICCPR provides for the right to found a family. Further provisions can be found in virtually all core human rights treaties[161] as well as the fundamental conventions of the International Labour Organisation.[162]

At the regional level, relevant legal instruments include the European Convention for the Protection of Human Rights and Fundamental Freedoms (EConHR)[163] and the European Social Charter.[164] While the EConHR guarantees only civil and political rights reflecting those covered in the UDHR, it is the European Social Charter that fully addresses social rights such as the right to make a living (Article 1), the right to safe and healthy working conditions (Articles 2 and 3), the right to a fair remuneration, the right to freedom of association (Article 5), the right of employed women to protection (Article 8), and among others the right to social security and welfare (Articles 12–14).[165] The Charter of Fundamental Rights of the European Union (EU Charter)[166] brings together in one document all the fundamental rights protected in the European Union (EU). For example, the EU Charter

---

[161] International Convention on the Protection of the Rights of All Migrant Workers and Members of their Families 1990; International Convention on the Elimination of All Forms of Racial Discrimination 1965; Convention on the Rights of the Child 1989; Convention on the Elimination of All Forms of Discrimination against Women 1979; Convention against Torture and Other Cruel, Inhuman or Degrading Treatment or Punishment 1987.

[162] Convention C182 – Convention concerning the Prohibition and Immediate Action for the Elimination of the Worst Forms of Child Labour 1999; Convention C138 – Convention concerning Minimum Age for Admission to Employment 1973; Convention C111 – Convention Concerning Discrimination in Respect of Employment and Occupation 1958; Convention C105 – Convention concerning Forced or Compulsory Labour 1957; Convention C100 – Equal Remuneration Convention 1951; Convention C098 – Convention concerning the Right to Organise and Collective Bargaining 1949; Convention C029 – Convention concerning Forced or Compulsory Labour 1930; Convention C087 – Convention concerning Freedom of Association and Protection of the Right to Organise 1948.

[163] European Convention for the Protection of Human Rights and Fundamental Freedoms 1950.

[164] European Social Charter 1961.

[165] ibid; European Convention for the Protection of Human Rights and Fundamental Freedoms 1950.

[166] Charter of Fundamental Rights of the European Union 2009.

entrenches all the rights found in the case law of the Court of Justice of the EU, the rights and freedoms covered in the EConHR and other rights and principles that result from common constitutional traditions of EU Member States and other international instruments. Title IV on 'Solidarity' covers, among others, the right to collective bargaining (Article 27), the right to fair and just working conditions (Article 31), the prohibition of child labour and the protection of young people at work (Article 32), the right to social security (Article 34) and the right to a 'high level of environmental protection' (Article 37).[167]

The Arab Charter on Human Rights[168] seeks to largely reaffirm the principles enshrined in the UN Charter, the UDHR, the ICCPR, and the ICESCR. The Arab Charter on Human Rights recognises the right to private property (Article 25), the right to peaceful assembly (Article 28), the right to form trade unions (Article 29), the right to social security (Article 30) and the right to a fair wage (Article 32). In September 2014, a ministerial meeting for the League of Arab Nations[169] approved the Statute of the Arab Court of Human Rights, which will be based in Bahrain and will be charged with the implementation of the Arab Charter. One of the main flaws of the Charter is that only States can bring complaints. The Member States of the Association of Southeast Asian Nations (ASEAN)[170] have also adopted a human rights declaration,[171] and the economic, social and cultural rights of the UDHR are reaffirmed in this declaration in General Principles 26–34. In addition, General Principle 35 enshrines the right to development, whereby this right must be fulfilled in order 'to meet equitably the developmental and environmental needs of present and future generations'. The African Charter of Human Rights,[172] to which all States situated on the African continent are members, also reaffirms the principles of the UN Charter, the UDHR, the ICCPR and the ICESCR. The American Convention on Human Rights[173]

[167] ibid.

[168] Arab Charter on Human Rights 2008.

[169] Egypt, Iraq, Jordan and Yemen all joined created the Arab League in 1945. Other States joined later: Algeria (1962), Bahrain (1971), Comoros (1993), Djibouti (1977), Kuwait (1961), Libya (1953), Mauritania (1973), Morocco (1958), Oman (1971), Qatar (1971), Somalia (1974), Southern Yemen (1967), Sudan (1956), Tunisia (1958) and the United Arab Emirates (1971). The Palestine Liberation Organization was admitted in 1976. In January 2003 Eritrea joined the Arab League as an observer.

[170] ASEAN Member States: Brunei Darussalam, Cambodia, Indonesia, Laos, Malaysia, Myanmar, Philippines, Singapore, Thailand and Vietnam.

[171] ASEAN Human Rights Declaration 2012.

[172] The African Charter on Human and Peoples' Rights (Banjul Charter) 1981.

[173] The American Convention on Human Rights 1978.

has similar provisions, although it is through the Protocol of San Salvador that the ambit of the economic, social and cultural rights are significantly expanded.[174]

1.5.2 *General Comments on the 'Respect, Protect and Fulfill' Framework*

The generally accepted view is that States are the main subjects of international law. As subjects of international law, States become parties to treaties, which are one of the main sources of international law.[175] Consequently, under the principle of *pacta sunt servanda*, this means that States have a legal obligation to comply with the provisions of the treaties that they choose to be party to. As far as the realisation and justiciability of human rights standards is concerned, the obligations of States in this area have been widely accepted as belonging to a framework, which is composed of three elements. That is, States have an obligation to '*respect, protect* and *fulfill* human rights'.[176] This is also known as the 'typology' of States' obligations to respect human rights, which has been developed by the former special rapporteur of the UN Sub-Commission on Prevention of Discrimination and Protection of Minorities, Asbjorn Eide, in his report dealing with the right to food, although it is the political philosopher Henry Shue who must be given credit for actually creating this framework.[177] Since then, this framework been widely accepted. The 'respect, protect, fulfill' framework is supported by the wording of Article 2(1) of the ICCPR, which provides that each State Party 'undertakes to *respect* and to *ensure* to all individuals within its territory and subject to its jurisdiction, the rights recognised in the present covenant'.[178] The respect, protect, fulfill framework is adopted by the UNGPs[179] and forms part of Pillar I and

---

[174] Additional Protocol to the American Convention on Human Rights in the Area of Economic, Social and Cultural Rights (Protocol of San Salvador) 1988.

[175] Hugh Thirlway, *The Sources of International Law* (Oxford University Press 2014) 31–44. See also the Statute of the International Court of Justice, Article 38(1).

[176] Schutter (n 146) 280–291; UN Committee on Economic, Social and Cultural Rights, General comment No. 24 (2017) on State obligations under the International Covenant on Economic, Social and Cultural Rights in the context of business activities, 10 August 2017, E/C.12/GC/24 paras 10–24.

[177] Henry Shue, 'The Interdependence of Duties' in Philip Alston and Katarina Tomasevski (eds), *The Right to Food* (Martinus Nijhoff 1984) 83–84.

[178] Emphasis added.

[179] Human Rights Council, 'Towards Operationalizing the "Protect, Respect and Remedy" Framework; Report of the Special Representative of the Secretary-General on the Issue of Human Rights and Transnational Corporations and Other Business Enterprises' (2009) A/HRC/11/13 para 2.

Pillar III of the Guiding Principles on Business and Human Rights (UNGPs).[180]

1.5.3 *The Nature of States' Obligations to 'Respect, Protect and Fulfill' Human Rights*

The obligations to respect, protect and fulfill human rights are both of a positive and negative nature. In this context, the UN Human Rights Commissioner stated that

> all human rights – economic, civil, social, political and cultural – impose negative as well as positive obligations on States, as is captured in the distinction between duties to respect, protect and fulfill. *The duty to respect* requires the duty bearer to refrain from interfering with the enjoyment of any human right. *The duty to protect* requires the duty-bearer to take measures to prevent violations of any human right by third parties. *The duty to fulfill* requires duty-bearer to adopt appropriate legislative, administrative and other measures toward the full realization of human rights.[181]

On the one hand, the *duty to respect* implies that States have a *negative* obligation to refrain from interfering with the enjoyment of any human rights. The text of both Articles 2(1) of the ICCPR and the ICESCR evidence the negative nature of this obligation,[182] as does the clarification provided by the General Comment No. 31 of the UN Human Rights Committee:

> The legal obligation under article 2, paragraph 1 is both negative and positive in nature. State Parties must refrain from violation of the rights recognised by the Covenant, and any restriction on any of those rights must be permissible

---

[180] Ruggie, 'Guiding Principles on Business and Human Rights: Implementing the United Nations "Protect, Respect and Remedy" Framework (Report of the Special Representative of the Secretary-General on the Issue of Human Rights and Transnational Corporations and Other Business Enterprises)' (n 92).

[181] 'Principles and Guidelines for a Human Rights Approach to Poverty Reduction Strategies' (Office of the United Nations high Commissioner for Human Rights 2012) HR/PUB/06/12 para 48.

[182] The words in ICESCR Articles 2(1) are similar in nature: 'Each State Party to the present Covenant, undertakes to take steps, individually and through international assistance and co-operation, especially economic and technical, to the maximum of its available resources, with a view to achieving progressively the full realization of the rights recognised in the present Covenant by all appropriate means, including particularly the adoption of legislative measures.' Article 2(2) provides that: 'The States Parties to this present Covenant undertake to guarantee that the rights enunciated in the present Covenant will be exercised without discrimination of any kind as to race, colour, sex, language, religion, political, or other opinion, national or social origin, property, birth or other status.'

under the relevant provision of the Covenant. Where such restrictions are made, States must demonstrate their necessity and only take such measures as are proportionate to the pursuance of legitimate aims in order to ensure continuous and effective protection of Covenant Rights.[183]

According to General Comment No. 24, in the context of business activities, a State would breach its obligation to respect human rights if it prioritises business interests over human rights 'without adequate justification', or if it pursues policies that impact on those rights in a negative manner, such as by ordering forced evictions in order to start investment projects.[184] On the other hand, *the duty to protect* and *the duty to fulfill* imply *positive* obligations that apply to 'all human rights'.[185] John Ruggie has summarised the State duty to protect in the following manner:

The State duty to protect is a standard of conduct, and not a standard of result. That is, States are not held responsible for corporate-related human rights abuses per se, but may be considered in breach of their obligations where they fail to take appropriate steps to *prevent* it and to *investigate, punish* and *redress* it when it occurs. Within these parameters, States have discretion as to how to fulfill their duty. The main human rights treaties generally contemplate legislative, administrative and judicial measures. The treaty bodies have recommended to States such measures as adopting anti-discrimination legislation and governing employment practices; consulting with communities before approving mining and logging projects, monitoring

---

[183] UN Human Rights Committee (HRC), General comment no. 31, The nature of the general legal obligation imposed on States Parties to the Covenant, 26 May 2004, CCPR/C/21/Rev.1/Add.13 para 6.

[184] UN Committee on Economic, Social and Cultural Rights, General comment No. 24 (2017) on State obligations under the International Covenant on Economic, Social and Cultural Rights in the context of business activities, 10 August 2017, E/C.12/GC/24 paras 12–14; Daniel Augenstein, 'State Responsibilities to Regulate and Adjudicate Corporate Activities under the European Convention on Human Rights' [2011] Submission to the Special Representative of the United Nations Secretary-General (SRSG) on the issue of Human Rights and Transnational Corporations and Other Business Enterprises.

[185] UN Committee on Economic, Social and Cultural Rights, General comment No. 24 (2017) on State obligations under the International Covenant on Economic, Social and Cultural Rights in the context of business activities, 10 August 2017, E/C.12/GC/24 paras 14–24; Human Rights Council, 'Towards Operationalizing the "Protect, Respect and Remedy" Framework; Report of the Special Representative of the Secretary-General on the Issue of Human Rights and Transnational Corporations and Other Business Enterprises' (n 181) para 13; Guiding Principles on Business and Human Rights: Implementing the United Nations 'Protect, Respect and Remedy' Framework 2011 Guiding Principle 1.

and addressing the human rights impacts of such projects; and encouraging business to develop codes of conduct that include human rights.[186]

As emphasised by John Ruggie, while States ultimately have discretion concerning the exact method used for the fulfillment of their duty to protect, the main avenues by which this obligation can be fulfilled is the passing of legislative, administrative, judicial, financial, educational and social measures to this effect.[187] More recently, the text of Principle 3 of the UNGPs also reinforces this approach.[188] In accordance with General Comment No. 3, States must take those measures 'by all appropriate means', a phrase which 'must be given its full and natural meaning',[189] being required to justify why a particular type of measure was taken over another.[190] The appropriateness of the measure in question is a determination that will ultimately be made by the Committee on Economic, Social and Cultural Rights (Committee).[191] This means that while States have some discretion concerning the type of measures to be taken, this discretion is not absolute. Generally, the obligation to protect against human rights abuses implies *substantive obligations*,[192] which are often implemented through specific legislation (such as legislation that deals with the protection of children, women, indigenous people, etc.), *procedural obligations*[193] to investigate and punish human rights abuses and lastly an

---

[186] Human Rights Council, 'Towards Operationalizing the "Protect, Respect and Remedy" Framework; Report of the Special Representative of the Secretary-General on the Issue of Human Rights and Transnational Corporations and Other Business Enterprises' (n 181) para 14. (Emphasis added. Footnotes omitted).

[187] UN Committee on Economic, Social and Cultural Rights (CESCR), General comment No. 3: The Nature of States Parties' Obligations (Art. 2, Para. 1, of the Covenant), 14 December 1990, E/1991/23 para 7.

[188] Guiding Principles on Business and Human Rights: Implementing the United Nations 'Protect, Respect and Remedy' Framework.

[189] UN Committee on Economic, Social and Cultural Rights (CESCR), General Comment No. 3: The Nature of States Parties' Obligations (Art. 2, Para. 1, of the Covenant), 14 December 1990, E/1991/23 para 3.

[190] ibid para 4.

[191] ibid.

[192] *Case of López Ostra v Spain* (European Court of Human Rights, Application No 16798/90) [51–53]; *Case of Tatar v Romania* (European Court of Human Rights, Application No 67021/01) [88].

[193] *Case of Hatton & others v United Kingdom* (European Court of Human Rights, Grand Chamber, Application No 36022/97) [104]. ('In connection with the procedural element of the Court's review of cases involving environmental issues, the Court is required to consider all the procedural aspects, including the type of policy or decision involved, the extent to which the views of individuals (including the applicants) were taken into account throughout the decision-making procedure, and the procedural safeguards available.').

obligation to *monitor* and inform high-risk activities.[194] States must take the necessary steps 'to the maximum of its available resources', but the economic discrepancies between the various States has been recognised. Nevertheless, no State can invoke a lack of resources, unless it is proven that 'every effort' was made to 'use all resources that are at its disposition in an effort to satisfy, as a matter of priority', at least the minimum obligations imposed by the ICESCR.[195] Such minimum obligations have been considered to be the provision of 'essential foodstuffs, of essential primary health care, of basic shelter and housing, or of the most basic forms of education'.[196] Some commentators have argued that the right to water and the right to health should also form part of those minimum obligations.[197] As a framework, the 'typology of human rights' obligations imposes duties on States to respect, protect and fulfill human rights. Those duties are both of a negative and positive nature. The duty to respect is negative in nature, while the duty to protect and the duty to fulfill are positive in nature. The duty to respect implies a negative obligation to refrain from doing anything that could interfere with the enjoyment of rights. The duties to protect and to fulfill are positive in nature in that States must take appropriate measures to ensure the protection and fulfillment of human rights. While ultimately States have discretion on the exact way to implement their obligation to protect, respect and fulfill human rights, it is expected that this is achieved by adopting legislative, administrative, judicial, financial, educational and social measures to this effect.

In light of the connection between the State and its SOEs, under the State duty to protect human rights, States have an obligation to ensure that they appropriately regulate their SOEs. Another relevant issue to consider is the political power and 'clout' that sits behind SOEs, which, in effect, amounts to

---

[194] Stephanie Lagoutte, 'The State Duty to Protect against Business-Related Human Rights Abuses. Unpacking Pillar 1 and 3 of the UN Guiding Principles on Human Rights and Business' (Danish Institute for Human Rights 2014) 2014/1 13; 'Indigenous and Tribal Peoples' Rights over Their Ancestral Lands and Natural Resources: Norms and Jurisprudence of the Inter-American Human Rights System' (Inter-American Commission on Human Rights 2009) OEA/Ser.L/V/II. Doc. 56/09.

[195] UN Committee on Economic, Social and Cultural Rights (CESCR), General comment No. 3: The Nature of States Parties' Obligations (Art. 2, Para. 1, of the Covenant), 14 December 1990, E/1991/23 para 10.

[196] ibid para 10.

[197] Chiara Macchi, 'Right to Water and the Threat of Business: Corporate Accountability and the State's Duty to Protect' (2017) 35 Nord. J. Hum. Rights 186; Andrew Clapham and Mariano Garcia Rubio, 'The Obligations of States with Regard to Non-State Actors in the Context of the Right to Health' [2002] Health and Human Rights Working Paper Series.

an information asymmetry, when compared to privately owned entities. Since States generally have at their disposal means that are above and beyond those usually available to private entities, they are in the best position to know exactly how the entities in question are performing and if their activities could have the potential to interfere with the State's obligations to respect, protect and fulfill human rights.

1.5.4 *The Relationship between Human Rights, International Law and State Corporate Ownership*

International bodies are beginning to recognise that a special link may exist between State corporate ownership and human rights and that State corporate ownership can play an important regulatory function in a human rights context.[198] For example, in General Comment No. 24 the UN Committee on Economic, Social and Cultural Rights stated that business activities included all the activities of business entities whether domestic or transnational or whether they are private or State-owned.[199] General Comment No. 16,[200] made by the UN Committee on the Rights of the Child (CRC) recognises that States have certain international obligations[201] regarding the impact of business activities on the rights of children and applies to '*all business enterprises*, both national and transnational, regardless of size, sector, location, ownership and structure'.[202] The purpose of the General Comment is to provide guidance to States on how they should organise the activities of business enterprises, in order to ensure that the rights of children are protected and that a remedy is provided in situations where infringement occurs. As far as State ownership is concerned, the General Comment states that

---

[198] Larry Catá Backer, 'Sovereign Investing and Markets Based Transnational Rule of Law Building: The Norwegian Sovereign Wealth Fund in Global Markets' (2013) 29 Am. Univ. Int. Law Rev. 1. The potential regulatory function of State ownership was also recognised by John Ruggie as early as 2006.

[199] UN Committee on Economic, Social and Cultural Rights, General comment No. 24 (2017) on State obligations under the International Covenant on Economic, Social and Cultural Rights in the context of business activities, 10 August 2017, E/C.12/GC/24 para 3.

[200] UN Committee on the Rights of the Child (CRC), General comment No. 16 (2013) on State obligations regarding the impact of the business sector on children's rights, 17 April 2013, CRC/C/GC/16.

[201] Those obligations arise mainly out of the Convention on the Rights of the Child (1989), the Optional Protocol on the Sale of Children, Child Prostitution and Child Pornography (2002) and the Optional Protocol on the Involvement of Children in Armed Conflict (2002).

[202] UN Committee on the Rights of the Child (CRC), General comment No. 16 (2013) on State obligations regarding the impact of the business sector on children's rights, 17 April 2013, CRC/C/GC/16 3. (Emphasis added).

States should lead by example requiring all State-owned enterprises to undertake child rights due diligence and to publicly communicate their reports on their impact on children's rights, including regular reporting. States should make public support and services, such as those provided by an export credit agency, development finance, and investment insurance conditional on business' carrying out child rights due diligence.[203]

In addition to the due diligence obligation outlined above, the CRC makes a broad recommendation that 'States should not invest public finances and other resources in business activities that violate children's rights'.[204] The CRC has also made a direct recommendation to Sweden that 'State corporations, including the State pension funds, that invest abroad or operate through subsidiaries and associates in foreign countries, comply with due diligence requirements to prevent and protect children in those countries'.[205] As far as the legal status of such comments is concerned, it should be noted that the Convention on the Rights of the Child is one of the most widely ratified treaties. With regard to the source of authority, commentators have argued that since the CRC is a competent treaty body, its power to 'issue general comments is now accepted by States'.[206] Nevertheless, comments made by the UN treaty bodies remain non-binding, although they do carry 'enormous political and moral weight' which could contribute to the 'elaboration of standards and possible future custom within the complex matrix of international law'.[207]

The UN Human Rights Council has also issued a report that examines the duty of States to protect against human rights abuses in entities that are owned and controlled by the State.[208] The report acknowledges that 'not enough importance has been paid' to the human rights responsibilities of SOEs:

---

[203] ibid 17.

[204] UN Committee on the Rights of the Child (CRC), General comment No. 16 (2013) on State obligations regarding the impact of the business sector on children's rights, 17 April 2013, CRC/C/GC/16.

[205] 'Consideration of Reports Submitted by States Parties under Article 12, Paragraph 1, of the Optional Protocol to the Convention on the Rights of the Child on the Sale of Children, Child Prostitution and Child Pornography' (Committee on the Rights of the Child 2012) CRC/C/OPSC/SWE/CO/1 4.

[206] Paula Gerber, Joanna Kyriakakis and Katie O'Byrne, 'General Comment No. 16 on State Obligations Regarding the Impact of the Business Sector on Children's Rights: What Is Its Standing, Meaning and Effect' (2013) 14 Melb. J. Int'l L. 93, 99.

[207] ibid 99, 101, 102.

[208] Human Rights Council, 'Report of the Working Group on the Issue of Human Rights and Transnational Corporations and Other Business Enterprises' (n 106).

Yet, most States do not seem to fully understand what taking additional steps to protect against human rights abuse by State-owned enterprises means in practice. Nor does it seem obvious to many State-owned enterprises that they have a responsibility to respect human rights . . . .. States, as primary duty bearers under international human rights law, should lead by example. To show leadership on business and human rights requires action and dedicated commitment on many fronts. It also includes using all the means at the disposal of States to ensure that the enterprises under their ownership or control fully respect human rights throughout their operations. There is untapped potential for State-owned enterprises to be champions of responsible business conduct, including respect of human rights. The Working Group calls on States and State-owned enterprises to demonstrate leadership in this field.[209]

The report also notes that SOEs have been the 'least responsive' to requests for information by human rights bodies.[210] The report attempts to define SOEs and outlines the State's duty to protect against abuse by SOEs as well as providing certain suggestions for operationalising the requirements of Principles 4, 5 and 6 of the UNGPs,[211] such as the need for capacity building, transparency, reporting, the performance of human rights due diligence and to ensure access to remedy.[212] The purpose of this report is to fill gaps and to provide guidance to the implementation of Principles 4, 5 and 6 of the UNGPs, which requires States to take 'additional steps' in the context of SOEs. The rationale for imposing additional requirements on States is based on the close connection between the SOE and the State that owns them, as well as on matters of policy coherence, legitimacy and credibility. States should not 'ask less of companies that are closely associated with it, than it asks of private businesses' since the 'human rights record of a State-owned enterprise is often associated with that of the State and vice-versa'.[213] The Committee on Economic, Social and Cultural Rights has also made reference to SOEs in General Comment No. 14 whereby 'States should also refrain from unlawfully polluting air, water and soil, e.g. through industrial waste from State-owned facilities'.[214] The Committee on the Elimination of Discrimination against Women also makes periodic suggestions to States,

---

[209] ibid 22.
[210] ibid 4, 6.
[211] For an in-depth discussion of the UNGPs in the context of SOEs, see Chapter 3.
[212] Human Rights Council, 'Report of the Working Group on the Issue of Human Rights and Transnational Corporations and Other Business Enterprises' (n 106) 12–19.
[213] ibid 8.
[214] UN Committee on Economic, Social and Cultural Rights (CESCR), General comment No. 14: The Right to the Highest Attainable Standard of Health (Art. 12 of the Covenant), 11 August 2000, E/C.12/2000/4 2000 10.

which are aimed at 'increasing the representation of women in decision-making positions in State-owned companies'.[215]

1.6 INTERIM CONCLUSION

This chapter has shown that State corporate ownership is undergoing a period of revival and transformation. State corporate ownership has a long history in the economies of many States, and although it was not a popular form of economic organisation during the 1970s, 1980s and 1990s, it has recently gone through a phase of revival. This revival phase has brought along significant changes to the ways States own companies. Probably the most important change is that States have begun to internationalise their activities again through a multitude of vehicles specifically designed for this purpose. While the traditional concerns associated with State ownership relate to unfair competition, national security and resource security, as the internationalisation of State-ownership increased, it became apparent that there may be specific human rights challenges associated with the activities of SOEs. In this context, new concerns emerged about how States should exercise their ownership function and what type of owner the State should ultimately be. From an international law perspective, the obligations of States to respect, protect and fulfill human rights and the special link that exists between the State and their SOEs, indicates that State corporate ownership could have an important regulatory function in a human rights context.

---

[215] 'List of Issues and Questions in Relation to the Combined Eighth and Ninth Periodic Reports of Portugal' (Committee on the Elimination of Discrimination against Women 2015) CEDAW/C/PRT/Q/8-9 2.

2

State-Owned Entities as a Sui Generis 'Participant' in International Law

2.1 INTRODUCTION

This chapter argues that SOEs are a sui generis 'participant' in international law. After an introduction to the concept of legal personality in international law and to the long-standing debates and remaining challenges associated with the recognition of corporations as subjects of international law, the chapter continues with an analysis of the differences between SOEs and POEs. The sui generis character of SOEs can be ascertained from their belonging to the public domain, from their role and rationale for existence and from the creation of entirely separate regulatory regimes to specifically address some of the challenges associated with State corporate ownership. From an international law perspective, the recognition of SOEs as sui generis participants could have two main consequences. First, it demonstrates the increasing heterogeneity and complexity of the notion of participation in the international legal system. Second, from a human rights perspective, the corporate 'responsibility' to respect human rights may be elevated to the level of a 'duty' in the case of SOEs. Overall, this chapter demonstrates that international law has an inherent capacity to expand on certain well-entrenched conceptual frameworks and to adapt to new ideas.

2.2 THE CONCEPT OF LEGAL PERSONALITY IN INTERNATIONAL LAW

Legal personality is one of the most 'mysterious' and controversial concepts in international law, having been the subject of debate for many centuries.[1] In a

---

[1] Robert McCorquodale, 'The Individual and the International Legal System' in Malcolm D Evans (ed), *International Law* (4th edn, Oxford University Press 2014) 280; Fleur Johns (ed), *International Legal Personality* (Ashgate 2010); Janne Elisabeth Nijman, *The Concept of International Legal Personality: An Inquiry into the History and Theory of International Law*

similar way to municipal law, the concept of legal personality in international law is used to distinguish between the actors that belong to the international legal system and those that are excluded from it.[2] The process of *how* one becomes a legal person determines *who* is ultimately endowed with rights and obligations on the international plane, as well as the *consequences* that follow from such endowment. A full subject of international law is endowed with *substantive* rights and obligations and has the *procedural capacity* to maintain those rights, by bringing international claims to defend them, and to be responsible for breaches of its obligations, by being subjected to claims by third parties. If procedural capacity is absent, then an entity is considered as having restricted legal personality, which may ultimately be dependent on the 'agreement or acquiescence of recognised legal persons and opposable on the international plane only to those agreeing or acquiescent'.[3] The capacity to make claims with respect to breaches of international law, the capacity to enter into treaties that are valid on the international plane and the enjoyment of privileges and immunities from national jurisdictions are some of the areas where questions relating to the concept of legal personality in international law have traditionally arisen.[4] In addition, legal personality is also relevant to the question whether treaties apply to individuals, the capacity of international organisations, the rights and duties of non-State actors under customary international law and the legal nature of State contracts.[5] The undeniable

---

(TMC Asser Press 2004); Andrea Bianchi (ed), *Non-State Actors and International Law* (Routledge 2017); Jean d'Aspremont (ed), *Participants in the International Legal System: Multiple Perspectives on Non-State Actors in International Law* (Taylor & Francis 2011); Catherine M Brölmann and Janne Elisabeth Nijman, 'Legal Personality as a Fundamental Concept for International Law' in Jean D'Aspremont and Sahib Singh (eds), *Concepts for International Law* (Edward Elgar 2019); Wilhelm G Grewe, *The Epochs of International Law* (Walter de Gruyter 2013) 302; James Crawford, *Chance, Order, Change: The Course of International Law, General Course on Public International Law* (Hague Acad of Internat Law 2014) 192–211. (Grewe notes that: 'It was a matter of controversy in international legal theory during the nineteenth century whether the great trading companies were "subjects" of international law, whether they held a "sovereignty" of their own, or whether they were merely "organs" of their parent country. In general, the latter view was taken and the entire problem was considered to be a matter of domestic public law. However, the questions which were asked actually missed the issue. Although the trading companies could not be squeezed into the continental European notion of "State", they were nevertheless a phenomenon of relevance to international law. Their very function was to prevent the transfer of the concept of "State to the non-European world."').

[2]   Roland Portmann, *Legal Personality in International Law* (Cambridge University Press 2010) 19.
[3]   Crawford, *Brownlie's Principles of Public International Law* (Oxford University Press 2012) 115.
[4]   ibid.
[5]   Portmann (n 2) 3.

importance and complexity of the issues involved have led to varied conceptualisations and interpretations of the concept of legal personality. By tracing
the intellectual origins, historical development and practical application of
this concept, Roland Portmann has identified five different 'conceptions' of
legal personality in international legal argument: the 'States-only conception',
the 'recognition conception', the 'individualistic conception', the 'formal
conception' and the 'actor conception'.[6] While the following paragraphs
succinctly summarise the five different 'conceptions' of legal personality, they
are intended to be read not as a mere synthesis but as the starting point for
further reflection, as well as the necessary background for the remainder of
this chapter.

According to the States-only conception, the international community is
composed only of States and international law is created exclusively through
State will. Under this view, no other entities are present in the international
realm and individuals are non-existent on the international plane. Since only
States can create international law – through consent – it is only States that
can be bound by it. At the basis of this conception is a view of the State as a
historical fact absorbing individuals, and of the individual who can only come
'to its full existence and moral standing as part of the State'.[7] The philosophical underpinning of this conception is largely based on Hegel's views of the
State as an 'organism',[8] and of international law as applicable only between
States.[9] The States-only conception of international legal personality sits at the
basis of the positivist school of thought, having been endorsed by scholars such
as, among others, Heinrich Triepel[10] and Lassa Oppenheim,[11] while in legal

---

[6] ibid 242–243.
[7] ibid 55, 42–80.
[8] Georg Wilhelm Fredrich Hegel, *Hegel: Elements of the Philosophy of Right* (Cambridge
University Press 1991) 347.
[9] ibid 366. ('International law applies to the *relations* between independent states. What it
contains *in and for itself* therefore assumes the form of an *obligation*, because its actuality
depends on *distinct and sovereign wills*.').
[10] Jörg Kammerhofer, 'Hans Kelsen in Today's International Legal Scholarship' in Jörg
Kammerhofer and Jean D'Aspremont (eds), *International Legal Positivism in a Post-Modern
World* (Cambridge University Press 2014) 91. ('The will whose content will form the legal rule,
the will from which the legal rule flows, we call source of law . . . . What kind of will is able to
create international law with binding force? This will can only be the will of states. . . Only the
common will of many states, joined as a unity of will through a unification of will, can be the
source of international law.' Translation from German by the author of this book chapter from
Heinrich Triepel, *Völkrrecht und Landesrecht* (C. L. Hirschfeld 1899) 27–32).
[11] Lassa Oppenheim, *International Law: A Treatise*, vol 1 (2nd edn, Longmans, Green and Co
1912) 107. ('The conception of International Persons is derived from the conception of the Law
of Nations. As this law is the body of rules, which the civilised States consider legally binding in
their intercourse, every State which belongs to the civilised States, and is, therefore, a member

practice it can be found, among others, in cases such as the *SS Lotus*[12] and the *Mavrommatis Palestine Concessions*.[13] In this view, law is a system of rules that must be distinguished from other non-legal considerations, such as moral or ethical arguments.[14] States are the 'gatekeepers' of the international legal system and maintain a 'monopoly on access to rights, obligations and capacities'.[15] Individuals cannot be subjects of international law; individuals are mere objects of international law.[16] However, this view only addresses what may be called traditional positivism. More modern forms of positivism have emerged, and the doctrinal thinking has developed into a more nuanced approach, where the main concern is still with the derivation of a rule, but there is also the acknowledgement that the rule may be derived from sources of law, which are not necessarily 'wedded' to State consent.[17] Modern positivism allows for rules to be derived from State practice in general. This State practice can be said to incorporate interactions between States, domestic legislation, judicial decisions, diplomatic dispatches, internal memoranda, ministerial statements and the practice of international organisations.[18]

The recognition conception of international legal personality is a continuum of the States-only conception. According to this view, the presumption is that States are still the only recognised persons in the international realm and that international law can only emanate from State will. However, given

of the Family of Nations, is an International Person. Sovereign States exclusively are International Persons – i.e. subjects of International Law.').

[12] *SS Lotus (France v Turkey)* (Permanent Court of International Justice, 1927 PCIJ (ser A) No 10 (Sept 7)) [41]. ('International law governs relations between independent States. The rules of law binding upon States therefore emanate from their own free will as expressed in conventions or by usages generally accepted as expressing principles of law and established in order to regulate the relations between these co-existing independent communities or with a view to the achievement of common aims. Restrictions upon the independence of States cannot therefore be presumed.').

[13] *The Mavrommatis Palestine Concessions (Greece v UK)* (Permanent Court of International Justice, 1924 PCIJ (ser B) No 3 (Aug 30)) [21]. (This case, however, does not expressly exclude the fact that the individual can be the bearer of rights in international law: 'It is an elementary principle of international law that a State is entitled to protect its subjects, when injured by acts contrary to international law committed by another State, from whom they have been unable to obtain satisfaction through the ordinary channels. By taking up the case of one of its subjects and by resorting to diplomatic action or international judicial proceedings on his behalf, a State is in reality asserting its own rights – its right to ensure, in the person of its subjects, respect for the rules of international law.').

[14] Kate Parlett, *The Individual in the International Legal System: Continuity and Change in International Law* (Cambridge University Press 2011) 41.

[15] ibid 348.

[16] Oppenheim (n 11) 366.

[17] Parlett (n 14) 41.

[18] ibid.

their position as the 'highest authorities in the international realm', States can overcome this presumption by creating and recognising non-State entities as limited international legal persons. In this case, international legal personality is acquired with the consent of the State of nationality. The recognition conception confirms the fundamental view of the State as a historical fact that precedes law, but it introduces – as a corrective measure – the argument that an interpretation of the law must be realistically attuned to current social conditions and the development of society.[19] Georg Jellinek and Max Huber, among others, have supported the recognition conception.[20] In legal practice, the recognition conception is encountered in the context of international organisations and entities that hold special status in international law (the Holy See, the Order of Malta, 'governments-in-exile' and territories whose title is undetermined but still have international legal identity).[21] The *Reparation for Injuries Suffered in the Service of the United Nations* advisory opinion, where the ICJ declared the UN as an international legal person, is the most important manifestation in legal practice of the recognition conception.[22]

The individualistic conception of international legal personality can be considered as a revival of natural law concepts and emerged as a response to positivist legal thought.[23] Under the individualistic conception, the individual human being is the 'ultimate' international legal person and has rights and obligations in the international legal sphere. The development of this view of legal personality was heavily influenced by the atrocities committed during World War II and was promoted by Hersch Lauterpacht,[24] Georges Scelle[25]

---

[19] Portmann (n 2) 85.

[20] ibid 95.

[21] ibid 99–125; Crawford, *Brownlie's Principles of Public International Law* (n 3) 121–122, 124–126.

[22] *Reparations for Injuries Suffered in the Service of the United Nations* 19 (International Court of Justice, Advisory Opinion: ICJ Reports 1949, p 174) 178–179. ('The subjects of law in any legal system are not necessarily identical in their nature or in the extent of their rights, and their nature depends upon the needs of the community. Throughout its history, the development of international law has been influenced by the requirements of international life, and the progressive increase in the collective activities of States has already given rise to instances of action upon the international plane by certain entities which are not States. This development culminated in the establishment in June 1945 of an international organization whose purposes and principles are specified in the Charter of the United Nations. But to achieve these ends the attribution of international personality is indispensable.').

[23] Parlett (n 14) 38–45.

[24] Hersch Lauterpacht, *International Law: Being the Collected Papers of Hersch Lauterpacht (Volume 2, Part I International Law in General)* (Elihu Lauterpacht ed, Cambridge University Press 1975) 487–537.

[25] Georges Scelle, *Précis de droit des gens: Principes et systématique* (Librairie du Recueil Sirey (société anonyme) 1932) 42. (['L]es individus seuls sont sujets de droit en droit international public.').

and more recently by Judge Augusto Cançado Trindade.[26] Its main manifestations in legal practice can be found in the judgment of the International
Military Tribunal at Nuremberg (which sentenced twelve Nazi defendants to
death and seven to imprisonment for the commission of international crimes),
the civil responsibility of private parties for *jus cogens* violations under the US
Alien Tort Statute (which has repeatedly confirmed that private entities can
violate norms *jus cogens*) and the development of international human rights
law by the ECHR.[27] The individualistic conception rejects both the States-
only conception and the recognition conception and holds that a State must
be viewed not as a 'mystical entity' but as a corporate entity that is created by
individuals in order to pursue certain interests. This view further posits that the
sources of international law include general principles of law, which means
that international law is not exclusively dependent on State will.[28] From a
philosophical perspective, the 'individualistic conception of international law'
can be associated with Immanuel Kant's cosmopolitan views of a 'universal
community'. In international law, the manifestations of cosmopolitanism can
be best observed through other associated concepts such as global citizenship,
internationalism and individualism.[29] Arguably, the ICJ opened the door for
the direct application of international law to individuals in the *Jurisdiction of
the Courts of Danzig* advisory opinion (although some commentators have
argued otherwise),[30] where the Court stated that 'it cannot be disputed that the
very object of an international agreement, according to the intention of the
contracting Parties, may be the adoption by the Parties of some definite rules
creating individual rights and obligations and enforceable by the national
courts'.[31] This position seems to have been later confirmed by the ICJ in the
LaGrand case, where it held that Article 36(1)(b) of the Vienna Convention
on Consular Relations 'creates individual rights'.[32]

Under the formal conception of legal personality, there are no preconceived
notions as to who may be an international legal person: anyone who is the addressee
of an international norm that contains rights, duties or capacities can, in principle,

---

[26] Antônio Augusto Cançado Trindade, *International Law for Humankind: Towards a New Jus
Gentium* (Brill Nijhoff 2010) 213–273.

[27] Portmann (n 2) 154–172.

[28] Trindade (n 26) 55–84.

[29] Parlett (n 14) 43.

[30] Portmann (n 2) 68–73.

[31] *Jurisdiction of the Courts of Danzig* (Advisory Opinion) (Permanent Court of International
Justice, 1928, PCIJ (ser B) No 15) 17–18.

[32] *LaGrand (Germany v United States of America)* (International Court of Justice, Judgment, I C
J Reports 2001, p 466) [77].

be an international legal person. There are no further consequences that follow on from being deemed an international legal person, and those that hold international legal personality do not possess fundamental rights and duties nor is the capacity to contribute to international law automatically bestowed on them.[33] In the formal conception, law can only be properly called so if it is empirically observable and divorced from theology, ethics and morals. This conception was initially formulated by Hans Kelsen,[34] and since then, it has been advocated by international lawyers such as, among others, Paul Guggenheim and Julio Barberis.[35]

According to the actor conception, all entities that exercise 'effective power' in the international 'decision-making process' have international legal personality. In the international sphere one may find a multitude of 'actors' that exercise 'effective power', such as, among others, armed groups, non-governmental organisations and corporations. The basic propositions that underpin the actor conceptualisation is that international law is not a set of rules but an authoritative decision-making process and that it is ultimately the exercise of effective power that determines the ambit of participation.[36] The origins of the actor conception can be found in American realism and in the creators of the New Haven School (Myers S. McDougal, Harold D. Laswell and Michael Reismann), who viewed law as an interdisciplinary decision-making process, which included political science, sociology and philosophy. In contemporary international legal thought, it is Rosalyn Higgins that can be credited with bringing this theory into the mainstream. Judge Higgins encouraged lawyers to escape from the 'intellectual prison' erected by the subject–object dichotomy and extended to them an invitation to entertain the possibility that States along with other actors such as international organisations, individuals and corporations are 'participants' in international law.[37] The actor conception of international legal personality can be found in the works of

---

[33] Portmann (n 2) 172–207, 177.

[34] Hans Kelsen, *General Theory of Law and State* (The Lawbook Exchange, Ltd 2007) 342. ('All law is regulation of human behaviour. The only social reality to which legal norms can refer are the relations between human beings. Hence, a legal obligation as well as a legal right cannot have for its contents anything but the behaviour of human individuals. If, then, international law should not obligate and authorise individuals, the obligations and rights stipulated by international law would have no contents at all and international law would not obligate or authorise anybody to do anything.').

[35] Portmann (n 2) 173.

[36] ibid 213, 208–243.

[37] Rosalyn Higgins, *Problems and Process: International Law and How We Use It* (Clarendon Press 1994) 49–50. ('Finally, the whole notion of "subjects" and "objects" has no credible reality, and in my view no functional purpose. We have erected an intellectual prison of our own choosing and then declared it to be an unalterable constraint.').

John Dugard, Ane-Marie Slaughter, Robert McCorquodale and Andrew Clapham,[38] while its manifestations in legal practice can be observed from jurisprudence such as the *Bank for International Settlements* arbitration.[39] Some of the scholars that endorse the actor conception have also suggested that it is generally 'unhelpful' to focus on the notion of who can be a 'subject' of international law and that it might be better to instead focus on the 'capacity' of those actors to bear rights and obligations.[40] The term 'non-State actor' is also used when one discusses the notion of participation in international law. Yet, the usage of the term 'non-State actor' is in itself problematic – as Phillip Alston notes – because this terminology has been 'intentionally adopted in order to reinforce the assumption that the State is not only the central actor, but also the indispensable and pivotal one around which all other entities revolve'.[41] On the same issue, Judge Cançado Trindade notes:

It appears quite clear nowadays that there is nothing intrinsic to International Law that would impede, or render it impossible, to non-State 'actors' to be endowed with international legal personality and capacity. Yet, part of the contemporary legal doctrine keeps on referring to individuals as 'actors' (rather than subjects) in the international legal order. This is not a juridical term, it is rather a term of art, to which no specific juridical contents and consequences are necessarily attached. To call individuals 'actors' in International Law is nothing but a platitude. They are true subjects of International Law, bearers of rights and duties which emanate directly therefrom. It is perfectly possible to conceptualize as subject of International Law any person or entity, *titulaire* of rights and bearer of obligations, which emanate directly from International Law.[42]

At this point in time, it can be asserted with a relatively high degree of confidence that there are likely to be few adherents to the States-only

---

[38] Portmann (n 2) 209–210; Robert McCorquodale, 'Sources and the Subjects of International Law: A Plurality of Law-Making Participants' in Samantha Besson and Jean d'Aspremont (eds), *The Oxford Handbook on the Sources of International law* (1st edn, Oxford University Press 2017); Robert McCorquodale, 'An Inclusive International Legal System' (2004) 17 Leiden J. Int. Law 477; Andrew Clapham, *Human Rights in the Private Sphere* (Clarendon Press 1996); Matthias Herdegen, *Principles of International Economic Law* (Oxford University Press 2013) 25–27.

[39] *Dr Horst Reineccius & Ors v Bank for International Settlements* (Permanent Court of Arbitration, 2003, Final Award).

[40] Clapham (n 38) 60–61, 63–68, 70–73; Trindade (n 26) 243–373.

[41] Philip Alston, 'The "Not-a-Cat" Syndrome: Can the International Human Rights Regime Accommodate Non-State Actors?' in Philip Alston (ed), *Non-State Actors and Human Rights* (Oxford University Press 2005) 3.

[42] Trindade (n 26) 240.

conception of international legal personality. However, another issue that must be taken into consideration is that changes within the existing structures of international law have often occurred because of the need to provide 'practical solutions to manage certain problems, rather than by reference to some overriding theoretical framework or pursuit of a structurally different system'.[43] Consequently, the development of new theories, or the changes that have occurred within existing ones, can be considered as a by-product of the practical need to address certain problems rather than as an attempt to make changes to the structure of international law *through* the use of a particular theory.[44] This can be observed, for example, from the historical developments concerning the position of the individual in the international legal system and from the recognition of international organisations as subjects of international law. Furthermore, with regard to the position of the individual in the international legal system, two observations are in order. First, the notion of 'individual' should be understood broadly to include not only human beings but also groups of persons, such as indigenous populations, non-governmental organisations and corporations.[45] Second, one should also note the gradual change that has occurred starting from the nineteenth century, when individuals were perceived as having no standing or participatory rights in the international legal system, to the intermediate position during the interwar period following the *Danzig* opinion, to the post-1945 international legal system which recognises that individuals have direct rights and obligations in international law.[46]

Overall, the emergence and increasing importance of international organisations on the international plane, particularly after World War II, opened the door to a more nuanced approach to the doctrine of subjects. The subjects of international law are thus different, according to their nature and their rights and obligations. States have full capacity with regard to rights and obligations, while other subjects can have a lesser status and more limited capacities, rights and obligations.[47] Yet, this approach is problematic too,

---

[43] Parlett (n 14) 365.
[44] ibid.
[45] McCorquodale, 'The Individual and the International Legal System' (n 1) 281.
[46] Parlett (n 14) 343–353. For example, individuals are the holders of enforceable rights, among others, under international human rights law, in international investment law and in the context of international armed conflict under the Geneva Conventions and the Additional Protocols.
[47] Vincent Chetail, 'The Legal Personality of Multinational Corporations, State Responsibility and Due Diligence: The Way Forward' in Denis Alland and others (eds), *Unity and Diversity of International Law: Essays in Honour of Professor Pierre-Marie Dupuy* (Brill 2014) 110.

insofar as in international law there are no objective criteria for determining what rights, obligations and capacities a particular subject has.[48] The complex nature of this topic has prompted some scholars to fully reject the subject–object dichotomy and terminology as having no 'credible reality' or 'functional purpose'.[49] In international law, there are no 'subjects' or 'objects' but a multitude of 'participants' such as States, individuals, international organisations, multinational corporations and private non-governmental groups, as Rosalyn Higgins notes:

> In the way our world is organised, it is States, which are mostly interested in, for example, sea-space, or boundaries or treaties; it is thus States which advance claims and counterclaims about these. Individuals' interests lie in other directions: in protection from the physical excess of others, in their personal treatment abroad, in the protection abroad of their property interests, in fairness and predictability in their international business transactions and in securing some external support for the establishment of a tolerable balance between their rights and duties within their national state. Thus, the topics of minimum standard of treatment of aliens, requirements as to the conduct of hostilities and human rights, are not simply exceptions conceded by historical chance within a system of rules that operates between states. Rather, they are simply part and parcel of the fabric of international law, representing the claims that are naturally made by individual participants in contradistinction to state-participants.[50]

To conclude, this section has demonstrated that there are many different ways of looking at the same problem. As a result of the inherently 'parochial' nature of law, 'the legal scholar – even the nihilist – is necessarily an activist advocating a certain vision of the law, and hence, a given way to make sense of the world'.[51] Nevertheless, caution must be exercised when one endorses a particular view or theory because of the limited perspective that any such theory can realistically offer, as Andrea Bianchi notes:

> Theories are ways of worldmaking …. The worlds they construct are the worlds of their own making. They do not offer subjective explanations of a reality that has a discrete and objective existence. They constitute the reality

---

[48] Parlett (n 14) 354.
[49] Higgins (n 37) 49.
[50] ibid 50. Quoting Rosalyn Higgins, 'Conceptual Thinking about the Individual in International Law' (1978) 4 Br. J. Int. Stud. I at 5–6.
[51] Jörg Kammerhofer and Jean D'Aspremont, 'Introduction: The Future of International Legal Positivism' in Jörg Kammerhofer and Jean D'Aspremont (eds), *International Legal Positivism in a Post-Modern World* (Cambridge University Press 2014) 1–2.

they intend to describe by representing it and constructing it on the basis of their own presuppositions and theoretical tenets. Hence, it is important to make the effort to understand these different worlds from their own internal perspective, from the premises they start from, and against the backdrop of their fundamental tenets. This is no easy task, as we are all 'positioned': we all look at international law from our own standpoint, which is the result of our intellectual upbringing, the set of presuppositions and beliefs we adhere to, as well as our personal history that makes us sensitive to some issues rather than others. Yet, I believe that mere awareness of this issue is a great advantage to anyone who would like to broaden his or her intellectual horizon. At the very least, knowledge of such diversity of theories and methodologies should bring about more humbleness, and tolerance for those who do not share our own beliefs.[52]

2.3 CORPORATIONS AS 'SUBJECTS' OF INTERNATIONAL LAW

When considering the question whether corporations can be subjects of international law, it must be acknowledged, as a starting point, that in international law there is no centralised law of corporations. While most, if not all, municipal legal systems have specific laws that deal with the rights and obligations of corporations, in international law no such centralised law can be found. Consequently, the endowment of corporations with international personality would be dependent on the adoption of one of the conceptions of legal personality discussed in Section 2.2. Yet, one must be wary of 'facile generalisations on the subject of legal personality' and under this view – which to a certain extent is still recognised as being orthodox – corporations are still not considered as subjects of international law.[53] As such, if one adopts the States-only conception, the answer to this question would be that, since the main aim of international law is to regulate the relationships between sovereign States, and more recently international organisations,[54] international law is not, and cannot be concerned about the regulation of corporations, regardless of whether they are national, multinational, private or State-owned. The resistance of recognising corporations as subjects of international law is due to several concerns: first, there is the fear that corporations may interfere in the political and economic affairs of States; second, there is the concern that they

---

[52] Andrea Bianchi, *International Law Theories: An Inquiry into Different Ways of Thinking* (Oxford University Press 2016) 16. (References omitted).

[53] Crawford, *Brownlie's Principles of Public International Law* (n 3) 126; Malcom Shaw, *International Law* (Cambridge University Press 2008) 182.

[54] *Reparations for Injuries Suffered in the Service of the United Nations* (n 22).

may be able to 'trigger excessive diplomatic protections';[55] and third, there is the fear that corporations may 'reduce the power of states and their traditionally dominant position in international law'.[56]

Under the recognition conception, a corporation could be considered a 'limited' subject of international law. In the *Legality of the Use of Nuclear Weapons in Armed Conflict* advisory opinion, the ICJ said that 'the Court need hardly point out that international organisations are subjects of international law which do not, unlike States, possess a general competence'.[57] In the view of the Court, international organisations were governed not only by the 'principle of speciality' according to which States endowed express powers on those organisations in order to fulfill their tasks, but also with 'implied powers' in order to achieve their objectives.[58] The recognition conception of legal personality has been applied to corporations in the *Texaco/Calasiatic*[59] award where two American companies (Texaco and Calasiatic) were declared international legal persons for the purposes of the contract that those two entities concluded with Libya. In that case, sole arbitrator René-Jean Dupuy stated that while Texaco and Calasiatic were not States and their concessions with Libya were not treaties, 'the legal order from which the contract derived was international law' so

> stating that the contract between a State and a private person falls within the international legal order means that for the purposes of interpretation and performance of the contract, it should be recognised that a private contracting party has specific international capacities. But, unlike a State, the private person has only a limited capacity and his quality as a subject of international law does enable him only to invoke, in the field of international law, the rights which he derives from the contract.[60]

There is no reason why corporations cannot be subjects of international law under the individualistic conception. Since both international and domestic law recognise corporate entities, this could 'support the idea of treating [corporations] the same as a natural person, with the result that businesses

---

[55] Clapham (n 38) 78.
[56] Chetail (n 47) 111.
[57] *Legality of the Use by a State of Nuclear Weapons in Armed Conflict* (International Court of Justice, Advisory Opinion, ICJ Reports 1996, p 66) [25].
[58] ibid.
[59] *Texaco Overseas Petroleum Company and California Asiatic Oil Company v The Government of the Libyan Arab Republic* ((Ad hoc Award, Arbitrator: René-Jean Dupuy, 19th January 1977) International Legal Materials 1978 1).
[60] ibid 47.

would be responsible for the same international crimes as individuals'.[61] In the context of claims under the Alien Torts Statute (ATS),[62] courts in the United States have held numerous times that private individuals can violate norms *jus cogens*. While initially this line of reasoning was applicable only to conduct exercised on behalf of a State,[63] it was later extended to include violations of norms *jus cogens* by private individuals[64] and also arguably to foreign corporations.[65] However, it should be noted that while the individualistic conception has maintained under the ATS – in that the statute is still applicable to both individuals and corporations – its extraterritorial reach has been restricted since the decision in *Kiobel v Dutch Petroleum*, where it was held that there was a presumption against the extraterritorial application of the ATS, unless the claim 'touches and concerns' the territory of the United States.[66] It is likely that for a claim to 'touch and concern' the United States, the wrongful conduct must have occurred in the United States and that it must also have been a violation of international law.[67]

---

[61] Steven R Ratner, 'Corporations and Human Rights: A Theory of Legal Responsibility' (2001) 111 Yale L.J. 443, 494.

[62] Alien Tort Statute (28 US Code 1350).

[63] *Filártiga v Peña-Irala* (United States, Court of Appeals (1980) 630 F2d 876); *Tel-Oren v Libyan Arab Republic* ((United States, Court of Appeals, District of Columbia Circuit (1984) 726 F2d 774 (DC Cir 1984)).

[64] *Kadic v Karadžic* (United States, Court of Appeals, Second Circuit (1995) 70 F3d 232) 239. ('We do not agree that the law of nations, as understood in the modern era, confines its reach to state action. Instead, we hold that certain forms of conduct violate the law of nations whether undertaken by those acting under the auspices of state or only as private individuals.' Per Newman C.J.).

[65] *Doe v Unocal* (United States, Court of Appeals, 9th Circuit (2002) 395 F3d 932); *Presbyterian Church of Sudan v Talisman Energy* (United States, Court of Appeals, Second Circuit (2009) 582 F3d 244) 48 (footnote 12). ('We will also assume, without deciding, that corporations such as Talisman may be held liable for the violations of customary international law that plaintiffs allege.').

[66] *Kiobel v Royal Dutch Petroleum Co* ((United States Supreme Court, 2013)133 S Ct 1659). (The restrictive interpretation of the Alien Tort Statute was started in *Sosa v Alvarez-Machian* (United States, Supreme Court (2004) 542 U.S. 692) where the Supreme Court stated that extraterritorial jurisdiction under the ATS was only permissible in a limited number of circumstances, which were 'specific, universal and obligatory'. The approach taken in *Kiobel* was recently confirmed in *Joseph Jesner v Arab Bank* (United States, Supreme Court (2018) 138 S. Ct. 1386) where the Supreme Court said that 'foreign corporations may not be defendants under the Alien Tort Statute'.).

[67] P Sean Morris, 'Lex Internationalis: Kiobel, Empires, and the Color of Human Rights' (2015) 7 Geo. JL & Mod. Critical Race Persp. 71; Robert McCorquodale, 'Waving Not Drowning: Kiobel Outside the United States' (2013) 107 Am. J. Int. Law 846; Caroline Kaeb and David Scheffer, 'The Paradox of Kiobel in Europe' (2013) 107 Am. J. Int. Law 852; Sarah H Cleveland, 'After Kiobel' (2014) 12 J. Int. Crim. Justice 551.

Since under the formal conception the international legal system is completely open, corporations would be subjects of international law as long as a norm can be identified which confers rights, duties or capacities to that entity.[68] For example, international investment law gives *direct* rights to investors, while norms *jus cogens* are also *directly* applicable to corporations.[69] There are also norms that apply to corporations *indirectly* such as those that can be found in anti-corruption, anti-bribery and anti-discrimination conventions and under human rights conventions.[70] While, strictly, it would be incorrect to refer to the notion of 'subjects' under the actor conception, it is clear that the notion of 'participation' covers corporations. The actor conception is best evidenced through the workings of the international corporate social responsibility movement that has been developing since the end of the last century, specifically to address the accountability gaps that are associated with transnational corporations, and which has engaged a multitude of actors, such as international organisations, non-governmental organisations, trade unions, national governments and corporations, and which is a development that further entrenches the role that international law has to play in this area. In the context of the corporate responsibility of transnational corporations for human rights violations,[71] there is a considerable amount of literature that endorses the actor conception,[72] while in

---

[68] Portmann (n 2) 174.

[69] Rome Statute of the International Criminal Court 2002. (Article 1 states that the International Criminal Court (ICC) has jurisdiction over 'persons' without distinguishing between individuals or other legal entities. In accordance with Article 5 the ICC only has jurisdiction over the 'most serious crimes of concern to the international community as a whole' such as genocide, crimes against humanity, war crimes and the crime of aggression. For the exercise of jurisdiction see Articles 12, 13, 14 and 15.).

[70] Carlos Manuel Vázquez, 'Direct vs. Indirect Obligations of Corporations under International Law' 43 Colum. J. Transnat'l L. 928.

[71] Jennifer A Zerk, *Multinationals and Corporate Social Responsibility: Limitations and Opportunities in International Law* (1st pbk. edn, Cambridge University Press 2011); Surya Deva and David Bilchitz (eds), *Human Rights Obligations of Business: Beyond the Corporate Responsibility to Respect?* (Cambridge University Press 2013); Nadia Bernaz, *Business and Human Rights: History, Law and Policy: Bridging the Accountability Gap* (Routledge 2017); Clapham (n 38) 195–266; Lee McConnell, *Extracting Accountability from Non-State Actors in International Law: Assessing the Scope for Direct Regulation* (Taylor & Francis 2016); Adam McBeth, *International Economic Actors and Human Rights* (Routledge 2009); Lene Bomann-Larsen and Oddny Wiggen, *Responsibility in World Business: Managing Harmful Side-Effects of Corporate Activity* (United Nations University Press 2004); Peter T Muchlinski, *Multinational Enterprises and the Law* (2nd edn, Oxford University Press 2007).

[72] Andrea Bianchi (ed), *Non-State Actors and International Law* (Routledge 2017); Alston (n 41); Clapham (n 38); McConnell (n 71); Math Noortmann, August Reinisch and Cedric Ryngaert, *Non-State Actors in International Law* (Bloomsbury 2015); Robert McCorquodale, *International Law beyond the State: Essays on Sovereignty, Non-State Actors and Human Rights*

jurisprudence, the actor conception can be found in the *Bank of International Settlements* arbitration where the tribunal stated the following:

> Now, obviously the Bank is not a State. If public interest were understood as meaning the public interest of a state, the Bank's actions could not meet the public interest test and would be *eo ipso* unlawful. The reason for this conclusion would not derive from the nature and purpose of the action, but from the fact that the Bank is not a state . . .. When applied to an actor which is an international entity, but is not a state, public interest must be understood, *mutatis mutandis*, as an action rationally, proportionally and necessarily related to the performance of one of the legitimate international public purposes of the *actor* undertaking it.[73]

Overall, despite criticism, the notion of 'participation' and 'participants' in the international legal system is not only inherently flexible, but it also realistically reflects the international legal system in its present form.[74] Its usage, however, does not necessarily imply that one exclusively adopts the view of international law as a 'process',[75] nor does it assume that corporations have identical rights and obligations as other participants in the international system, such as States. In this sense, corporations can be viewed as having a 'limited international personality':

> As long as we admit that individuals have rights and duties under customary international human rights law and international humanitarian law, we have to admit that legal persons may also possess the international legal personality necessary to enjoy some of these rights, and conversely to be prosecuted or held accountable for violations of the relevant international duties.[76]

Furthermore, except perhaps for the States-only conception, the notion of participation can be found in all the other approaches to the concept of international legal personality discussed above. According to the recognition conception as established by the *Reparation for Injuries Suffered in the Service of the United Nations*, the notion of participation is implied in the acknowledgement that the subjects of international law vary according to their nature, rights and obligations. The formal conception of international law as an open

---

(CMP 2011); Higgins (n 37); McCorquodale, 'An Inclusive International Legal System' (n 38); Robert McCorquodale, 'Beyond State Sovereignty: The International Legal System and Non-State Participants' (2006) Revista Colombiana de Derecho Internacional.

[73] *Dr. Horst Reineccius & Ors v Bank for International Settlements* (n 39) [150].

[74] McCorquodale, 'The Individual and the International Legal System' (n 1) 300–301.

[75] McCorquodale, 'Sources and the Subjects of International Law: A Plurality of Law-Making Participants' (n 38) 754.

[76] Clapham (n 38) 78–79. (Footnotes omitted).

system also acknowledges that no entities are excluded from it and that, as long as there is an international norm that addresses that entity, international legal personality automatically follows from it. The individualistic conception endorses the notion of participation by recognising that individuals have rights, obligations and capacities on the international plane that are independent from State will, as is the case in the context of norms *jus cogens*.[77] Consequently, it is now becoming an increasingly accepted proposition that in international law one can find – in the words of Robert McCorquodale – a 'plurality of law-making participants', which ended the 'Dark Ages of international legal ideas', when it was believed that only States could have the status of subjects of international law.[78] In light of this discussion, for the remainder of this monograph the notion of 'participant' and 'participation' will be used.

2.4 STATE-OWNED ENTITIES AS A SUI GENERIS PARTICIPANT IN INTERNATIONAL LAW

2.4.1 *State-Owned Entities in International Law*

Rajavuori remarks that 'SOEs provide promising ground for investigating dynamics and consequences of international legal personality for conceptual, doctrinal, historical and theoretical reasons'.[79] The remainder of this chapter will thus look at SOEs through the prism of the concept of legal personality in international law. From the perspective of general international law, the status of SOEs can be ascertained by analogy to corporations in general; both public and private corporations are considered as belonging to the broader category of corporations, with no express distinction being made between the two (e.g., POEs and SOEs). In fact, 'customary international law assumes that trading activities are in the hands of private enterprises'.[80] On this apparent conflation between the private and the public spheres, Hu makes the following remarks:

---

[77] McCorquodale, 'The Individual and the International Legal System' (n 1) 286. ('It can be concluded, therefore, that although originally based on the agreement of States, individuals now have some distinct rights in the international legal system, ranging from a person's right to freedom from torture to the protection of a group of individuals under the right of self-determination.').

[78] McCorquodale, 'Sources and the Subjects of International Law: A Plurality of Law-Making Participants' (n 38) 749.

[79] Mikko Rajavuori, 'Making International Legal Persons in Investment Treaty Arbitration: State-Owned Enterprises along the Person/Thing Distinction' (2017) 18 Ger. Law J. 1185. (Rajavuori examines the legal personality of SOEs from the perspective of international investment law.).

[80] Wolfgang Friedmann, 'Changing Social Arrangements in State-Trading States and Their Effect on International Law' (1959) 24 Law & Contemp. Probs. 350, 354.

The conflation between the state and the market has significant implications, not just for the economy, but for international law as well. States, international organisations, and international lawyers need to clarify whether SEs [State enterprises] are public or private. This classification is vital for proper regulation and treatment of their cross-border activities, but also for deciding on the jurisdiction and liability when their activities turn to disputes. Unfortunately, identifications of SEs tend to conflict with each other in different areas of international law.[81]

While in international law a distinction is made between the *ownership* and *control*[82] of a corporate entity, the *ownership* of an entity – whether public or private – nevertheless appears to be a criterion that is sidelined. This position can be inferred from the Commentaries to the International Law Commission's Articles on the Responsibility of States for International Wrongful Acts (ILC Articles):

> Questions arise with respect to the conduct of companies or enterprises, which are State-owned and controlled. If such corporations act inconsistently with the international obligations of the State the question arises whether such conduct is attributable to the State. In discussing this issue it is necessary to recall that international law acknowledges the general separateness of corporate entities at the national level, except in those cases where the 'corporate veil' is a mere device or a vehicle for fraud and evasion. The fact that the State initially establishes a corporate entity, whether by special law or otherwise, is not a sufficient basis for the attribution to the State of the subsequent conduct of that entity. Since corporate entities, although owned by and in that sense subject to the control of the State are considered to be separate, *prima facie* their carrying out their activities is not attributable to the State unless they are exercising elements of governmental authority.[83]

---

[81] Shixue Hu, 'Clash of Identifications: State Enterprises in International Law' 19 UC Davis Bus. L.J. 171, 174–175.

[82] Doreen Lustig, *Veiled Power: International Law and the Private Corporation, 1886–1981* (Oxford University Press 2020). (By using the example of the *Anglo-Iranian Oil Co. case (jurisdiction)* (International Court of Justice, Judgment of July 22nd, 1952: ICJ. Reports 1952, p. 93) and *Case Concerning Barcelona Traction, Light and Power Company, Limited (Belgium v Spain)* (International Court of Justice, Judgment, ICJ. Reports 1970, p. 3), Lustig argues that the ICJ 'based its decisions on the corporate law principle of the separation between ownership and control. By addressing the corporate personality as a separate entity from its public (British state) or private (Belgian citizens) shareholders, it empowered the position of the State vis-à-vis the corporate entity'.).

[83] International Law Commission, *Draft Articles on Responsibility of States for Internationally Wrongful Acts, with Commentaries* (Yearbook of the International Law Commission, vol II, part 2, 2001) 48.

Thus, the general position can be said to be that it matters less *who* owns an entity, than whether elements of *governmental authority* were exercised in a given case. Apart from the exercise of governmental authority, there are also other matters that may be taken into consideration – at least for the purposes of State responsibility – in order to determine the degree of State involvement into the affairs of an entity, such as whether the entity in question had the *status* of a State organ (de jure or de facto) and whether the entity was under the *effective control* of the State, as Chapter 5 will further elaborate. While the ICJ has dealt with corporations in several cases mainly involving diplomatic protection issues,[84] so far, the Court has not expressly addressed State corporate ownership or SOEs. For clarity, the position adopted in this monograph is not that the corporate veil of an entity should be discarded, since that would go against a basic principle of corporate law which states that a corporation has personality, rights and obligations that are distinct from its shareholders,[85] a status quo that is fully recognised in international law.[86] The position adopted here is that *who* owns an entity matters (e.g., if an entity is privately or publicly owned) and that *ownership* is an important criterion that should be taken into consideration in a given set of circumstances. For example, human rights treaty bodies and judicial bodies, such as the ECHR, adopt a different approach to this issue[87] and in the practice of the ECHR and that of human rights treaty bodies *who owns an entity matters* and is an important criterion for determining the rights and obligations of the State that owns a given entity.[88] For example, *Leo R. Hertzberg, Ulf Mansson, Astrid Nikula and Marko and Tuovi v Finland* was a case heard by the Human Rights Committee under

---

[84] *Case Concerning Barcelona Traction, Light and Power Company, Limited (Belgium v Spain)* (n 82); *Anglo-Iranian Oil Co case (jurisdiction)* (International Court of Justice, Judgment, 22 July 1952, ICJ Reports 1952, p 93); *Ahmadou Sadio Diallo (Republic of Guinea v Democratic Republic of the Congo)* (International Court of Justice Preliminary Objections, Judgment, ICJ Reports 2007, p 582); *Ahmadou Sadio Diallo (Republic of Guinea v Democratic Republic of the Congo)* (International Court of Justice, Merits, Judgment, ICJ Reports 2010, p 639).

[85] *Salomon v Salomon* (United Kingdom, House of Lords [1897] AC 22).

[86] *Case Concerning Barcelona Traction, Light and Power Company, Limited (Belgium v Spain)* (n 82) 38–39, 57–58; *Anglo-Iranian Oil Co. case (jurisdiction)* (n 82) 112; *Ahmadou Sadio Diallo (Republic of Guinea v Democratic Republic of the Congo)* (n 84) paras 61–65; *Ahmadou Sadio Diallo (Republic of Guinea v Democratic Republic of the Congo)* paras 99–105.

[87] *Case of Heinisch v Germany Germany* (European Court of Human Rights, Fifth Section, Application No 28274/08).

[88] ibid 71; *Leo R Hertzberg, Ulf Mansson, Astrid Nikula and Marko and Tuovi v Finland* (Human Rights Committee, Communication No 61/1979, UN Doc CCPR/C/OP/1 (1985), at p. 124, para 91) [9.1]; Mikko Rajavuori, 'How Should States Own? Heinisch v. Germany and the Emergence of Human Rights-Sensitive State Ownership Function' (2015) 26 Eur. J. Int. Law 727.

Article 19 of the ICCPR (freedom of expression) and Articles 1 (right of the Human Rights Committee to receive communications from a State party and exhaustion of domestic remedies) of the Optional Protocol of the ICCPR.[89] The authors of the Communication complained that the Finnish authorities, includ-ing organs of the State-owned and controlled Finnish Broadcasting Company, interfered with their right to freedom of expression by imposing sanctions or censoring participants in radio and TV programmes that dealt with homosexuality. In its analysis of the merits of the Communication, the Human Rights Committee started 'from the *premise* that the State party is responsible for the action of the Finnish Broadcasting Company (FBC), in which the State holds a dominant stake (90 percent) and which is placed under specific government control'.[90] While ultimately the Human Rights Committee held that there was no violation in this case, it is interesting to note that it started its analysis from the *premise* that by virtue of its State ownership of the FBC, Finland was responsible for its actions.

The rest of this chapter thus argues that SOEs and POEs should be distinguished for several reasons. First, from a conceptual point of view, SOEs belong to the public domain, while POEs belong to the private domain; second, State ownership has a different role and rationale from private owner-ship; third, State ownership involves a different type of ownership rights; fourth, the existence of separate regulatory regimes to deal with the challenges associated with SOEs further emphasise their conceptually different nature. Consequently, by virtue of those distinguishing characteristics SOEs are a sui generis participant in international law, which belong to the broader category of corporations, but which are nevertheless distinct from POEs.

2.4.2 *Differentiating between State-Owned Entities and Privately Owned Entities*

2.4.2.1 The First Level of Differentiation: Conceptually, State-Owned Entities and Privately Owned Entities Belong to Different Domains

This section explores the first level of differentiation between SOEs and POEs, by looking at the distinction between the public and the private spheres. It is argued that due to the connection with the State that owns them – from a conceptual point of view – SOEs are fundamentally

---

[89] Leo R. Hertzberg, Ulf Mansson, Astrid Nikula and Marko and Tuovi v Finland (Human Rights Committee, Communication No 61/1979, UN Doc CCPR/C/OP/1 (1985), at page 124, paragraph 9.1. (Emphasis added).
[90] ibid.

entrenched in the public domain and cannot be part of the private domain, even if States create SOEs as entities with a separate legal personality and with corporate governance mechanisms that are independent from the State. To be sure, States often create SOEs that are governed by general corporate law, just like any other POEs.[91] Yet, it would be wrong to regard those entities as being 'private' entities from a conceptual point of view. Often, the fact that an SOE engages in international commercial activities is a clear indication of the importance that the particular SOEs have for the home State. Even if, technically, some SOEs may be created as legal entities that are governed by private law, *conceptually* they cannot be considered as 'private entities'. An SOE cannot be a 'private' entity, *because* the State owns it:

> L'État ne passe aucun acte, n'intervient dans aucun rapport juridique, sans que l'acte soit, directement ou indirectement, motivé par la nécessité de maintenir sa haute mission gouvernementale . . . . Il comprend bien ou mal sa mission; cela importe peu. Si l'on va au fond des choses, il ne peut jamais se presenter exclusivement comme personne priveé.[92]

To a certain extent, the artificiality of this distinction seems to be acknowledged even at a domestic level in certain States, *by* the domestic law applicable to SOEs. For example, in Article 4 the Vietnamese law on State-owned enterprises states that

> (1) State companies shall operate pursuant to this Law and other relevant laws. If there is a difference between the provisions of this Law and those of another relevant law on the same issue within the governing scope and applicable entities of such other relevant law, the provisions of such other law shall apply. (2) If there is a difference between the provisions of this Law and those of relevant laws on the rights and obligations of State owners of State companies with respect to State companies; or if the provisions on the relationship between the State owner and the authorized representative of the State's capital contribution portion are different in this Law, in the Law on Enterprises, in the Law on Foreign Investment in Vietnam and in equivalent laws on enterprises to which the State contributes capital, then this Law shall apply.[93]

---

[91] World Bank Publications, *Corporate Governance of State-Owned Enterprises: A Toolkit* (World Bank 2014) 31. (SOEs in Bhutan, Chile, Ghana, India, Malaysia, Pakistan, Peru, Serbia, South Africa and Zambia operate under general company law.)

[92] Alfred Chrétien, Paul Nachbaur, *Principes de droit international public* (1893), as quoted in: Hersch Lauterpacht, 'The Problem of Jurisdictional Immunities of Foreign States' (1951) 28 Brit. Yearb. Int'l L 224.

[93] Law on State-Owned Enterprises 2003. (Under Article 1(a) a 'State owned enterprise means an economic organisation in which the State owns the entire charter capital or holds the

Consequently, in Vietnam, if an SOE is created as an entity governed by general corporate law, that SOE will be treated as any POE, but only up to the point when the *rights and obligations* of the SOE come into consideration. When the *rights and obligations* of a particular SOE would come into consideration, the special law on SOEs would apply. Furthermore, it is important to note that even those SOEs that are created under general law often have special corporate governance codes and special ownership policies or guidelines that guide their day-to-day operation and which further underline their sui generis nature.[94] It is also usual for States to create a special legal framework applicable to SOEs.[95]

The best way to understand how SOEs are part of the 'public' domain is to delve deeper into the distinction between the public and private spheres, a distinction that is present in most, if not all, domestic legal systems and in international law. Furthermore, the distinction between public and private spheres of activity is also present in various economic ideologies and is central to liberalism and Western legal thought[96] and has been defined as

> notions that legitimize or delegitimize legal regulative 'intervention' in different spheres of human activity . . . . Roughly speaking, the liberal idea that has haunted legal consciousness since the late nineteenth century, or since 'markets became central legitimizing institutions', is that legal intervention in the private sphere (namely, the family and the economic market) is unjustified and should be limited (in the market) or nonexistent (in the family), while in the public sphere (state) legal intervention is welcome and necessary.[97]

The literature that deals with the public/private distinction is vast. In fact, one author said that 'probably too much has been written about [it]'.[98] The

---

controlling shareholding or controlling capital contribution, and which is organised in the form of a State company, shareholding company or limited liability company.').

[94] World Bank, *Corporate Governance of State-Owned Enterprises: A Toolkit* (World Bank 2014) 31, 59–65. (SOEs in Bhutan, Chile, Ghana, India, Malaysia, Pakistan, Peru, South Africa and Zambia operate under general company law, but also under special corporate governance codes and guidelines specifically designed for SOEs. There are many other countries that have developed similar governance codes that apply exclusively to SOEs (In this publication, see in particular page 60)).

[95] ibid 30. (Egypt, Korea, Serbia, Turkey are cited in this research as having separate legal regimes for their SOEs. There are also others States with separate legal regimes for their SOEs such as: Romania, China, Australia, Norway, Sweden, France and Russia, etc.).

[96] Hilary Charlesworth, 'The Public/Private Distinction and the Right to Development in International Law' (1988) 12 Aust. YBIL 190, 190–191.

[97] Hila Shamir, 'The Public/Private Distinction Now: The Challenges of Privatization and of the Regulatory State' (2014) 15 Theor. Inq. Law 1, 4–5. (Footnotes omitted).

[98] ibid 2.

history of the public/private divide is punctuated by ups and downs,[99] with some scholars vilifying it and calling for its abolition,[100] some defending it,[101] others calling it irrelevant,[102] while some warn of the danger of making such distinctions in the first place.[103] Although some commentators are calling the distinction irrelevant[104] and some have even proclaimed it dead,[105] it still seems to be 'ruling us from the grave', as Duncan Kennedy acknowledged.[106] To name a few current encounters, at the domestic level the public/private distinction is present in labour law,[107] environmental law[108] and in the context of family law,[109] often from a feminist perspective.[110] Some commentators have called the interaction between the public and private spheres 'essential' for statehood, as 'without the former, there would be no democracy, while there would be no freedom without the latter'.[111] At the international level, the distinction is fundamental and 'define[s] the scope of international law' by carving out entirely different spheres of activity, such as public international law, which deals with the law that governs relationships between States and private international law, which deals with conflicts between domestic legal systems.[112] Specifically, at the international level, scholars have analysed the dichotomy from a global governance perspective;[113] it is discussed in human

---

[99] Duncan Kennedy, 'The Stages of the Decline of the Public/Private Distinction' (1981) 130 U. Pa. L. Rev. 1349; Juan Manuel Amaya Castro, 'Human Rights and the Critiques of the Public-Private Distinction' (Vrije Universiteit Amsterdam, Faculty of Law 2010).

[100] Ruth Gavison, 'Feminism and the Public/Private Distinction' (1992) 45 Stan. L. Rev. 1, 1–2; Christine Chinkin, 'A Critique of the Public/Private Dimension' (1999) 10 Eur. J. Int. Law 387.

[101] Matthias Goldmann, 'A Matter of Perspective: Global Governance and the Distinction between Public and Private Authority (and Not Law)' (2016) 5 GlobCon 48.

[102] Christopher D Stone, 'Corporate Vices and Corporate Virtues: Do Public/Private Distinctions Matter?' (1982) 130 U. Pa. L. Rev. 1441.

[103] Clapham (n 38) 124–133.

[104] Stone (n 102).

[105] Kennedy (n 99) 1353.

[106] ibid.

[107] Karl E Klare, 'The Public/Private Distinction in Labor Law' (1982) 130 U. Pa. L. Rev. 1358.

[108] Yishai Blank and Issi Rosen-Zvi, 'The Persistence of the Public/Private Divide in Environmental Regulation' (2014) 15 Theor. Inq. Law 199.

[109] Robert H Mnookin, 'Public/Private Dichotomy: Political Disagreement and Academic Repudiation' (1981) 130 U. Pa. L. Rev. 1429, 1430–1431.

[110] Gavison (n 100); Frances E Olsen, 'The Family and the Market: A Study of Ideology and Legal Reform' [1983] Harv. L. Rev. 1497.

[111] Goldmann (n 101) 56.

[112] Charlesworth (n 96) 195.

[113] Axel Marx, 'The Public-Private Distinction in Global Governance: How Relevant Is It in the Case of Voluntary Sustainability Standards?' (2017) 3 CJGG 1; Goldmann (n 101); L Casini, '"Down the Rabbit-Hole": The Projection of the Public/Private Distinction beyond the State' (2014) 12 Int. J. Const. Law 402.

rights,[114] in international investment arbitration[115] (through the lens of the principle of subsidiarity,[116] stabilisation clauses and umbrella clauses),[117] in State responsibility (it sits at the heart of the concept of attribution)[118] and in sovereign immunity (via the distinction made between sovereign acts and commercial acts).[119] The public/private distinction is also present at the EU level; however, there it seems to have evolved from an initially formal to a currently functional approach.[120]

For clarification, it is important to draw attention to the fact that there are actually two public/private dichotomies in place. The first deals with the dichotomy between the *market*, which has a public character, and the *family* which is private; and the second deals with the differences between the *State*, which is public, and the *civil society* (composed of family *and* the market) which is private. This section addresses the second dichotomy, which is encountered between the *State* and the *market*. Frances Olsen explains this issue as follows:

> In discourse on the market, the state/civil society dichotomy appears as the issue of state regulation of the economy; in discourse on the family it appears as the issue of state interference in the family. The classic laissez-faire arguments against state regulation of the free market find a striking parallel in the arguments against state interference with the private family. The two sets of arguments, and the ideals that underlie them, share a great deal more than just hostility to government. Both are constructed of similar elements and subject to similar attacks; our understanding of each is enriched by our understanding of the other.[121]

---

[114] Celina Romany, 'Women as Aliens: A Feminist Critique of the Public/Private Distinction in International Human Rights Law' (1993) 6 Harv. Hum. Rts. J. 87; Donna Sullivan, 'The Public/Private Distinction in International Human Rights Law' in Julie Peters and Andrea Wolper (eds), *Women's Rights, Human Rights: International Feminist Perspectives* (Routledge 1995).

[115] Julie A Maupin, 'Public and Private in International Investment Law: An Integrated Systems Approach' (2013) 54 Va. J. Int'l L. 367, 373.

[116] Markus Jachtenfuchs and Nico Krisch, 'Subsidiarity in Global Governance' (2016) 79 Law Contemp. Probl. 1; Rene Uruena, 'Subsidiarity and the Public-Private Distinction in Investment Treaty Arbitration' (2016) 79 Law Contemp. Probl. 99, 100.

[117] Gus Van Harten, 'The Public – Private Distinction in the International Arbitration of Individual Claims against the State' (2007) 56 Int'l & Comp. L.Q. 371, 375.

[118] Chinkin, 'A Critique of the Public/Private Dimension' (n 100); Ciara Hackett and Luke Moffett, 'Mapping the Public/Private-Law Divide: A Hybrid Approach to Corporate Accountability' (2016) 12 Int. J. Law Context. 312.

[119] Hazel Fox and Philippa Webb, *The Law of State Immunity* (3rd edn, Oxford University Press 2013) 395–412.

[120] Okeoghene Odudu, 'The Public/Private Distinction in EU Internal Market Law' (2003) 62 ECLR 62.

[121] Olsen (n 110) 1501–1502.

The distinction between public and private spheres traces its roots back to the medieval period and was primarily caused by the emergence of the nation-state when ideas of a 'distinctly public realm' came into being due to changes in political and legal thought.[122] However, as a 'reaction' to the 'unrestrained power' of monarchs and later parliaments to legislate, 'there developed a countervailing effort to stake out distinctively private spheres free from the encroaching power of the State'.[123] For example, in English law, this distinction was evident by the late medieval period, where the king held land in two capacities: first, as a feudal lord and second, as king.[124] The king could sell the land held as a feudal lord, but not that land held in his power as king, because that was public land. Whilst the public/private distinction had a relatively slow evolution during the next several hundred years, it was during the nineteenth century when the 'virtual obsession' with separating public and private spheres occurred. The fundamental rift between the public and the private sphere appears to have been caused by the emergence of the market as a social mode of organisation.[125] This rift made a clear distinction between public law, which was composed of constitutional criminal and administrative law, and private law, which encapsulated property law, contract, and commercial law. The case that firmly entrenched the public/private division in Western legal discourse, and subsequently the role of the private corporation at the center of American free market ideology, is *Trustees of Dartmouth College v Woodward*.[126] This case considered the grant of a royal charter by King George III to the Dartmouth College in 1769. The charter outlined the purpose of the school and the governance structure. In 1816, the legislature of the State of New Hampshire purported to alter the charter of Dartmouth College by passing a law, which in essence changed the nature of the school from a private body to a public institution. The duties of the trustees and the procedure for choosing them were also changed. This led the existing trustees to file a suit, which claimed the unconstitutionality of the State legislation. Specifically, the trustees claimed that the United States Constitution prevented a State from 'impairing' a contract.[127] The Supreme Court, by a 5-1

---

[122] Morton J Horwitz, 'The History of the Public/Private Distinction' (1982) 130 U. Pa. L. Rev. 1423, 1423.

[123] ibid.

[124] ibid.

[125] ibid 1424–1425. (Footnotes omitted).

[126] *Trustees of Dartmouth College v Woodward* (United States, Supreme Court (1819) 17 US 518).

[127] ibid 625. ('But the American people have said in the Constitution of the United States that "no State shall pass any bill of attainder, *ex post facto law*, or law impairing the obligation of contracts". In the same instrument, they have also said, "that the judicial power shall extend to

majority decision, agreed with the trustees, reinforced the fundamental belief in the sanctity of contracts, and struck down the State law, with Dartmouth College continuing as a private institution. The effect of this decision was an improvement in the business environment, by ensuring that State governments are not able to interfere with private business.

The public/private distinction is still present in contemporary legal thought, albeit fundamentally changed, and has been likened to a 'reservoir':

> [If contemporary legal thought] introduced the distinction, and its social critique constituted a (complicated) attempt to 'empty' the private, the current moment can be roughly characterized by an attempt to 'empty' the public and use considerations thought to be private as the measure of all things, including public services and institutions. This can be seen in labor market deregulation, the rolling back of various social security benefits and welfare state functions, and the widespread privatization across the Western world. What were once understood to be strictly state functions are increasingly contracted out, delegated, or simply relegated to what were once understood to be strictly private entities. From military contractors, to prisons, to social security and charter schools, an intermediate space between the state and the governed has opened up and become populated with myriad 'private' entities.[128]

As such, in its current complex form, the public/private distinction presents many challenges to those that have deal with it. Chiefly among those are the inherent difficulties in actually identifying the scope of what acts are public and what acts are private, the method of doing so and who has authority to do this.[129] Functions that have been traditionally performed by the State, such as police and the military forces, have been privatised in many States and private actors now provide services once provided by public actors.[130]

Returning to SOEs, their emergence as actors in their own right in the international sphere has its own difficulties from the perspective of the public/private divide. If an SOE is created by domestic law in a given State and charged with the purpose of fulfilling a *public interest*, such as securing the financial future of future generations, as many SWFs are, or to be officially

---

all cases in law and equity arising under the Constitution". On the judges of this Court, then, is imposed the high and solemn duty of protecting, from even legislative violation, those contracts which the Constitution of our country has placed beyond legislative control; and however irksome the task may be, this is a duty from which we dare not shrink.').

[128] Shamir (n 97) 9.

[129] ibid 11.

[130] Laura A Dickinson, 'Government for Hire: Privatizing Foreign Affairs and the Problem of Accountability under International Law' (2005) 47 Wm. & Mary L. Rev. 135, 138–139.

part of a strategy designed to secure the home State's access to natural resources, it is challenging to understand how the same entity – when it moves from the domestic to the international sphere – becomes a *private actor*.[131] At the international level, the public/private distinction plays itself out on three levels and it 'may refer in turn, or simultaneously to the *legal regime*, the *legal status of the actors* or the *interests at stake*'.[132] For example, a finding (or not, as the case may be) that an SOE is a protected 'investor' under an investment treaty in effect determines access to the arbitration regime in itself.[133] The legal status of the actors and the interests at stake also has a role in determining ultimate liability and the availability of immunities as Chapter 4 demonstrates. In this context, central to the concept of State responsibility are the acts that can be attributed to the State in question. Acts and omissions that *can* be attributed to the State ultimately determine responsibility. Generally, 'purely private conduct' is not attributable to the State,[134] unless the State 'acknowledges and adopts the conduct in question as its own'.[135] Christine Chinkin summarises these issues in the following manner:

> The dichotomy between internationally wrongful acts or omissions that incur state responsibility through attribution to the state from those that do not, is one of the ways in which international law rests 'on a variety of distinctions between public and private worlds'. Although the Draft Articles do not espouse the language of public/private, this distinction brings into the law of state responsibility the reserved domain from international intrusion … . The retention of immunity from suit within the domestic court of another state for governmental acts (*jure imperii*) asserts the international quality of those acts, while its denial for private of commercial acts (*jure gestionis*) locates them within the national, domestic arena.[136]

---

[131] S Hu, 'Clash of Identifications: State Enterprises in International Law' 19 UC Davis Bus. L.J. 171, 175–176; *Beijing Urban Construction Group Company Limited v Yemen* (ICSID Case No ARB/14/30 (Decision on Jurisdiction)).

[132] Casini (n 113) 408. (Emphasis added. Footnotes omitted).

[133] Mihaela M Barnes, 'International Investment Law and State-Owned Entities: Recurrent Key Issues and Future Directions' in Lisa E Sachs and others (eds), *2018 Yearbook of International Investment Law and Policy* (Oxford University Press 2019).

[134] Higgins (n 37) 153.

[135] International Law Commission, *Draft Articles on Responsibility of States for Internationally Wrongful Acts, with Commentaries* (n 83) 52–54. (See, in particular, Article 11 of the ILC Articles: 'Conduct which is not attributable to a State under the preceding articles shall nevertheless be considered an act of that State under international law if and to the extent that the State acknowledges and adopts the conduct in question as its own.').

[136] Chinkin, 'A Critique of the Public/Private Dimension' (n 100) 389.

In other words, 'classifying an act as public or private determines what kind of legitimacy it requires', with a public act requiring a higher degree of legitimacy than a private one.[137] A public act would ultimately be tied to the political process and the State, while a private act would not necessarily be so.[138] However, this issue further increases in complexity in States, which do not necessarily have a market economy or a political system that is based on democratic principles. For example, Chinese scholars rejected the public/private distinction initially and considered it as being a 'distinction made in bourgeois law that should be replaced by a new socialist legal system, which would acknowledge no such difference'.[139] As a consequence of China's recent increased openness to the world, the situation has changed, and the public/private distinction is now recognised. However, due to ideological constraints inherited from the pre-reform era,[140] it was not initially easy to give meaning to the distinction, and many debates were waged in relation to it, mainly for the purpose of the recognition of private ownership.[141]

A further illustration of the difficulties associated with the public/private distinction as applicable to SOEs can also be discerned from the *US – Definitive Anti-Dumping and Countervailing Duties on Certain Products from China*.[142] This is a WTO dispute in which China claimed that the US imposed countervailing duties on certain products from China that were in breach of the Agreement on Subsidies and Countervailing Measures (SCM Agreement). Central to this case was the question whether China's State-owned enterprises and State-owned commercial banks are 'public' or 'private bodies'. The US imposed the countervailing duties on certain products from China as a result of an investigation by the US Department of Commerce (USDOC), which found, among others, that China provided subsidies in the form of preferential interest rates to one producer.[143] China claimed that the USDOC's determination that certain Chinese State-owned commercial banks were public bodies was inconsistent with Article 1.1(a)(1) of the SCM

---

[137] Goldmann (n 101) 48.

[138] ibid 57.

[139] Xingzhong Yu, 'State Legalism and the Public/Private Divide in Chinese Legal Development' (2014) 15 Theor. Inq. Law 27, 27, 32–33.

[140] ibid 34.

[141] ibid 28.

[142] *United States – Definitive Anti-Dumping and Countervailing Duties on Certain Products from China (Panel Report)* (World Trade Organisation (WT/DS379/R 22 October 2010); United States – Definitive Anti-Dumping and Countervailing Duties on Certain Products from China (Appellate Body Report) (World Trade Organisation (WT/DS379/AB/R 11 March 2011)).

[143] *United States – Definitive Anti-Dumping and Countervailing Duties on Certain Products from China (Panel Report)* (n 142) paras 2.4–2.5.

Agreement, which provided that a 'subsidy shall be deemed to exist if there is a financial contribution by a government or any *public body* within the territory of a Member'. In its investigation, the Panel interpreted the term 'public body' to mean 'any entity controlled by a government'[144] and in the Panel's view, *ownership* was a key feature that determined whether a body was public or not. The Panel further said that this was the 'correct interpretation, which emerged from an analysis of the ordinary meaning of the term in its context and in the light of the object and purpose' of the SCM Agreement.[145] Consequently, the Panel sided with the USDOC and considered majority government-ownership of a certain body as a key factor in determining its 'public' nature.[146] The Panel said:

> We recall, however, our conclusion that a public body is any entity controlled by a government, and in this regard *we consider government ownership to be highly relevant (indeed potentially dispositive)* evidence of government control. Here we note in particular the everyday financial concept of a 'controlling interest' in a company. The technical definition of what is needed for a controlling interest is a *maximum* of 50 per cent plus one share of the voting stock of a company, with the possibility that a *much smaller* voting block can be controlling, depending on how dispersed the ownership of the remaining shares is, and the extent to which the other shareholders participate in voting. We see no reason to consider that the concept that 'control' of a company resides with its majority owner, which is uncontested in the private sector, would be inapplicable to government-owned companies. Logically, quite the reverse should be true, given the generalized power of governments over economic affairs within their territories. As such, we consider that, on its own, majority government ownership is *clear and highly indicative* evidence of government control, and thus of whether an entity is a public body for purposes of the SCM Agreement.[147]

The Appellate Body rejected the finding of the Panel, whereby majority government ownership was to be regarded as the key indicator of a body's public character and instead said that the concept of 'public body' was better viewed as sharing certain features with the concept of 'government', whereby the possession and exercise of *governmental authority* was instead the key factor.[148] The Appellate Body further clarified that, in this determination, panels and investigating authorities must instead look at the *core features* of

---

[144] ibid para 8.94.
[145] ibid.
[146] ibid paras 8.99–8.142.
[147] ibid paras 8.134–8.135. (Emphasis added).
[148] *United States – Definitive Anti-Dumping and Countervailing Duties on Certain Products from China (Appellate Body Report)* (n 142) paras 317–318.

the entity concerned and *its relationship with the government*. In this context, the Appellate Body recognized that 'no two governments are alike' and that 'the precise contours and characteristics of a public body are bound to differ from entity to entity, State to State, and case to case'.[149] The *relationship* of the entity with the government and its investiture with *governmental authority* now appears to be the key factors, which determine whether a body is to be considered public, while *government ownership* takes secondary importance. Even if one was to accept that governmental authority *should* take precedence over government ownership, the Appellate Body seems to have failed to consider the special nature of the Chinese SOEs. While the governance of Chinese SOEs has been through many reforms during the last few decades – in that if once SOEs were considered as simply an extension of the government, they now enjoy relatively increased autonomy and may have responsibility to make decisions based on market considerations – there is no denying that, in fact, Chinese SOEs are unique and 'vastly different from the conventional expectation of government-enterprise relationship'.[150]

Overall, it is difficult to envisage how economic activity conducted by a State can be of a 'private nature' as Hersch Lauterpacht elaborated, more than seventy years ago:

> Moreover, it is no longer generally accepted that the economic activities of the state – such as state management of industry, state buying, and state selling – are necessarily of a purely 'private-law nature'; that they are 'jure gestionis'; and that in engaging in them a state acts like a private person. In these and similar cases ostensibly removed from the normal field of its political and administrative activities, the state nevertheless acts as a public person for the general purposes of the community as a whole. This applies not only to states with a socialist economy where trading or management of industry have become a public function of the state. For the state always acts as a public person. It cannot act otherwise.[151]

To conclude, this section illustrates that, the public/private distinction is still important from a conceptual point of view in the context of SOEs. The public/private distinction can be found in general international law, in the rules of State responsibility and sovereign immunity, as well as in specialised regimes, such as international economic law. The difficulties in

---

[149] ibid para 317.
[150] Ming Du, 'China's State Capitalism and World Trade Law' (2014) 63 Int'l & Comp. L.Q. 409, 436.
[151] Hersch Lauterpacht, 'The Problem of Jurisdictional Immunities of Foreign States' (1951) 28 Brit. Yearb. Int'l L. 220, 224.

distinguishing between public and private spheres of activity, however, continue to this day. Despite those difficulties, this monograph takes the view that SOEs are part of the public sphere. Further justifications for this approach can be found in Sections 2.4.2.2–2.4.2.4.

2.4.2.2 The Second Level of Differentiation: A Different Role and Rationale for State Corporate Ownership

The section argues that SOEs are different to POEs because of the different role and rationale that underpins State ownership. Analyses of the economic and legal rationales for State ownership support this claim.

ECONOMIC RATIONALE FOR STATE CORPORATE OWNERSHIP In order to find the economic rationale for State ownership two questions must be asked. The first one is: Why must SOEs exist? The second question: Is the private sector unable to take over all the functions that SOEs are currently performing? SOEs have been a major topic of study, particularly in economic literature, where private ownership is generally considered as being superior to public ownership,[152] although it has been shown that in many cases publicly owned companies perform as well as private companies and that inefficiency is usually caused by lack of competition not by the type of ownership.[153] SOEs are usually portrayed as having fundamental issues with performance and efficiency, despite the occasional empirical study that shows the opposite,[154] or the fundamental belief encountered in States like Norway, that the 'government can be as good a capitalist as anybody'.[155] Nevertheless, whilst the

[152] Pierangelo Maria Toninelli (ed), *The Rise and Fall of State-Owned Enterprise in the Western World* (Cambridge University Press 2000); Daniel Shapiro and Steven Globerman, 'The International Activities and Impacts of State-Owned Enterprises' in Karl P Sauvant, Lisa E Sachs and Schmit Jongbloed PF Wouter (eds), *Sovereign Investment: Concerns and Policy Reactions* (Oxford University Press 2012) 99.

[153] Yair Aharoni, 'The Evolution of State-Owned Multinational Enterprise Theory' in Alvaro Cuervo-Cazurra (ed), *State-Owned Multinationals: Governments in Global Business* (Palgrave Macmillan 2018) 19–20. ('Many studies have delved into the relative performance of SOEs and privately owned firms. A common problem with these studies is that performance is measured in terms of one specific goal such as profits or efficiency. Only when performance is compared between SOEs and investor-owned firms in the same industry, and the only measuring rod is the profits of these firms, is it possible to reach definite conclusions as to the relative performance of the two types of ownership.').

[154] Gary D Bruton and others, 'State-Owned Enterprises around the World as Hybrid Organizations' (2015) 29 Acad. Manag. Perspect. 92, 102.

[155] Hans Christiansen, 'Balancing Commercial and Non-Commercial Priorities of State-Owned Enterprises' (OECD 2013) OECD Corporate Governance Working Papers 6 103;

raison d'être for POEs is profit maximisation, the same cannot be said about SOEs.[156] In order to answer the above questions, economic literature provides two broad reasons for the continued existence of State ownership: first, it is expected that in similar market circumstances, SOEs will act differently from private companies;[157] and second, some SOEs are established in order to pursue mainly non-commercial activities.[158] As an illustration of the first category, when States use 'defensive' policies, they can make the SOEs that they own 'maintain a larger share of employment, research and development or headquarter functions in the national economy' than private businesses would do in similar market circumstances.[159] A recent study conducted by the OECD,[160] which examined the rationale for State ownership in twenty-four jurisdictions, has concluded that whilst States may vary in the way they actually express their ownership rationale – by using either express legislation[161] or via government decision-making instruments[162] or both[163] – the overall *non-commercial objectives* for the ownership of SOEs fall into the following categories: (i) support for the national economy and for strategic interests;[164] (ii) ensuring continuing national ownership of enterprises;[165] (iii) the supply of certain public goods that the market cannot or does not want to supply; (iv) the set-up of 'natural' monopolies and (v) the creation of a State-owned monopoly (or oligopoly) where market regulation is deemed infeasible

---

'Opportunities for All: Human Rights in Norway's Foreign Policy and Development Cooperation' (2014) Meld. St. 10 (2014–2015) Report to the Storting (white paper) 60–61.

[156] Mike W Peng and others, 'Theories of the (State-Owned) Firm' (2016) 33 Asia Pac. J. Manag. 293; Cuervo-Cazurra and others, 'Governments as Owners: State-Owned Multinational Companies' (2014) 45 J. Int. Bus. Stud. 919.

[157] Christiansen (n 155) 3.

[158] ibid 6; Aharoni (n 153) 14–16.

[159] Christiansen (n 155) 7.

[160] OECD, *State-Owned Enterprise Governance: A Stocktaking of Government Rationales for State Ownership* (OECD 2015) 11; Oliver Hart, Andrei Shleifer and Robert W Vishny, 'The Proper Scope of Government: Theory and an Application to Prisons' (1997) 112 Q. J. Econ. 1127.

[161] Estonia, Germany, Hungary, Lithuania and Poland were used in the study as examples of countries that use express legislation to set out their State ownership rationale.

[162] Such as resolutions and decrees or policy statements. Five countries in the study express their State ownership rationale through resolutions and decrees: Chile, Finland, Norway, Sweden and Switzerland. Ireland and the Netherlands use policy statements to explain their State ownership rationale.

[163] The study cites The Czech Republic and Portugal.

[164] Aharoni (n 153) 16. ('Developing and newly independent states saw SOEs as a fast means to economic growth. SOEs were established when a weak private sector was unable or unwilling to create desired enterprises, because of a lack of funds, competent managers, or the necessary technology.').

[165] ibid. The growth of SOEs in postwar Europe was a response to the challenge of US multinationals.

or inefficient.[166] SOEs are also generally expected to comply with higher standards of corporate social responsibility.[167] In Norway, all SOEs are formally catalogued as being either 'sector-policy oriented' or 'commercial', and this categorisation is made by government policy subject to parliamentary approval.[168] Hungary maintains that all its SOEs exist for public policy reasons, while no categorisation exists in the Netherlands and New Zealand.[169] In China, all SOEs are owned by the State-Owned Assets Supervisory and Administration Commission of the State Council (SASAC), and have 'enormous economic and social obligations'.[170] For example, in China, SOEs have responsibilities for the healthcare and retirement benefits of hundreds of thousands of retirees and 'by the end of 2011, there were still more than 8,000 social institutions, including workplace hospitals and schools, run by central SOEs which incur billions in costs each year'.[171] To conclude, the existence of an economic rationale for State ownership at the domestic level can be categorised as being either policy oriented or commercially oriented, although it appears that generally the policy-oriented rationales will ultimately outweigh any commercial considerations.

LEGAL RATIONALE FOR STATE CORPORATE OWNERSHIP State corporate ownership is also recognised domestically in many jurisdictions either constitutionally or in separate legislation. For example, the history of China reveals that the concept of private property was never really that well developed, at least not locally.[172] While this situation changed after the 1978 reforms, when China opened its doors to the Western world, State ownership nevertheless still has a fundamental role to play in the Chinese economy.[173] The importance of this phenomenon can be observed not only from the fact that China is first in terms of the size and number of SOEs, but also in the fact that State ownership is still a recognised form of property ownership that is constitutionally protected. For example, Article 6 of the Chinese Constitution states that

---

[166] OECD, *State-Owned Enterprise Governance: A Stocktaking of Government Rationales for State Ownership* (n 160) 11; Hart, Shleifer and Vishny (n 160).

[167] Christiansen (n 155) 10–12.

[168] ibid 12.

[169] ibid 11–12.

[170] Gang Fan and Nicholas C Hope, 'Chapter 16: The Role of State-Owned Enterprises in the Chinese Economy' [2013] China US Focus 10 <www.chinausfocus.com> accessed 12 December 2020.

[171] ibid.

[172] Mo Zhang, 'From Public to Private: The Newly Enacted Chinese Property Law and the Protection of Property Rights in China' (2008) 5 Berkeley Bus. Law J. 317, 320.

[173] ibid.

the basis of the socialist economic system of the People's Republic of China is socialist public ownership of the means of production, namely, ownership by the whole people and collective ownership by the working people. The system of socialist public ownership supersedes the system of exploitation of man by man; it applies the principle of 'from each according to his ability, to each according to his work'. During the primary stage of socialism, the State adheres to the basic economic system with the public ownership remaining dominant and diverse sectors of the economy developing side by side, and to the distribution system with the distribution according to work remaining dominant and the coexistence of a variety of modes of distribution.[174]

Furthermore, through Article 7, SOEs gain constitutional protection:

The State-owned economy, that is, the socialist economy under ownership by the whole people, is the leading force in the national economy. The State ensures the consolidation and growth of the State-owned economy.[175]

There are many other jurisdictions where explicit rationales for State ownership can be found in express legislation.[176] It appears that the existence of such provisions does not actually seem to be directly tied to the presence of socialist or communist ideologies in that State. For example, Canada,[177] Australia[178] and New Zealand,[179] States that are not necessarily associated with either communism or socialism, have express legislation concerning various SOEs that come under the umbrella of 'Crown corporations'. Overall, for all the States surveyed,[180] the realisation of public policy objectives as well as the realisation of 'important' social, strategic or other public

---

[174] Constitution of the People's Republic of China 1982 Article 6.
[175] ibid Article 7. (Private property is also given constitutional protection. Article 13 provides that 'the State, in accordance with the law, protects the rights of citizens to private property and to its inheritance'. Article 11 also states that: 'individual, private and other non-public economies that exist within the limits prescribed by law are major components of the *socialist* market economy'.).
[176] OECD, *State-Owned Enterprise Governance: A Stocktaking of Government Rationales for State Ownership* (n 160); Ma Xili, 'Advancing Direct Corporate Accountability in International Human Rights Law: The Role of State-Owned Enterprises' (2019) 14 Front. Law China 43, 241–244, 266–271.
[177] Canada Pension Plan Investment Board Act (S.C. 1997, c. 40); Business Development Bank of Canada Act (S.C. 1995, c. 28).
[178] Australia Future Fund Act 2006 (Cth).
[179] Crown Entities Act 2004.
[180] Australia, Canada, China, New Zealand, Chile, Czech Republic, Estonia, Finland, Germany, Hungary, Ireland, Lithuania, Netherlands, Norway, Poland, Portugal, Slovenia, Sweden, Switzerland, Israel, Italy, Japan, Mexico, Slovak Republic, Turkey and the United Kingdom.

beneficial interests are the main reasons for the creation of SOEs.[181] There are also States where SOEs are organised as 'private' entities regulated by general corporate law. In such cases, the public purpose of an entity can be often ascertained by making further investigations into corporate governance codes or other similar instruments.

2.4.2.3 The Third Level of Differentiation: A Different Type of Property Rights

The public nature of SOEs can also be ascertained by looking at the nature of the property rights that are inherent in State ownership in general: property that is owned by POEs is of an inherently *private* nature, while property that is owned by SOEs is *public*. A preliminary discussion of the concept of property and the various types of property is thus a necessary requirement for an understanding of the concept of State corporate ownership and its implications. However, any such discussion will be ideologically charged, as William Blackstone noted over 250 years ago: 'there is nothing which so generally strikes the imagination and engages the affections of mankind as the right to property'.[182] This is because the concept of property, and the preferences given by some States to one type of property over another, sit at the heart of our whole societal ordering influencing the evolution of social and political institutions.[183] The inherent tensions between different types of property ownership (private ownership versus common ownership; private ownership versus public ownership) are central to the arguments presented in this section. For example, private ownership is fundamental to the development and survival of capitalism,[184] whereas to socialist and communist regimes, common and collective types of owners are preferred. For the purposes of this section, a broad conceptualisation of property will be adopted. As such, property is any type of right, interest or thing which is legally capable of ownership and which has a value.[185] From a legal point of view, the concept of property is concerned not so much with the definition of the thing, right or

---

[181] OECD, *State-Owned Enterprise Governance: A Stocktaking of Government Rationales for State Ownership* (n 160) 19–28.

[182] William Blackstone, *Commentaries on the Laws of England, Volume 2: A Facsimile of the First Edition of 1765–1769* (University of Chicago Press 1979).

[183] Samantha Hepburn, *Australian Principles of Property Law* (Routledge 2013) 5.

[184] Hugh Evander Willis, 'Capitalism, The United States Constitution and the Supreme Court' (1934) XXII Ky. L.J. 343, 343–344.

[185] Peter Butt, *Butterworths Concise Australian Legal Dictionary* (LexisNexis Butterworths 2004) 348.

the interest itself, but with the relationships that form between the property and its owner, and between the property, its owner and the world at large.[186] Viewed broadly, as Harold Demsetz notes, property rights are an 'instrument of society' which would have had no role 'in the world of Robinson Crusoe'.[187] A property relationship confers a legally enforceable bundle of rights entitling the holder to control an object or resource.[188] Most of the world's legal systems recognise three types of systems of ownership: common ownership, private ownership and State ownership.

Common ownership is a right, which can be exercised by all members of the community, and as such it 'denies the state or individual citizens the right to interfere with any person's exercise of communally-owned rights'.[189] The peculiarity of common property rights is that they are 'neither private nor public'.[190] From a legal point of view, the defining characteristic of common property is that 'the proprietary interest shared is in the nature of a usufruct or use right, not a discrete or severable right in the land itself. The common right *inter se* is not exclusive; however, the extent of the right may be regulated internally by custom or contract'.[191] The same characteristics can be observed from an economic point of view, where common property is generally defined as 'resources for which the exclusive title is in the hands of a group of individuals. This group has control over access to the resource, is frequently backed in this capacity by the State, and has general decision-making capacity over the resource'.[192] Consequently, one of the fundamental issues at play when dealing with common property is an understanding of the fact that common property is not 'everybody's property',[193] because the concept allows for the exclusion of those that are not members of the group of co-owners.[194]

---

[186] Hepburn (n 183) 1.
[187] Harold Demsetz, 'Toward a Theory of Property Rights' (1967) 57 Am. Econ. Rev. 347, 347.
[188] Michael A Heller, 'The Tragedy of the Anticommons: Property in the Transition from Marx to Markets' (1998) 111 Harv. L. Rev. 621, 662; Hepburn (n 183) 2.
[189] Demsetz (n 187) 354.
[190] John Page, 'Common Property and the Age of Aquarius' (2010) 19 Griffith L. Rev. 172, 176.
[191] ibid 177.
[192] DA Fuchs, *An Institutional Basis for Environmental Stewardship* (Springer Science & Business Media 2003) 49.
[193] Contrast with concepts such as 'common heritage of mankind' found in international law, which posits that certain global commons or elements regarded as beneficial to the whole of humanity should not be unilaterally exploited by States, corporations or individuals, but rather they should be exploited under an international agreement or regime for the benefit humanity at large. See in general Kemal Baslar, *The Concept of the Common Heritage of Mankind in International Law* (Martinus Nijhoff 1998).
[194] Siegfried V Ciriacy-Wantrup and Richard C Bishop, 'Common Property as a Concept in Natural Resources Policy' (1975) 15 Nat. Resources J. 713, 715.

Although at times much maligned and blamed for a series of 'social ills' including 'resource depletion, pollution, dissipation of economic surplus, poverty among resource users, backwardness in technology and misallocation of labor and capital', under the terminology 'tragedy of the commons', conceptually, common property is perhaps better understood as a 'social institution' often encountered in 'informal institutional arrangements based on custom, tradition, kinship and social mores', as was and still is the case in hunting and gathering societies, and is well entrenched in Anglo-Saxon common law and German law with a long history that stretches back to Roman law.[195]

Private ownership 'implies that the community recognises the right of the owner to exclude others from exercising the owner's private rights'.[196] The notion of *private property*, and an individual's natural law entitlement to it, came into Western legal philosophy through the writings of Plato who argued that 'a man may neither take what is another's, nor be deprived of what is his own'.[197] In contrast to Plato, Aristotle developed the concept of distributive justice according to which equals deserve to be treated as equals and unequals unequally.[198] In this context, Van der Vyver argues that

> the difference in emphasis that thus emerged from the respective legal theories of Plato and Aristotle – on the one hand the right of the individual to acquire property and to be protected in the free exercise of the entitlements of ownership, and on the other hand, the moral claim to an equal share in the distribution of goods – up to this day remains critical in the philosophical discourse on the property of private title to, for instance, immovable things, the means of production and strategic materials. The dichotomy between the accumulation of wealth through one's enterprising labours and maintaining economic equality constitutes the core of the dispute between capitalism and socialism.[199]

Later on, Platonian philosophical thought was continued through the works of John Locke whose natural rights theory sought to justify the concept of private property. Under this view, property was originally owned in common by all men, but man had a *'natural right'* to appropriate for his own private

---

[195] ibid 713–715; Richard Perruso, 'Development of the Doctrine of Res Communes in Medieval and Early Modern Europe, The' (2002) 70 Tijdschrift voor Rechtsgeschiedenis 69; Heller (n 188).

[196] Demsetz (n 187) 354.

[197] Plato, *The Republic of Plato* (Basic Books 1991) 112.

[198] Aristotle, *Nicomachean Ethics* (Hackett 2014) 81.

[199] JD Van der Vyver, 'Ownership in Constitutional and International Law' [1985] Acta Juridica 119, 120.

use, the property created as a result of *his labor*.[200] This is known as the labor theory of property, which in essence is 'liberal and anti-authoritarian' thus opposing divine rule and defending private property.[201] Locke's natural right philosophy was thus fundamental to the creation of the middle class and liberalism, and to the discarding of old societal orderings such as feudalism and royal privilege. In contrast to John Locke, Thomas Hobbes viewed the sovereign as the ultimate source from which all property rights arise, since the sovereign 'prescribes the Rules, whereby every man may know, what Goods he may enjoy and what Actions he may doe, without being molested by his fellow subjects'.[202] Pierre-Joseph Proudhon further refined John Locke's arguments and made a further distinction between *personal property*, which is obtained by virtue of one's labor (thus, up to this point sharing John Locke's views) and *other private property*, which in the context of the scarcity of resources is viewed as *beyond one's needs*.[203] At the opposite end, Karl Marx sees private property as 'the product, the necessary result of alienated labor, of the external relation of the worker to nature and to himself'.[204] Marx noted that capitalism itself was prone to contradictions because it is, in effect, expropriatory. Capitalism socialises production whereby the workers who produce all the goods are nothing more than wage slaves for life – in Marx's view – since they do not own any of the things that they produce. The way to solve this situation, in Marx's view, was to abolish bourgeois private property.[205]

In the case of *State ownership*,[206] 'the State may exclude anyone from the use of a right as long as the State follows accepted political procedures for determining who may not use State-owned property'.[207] Ultimately, however, State ownership is in fact a form of public property. Since ownership generally is 'premised on the vesting of property rights in a recognizable entity' which is the 'right to have and dispose of possession and enjoyment of the subject

---

[200] John Locke, *Two Treatises of Government* (C and J Rivington 1824) 146–147.
[201] Pierre-Joseph Proudhon, *What Is Property?: An Inquiry into the Principle of Right and of Government* (BR Tucker 1876) 42–84; Elias N Stebek, 'Conceptual Foundations of Property Rights: Rethinking De Facto Rural Open Access to Common-Pool Resources in Ethiopia' (2011) 5 Mizan L. Rev. 1, 10–11.
[202] Thomas Hobbes, *Hobbes: Leviathan: Revised Student Edition* (Cambridge University Press 1996) 125.
[203] Stebek (n 201) 13.
[204] Karl Marx, *Economic and Philosophic Manuscripts of 1844* (Prometheus Books 1988).
[205] Karl Marx, *Capital: A Critique of Political Economy* (Penguin UK 2004).
[206] 'State ownership' was defined in Section 1.1 as the *public* or *government* ownership of a corporation or of any other asset.
[207] Demsetz (n 187) 354.

matter',[208] this means that in the case of State property, the ownership entity is public, which is the State itself, or an agency of the State or an SOE. However, as one author notes:

[T]his assumption poses further questions; does the state or state agency own the land absolutely, or pursuant to some trust for and on behalf of its citizens? ... An implied trust seemingly results from state ownership ... while the nominal owner may be the state, the title is a threadbare one. The true beneficial owner, illusory or otherwise, is the people.[209]

Thus, when viewed in this manner, when one refers to State ownership, one in effect refers to the beneficiaries in whom all the rights associated with ownership ultimately rest. As such, this prompts us to take a deeper look at the function of State ownership and how this function should be exercised. In this context, the way in which States should own, and how the function of State ownership should be discharged are all interconnected issues. As has already been discussed above, in the WTO case of *US – Definitive Anti-Dumping and Countervailing Duties on Certain Products from China*,[210] there is a blurred line between the pursuance of economic activities, public policy objectives and the exercise of governmental authority or governmental functions. Another example of this lingering confusion can be found in the drafting of the OECD Guidelines on Corporate Governance of State-Owned Enterprises which states that: 'the Guidelines are applicable to all SOEs pursuing economic activities, either exclusively or together with the pursuit of public policy objectives or the exercise of governmental authority or a governmental function'.[211] Nevertheless, despite the persisting confusion, it has been acknowledged that

the members of the public whose government exercises the ownership rights are the ultimate owners of SOEs. This implies that those who exercise ownership rights over SOEs owe duties toward the public that are not unlike the fiduciary duties of a board toward the shareholders and should act as trustees of the public interest. High standards of transparency and accountability are needed to allow the public to assure itself that the state exercises its powers in accordance with the public's best interest.[212]

---

[208] John Page, 'Towards an Understanding of Public Property' in Nicholas Hopkins (ed), *Modern Studies in Property Law*, vol 7 (Bloomsbury 2013) 204, 208.

[209] ibid.

[210] *United States – Definitive Anti-Dumping and Countervailing Duties on Certain Products from China (Panel Report)* (n 142); *United States – Definitive Anti-Dumping and Countervailing Duties on Certain Products from China (Appellate Body Report)* (n 142).

[211] OECD, *OECD Guidelines on Corporate Governance of State-Owned Enterprises* (OECD 2015) 16.

[212] ibid 29. (Emphasis added).

Overall, the difference between SOEs and POEs is also evidenced by the fundamental difference in the nature of the property rights that are found in those two types of ownership. Private ownership is inherently private in nature, while State ownership is inherently public. Since the public ultimately owns all State property, the State must always act with the public's interests in mind, a situation that is not present in the case of private ownership.

2.4.2.4 The Fourth Level of Differentiation: Separate Regulatory Regimes

The difference between SOEs and POEs also becomes apparent when one examines the various regulatory regimes, which contain specific provisions for SOEs. At the international level, separate rules that apply to SOEs can be found in international economic law – and its subfields such as trade, investment, competition law, taxation law – in general international law in matters concerning the responsibility of States for internationally wrongful acts, in sovereign immunity and also in human rights law.[213] For example, in international trade law, Article XVII of the GATT, as well as the Understanding on the Interpretation of General Agreement on Tariffs and Trade Article XVII refer specifically to 'State Trading Enterprises'.[214] Similar wording is found in the Agreement on Agriculture[215] and in the Subsidies and Countervailing Measures Agreement.[216] The Canada – European Union Comprehensive Economic and Trade Agreement,[217] the North-American Free Trade Agreement[218] and the Comprehensive and Progressive Agreement for Trans-Pacific Partnership[219] all have specific provisions that deal with SOEs. Similar provisions exist at the EU level in Article 106 (1) (ex Article 86) of the Treaty on the Functioning of the European Union (TFEU), which states that 'public undertakings' to which Member States grant special or exclusive rights, shall at all times be subjected to the competition law provisions provided in Articles 18 (non-discrimination), and Articles 101 to 109 which establish the competition

---

[213] Barnes, 'International Investment Law and State-Owned Entities: Recurrent Key Issues and Future Directions' (n 133) 434; Leonardo Borlini, 'When the Leviathan Goes to the Market: A Critical Evaluation of the Rules Governing State-Owned Enterprises in Trade Agreements' (2020) 33 Leiden J. Int. Law 313.

[214] General Agreement on Tariffs and Trade (GATT) 1994.

[215] Agreement on Agriculture 1995 Article 4.

[216] Agreement on Subsidies and Countervailing Measures (SCM Agreement) 1995 Article 6.7.

[217] Comprehensive Economic and Trade Agreement 2017. See chapter 18.

[218] North American Free Trade Agreement 1994. See chapter 15.

[219] Comprehensive and Progressive Agreement for Trans-Pacific Partnership 2018. See chapter 17.

policy of the EU.[220] At the EU level, SOEs are also subject to the rules applicable to monopolies and State aid and a large share of case law concerning SOEs in the EU relates to State aid in the context of the so-called golden share cases.[221] There are also specific 'soft law' instruments that apply to SOEs. For example, the UNGPs[222] explicitly deal with the SOEs in Pillar I, Principles 4, 5 and 6, in the State duty to protect human rights under the terminology 'the State-business nexus'. Among other soft-law norms applicable expressly to SOEs, there are OECD Guidelines on the Corporate Governance of State-Owned Enterprises (OECD Guidelines for SOEs), the Extractive Industries Transparency Initiative and the Sovereign Wealth Funds Generally Accepted Principles and Practices as will be further elaborated in Chapter 3.

2.5 THE RECOGNITION OF STATE-OWNED ENTITIES AS A SUI GENERIS PARTICIPANT IN INTERNATIONAL LAW: OBSTACLES FROM INTERNATIONAL LAW?

Having observed that international law does not expressly distinguish between SOEs and POEs – yet the inherent differences between those entities supports the argument that a distinction should indeed be made – the question that remains is this: Are there any obstacles from international law itself that would impede such recognition? The remainder of this section argues that theoretically no such obstacles could be found to exist in international law. For example, as the preceding sections on the issue of legal personality have discussed, international law has recognised for a long time that that 'reference to states and similar political entities, to [international] organisations, and to individuals does not exhaust the tally of entities active on the international

---

[220] Consolidated Version of the Treaty on European Union and the Treaty on the Functioning of the European Union 2007.

[221] *C-367/98 Commission v Portugal* (European Court of Justice, Judgment of the Court 4 June 2002); *C-483/99 Commission v France* (European Court of Justice, Judgment of the Court, 4 June 2002); *C-503/99 Commission v Belgium* (European Court of Justice, Judgment of the Court, 4 June 2002); *C-463/00 Commission v Spain* (European Court of Justice, Judgment of the Court, 13 May 2003); *C-98/01 Commission v UK* (European Court of Justice, Judgment of the Court, 13 May 2003); *C-112/05 Commission v Germany* (European Court of Justice, Judgment of the Court (Grand Chamber) 23 October 2007); *C-463/04 and C-464/04 Federconsumatori v Comune di Milano* (European Court of Justice, Judgment of the Court (First Chamber) 6 December 2007).

[222] J Ruggie, 'Guiding Principles on Business and Human Rights: Implementing the United Nations "Protect, Respect and Remedy" Framework (Report of the Special Representative of the Secretary-General on the Issue of Human Rights and Transnational Corporations and Other Business Enterprises)' (2011) A/HRC/17/31.

scene'[223] and that 'throughout history, the development of international law has been influenced by the requirements of international life'.[224] Even without adopting the 'actor conception', or the notion of 'participation', international law has recognised that special types of entities – with distinct rights, obligations and capacities – may exist in the international sphere.[225] For example, international public corporations[226] and other types of 'intergovernmental corporations of private law' have been considered as a sui generis participant in the international sphere and have been distinguished from other entities such as traditional international organisations, multinational corporations, *'établissements publics internationaux'* and international public–private partnerships.[227] While it is indeed true that international public corporations have been created by States through treaties – which define their powers, rights, obligations and immunities – it should be noted that the existence of a treaty is not a necessary precondition for a given actor to exist or to participate on the international plane. From the perspective of international law, there would be thus no reason why SOEs could not be recognised as having sui generis status under the broader category of corporations. Such recognition is already present in many – if not most – of the world's municipal legal systems, as well as in some hard and soft international law norms, as illustrated in the immediately preceding sections. Furthermore, another issue that must be taken into consideration is the influence that SOEs have had on the development of international law itself, evidence of this fact being among many examples of the development of the doctrine of restrictive sovereign immunity and the *acta juris gestionis* exception to sovereign immunity – a development which occurred as a response to the increased internationalisation in the trading activities of many States, which ultimately used SOEs to achieve their economic and policy goals.[228]

---

[223] Crawford, *Brownlie's Principles of Public International Law* (n 3) 121.

[224] *Reparations for Injuries Suffered in the Service of the United Nations* (n 22) 178.

[225] Hersch Lauterpacht, 'The Subjects of International Law' in Elihu Lauterpacht (ed), *International Law: Volume 1, The General Works: Being the Collected Papers of Hersch Lauterpacht* (Cambridge University Press 1970) para 48. ('[T]he range of subjects of international law is not rigidly and immutably circumscribed by any definition of the nature of international law but is capable of modification and development in accordance with the will of States and the requirement of international intercourse.').

[226] Crawford, *Brownlie's Principles of Public International Law* (n 3) 122–123; W Friedmann, 'International Public Corporations' (1943) 6 Mod. L. Rev. 185; W Friedmann, 'The Legal Status and Organization of the Public Corporation' (1951) 16 Law Contemp. Probl. 576.

[227] Dotse A Tsikata, 'The International Public Corporation: A Concept More Relevant than Ever?' (2017) 14 IOLR 120, 134–137.

[228] Robert M Jarvis, 'The Tate Letter: Some Words Regarding Its Authorship' (2015) 55 Am. J. Leg. Hist. 465, 471; Fox and Webb (n 119) 131–165.

2.6 STATE-OWNED ENTITIES AS SUI GENERIS PARTICIPANT IN INTERNATIONAL LAW: CONSEQUENCES

2.6.1 Consequences for International Law in General: Increased Heterogeneity and Complexity of Participants

The emergence of SOEs as participants in the international legal system demonstrates the increasing heterogeneity and complexity of the notion of 'participation' on the international plane. At the same time, it also underscores the governance and accountability challenges that those particular 'participants' may have. For example, SOEs may have particular corporate governance issues – such as increased opacity, bribery and corruption – which arise, principally from the fact that usually their leadership is in the hands of government officials and not those of professional managers. Given that the boards of directors have fiduciary duties of care and of loyalty, if the leadership of SOEs is in the hands of government officials, there may be a conflict between the fiduciary duties that the directors owe to the SOE and its shareholders and the allegiance that those board members may have to their own political party.[229] For SOEs, the main aim of sound corporate governance principles is to ensure that they are 'at least as accountable to the general public as a listed company should be to its shareholders'.[230] For example, the OECD has long recognised some of the challenges facing the corporate governance of SOEs and has pointed to several areas of corporate governance that deserve specific attention: disclosure and transparency, decision-making (in particular the responsibilities of the boards of State-owned enterprises, as well as the equitable treatment of shareholders and other investors), accountability, the State's role as an owner and participant in the market place and the role of the State in promoting responsible business practices.[231] Apart for corporate governance challenges, and the specialised field of international economic law, SOEs pose additional challenges to several areas of international law such as sovereign immunities, State responsibility and human rights, as the remaining chapters in this monograph show. For clarity, it must be stated that the recognition of SOEs as a sui generis participant in international law does not mean that SOEs would be equal to States. Their recognition as sui generis participants would be envisaged in a more

---

[229] World Bank (n 94) 160–161.
[230] OECD, OECD Guidelines on Corporate Governance of State-Owned Enterprises (n 211).
[231] ibid.

'limited'[232] and functional manner. Overall, the recognition of SOEs as sui generis participants would demonstrate that international law has an inherent capacity to expand on certain well-entrenched conceptual frameworks and to adapt to new ideas in order to address some of the most pressing current challenges.

2.6.2 Consequences for State-Owned Entities: A 'Duty' to Respect Human Rights

This section argues that SOEs may have a 'duty to respect' human rights, which is different to the generally accepted corporate 'responsibility to respect' human rights. The section commences by introducing the general corporate responsibility to respect human rights and then asks the question: Are SOEs any different? A conclusion is reached that SOEs are indeed different by looking at certain doctrinal developments as well as relevant State practice.

2.6.2.1 General Comments on the Corporate Responsibility to Respect Human Rights

The UNGPs, adopted by the UN Human Rights Council are the latest and clearest expression of the corporate responsibility to protect human rights in international law. As a soft law instrument that is not legally binding for either States or corporations,[233] the UNGPs are considered a 'global standard' and have been generally well received by all actors involved such as States, businesses and civil society.[234] The UNGPs framework is composed of three

---

[232] Clapham (n 38) 78–79; Joost Pauwelyn, 'Is It International Law or Not, and Does It Even Matter?' in Joost Pauwelyn, Ramses A Wessel and Jan Wouters (eds), *Informal International Lawmaking* (Oxford University Press 2012) 144.

[233] Justine Nolan, 'The Corporate Responsibility to Respect Human Rights: Soft Law or Not Law?' in Surya Deva and David Bilchitz (eds), *Human Rights Obligations of Business: Beyond the Corporate Responsibility to Respect?* (Cambridge University Press 2013). (While this contribution 'highlights the many limitations of using soft law to hold corporations accountable for human rights violations, it also recognises [that] reliance on soft law can result in incremental change'.).

[234] Karin Buhmann, 'Navigating from "Train Wreck" to Being "Welcomed": Negotiation Strategies and Argumentative Patterns in the Development of the UN Framework' in Surya Deva and David Bilchitz (eds), *Human Rights Obligations of Business: Beyond the Corporate Responsibility to Respect* (Cambridge University Press 2013); Bernaz (n 71) 195; Surya Deva, *Regulating Corporate Human Rights Violations Humanizing Business* (1st pbk. edn, Routledge 2014) 110–113; Surya Deva, 'From Business or Human Rights to Business and Human Rights: What Next?' in Surya Deva and David Birchall, *Research Handbook on Human Rights and Business* (Edward Elgar 2020) <https://www.elgaronline.com/view/edcoll/9781786436399/9781786436399.00005.xml> accessed 7 August 2020.

pillars: Pillar I deals with the State duty to protect against human rights abuses by non-State actors including business (containing the 'State-business nexus', as already discussed), Pillar II deals with the responsibilities of corporations to respect human rights and Pillar III deals with the need to ensure that appropriate remedies exist to deal with those cases where there has been a violation of human rights. Even though the UNGPs do not create international legal obligations, they are the latest embodiment of global expectations about how States and corporations are expected to behave. In theory, it is also possible that in time, new customary norms will develop from the UNGPs, as some commentators have noted.[235]

In the UNGPs, the corporate responsibility to respect human rights is contained in Principles 11–15. UNGP 11 states that 'business enterprises should respect human rights'.[236] This in effect means that business enterprises 'should avoid infringing on the human rights of others and should address adverse human rights impacts with which they are involved'.[237] The Commentary to the UNGPs clarifies that the corporate responsibility to respect human rights is a 'global standard of conduct' that is expected of all business enterprises and which 'exists independently of States' abilities and/or willingness to fulfil their own human rights obligations, and does not diminish those obligations'. Yet the UNGPs ground the corporate responsibility to respect human rights in 'enlightened self-interest' rather than on a sense of a moral obligation, which could be characterised as representing an inherent weakness.[238] For example, Wesley Cragg considers that a justificatory foundation based on enlightened self-interest 'is not [enough of] a compelling reason' to respect human rights. Cragg further argues that instead corporations have both a direct and indirect moral obligation to respect human rights. The indirect moral obligation is 'imposed and mediated by the law' because 'corporations have an obligation to obey the law regardless of whether or not it can be shown in particular cases to be in their best economic or financial interests'.[239] The direct moral obligation is based on the argument that human rights are 'designed to protect

---

[235] Zerk (n 71) 263.
[236] Ruggie, 'Guiding Principles on Business and Human Rights' (n 222) 13.
[237] ibid.
[238] David Bilchitz and Surya Deva, 'The Human Rights Obligations of Business: A Critical Framework for the Future' in Surya Deva and David Bilchitz (eds) *Human Rights Obligations of Business: Beyond the Corporate Responsibility to Respect* (Cambridge University Press 2013) 12–13; Wesley Cragg, 'Ethics, Enlightened Self-Interest, and the Corporate Responsibility to Respect Human Rights: A Critical Look at the Justificatory Foundations of the UN Framework' (2012) 22 Bus. Ethics Q. 9, 10; Denis G Arnold, 'Transnational Corporations and the Duty to Respect Basic Human Rights' (2010) 20 Bus. Ethics Q. 371.
[239] Cragg (n 239) 19.

fundamental interests in which everybody has an interest', which ultimately means that corporations must respect human rights on the basis of a 'moral imperative'[240] rather than enlightened self-interest.[241] Other scholars have also argued that corporations' human rights obligations must be sourced in the nature of human rights themselves rather than on 'social expectations'.[242] Doing otherwise would be 'inconsistent with the logic of human rights, which entails duties upon those who have the capacity to violate them or assist in their realisation'.[243] Starting from the assumption that an international legal system that imposes legal obligations only upon States is not sufficient to protect human rights, Ratner imagines corporations as powerful entities that have direct obligations in international law to protect human rights[244] and he further argues that corporations have human rights obligations because they cooperate with States and because their activities infringe upon the human dignity of those with whom they have special ties.[245] Andrew Clapham also dismisses the notion that it is only States that can have human rights obligations and argues that corporations can also be the bearers of international obligations in the following way:

> States have adopted intentional texts which are addressed to corporations themselves and which specifically call for human rights to be respected by transnational corporations . . . . Although there are only rare instances of an international tribunal where a corporation could be the respondent in a dispute, corporations can still be the bearers of international duties. Lack of international jurisdictions to try a corporation does not mean that a corporation is under no international legal obligation . . . . It makes sense to speak of the separation between the *obligation* under international law and *international jurisdiction* to try the alleged offender. There are clearly violations of international criminal law that exist in the absence of any international jurisdiction to try them. The absence of an international jurisdiction to try corporations does not mean that transnational corporations cannot break international law.[246]

---

[240] The author recognises that this argument may create disagreements about the nature of morality itself.

[241] Cragg (n 239) 19.

[242] David Bilchitz, 'A Chasm between "Is" and "Ought"? A Critique of the Normative Foundations of the SRSG's Framework and the Guiding Principles' in Surya Deva and David Bilchitz (eds), *Human Rights Obligations of Business: Beyond the Corporate Responsibility to Respect?* (Cambridge University Press 2013) 120.

[243] ibid.

[244] Ratner (n 61) 449, 461.

[245] ibid.

[246] Clapham (n 38) 266–267. (Emphasis added. Footnotes omitted).

Surya Deva and Jennifer Zerk argue that corporations have human rights obligations because of their relation to and position in society.[247] Deva views corporations as organs that are critical to the operation of society generally. Departing from this general proposition, Deva further argues that corporations 'ought to comply with basic moral and legal norms of society in which they operate, for not doing so will lead to chaos and instability'.[248] Ethics scholars have asked the question whether corporations can be moral agents, and thus endowed with personality in a similar fashion to human beings, but the answers to those questions have been contradictory. Some of those scholars believe that corporations can sometimes be moral agents, if the decision-making structure that they have in place satisfies certain requirements,[249] while others argue the contrary.[250]

UNGP 14 states that 'the responsibility of business enterprises to respect human rights applies to all enterprises regardless of their size, sector, operational context, *ownership* and structure'[251] an issue that was further clarified by the UN Working Group on Business and Human Rights.[252] This means that a corporate responsibility to respect human rights will exist even when the State in question is unable or unwilling to fulfill their own human rights obligations. For SOEs, this has two implications. First, where an SOEs operates in a State that is unable or unwilling to fulfill its own human rights obligations, because of a lack of resources or unwillingness to do so, or for other reasons, the SOE still has a responsibility to respect human rights that arises independently of the legal framework present in the host State. Second, this responsibility also exists independently of how the home State of the SOE regulates corporate conduct within its own jurisdiction. The requirement for supply chain due diligence is iterated in UNGP 13, which states that business enterprises have a responsibility to avoid causing or contributing to adverse

---

[247] Deva, *Regulating Corporate Human Rights Violations* (n 234) 146. Citing Jennifer Zerk, *Multinational Enterprises and Corporate Social Responsibility: Limitations and Opportunities in International Law* (Cambridge University Press 2006) 32.

[248] ibid 147.

[249] Thomas Donaldson, *Corporations and Morality* (Prentice-Hall 1982) 30. (Corporations can qualify as moral persons when they have the capacity to use moral reasons in decision-making and when they can control not only overt corporate acts, but also the structure of polices and rules.).

[250] Patricia H Werhane, 'Corporate Moral Agency and the Responsibility to Respect Human Rights in the UN Guiding Principles: Do Corporations Have Moral Rights?' (2016) 1 BHRJ 5.

[251] Emphasis added.

[252] 'Leading by Example: The State, State-Owned Enterprises and Human Rights (Report of the Working Group on the Issue of Human Rights and Transnational Corporations and Other Business Enterprises)' (2016) A/HRC/32/45 9.

human rights impacts through their own activities or through the activities of others 'that are directly linked to their operations, products and services'.[253] While 'all business enterprises', regardless of 'size, sector, operational context, ownership and structure' have a responsibility to respect human rights, UNGP 14 expects larger businesses to do more in this context. UNGP 15 states that in order to meet their responsibility to respect human rights, corporations should have in place policies and processes appropriate to their size and circumstances, such as a human rights due-diligence process (that 'identifies, prevents and mitigates and accounts for how they address their impacts on human rights') as well as other processes 'that enable the remediation of any adverse human rights impacts', thus underlining that corporations can have an important role to play in the remediation of 'adverse human rights impacts' that have already occurred. The UNGPs further elaborate on the requirements for an appropriate policy commitment (UNGP 16), the parameters (UNGP 17) and essential components of 'human rights due diligence', such as the responsibility to *identify* actual or potential impacts, the *prevention and mitigation* of the impacts identified and *accounting* for the impacts and responses to them (UNGPs 18, 19, 20, 21).[254] 'Human rights due diligence' must also be context specific (UNGP 23). Furthermore, the results of the due diligence must be effectively integrated across the whole of the business enterprise and the response tracked and communicated to affected stakeholders. UNGP 22 provides that in a case where a business enterprise identifies that it has caused or contributed to adverse impacts, 'they should provide for or cooperate in the remediation through legitimate processes'.[255]

2.6.2.2 Are State-Owned Entities Different from the General Position?

Having considered the general corporate responsibility to respect human rights, this section asks whether this general position is applicable to SOEs in equal measure, or whether there are differences in its application. For clarity, the UNGPs do not mention SOEs specifically under Pillar II. As discussed in Section 2.4.2.4, SOEs are only mentioned under Pillar I, under the State duty to protect human rights in 'State-business nexus', but not in Pillar II, which could lead one to conclude that, as far as Pillar II is concerned, SOEs are placed in an identical position to POEs. That is, an SOE would have a responsibility to respect human rights, but no more than that. Yet it is

---

[253] Ruggie, 'Guiding Principles on Business and Human Rights' (n 222) 14.
[254] ibid 15–20; Olivier De Schutter and others, 'Human Rights Due Diligence: The Role of States' 55–57.
[255] Ruggie, 'Guiding Principles on Business and Human Rights' (n 222).

beginning to be recognised that SOEs are indeed in a different position to POEs.[256] For example, Larry Catá Backer argues that

> the conduct of economic activities through state owned enterprises (SOEs) function in a space where the public duty and private obligation meet, that is, where the legal duties of the state merge with the governance responsibilities of the private organisation. The SOE does not easily fit within the classical division of obligation, expressed in political legal theory, between public and private entities, and their respective relationship to law. States have a duty which is undertaken through law; enterprises have a responsibility which is imbedded in their governance. These fundamental divisions form part of the current international efforts to institutionalize human rights related norms on and through states and enterprises, and most notably through the U.N. Guiding Principles for Business and Human Rights. The problems of conforming to evolving norms becomes more difficult where states project their authority through commercial enterprises, that is where the societal (and economic) governance order of the enterprise is conflated with the political and legal order of the state.[257]

Backer further asserts that SOEs 'occupy a dual place within the UNGPs' in that they are an instrumentality of the State and thus 'potentially subject to the State duty to protect' and that they operate as 'commercial ventures being subject to the corporate responsibility to respect'.[258] This means that practically 'their owners have a duty in exercising their ownership responsibilities that may also be constrained by the State duty to protect human rights'.[259]

> [I]ssues of corporate personality, of sovereign immunity, of asset partition and of the mania for compartmentalization that marks certain approaches to global economic and financial regulation may well hobble the work of embedding human rights within the operation of states as owners and SOEs as public enterprises. More importantly it suggests the difficulty of the current strongly held consensus that the focus of regulatory governance must be grounded in and through a formally constituted enterprise, the SOE, rather than focusing on the regulation of economic activity irrespective of the

---

[256] Judith Schönsteiner, 'Attribution of State Responsibility for Actions or Omissions of State-Owned Enterprises in Human Rights Matters' (2019) 40 U. Pa. J. Int'l L. 42, 895. (Schönsteiner argues that SOEs are 'the only business entities which have, as of now, direct responsibilities under international law *lege lata*'.).

[257] LC Backer, 'The Human Rights Obligations of State-Owned Enterprises (SOEs): Emerging Conceptual Structures and Principles in National and International Law and Policy' (2017) 50 Vand. J. Transnat'l L. 1, 1–2.

[258] ibid 9.

[259] ibid.

form in which it is undertaken. Until those conceptual issues are considered the regulation of economic activities – SOEs, supply chains, multinational corporations, will remain elusive.[260]

The suggestion that SOEs might indeed be in a different position than POEs was even alluded to in the 2015–2016 report of the UN Working Group on Business and Human Rights which pointed to the fact that there might be situations when the acts of an SOE and the 'nature of its relationship with the State are more clearly associated with the State duty to respect'.[261] The report does not mention how one is to distinguish between such circumstances apart from the suggestion that the enterprise in question would be performing 'public functions', but no further definition is provided in this sense.[262] Yet it is unfortunate that the UNGPs mention the 'public function' requirement as this makes one think of the requirements for distinguishing between *acta jure imperii* and *acta jure gestionis*, or of the requirements for determining whether 'governmental authority' was in fact exercised for the purposes of attributing State responsibility, issues which, as will be discussed in Chapter 5, bring their own challenges. Nevertheless, what this would mean is that, in circumstances when the SOE exercises 'public functions', the corporate responsibility to respect human rights is in effect 'merged' with the State duty to protect.[263] When, however, the 'public function' is not exercised, the SOE in question would only have a responsibility to respect human rights.

The UN Working Group on Business and Human Rights has further stated that 'in addition to' the responsibility of SOEs to respect human rights, they are expected to also observe 'the highest standards of business conduct on par with listed companies'.[264] Since publicly listed companies have generally more onerous obligations under domestic law, in terms of disclosure and transparency, this analogy implies that SOEs will *always* have more onerous

---

[260] ibid.

[261] Human Rights Council, 'Report of the Working Group on the Issue of Human Rights and Transnational Corporations and Other Business Enterprises' (2013) A/HRC/23/32/Add.2 at 9.

[262] Larry C Backer, 'Human Rights Responsibilities of State-Owned Enterprises' in Surya Deva and David Birchall (eds), *Research Handbook on Human Rights and Business* (Edward Elgar 2020) 240–242.

[263] Larry C Backer, 'The Human Rights Obligations of State-Owned Enterprises (SOEs): Emerging Conceptual Structures and Principles in National and International Law and Policy' (2017) 50 Vand. J. Transnat'l L. 23.

[264] Human Rights Council, 'Report of the Working Group on the Issue of Human Rights and Transnational Corporations and Other Business Enterprises' (n 261) 10.

obligations.[265] In the last paragraph of the report, the Working Group reiterates that SOEs are required to respect human rights regardless whether their activities are 'purely commercial or related to specific public purposes'.[266] Backer again points out that the distinction between the 'public' and 'commercial' activities might not be in the best overall interest of the UNGPs and further argues that the UNGPs seek to embed respect for human rights in all economic activities, regardless whether they are classified as public or private:

> The UNGP are meant to frame the way that human rights ought to be deeply embedded within the structures of economic activity. To add contingencies about the scope and manner of that protection on the basis of the character of the activity is at best ill advised. First, the "performs public functions" stand is itself ambiguous. Public functions are understood quite differently depending on the political economy of a state, its traditions and its operations. Moreover, such a standard is at best difficult to implement and monitor. The United States' Supreme Court's efforts to distinguish between traditional governmental functions and ordinary economic activity proved a too difficult task to undertake in any principled way. Adding the complication of differences among states, the resulting variation in the scope of coverage might well be used to undermine the coherence of the human rights project itself.[267]

Another way to look at this problem is to consider the close connection between the State and its SOEs. Ultimately, all SOEs are run in the public interest by virtue of the fact that it is the public that owns them as was discussed earlier in this chapter. Even if an SOE is created for a purely commercial purpose, that is, to make a profit, its ultimate purpose is public since its profits and assets upon liquidation go into the public purse.[268] Furthermore, since the expectation has been that SOEs 'should lead by example'[269] it is difficult to see how this could be done only in certain circumstances (when the State acts in a public capacity), but not in other circumstances (when the State acts in a 'purely commercial' capacity). Another issue to consider in this discussion is that the obligations imposed on States under Pillar I make no such distinctions. That is, a State is not required to take 'additional steps' to protect against human rights

---

[265] ibid. The report refers to 'accounting standards, disclosure, compliance and auditing standards'.

[266] ibid.

[267] Backer, 'The Human Rights Obligations of State-Owned Enterprises (SOEs)' (n 263) 25; Backer, 'Human Rights Responsibilities of State-Owned Enterprises' (n 262) 240–242.

[268] OECD, *OECD Guidelines on Corporate Governance of State-Owned Enterprises* (n 211) 29.

[269] Human Rights Council, 'Report of the Working Group on the Issue of Human Rights and Transnational Corporations and Other Business Enterprises' (n 261) 12.

abuses by SOEs, except only in certain circumstances. UNGP 4 does not mention this possibility. States are required to take 'additional steps' to ensure that human rights are protected by all SOEs, whatever their function or purpose may be. The extension of this duty to privatised entities and to procurement activities under UNGPs 5 and 6 further reinforces this conclusion. Given that more is expected of States under the 'State-business nexus' and considering that ultimately all SOEs are run in the public interest, it can only be concluded that, as far as the corporate responsibility to protect is concerned, more is expected of SOEs in general. Consequently, the corporate responsibilities of SOEs are superior to those of POEs and should be likened with a *duty to respect*, rather than solely with a responsibility to respect as is the case with POEs. The 'merger'[270] of the 'duty to protect' with the 'corporate responsibility to respect' as applicable to SOEs may have the net effect of bypassing what Surya Deva calls the 'cages of protect and respect' that have been artificially created by the UNGPs:

> If there are some companies owned or controlled by states, it is plausible to argue that the state duty to respect should (also) apply to such situation, for such companies are in effect part of the state machinery. Principle 4, however, deals with such a scenario only within the rubric of the state duty to protect against human rights abuses. That is a regressive idea, because public sector companies may already have an *obligation* to respect human rights. For instance under the Indian constitutional law jurisprudence, public companies are obliged to respect fundamental rights enumerated in the Constitution.[271]

Consequently, in international law one may encounter certain corporate entities, such as SOEs, which have obligations to respect human rights rather than a mere 'responsibility' to do so. This could bring the discourse one step closer to recognising that corporations have an obligation under international law – rather than a mere responsibility – to respect human rights.[272]

2.7 INTERIM CONCLUSION

This chapter began with a narrative of the concept of legal personality in international law. The different conceptualisations of this notion throughout

---

[270] Backer, 'The Human Rights Obligations of State-Owned Enterprises (SOEs)' (n 263) 23.

[271] Surya Deva, 'Treating Human Rights Lightly: A Critique of the Consensus Rhetoric and the Language Employed by the Guiding Principles' in Surya Deva and David Bilchitz (eds), *Human Rights Obligations of Business: Beyond the Corporate Responsibility to Respect* (Cambridge University Press 2013) 95–96.

[272] Schönsteiner (n 256).

history have shown how international law has had to find ways to address the emergence of participants that were not initially envisaged as forming part of the system. The evolution from the States-only conception, to the recognition conception and individualistic conception, later followed by the formal conception and the actor conception are all manifestations of a system that attempts to offer practical solutions to manage the challenges associated with the emergence of new types of participants in the international system, such as international organisations, individuals, non-governmental organisations and corporations. Based on several distinguishing characteristics the chapter then argued that SOEs are a sui generis 'participant' in international law, belonging to the broader category of corporations, but being nevertheless distinct from privately owned entities. Support for this assertion can be found from the fact that conceptually SOEs belong to the public domain, from their role and rationale for existence and from the emergence of entirely separate regulatory regimes that attempt to address some of the challenges linked with SOEs. There is nothing inherent in the international legal system that presents itself as an insurmountable obstacle against recognition. While the emergence of SOEs as participants in the international legal system demonstrates the increasing heterogeneity and complexity of the notion of participation on the international plane, it also underlines that the international legal system must continue to adapt in order to address new challenges, an issue that was recognised by the ICJ in the *Reparations for Injuries* advisory opinion, when it emphasised that the concept of whom may be a 'subject' is not static and that its nature depended 'upon the needs of the community'[273] and more recently by the General Court of the European Union when it distinguished between 'countries' and 'States' and stated that 'international society is not made up of States alone … [but] is composed of various actors'.[274] As a consequence of the recognition of SOEs as sui generis category of participant, those entities may have an obligation to respect human rights, rather than just a mere 'responsibility' to do so. This chapter demonstrates how switching the focus from one type of actor (private corporations) to a similar, but ultimately different, type of actor (SOEs) has the benefit of offering new perspectives and insights into the broader challenges associated with the regulation of corporations for human rights violations and on the role that international law has to play in this context.

---

[273] *Reparations for Injuries Suffered in the Service of the United Nations* (n 22) para 179.
[274] *Case T-370-19 Kingdom of Spain v European Union* (General Court of the European Union, Ninth Chamber, 23 September 2020) [29].

3

State-Owned Entities and Norm Development in International Law

International, Regional and Domestic Approaches to Regulation

3.1 INTRODUCTION

The purpose of this chapter is to examine the various approaches that have been taken to regulate SOEs from a human rights perspective and to determine their effect on international law. To this end, selected instruments that concern the regulation of SOEs are analysed on three levels: international, regional and domestic. At the international level, the chapter analyses the United Nations Guiding Principles on Business and Human Rights (UNGPs), the OECD Guidelines for Multinational Enterprises, the OECD Guidelines on the Corporate Governance of State-Owned Enterprises, the OECD Common Approaches for Officially Supported Export Credits and Environmental and Social Due Diligence, the ILO Tripartite Declaration concerning Multinational Enterprises, the Extractive Industries Transparency Initiative, the Sovereign Wealth Funds Generally Accepted Principles and Practices (Santiago Principles) and the UN Global Compact. It will be observed that some of those instruments are specifically designed for SOEs (e.g., the OECD Guidelines on the Corporate Governance of State-Owned Enterprises and the OECD Common Approaches for Officially Supported Export Credits and Environmental Social Due Diligence), while others only have specific provisions that apply to SOEs (the UNGPs and the Extractive Industries Transparency Initiative). Some instruments do not have any specific provisions that apply to SOEs, but it has been further elaborated that they apply to SOEs in equal measure (e.g., the OECD Guidelines for Multinational Enterprises and the ILO Tripartite Declaration concerning Multinational Enterprises and Social Policy). At the regional level, the chapter examines what might prove to be a key regulatory opportunity for the human rights dimension of State ownership: public procurement, which is analysed mainly through the prism of the EU Public Procurement Directives. The section on domestic approaches to

SOE regulation examines measures that have been taken by several States that have addressed the human rights dimension of State corporate ownership. Overall, the ultimate aims of this chapter are to demonstrate how State corporate ownership is regulated on several levels through a complex web of regulatory instruments and to determine the effect that the emergence of those regimes could have on international law.

3.2 GENERAL REMARKS ON REGULATORY THEORY

Although there is no generally accepted definition of regulation,[1] this process has been generally understood to include 'all forms of pressure to change the course of events' and thus goes 'beyond legal rules and mechanisms' to include all 'political, social, economic and psychological pressures' to achieve a desired end.[2] Generally, literature makes a distinction between economic and social regulation.[3] The rationale for social regulation is based on human rights or on other welfare considerations,[4] while economic regulation is either structural or conduct regulation and is based on general public interest considerations.[5] Structural regulation addresses market structure and classic examples are the entry and exit rules for individuals providing certain professional services. The special screening procedures designed for the admission of sovereign investment is another example of structural regulation. Conduct regulation is used for influencing market behaviour, for example, by setting prices. The provision (or not, as the case may be) of State aid to SOEs is an example of conduct regulation. Broadly speaking, the rationale for economic regulation assumes that regulation generally is 'second-best' and it is principally designed to address certain market failures such as monopolies, the presence of externalities, information asymmetries, predatory pricing and instances of unequal bargaining power. By implication, this approach to

---

[1] Robert Baldwin, Martin Cave and Martin Lodge, *Understanding Regulation: Theory, Strategy, and Practice* (Oxford University Press 2012) 2.
[2] Hilary Charlesworth, 'A Regulatory Perspective on the International Human Rights System' in Peter Drahos (ed), *Regulatory Theory: Foundations and Applications* (ANU Press 2017) 361.
[3] Baldwin, Cave and Lodge (n 1) 15–23; Tony Prosser, *The Regulatory Enterprise: Government, Regulation, and Legitimacy* (Oxford University Press 2010) 1–2; Johan Den Hertog, 'General Theories of Regulation', in Boudewijn Bouckaert and Gerrit de Geest (eds), *Encyclopedia of Law and Economics, Vol. III, The Regulation of Contracts* (Edward Elgar 2000) 224.
[4] Baldwin, Cave and Lodge (n 1) 16; Prosser *The Regulatory Enterprise: Government, Regulation, and Legitimacy* (n 3) 16. (Prosser argues that there are in fact four types of models of regulation: (a) regulation for economic efficiency and consumer choice, (b) regulation to protect rights, (c) regulation for social solidarity and (d) regulation as deliberation.)
[5] Baldwin, Cave and Lodge (n 1) 15; Den Hertog (n 3) 224.

regulation is narrow since it assumes that 'regulation is always a second-best solution, and the idea that there is an independent, cultural, or social justification for regulation as an alternative to markets has no place' under this approach.[6] This means that regulation is viewed as 'an always regrettable means of correcting market failures',[7] and by having efficiency as an ultimate goal, is intrinsically utilitarian.[8] Social regulation acts as a response mechanism to economic regulation and its main rationales are to protect human rights and to advance social solidarity.[9] Social regulation models question the assumptions behind the thinking in economic regulation that 'market solutions are always the best way to deal with decisions on the allocation of goods and services, and that non-market failure rationales for regulating are essentially arbitrary'.[10] Social regulation is thus broader than economic regulation[11] and touches upon two main areas: human rights and social solidarity.[12] Human rights regulation takes an individualistic perspective, which has at its core human dignity.[13] Human rights–based regulation is operationalised either directly through standards that have been developed and are enforced for this purpose, indirectly by restricting decision-making on certain matters or procedurally, whereby those affected by decisions are given means to participate in the decision-making process.[14] Social solidarity regulation takes a communitarian view of regulation, whereby it is the community's duty as a whole 'to secure inclusiveness, resting both on a moral sense of equal citizenship, and a more prudential goal of minimizing social fragmentation'.[15] Perhaps the best example of social solidarity regulation is the assurance of utility services to which the whole community has access, irrespective of income or location. The promotion of sustainability is also based on social solidarity concepts.[16] At the international level, SOEs have been regulated from both an economic and social perspective. For example, norms that

---

[6]   Tony Prosser, 'Regulation and Social Solidarity' (2006) 33 J. Law Soc. 364, 368–369.

[7]   Prosser, *The Regulatory Enterprise: Government, Regulation, and Legitimacy* (n 3) 1.

[8]   ibid 13.

[9]   ibid 2; Prosser, *The Regulatory Enterprise: Government, Regulation, and Legitimacy* (n 3); Baldwin, Cave and Lodge (n 1) 22.

[10]   Baldwin, Cave and Lodge (n 1) 22; Prosser (n 3).

[11]   Prosser, *The Regulatory Enterprise: Government, Regulation, and Legitimacy* (n 3) 3.

[12]   ibid 13–17.

[13]   Roger Brownsword, 'What the World Needs Now: Techno-Regulation, Human Rights and Human Dignity' in Roger Brownsword (ed), *Global Governance and the Quest for Justice*, Vol IV: Human Rights (Oxford University Press 2004).

[14]   Prosser, *The Regulatory Enterprise: Government, Regulation, and Legitimacy* (n 3) 14.

[15]   ibid 15–16.

[16]   ibid 17.

regulate SOEs from an economic perspective can be found in free trade agreements and in bilateral investment treaties and they largely seek to address the advantages that States bestow on SOEs such as direct subsidies, concessionary financing, informational advantages, State-backed guarantees and other preferential regulatory treatment. The rest of this chapter will examine various selected instruments that regulate SOEs from a human rights perspective on three levels: international, regional and domestic.

3.3 INTERNATIONAL APPROACHES TO THE REGULATION OF STATE-OWNED ENTITIES

3.3.1 *The United Nations Guiding Principles on Business and Human Rights (UNGPs)*

The UNGPs have been developed under the auspices of the UN by John Ruggie, special representative of the Secretary-General (SRSG) on the issue of human rights and transnational corporations. The UNGPs form the central part of the report presented by John Ruggie to the UN Human Rights Council[17] and have been unanimously endorsed by the UN Human Rights Council in Resolution 17/4 on 16 June 2011.[18] The principal achievement of the SRSG was to 'break the stalemate and to forge a broad consensus around his proposals', an approach that was rooted in 'principled pragmatism'.[19] Nevertheless, commentators have argued that the 'focus on consensus-building has arguably resulted in dilution of the framework's robustness in promoting corporate human rights responsibilities'.[20] The UNGPs rest on three pillars: under Pillar I, States have a duty to *protect* against human rights abuses by non-State actors, including businesses. According to Pillar II, businesses have a responsibility to *respect* human rights, while Pillar III provides that there is the need to ensure that

---

[17] John G Ruggie, 'Guiding Principles on Business and Human Rights: Implementing the United Nations "Protect, Respect and Remedy" Framework (Report of the Special Representative of the Secretary-General on the Issue of Human Rights and Transnational Corporations and Other Business Enterprises, John Ruggie)' (Human Rights Council, Seventeenth Session, Agenda Item 3 2011) A/HRC/17/31.

[18] General Assembly, Human Rights Council, Human Rights and Transnational Corporations and other Business Enterprises (A/HRC/RES/17/4).

[19] Surya Deva, *Regulating Corporate Human Rights Violations: Humanizing Business* (1st pbk. edn, Routledge 2014) 105.

[20] ibid; Surya Deva, 'Treating Human Rights Lightly: A Critique of the Consensus Rhetoric and the Language Employed by the Guiding Principles' in Surya Deva and David Bilchitz (eds), *Human Rights Obligations of Business: Beyond the Corporate Responsibility to Respect* (Cambridge University Press 2013).

appropriate *remedies* exist in cases where there has been an actual breach of those duties and responsibilities.[21] UNGPs 1–10 deal with the State 'duty to protect' against human rights abuses, and discuss SOEs as part of the 'State-business nexus', UNGPs 11–24 deal with the 'corporate responsibility' to respect, including the requirement to conduct human rights due diligence (UNGP 17), while UNGPs 25–31 deal with 'access to remedy', which includes both State-based judicial and non-judicial grievance mechanisms, as well as non-State based grievance mechanisms including operational-level grievance mechanisms that are created by corporations. Although the UNGPs constitute an important step in the development of a framework that seeks to ensure that businesses respect human rights, the way that the three pillars have been developed has attracted criticism:

> Out of the three-fold duty typology, the SRSG has selected only one type of duty each for states and companies: whereas states have a duty to protect, companies have a responsibility to respect. This compartmentalized approach has several adverse implications for human rights. For one it ignores the crucial link between states' duty to 'protect' human rights and corporate responsibility to 'respect' human rights. How can states enforce human rights obligations against corporations when the latter merely have a responsibility (not duty) to respect human rights in the first place? Moreover, this approach has shifted the focus of debate from the human rights obligations *of companies* to the obligations *of states*. The real issue is: should companies have independent 'obligations' along with states? The SRSG has responded by moving corporate obligations to the background and framing them in terms of 'responsibility'. Apart from putting an artificial limit on states' human rights obligations (and thus excluding the duties to protect and fulfill human rights), this approach has also unduly narrowed down the scope of corporate obligations. There are good reasons to contend that companies should have the 'protect' and 'fulfill' type of duties in certain situations. This pragmatic choosing of duties by the SRSG has also created a *conceptual anarchy*, because the Guiding Principles have ended up conflating the concepts of 'protect' and 'respect' with duties belonging to other categories.[22]

Further criticisms relate to the extent of the corporate human rights responsibilities, since the UNGPs only refer to 'internationally recognised human rights', being in the opinion of the SRSG those included in the International

---

[21] Ruggie, 'Guiding Principles on Business and Human Rights: Implementing the United Nations "Protect, Respect and Remedy" Framework (Report of the Special Representative of the Secretary-General on the Issue of Human Rights and Transnational Corporations and Other Business Enterprises, John Ruggie)' (n 17) 6.

[22] Deva, *Regulating Corporate Human Rights Violations* (n 19) 110. (References omitted).

Bill of Rights and the principles set out in the International Labour Organization's Declaration on Fundamental Principles and Rights at Work, which could mean that the rights of vulnerable groups such as women, children and indigenous people are not expressly included in the ambit of the UNGPs.[23] Other problematic terminology introduced by UNGPs that has attracted criticism relates to specific language such as 'impact' rather than 'violation', 'human rights risks' rather than 'human rights violations', and the lack of suggestions on how to deal with challenges posed by *forum non conveniens* and separate legal personality.[24]

The UNGPs deal with the 'State-business nexus' in Principles 4, 5 and 6.[25] For example, Principle 4 states that

> States should take *additional steps to protect against human rights abuses by business enterprises that are owned or controlled by the State*, or that receive substantial support and services from State agencies such as export credit agencies and official investment insurance or guarantee agencies, including, where appropriate, by requiring human rights due diligence.[26]

Furthermore, States do not relinquish their international human rights obligations when they privatise the delivery of certain services, or when they enter into commercial transactions such as those for the procurement of goods and services as Principles 5 and 6 clarify. The human rights obligations of States continue in all those circumstances, and it is the duty of States to ensure that the performance of certain services or contractual obligations are undertaken in a manner that ensures consistency with those obligations.[27] Thus, as previously discussed in Chapter 2, under the framework of the UNGPs, the human rights obligations that States have on behalf of their own SOEs are unique. This is because when SOEs engage in business activities they trigger a concomitant application of all three pillars of the 'protect, respect, remedy'

---

[23] ibid 112–113.

[24] ibid 113; Robert McCorquodale, 'Survey of the Provision in the United Kingdom of Access to Remedies for Victims of Human Rights Harms Involving Business Enterprises' (British Institute of International and Comparative Law 2015) 11.

[25] Mihaela M Barnes, 'The United Nations Guiding Principles on Business and Human Rights, the State Duty to Protect Human Rights and the State-Business Nexus' (2018) 15 Brazilian J. Int. Law 42.

[26] Ruggie, 'Guiding Principles on Business and Human Rights: Implementing the United Nations "Protect, Respect and Remedy" Framework (Report of the Special Representative of the Secretary- General on the Issue of Human Rights and Transnational Corporations and Other Business Enterprises, John Ruggie)' (n 17) 9. (Emphasis added).

[27] ibid 10.

framework. While a POE might have only the responsibility to respect human rights, in the case of SOEs this responsibility should be viewed concomitantly with a State's duty to protect human rights, and to ensure the existence of the adequate remedy. This line of reasoning is supported by the commentary to the UNGPs which states that

> where a business enterprise is controlled by the State or where its acts can be attributed otherwise to the State, an abuse of human rights by the business enterprise may entail a violation of the State's own international law obligations. Moreover, the closer a business enterprise is to the State, or the more it relies on statutory authority or taxpayer support, the stronger the State's policy rationale becomes for ensuring that the enterprise respects human rights. Where States own or control business enterprises, they have greatest means within their powers to ensure that relevant policies, legislation and regulations regarding respect for human rights are implemented.[28]

At the national level, the implementation of the UNGPs is to be conducted though the creation of a National Action Plan (NAP). The UN Working Group on Business and Human Rights (Working Group) 'encourages all States to develop, enact and update a NAP on business and human rights as part of the State responsibility to disseminate and implement the UNGPs'.[29] At the time of writing, many States have already produced a NAP, while other are in the process of doing so.[30] The Working Group defines a NAP as an 'evolving policy strategy developed by a State to protect against adverse human rights impacts by business enterprises in conformity with the UNGPs', and which fulfills the following four essential criteria: first, it needs to be based on the UNGPs; second, it is context-specific and address a State's actual and potential business-related human rights abuse; third, a NAP must be developed in a transparent and inclusive process; and fourth, a NAP needs to be regularly reviewed and updated.[31] In the context of the 'State-business

---

[28] ibid 9.

[29] 'OHCHR | State National Action Plans on Business and Human Rights' <https://www.ohchr .org/EN/Issues/Business/Pages/NationalActionPlans.aspx> accessed 10 August 2020; Human Rights Council, 'Report of the Working Group on the Issue of Human Rights and Transnational Corporations and Other Business Enterprises' (2013) A/HRC/23/32/Add.2 21; 'Outcome of the Seventh Session of the Working Group on the Issue of Human Rights and Transnational Corporations and Other Business Enterprises (A/HRC/WG.12/7/1)'.

[30] 'National Action Plans on Business and Human Rights' (*National Action Plans on Business and Human Rights*) <https://globalnaps.org/> accessed 10 August 2020; 'OHCHR | State National Action Plans on Business and Human Rights' (n 29).

[31] UN Working Group on Business and Human Rights, 'Guidance on National Action Plans on Business and Human Rights' (United Nations 2016) i.

nexus', a successful NAP would ensure that the UNGPs are implemented by SOEs and that human rights conditionalities are integrated throughout the activities of SOEs.[32] The UNGPs also provide for comprehensive provisions with regard to access to remedy in Principles 25–31. For this purpose, the UNGPs encourage States to ensure, 'through judicial, administrative, legislative or other appropriate means' that victims have access to effective remedy. The grievance mechanisms can be State-based, judicial or non-judicial. Another key issue to note is that the use of the OECD National Contact Points – as part of the State-based non-judicial mechanisms – is specifically addressed in the commentary to UNGP 25, thus providing for some integration between different regulatory mechanisms (OECD Guidelines for Multinational Enterprises and the UNGPs).

Overall, the UNGPs constitute a big and important step in ensuring that businesses behave responsibly, however, they also have their weaknesses. First, the UNGPs are voluntary, non-binding and do not impose new obligations on States or corporations under international or domestic law.[33] The UNGPs still maintain the State-centric approach to human rights by virtue of Pillar I and Pillar III. In this typology, corporations do not have obligations, which are legally enforceable, as a matter of international law, corporations merely have 'responsibilities' to respect human rights. Nevertheless, one of the novelties of the UNGPs is that they introduce extensive human rights due diligence requirements for corporations under Pillar II and those requirements could indeed play a preventative role in avoiding human rights abuses. However,

---

[32] ibid 23–25.
[33] Malcolm N Shaw, *International Law* (7th edn, Cambridge University Press 2014) 182–183. ('These Principles do not create international legal obligations as such. They emphasize the duty of states to respect, protect and fulfill the human rights of individuals and in particular to protect against human rights abuse within their territory and/or jurisdiction by third parties, including business enterprises. States must ensure that those affected by abuses taking place within their territory and/or jurisdiction must have access to an effective remedy. The principles declare that business enterprises should respect human rights, avoid infringing on the rights of others and should address adverse human rights impacts with which they are involved. The reference to human rights here refers to internationally recognised human rights. It is provided that the responsibility to respect human rights is a global standard of expected conduct for business enterprises. The realm is that of "soft law", of expectations, of anticipation not of binding international (as opposed to national) legal regulation. This responsibility to respect human rights requires that business enterprises avoid causing or contributing to adverse human rights impacts through their own activities and to seek to prevent or mitigate adverse human rights impacts that are *directly linked* to their operations, products or services by their business relationship.').

there are no penalties if due diligence is not undertaken. Second, the UNGPs do not solve any of the challenges posed by the activities of corporations that operate beyond the borders of their home State. Third, there are no enforcement mechanisms or any other means to control the implementation of the UNGPs for either States or for corporations. While some progress has been made in this regard, through the NAPs, the great majority of States still need to create NAPs. Fourth, securing access to remedy is still problematic, in that it entirely relies on existent domestic mechanisms and there is a lack of clarity as to what should happen if those mechanisms do not work appropriately. Fifth, as far as the State-business nexus is concerned, while the UNGPs do have specific provisions concerning the human rights dimension of State corporate ownership (e.g., States 'should take additional steps to protect against human rights abuses' by SOEs) this requirement is not framed in mandatory terms, and there are no penalties if States fail to do so. Yet, despite those inherent weaknesses, the UNGPs have been immensely successful and since their unanimous endorsement in 2011 by the UN Human Rights Council they have 'produced nothing less than a wave of lawmaking and standard-setting at the national, international, and corporate level'.[34] For example, the UNGPs have been referred to during the course of domestic litigation[35] and international arbitration,[36] and they have informed the creation of domestic[37] and regional legislation,[38] the setting of new standards by international organisations,[39] the development of guidances for specific sectors,[40] the beginning of a new treaty-making

[34] Steven R Ratner, 'Introduction to the Symposium on Soft and Hard Law on Business and Human Rights' (2020) 114 AJIL Unbound 163, 163.

[35] *Araya v Nevsun Resources Ltd* 1856 (2016 BCSC 1856); *Nevsun Resources Ltd v Araya* (Supreme Court of Canada, 2020 SCC5).

[36] *Urbaser SA and Consorcio de Aguas Bilbao Bizkaia, Bilbao Biskaia Ur Partzuergoa v The Argentine Republic* (ICSID Case No ARB/07/26 (Award)).

[37] Modern Slavery Act 2015; LOI n° 2017-399 du 27 mars 2017 relative au devoir de vigilance des sociétés mères et des entreprises donneuses d'ordre 2017 (2017-399).

[38] Regulation (EU) 2017/821 of the European Parliament and of the Council of 17 May 2017, laying down supply chain due diligence obligations for EU importers of tin, tantalum and tungsten, their ores, and gold originating from conflict-affected and high-risk areas; 'Draft Report with Recommendations to the Commission on Corporate Due Diligence and Corporate Accountability' (European Parliament, Committee on Legal Affairs 2020) 2020/2129 (INL); Markus Krajewski and others, 'Human Rights Due Diligence Legislation – Options for the EU' (European Union, Policy Department for External Relations 2020).

[39] OECD, *OECD Due Diligence Guidance for Responsible Supply Chains of Minerals from Conflict-Affected and High-Risk Areas* (OECD 2013).

[40] 'FIFA's Human Rights Policy (May 2017 Edition)'.

process[41] and are even beginning to influence the evolution of other areas of international law.[42]

3.3.2 *OECD Instruments*

3.3.2.1 The OECD Guidelines for Multinational Enterprises

The OECD Guidelines for Multinational Enterprises (OECD Guidelines)[43] are the 'leading standard on responsible business conduct worldwide'.[44] They were developed at the same time as the UN Draft Code, but unlike the UN Draft Code, their drafting process and approval by OECD Member States was ultimately successful. The OECD Guidelines are recommendations 'addressed by governments to multinational enterprises operating in or from adhering countries' and encourage businesses to behave in a responsible manner, not only by respecting the local laws but also internationally agreed standards.[45] The OECD Guidelines are applicable to POEs and SOEs in equal measure. For example, the guidelines state that SOEs 'are subject to the same recommendations as privately-owned enterprises, but public scrutiny is often magnified when the State is the final owner'.[46] An improvement that came with the 2011 revision is that the adhering States make a binding commitment to implement them.[47] The OECD Guidelines contain recommendations to multinational enterprises 'operating in or from' adhering countries that cover human rights, employment and industrial relations, environment, combating bribery, bribe solicitation and extortion and the

---

[41] Second Revised Draft, Legally Binding Instrument to Regulate, in International Human Rights Law, the Activities of Transnational Corporations and Other Business Enterprises (6 August 2020); Revised Draft, Legally Binding Instrument to Regulate, in International Human Rights Law, the Activities of Transnational Corporations and Other Business Enterprises (16 July 2019); Legally Binding Instrument to Regulate, in International Human Rights Law, the Activities of Transnational Corporations and Other Business Enterprises (Zero Draft 16 July 2018).

[42] 'UNCTAD's Reform Package for the International Investment Regime (2018 Edition)'.

[43] *OECD Guidelines for Multinational Enterprises, 2011 Edition* (OECD 2011).

[44] OECD, 'Annual Report on the OECD Guidelines for Multinational Enterprises 2016' (OECD 2017) 7.

[45] *OECD Guidelines for Multinational Enterprises, 2011 Edition* (n 43) 3.

[46] ibid.

[47] ibid 13. ('The Guidelines provide voluntary principles and standards for responsible business conduct consistent with applicable laws and internationally recognised standards. However, the countries adhering to the Guidelines make a binding commitment to implement them in accordance with the Decision of the OECD Council on the OECD Guidelines for Multinational Enterprises. Furthermore, matters covered by the Guidelines may also be the subject of national law and international commitments.').

protection of consumer interests, and they also have provisions relating to the need to respect science, technology, consumer protection and the taxation policies of the countries in which they operate. The General Policies of the OECD Guidelines recommend that enterprises fully take into account the 'established policies of the countries in which they operate' and in this context they should 'refrain from seeking or accepting exemptions not contemplated in the statutory or regulatory framework related to human rights, environmental, health, safety, labour, taxation, financial incentives or other issues'. Multinational enterprises are also encouraged to make 'high quality' disclosures on 'environmental and social' issues.[48] Another improvement brought by the 2011 revision is the recommendation that 'in countries where domestic laws and regulation conflict with the principles and standards of the OECD Guidelines, enterprises should seek ways to honor such principles and standards to the fullest extent which does not place them in violation of domestic law'.[49]

The section on human rights, another improvement of the 2011 revision, clarifies that it is States that have a 'duty to protect' human rights, while enterprises only have a 'responsibility to respect' human rights, an approach that is similar to that of the UNGPs. For this purpose, enterprises should have a human rights policy and should carry out human rights due diligence and 'provide for or co-operate through legitimate processes in the remediation of adverse human rights impacts'.[50] The section on industrial relations provides, among others, that enterprises should contribute to the abolition of forced or compulsory labour, respect the rights of workers to join trade unions and observe standards of employment that are 'not less favourable than those observed by comparable employers in the host country'.[51] Enterprises are also expected to take 'immediate and effective measures to secure the prohibition and elimination of the worst forms of child labour as a 'matter of urgency'.[52] Since the 2011 revision, international labour standards are applicable to the operations of multinational enterprises as opposed to the application of the standards prevailing in the host State, as was the case until 2011.

One unique feature of the OECD Guidelines is that they create National Contact Points (NCPs), which are in effect agencies that promote and implement the Guidelines, and which offer mediation and conciliation for

---

[48] ibid 29.
[49] ibid 17.
[50] ibid 31.
[51] ibid 36.
[52] ibid.

resolving disputes.[53] Adhering States are given flexibility on how to organize their NCP and are permitted to seek the input of social partners, the government, the business community, worker organisations, NGOs or other interested parties.[54] There are currently forty-nine States that have established NCPs.[55] The Specific Instances procedure is of particular importance because it creates a mechanism to deal with complaints of alleged violation of the OECD Guidelines by multinational enterprises. The NCP are expected to deal with such matters in an 'impartial, predictable, equitable' manner that is compatible with the broader principles and standards of the Guidelines.[56] After an initial assessment of the complaint, the NCP must offer 'good offices to help the parties involved to resolve those issues'.[57] The next step is a consultation procedure that must be made publicly available through the means of a 'statement' or 'report', taking into consideration the need to protect business and confidential information.[58] A statement usually describes the issues raised and whether those issues were worthy of further consideration. A report is more detailed, but its content is ultimately agreed upon by the parties and describes the issues raised, the procedures initiated and whether an agreement was reached. A statement is also issued when the parties are unwilling to participate in the procedures.[59] NCPs report regularly to the Investment Committee of the OECD, who gives guidance on the interpretation of the OECD Guidelines and on other matters.[60]

The non-governmental organisation OECD Watch, which has compiled statistics for 2001–2015, monitors the activity of the NCPs.[61] According to those statistics, most of the cases filed have come from the UK (seventy-two cases), followed by the United States (thirty-three cases) and the Netherlands (twenty-eight cases). The data also indicates that most cases are rejected (43 per cent), while 26 per cent of cases are concluded with an NCP Statement and only 9 per cent with an agreement between the parties. Most cases filed deal with complaints alleging human rights violations, followed by complaints relating to labour rights and the environment. The mining, oil and gas sectors are the

---

[53] ibid 68.
[54] ibid 71.
[55] 'National Contact Points – Organisation for Economic Co-Operation and Development' <http://mneguidelines.oecd.org/ncps/> accessed 11 August 2020.
[56] *OECD Guidelines for Multinational Enterprises, 2011 Edition* (n 43) 72.
[57] ibid.
[58] ibid 73.
[59] ibid.
[60] ibid 75.
[61] 'Case Database – OECD Watch Case Database' <https://complaints.oecdwatch.org/cases> accessed 11 August 2020.

source of the highest numbers of complaints, followed by financial institutions, agriculture companies and garment companies. Cases against significant SOEs have also been lodged. For example, in *Norwegian Climate Network et al v Statoil*[62] the complainants alleged that the Statoil, a Norwegian SOE, breached the environment chapter of the OECD Guidelines by investing in the oil sands of Alberta and, consequently, contributing to Canada's violations of international obligations to reduce greenhouse gas emissions in the period 2008–2012. It was pointed out in the complaint that Statoil, as an SOE, had a 'particular responsibility to withdraw from extractions that undermine other Norwegian climate obligations' and that, consequently, it should 'withdraw from all oil sands production in Canada, based on its incompatibility with the sustainability provisions of the Guidelines'. Statoil confirmed its activities in Canada and submitted in its defence that it did not have any obligations to assess whether Canada complied with its own international obligations. The NCP dismissed the case and found that the complainants 'failed to show on what basis it is the responsibility of Statoil to ensure that Canada meets its targets and how this particular company has specifically contributed to and is responsible for Canada's level of GHG emissions'. *Greenpeace Germany v Vattenfall*,[63] another case involving an SOE, had similar facts, but the case was also ultimately dismissed. In *Lok Shakti Abhiyan et al. v Government Pension Fund*,[64] the complainants alleged that POSCO, one of the largest steel-making multinationals in the world, failed to carry out comprehensive human rights due diligence and environmental assessments for its proposed iron ore mine and steel manufacturing plant in the State of Odisha, India. The proposed iron ore mine and steel plant would have led to the displacement of close to 20,000 people, including legally protected indigenous groups. The complainant also argued the responsibility of the Dutch pension funds and that of the Norges Bank Investment Management, as investors in POSCO. The Dutch NCP accepted the complaint and organized several meetings between the parties. A joint final statement was issued, whereby the Dutch pension funds committed to 'exercise their leverage to bring POSCO's business practices in line with international standards'. This statement also confirmed that the Guidelines apply to minority shareholdings, an important precedent, a position which was also confirmed by the Norwegian NCP. The Korean NCP rejected the complaint

---

[62] *Norwegian Climate Network et al v Statoil* (NCP Norway, NCP Canada, 28 November 2011).
[63] *Greenpeace Germany v Vattenfall* (NCP Germany, 29 October 2009).
[64] *Lok Shakti Abhiyan et al. v Government Pension Fund* (NCP Norway, NCP Netherlands, NCP Korea, 9 October 2012).

made against POSCO on the basis that it was ultimately the responsibility of the Indian authorities to investigate the matter. The Dutch NCP explored the possibility of organising a joint mission to India with the Norwegian and Korean NCPs, but this did not take place. In *Canada Tibet Committee v China Gold Int. Resources*,[65] the Chinese State media announced that eighty-three miners were buried in a major landslide at the Gyama Copper Polymetallic Mine located in Central Tibet. There were no survivors after the event. The mine belonged to a wholly owned subsidiary of China Gold International Resources (China Gold), a company listed on the Toronto and Hong Kong Stock Exchanges, and which was also partly State-owned. The Chinese government stated that the events at the mine occurred as a result of a natural disaster, a fact that was disputed by the complainants, who alleged that it was a man-made disaster and that 'the company had ignored previous warnings and local protests' in this context. The Canadian NCP confirmed that China Gold was unwilling to participate in the process, despite multiple requests from the Canadian NCP. A statement was issued which concluded that 'China Gold had not demonstrated that it is operating in a manner that can be considered to be consistent with the OECD Guidelines'. The Canadian NCP withdrew Trade Commissioner Services and other Canadian advocacy support abroad and made a final statement and recommendation to China Gold about the requirement to undertake human rights due diligence concerning the potential impacts of its future activities.

The 2011 revision has brought significant changes to the OECD Guidelines, but some challenges remain. For example, all proceedings and outcomes are confidential, which creates opacity, an issue that has been acknowledged by the OECD.[66] Furthermore, the NCPs continue to lack 'teeth'[67] and if their recommendations are not complied with, there is not much that can be done to ensure compliance. As some of the cases above have shown, the practice of the NCPs has been hesitant to begin with, however, more recently, certain measures have been taken against some companies. Although it has taken a long time to reach this stage, the growing practice in this area demonstrates that the role and effectiveness of the NCPs is improving. To conclude, it must be recalled that that the OECD Guidelines and the NCPs are still to this day the only 'government-backed international instrument for responsible business conduct with a built-in non-

---

[65] *Canada Tibet Committee v China Gold Int Resources* (NCP Canada, 29 January 2014).
[66] OECD, 'Implementing the OECD Guidelines for Multinational Enterprises: The National Contact Points from 2000 to 2015' (OECD 2016) 15.
[67] Deva, *Regulating Corporate Human Rights Violations* (n 19) 88.

judicial grievance mechanism'[68] and that by virtue of this government backing, it has the potential to continually improve and evolve.

3.3.2.2 The OECD Guidelines on the Corporate Governance of State-Owned Enterprises

Corporate governance is generally concerned with the accountability of corporations; however, there is no generally accepted definition of this notion. Most definitions are found along a spectrum from the relatively narrow – based on agency theory – to inclusive approaches, based on stakeholder theory.[69] For the purposes of this section, and in accordance with a growing trend, a broad definition of the concept will be adopted.[70] As such, corporate governance is defined as 'a system of checks and balances, both internal and external to companies, which ensures that companies discharge their accountability to all their stakeholders and act in a socially responsible way in all areas of their business activities'.[71]

SOEs have particular corporate governance challenges, which arise principally from the fact that usually their leadership is in the hands of government officials and not professional managers. Given that the boards of directors have fiduciary duties of care and of loyalty, if the leadership of SOEs is in the hands of government officials, there may be a conflict between the fiduciary duties that the directors owe to the SOE and its shareholders and the allegiance that board members may have to their own political party.[72] For SOEs, the main aim of sound corporate governance principles is to ensure that they are 'at least as accountable to the general public as a listed company should be to its shareholders'.[73] The OECD has long recognised some of the challenges facing the corporate governance of SOEs and has pointed to several areas of corporate governance that deserve specific attention: disclosure and transparency, decision-making (in particular the responsibilities of the boards of State-owned enterprises, as well as the equitable treatment of shareholders and other investors), accountability, the State's role as an owner and participant in the

---

[68] 'Implementing the OECD Guidelines for Multinational Enterprises: The National Contact Points from 2000 to 2015' (n 66) 29.

[69] Jill Solomon, *Corporate Governance and Accountability* (John Wiley & Sons 2007) 12.

[70] ibid 14.

[71] ibid.

[72] OECD, *OECD Guidelines on Corporate Governance of State-Owned Enterprises* (OECD 2015) 14.

[73] OECD, *OECD Guidelines on Corporate Governance of State-Owned Enterprises* (OECD 2015).

market place and the role of the State in promoting responsible business practices. Consequently, the OECD Guidelines on the Corporate Governance of State-Owned Enterprises (OECD Guidelines on SOEs) seek to address the particular challenges concerning the corporate governance of SOEs. In addition, the OECD Guidelines on SOEs also contain a chapter on stakeholder relations and responsible business, which makes general recommendations to SOEs 'to observe high standards of responsible business conduct' with regard to the environment, employees, public health and safety and human rights, and refer specifically to the standards of the OECD Guidelines for Multinational Enterprises, the ILO Declaration on Fundamental Principles and Rights at Work and the UNGPs.[74] While the OECD Guidelines on SOEs are considered the 'internationally agreed standard for how governments should exercise the state ownership function to avoid the pitfalls of both passive ownership and excessive state intervention',[75] not all States that have a significant State ownership sector use them as a standard.

The Guidelines on SOEs are applicable to both the domestic as well as international activities of SOEs. Recognising the increased importance of SOEs domestically as well as internationally, the Guidelines have three aims: to professionalise the State as an owner; to ensure that SOEs operate efficiently, transparently and in an accountable manner and that a level playing field is maintained between private enterprises and SOEs.[76] The OECD Guidelines on SOEs were first developed in 2005 alongside the G20/OECD Principles of Corporate Governance.[77] Following ten years of implementation experience and new developments, they were updated in 2015. Although exclusive in their application to SOEs, the Guidelines are a complement to other OECD instruments that apply to the private sector such as the G20/OECD Principles on Corporate Governance; the OECD Guidelines for Multinational Enterprises, discussed above;[78] the OECD Policy Framework for Investment;[79] the OECD and World Bank Competition Assessment Toolkits[80] and other similar recommendations and

---

[74] ibid 60.
[75] ibid 3.
[76] ibid 7, 11.
[77] *G20/OECD Principles of Corporate Governance 2015* (OECD 2015).
[78] *OECD Guidelines for Multinational Enterprises, 2011 Edition* (n 43).
[79] *Policy Framework for Investment, 2015 Edition* (OECD 2015).
[80] OECD, *Competition Assessment Toolkit Volume I: Principles* (Version 3, 2016); OECD, *Competition Assessment Toolkit Volume II: Guidance* (Version 3, 2016); OECD, *Competition Assessment Toolkit Volume III: Operational Manual* (Version 3, 2015); World Bank, *Corporate Governance of State-Owned Enterprises: A Toolkit* (World Bank 2014).

guidances.[81] The OECD Guidelines for SOEs aim to 'devise a robust model for the ideal State shareholder' and 'seek to support economic efficiency, sustainable growth and financial stability by rationalizing relationships between a company's management, board, shareholders and stakeholders'.[82] They are non-binding recommendations with no implementation or monitoring mechanisms. Consequently, governments that have a significant share of ownership in their economies may or may not adhere to them. Overall, their purpose is to 'insulate SOEs institutionally from day-to-day political interference'.[83]

3.3.2.3 OECD Common Approaches for Officially Supported Export Credits and Environmental and Social Due Diligence

The OECD Common Approaches for Officially Supported Export Credits and Environmental and Social Due Diligence (OECD Common Approaches)[84] are a set of non-binding recommendations that apply to officially recognised ECAs for addressing the environmental and social aspects that relate to exports of capital, goods and services and the locations to which these are destined. Noting the significant developments that have occurred since the 2007, the 2016 version of the OECD Common Approaches makes reference to the OECD Guidelines for Multinational Enterprises, the 1998 ILO Declaration on Fundamental Principles and Rights at Work and the UN Framework Convention on Climate Change. The main objectives of the OECD Common Approaches are to promote policy coherence, to develop common procedures and processes relating to the review of environmental and social issues in the activities of ECAs, to promote good practices and consistent review and assessment processes for projects, to enhance the efficiency of official support procedures, to promote a global level playing field for officially supported ECAs and to increase awareness and understanding of the instruments.[85] Adherents are encouraged to screen all applications for export credit in order to identify which applications must be subsequently

---

[81]   OECD, *Boards of Directors of State-Owned Enterprises: An Overview of National Practices* (OECD 2013); OECD, *Accountability and Transparency: A Guide for State Ownership* (OECD 2010).

[82]   Mikko Rajavuori, Governing the Good State Shareholder UTULAW, Research Paper Series 2/ 2017 3, 10.

[83]   ibid 12.

[84]   OECD Common Approaches for Officially Supported Export Credits and Environmental and Social Due Diligence (TAD/ECG(2016)3) 2016.

[85]   ibid 5–6.

reviewed.[86] Among others, the screening must take into account the value of the transaction, the location, the industry sector and the likelihood that there could be severe project-related human rights and environmental impacts occurring in that particular project.[87] The environmental and social review must be conducted in accordance with international standards.[88] Following this, the information resulting from the screening and review of a project is evaluated and a decision is made whether to decline, provide official support or to request additional information.[89] The exchange and disclosure of information between adherents is encouraged[90] as is the reporting and monitoring of the implementation of the OECD Common Approaches instrument in general.[91]

3.3.3 *The ILO Tripartite Declaration concerning Multinational Enterprises*

The ILO Tripartite Declaration of Principles concerning Multinational Enterprises and Social Policy (ILO Tripartite Declaration)[92] seeks to offer 'social policy guidelines in a sensitive and highly complex area of activities' relating to employment, training, conditions of work and life and industrial relations with the objective of realising 'decent work for all'.[93] The term 'multinational' is loosely defined to include 'fully or partially state-owned or privately owned [enterprises] which own or control production, distribution, services or other facilities outside the State in which they are based [and] they may be large or small, and can have their headquarters in any part of the world', thus including SOEs in their ambit.[94] It is 'tripartite' in that the Declaration is the outcome of a negotiated solution between government, employers and workers' organisations. The Tripartite Declaration was first adopted in 1977; it has undergone significant revisions in 2000, 2006 and 2017 and is largely based on principles contained in the ILO Conventions and Recommendations. The 2017 revision sought to respond to 'new economic realities' brought about by increased international trade and investment and

---

[86] ibid 8.
[87] ibid 6–7.
[88] ibid 8–11.
[89] ibid 11–12.
[90] ibid 12–13.
[91] ibid 13–15.
[92] ILO Tripartite Declaration of Principles concerning Multinational Enterprises and Social Policy 2017.
[93] ibid v.
[94] ibid 3.

the growth of supply chains.[95] It takes account of recent development in labour standards and new international legal instruments in this area, such as the ILO Declaration on Social Justice for a Fair Globalisation, the International Labour Conference Conclusions concerning decent work in global supply chains, the promotion of sustainable enterprises, the goals and targets of the 2030 Agenda for Sustainable Development, the Addis Ababa Action Agenda on financing for development, the Paris Agreement concerning climate change and the latest revision of the OECD Guidelines for Multinational Enterprises.[96] Of particular importance is the fact that the Tripartite Declaration makes express reference to the UNGPs and the need to integrate human rights due diligence into the operations of multinationals. The Tripartite Declaration also calls on multinational enterprises to 'fully take into account established general policy objectives of the countries in which they operate' and on both home and host States to 'promote good social practices, having regard to social and labour law, regulations and practices in host countries as well as to international standards'.[97] There are express provisions on measures to promote employment (paragraphs 13–21); social security (paragraph 22); elimination of forced or compulsory labour (paragraphs 23–25); the effective abolition of child labour (paragraphs 26–27); equality of opportunity and treatment (paragraphs 28–31); measures to promote security of employment (paragraphs 32–40); measures relating to decent wages, benefits and conditions of work, safety and health (paragraphs 41–46) and measures to promote harmonious industrial relations, particularly with regard to freedom of association and the right to organise collective bargaining (paragraphs 47–64). A significant change from the 2006 version is the addition of specific provisions relating to access to remedy and the appropriate means to examine grievances. For example, paragraphs 64 and 65 state that

> 64. As part of their duty to protect against business-related human rights abuses, governments should take appropriate steps to ensure, through judicial, administrative, legislative or other appropriate means, that when such abuses occur within their territory and/or jurisdiction any affected worker or workers have access to effective remedy.

---

[95] 'ILO Revises Its Landmark Declaration on Multinational Enterprises' (17 March 2017) <http://www.ilo.org/global/about-the-ilo/newsroom/news/WCMS_547615/lang–en/index.htm> accessed 12 August 2020.
[96] ILO Tripartite Declaration of Principles concerning Multinational Enterprises and Social Policy 1.
[97] ibid 5.

65. Multinational enterprises should use their leverage to encourage their business partners to provide effective means of enabling remediation for abuses of internationally recognised human rights.

Paragraph 66 provides for guidance in the processing of grievance claims, while paragraph 67 shifts the burden onto governments to ensure that free and speedy 'voluntary conciliation and arbitration mechanisms are available to assist in the prevention and settlement of industrial disputes'. Nevertheless, the ILO Tripartite Declaration has some significant shortcomings: its scope is declaratory in nature and there are no implementation or monitoring mechanisms.[98] The 2017 revision has brought some significant changes to the ILO Tripartite Declaration, with an increased focus on the prevention of human rights abuses in the context of labour relations. The express introduction of international labour standards in the operation of multinational enterprises in host States, the specific reference to the UNGPs and the need to conduct human rights due diligence are of particular importance in this context. The provisions on access to remedy are extremely significant from a redressive point of view, but the lack of implementation and monitoring mechanisms make their effectivity questionable.

3.3.4 *Sovereign Wealth Funds Generally Accepted Principles and Practices*

The IMF established the International Working Group of Sovereign Wealth Funds (IWG) in 2008 as a response to the controversy surrounding the activities of SWFs, particularly around the time of the 2007–2009 financial crisis.[99] The IWG was composed of twenty-six IMF member States that had an SWF.[100] At the third meeting of the IWG, in Santiago, 'a set of generally accepted principles and practices that properly reflects their investment practices and objectives' were agreed: the Sovereign Wealth Funds Generally

---

[98] Deva, *Regulating Corporate Human Rights Violations* (n 19) 90.

[99] Ronald J Gilson and Curtis J Milhaupt, 'Sovereign Wealth Funds and Corporate Governance: A Minimalist Response to the New Mercantilism' (2007) 60 Stan. L. Rev. 1345, 1360–1362; Sovereign Wealth Funds Generally Accepted Principles and Practices 'Santiago Principles' 2008.

[100] 'About Us | International Forum of Sovereign Wealth Funds' <https://www.ifswf.org/about-us> accessed 10 August 2020. The initial Member Countries were Australia, Azerbaijan, Bahrain, Botswana, Canada, Chile, China, Equatorial Guinea, Iran, Ireland, Korea, Kuwait, Libya, Mexico, New Zealand, Norway, Qatar, Russia, Singapore, Timor-Leste, Trinidad and Tobago, the United Arab Emirates and the United States. Permanent observers of the IWG were at the time Oman, Saudi Arabia, Vietnam, the OECD and the World Bank. Since then, Angola, Italy, Kazakhstan, Malaysia, Morocco, Nigeria and Rwanda have also joined.

Accepted Principles and Practices (Santiago Principles).[101] The guiding objectives that led to the drafting of the Santiago Principles were a concern for the stability of the global financial system, the need for compliance by SWFs with the relevant regulatory and disclosure requirements in the host State, the requirement to ensure that investments are made solely on the basis of financial considerations and a need to build a 'sound governance structure' that promotes operational control, risk management and accountability.[102] There are twenty-four principles that deal with three key areas of SWF management.[103] Principles 1–5 deal with the legal framework, the objectives of SWFs and the coordination of their investments with the State's macroeconomic policies. Principles 6–17 cover the institutional framework and governance structure, while principles 18–24 deal with the investment and risk management framework.[104] Although the Santiago Principles are voluntary in nature, they constitute a summary of what is considered to be the best practice for SWFs and all the members of the International Forum of Sovereign Wealth Funds (IFSWF) have endorsed them. The current members of IFSWF represent around a third of all SWFs. Following an extended debate about the regulation of SWFs,[105] which to a certain extent still continues,[106] the Santiago Principles have been generally well received.[107] Nevertheless, it has been specifically recognised that, in reality, they may be

---

[101] Sovereign Wealth Funds Generally Accepted Principles and Practices 'Santiago Principles' 1.
[102] ibid 4.
[103] ibid 7–9.
[104] ibid 11–25.
[105] Richard A Epstein and Amanda M Rose, 'The Regulation of Sovereign Wealth Funds: The Virtues of Going Slow' (2009) 76 U. Chi. L. Rev. 111; Larry C Backer, 'Sovereign Investing in Times of Crisis: Global Regulation of Sovereign Wealth Funds, State-Owned Enterprises, and the Chinese Experience' (2010) 19 Transnat'l L. & Contemp. Probs. 3; Joseph J Norton, 'The Santiago Principles and the International Forum of Sovereign Wealth Funds: Evolving Components of the New Bretton Woods II Post-Global Financial Crisis Architecture and Another Example of Ad Hoc Global Administrative Networking and Related Soft Rulemaking' (2009) 29 Rev. Banking & Fin. L. 465; Naveen Thomas, 'Regulating Sovereign Wealth Funds through Contract' (2013) 24 Duke J. Comp. & Int'l L. 459.
[106] Daniele Gallo, 'The Rise of Sovereign Wealth Funds (SWFs) and the Protection of Public Interest (s): The Need for a Greater External and Internal Action of the European Union' (2016) 27 Eur. Bus. Law Rev. 459; Jason Buhi, 'Negocio de China: Building upon the Santiago Principles to Form an Effective International Approach to Sovereign Wealth Fund Regulation' (2009) 39 Hong Kong L.J. 197.
[107] Anthony Wong, 'Sovereign Wealth Funds and the Problem of Asymmetric Information: The Santiago Principles and International Regulations' (2008) 34 Brook. J. Int'l L. 1081, 1098, 1103–1105.

limited in their ability to increase transparency,[108] since SWFs are not required to disclose individual investment positions.[109] Another concern is that they do not address certain intrinsic market risks that could be linked with sovereign investment, such as an en-masse withdrawal of funds from a host State's market or the requirement to make investments *only* on a commercial basis.[110] For example, Subprinciple 19.1 states that 'if investment decisions are subject to *other than* economic and financial considerations, these should be clearly set out in the investment policy and be publicly disclosed'. Broad critiques of the Santiago Principles underline the fact that there is too much focus on SWFs as entities and no focus on the relationship between SWFs and the recipient countries, the lack of a standard to measure compliance and enforcement and the failure to address asymmetric information problems that are faced by recipient countries.[111] Since their main purpose was to address transparency concerns relating to the investing activities of SWF, the Santiago Principles do not refer to human rights and nothing can be implied in this sense, apart from the disclosure requirements concerning investments made on *other than* financial considerations mentioned above. Nevertheless, there is a growing trend among SWFs to exclude certain companies from their investment universe in cases where there is the risk of severe environmental damage or of systematic violations of human rights. For example, Norges Bank either excludes certain companies from its investment universe or it places those entities on an observation list. Exclusions are currently made by the Executive Board of Norges Bank which acts on the recommendations of the Council of Ethics, appointed by the Ministry of Finance.[112]

3.3.5 *The Extractive Industries Transparency Initiative*

The Extractive Industries Transparency Initiative (EITI) is an international standard for transparency whose main purpose is to promote openness and accountability in the extractive industry sector.[113] The EITI was officially

---

[108] Adam D Dixon, 'Enhancing the Transparency Dialogue in the Santiago Principles for Sovereign Wealth Funds' (2013) 37 Seattle U. L. Rev. 581, 584.

[109] Paul Rose, 'Sovereigns as Shareholders' (2008) 87 N.C. L. Rev. 83, 89, 144.

[110] ibid 140.

[111] A Wong 'Sovereign Wealth Funds and the Problem of Asymmetric Information: The Santiago Principles and International Regulations' (2008) 34 Brook. J. Int'l L. 1081, 1105.

[112] 'Observation and Exclusion of Companies' (*Norges Bank Investment Management*) <https://www.nbim.no/en/the-fund/responsible-investment/exclusion-of-companies/> accessed 13 December 2020. Each case is accompanied by a justificatory decision.

[113] 'Who We Are' (*Extractive Industries Transparency Initiative*) <https://eiti.org/who-we-are> accessed 12 August 2020; Mihaela M Barnes, 'State-Owned Entities as Key Actors in the

launched by the United Kingdom Department for International Development at the Lancaster House Conference held in 2003, in London. This conference brought together representatives from government, business and the civil society and culminated with the adoption of a Statement of Principles.[114] The foundational ideas of what become the EITI are found, however, in academic work done in the 1990s and early 2000s by Professors Jeffrey Sachs,[115] Joseph Stiglitz,[116] Terry Lynn Karl[117] and Paul Collier,[118] which went beyond merely analyzing the concept of the 'Dutch Disease',[119] common to many countries heavily reliant on extractive industry revenues, and instead emphasised the complexity of natural resource governance generally.[120] Civil society organisations such as Global Witness, Human Rights Watch and Oxfam America followed up on the ideas of those academics and organised awareness campaigns, such as the now well-known 'Publish What You Pay', which emphasised the need for increased transparency for the revenues paid by companies in the extractive sector to the governments in the State of operation.[121]

Promotion and Implementation of the Agenda 2030 for Sustainable Development: Examples of Good Practices' [2019] Laws 9–10.

[114] 'The EITI Principles' (*Extractive Industries Transparency Initiative*, 27 January 2017) <https://eiti.org/document/eiti-principles> accessed 12 August 2020.

[115] Jeffrey D Sachs and Andrew M Warner, 'Natural Resource Abundance and Economic Growth' (National Bureau of Economic Research 1995); Macartan Humphreys and others, *Escaping the Resource Curse* (Columbia University Press 2007).

[116] Joseph E Stiglitz, 'On Liberty, the Right to Know, and Public Discourse: The Role of Transparency in Public Life' in Matthew J Gibney (ed), *Globalizing Rights: The Oxford Amnesty Lectures 1999* (Oxford University Press 2003); Joseph E Stiglitz, 'Making Natural Resources into a Blessing Rather than a Curse' in S Tsalik and A Schiffrin (eds), *Covering Oil: A Reporter's Guide to Energy and Development* (New York Revenue Watch, Open Society Institute 2005).

[117] Ian Gary and Terry Lynn Karl, *Bottom of the Barrel: Africa's Oil Boom and the Poor* (Catholic Relief Services 2003); Terry Lynn Karl, *The Paradox of Plenty: Oil Booms and Petro-States* (University of California Press 1997).

[118] Paul Collier, *The Bottom Billion: Why the Poorest Countries Are Failing and What Can Be Done about It* (Oxford University Press 2007).

[119] ibid 39–40. (The term 'Dutch Disease' relates to the relationship between the economic growth in a particular sector (in this case natural resources) and a decline in other sectors (such as manufacturing or services). The resource exports cause the country's currency to rise in value against other currencies, which in turn make that country's exports uncompetitive.).

[120] 'History of the EITI' (*Extractive Industries Transparency Initiative*) <https://eiti.org/history> accessed 12 August 2020.

[121] 'Publish What You Pay: History' <http://www.publishwhatyoupay.org/about/history/> accessed 12 August 2020.

Although it has its critics, and, at times, the initiative was received with hostility,[122] with open questions remaining in relation to its effectiveness,[123] in its short life since 2003, the EITI can be considered a success. As a 'soft law' instrument, the EITI Standard is now part of the transnational governance toolbox and at the time of writing there are fifty-three implementing States.[124] In its organic evolution, the EITI has turned the transparency aspiration into an expectation, with the focus now turning towards accountability.[125] The transition towards accountability was particularly emphasised in the 2016 version of the EITI Standard, which set new requirements for the full disclosure of the beneficial owners of companies involved in the extractive industries.[126] The EITI Standard was updated in 2019 to include new provisions on environmental,[127] social and gender impacts,[128] as well as other fiscal and legal issues, such as the disclosure of commodity sales data[129] and new contracts.[130] EITI also envisages civil society participation in the 'multi-stakeholder group'[131] that oversees its implementation and Requirement 1.3 provides for a broad engagement with the civil society in the EITI process. It should be noted, however, that the EITI Standard is a voluntary mechanism applicable only to States. Nevertheless, once a State becomes a member, companies involved in the extractive industries of that State are obliged to declare payments made to governments and, in order to match those disclosures, governments that have signed up to the EITI must also declare the amounts received from those companies.[132] Requirement 2.6 deals with State participation in the extractive

---

[122] Eric Fortineaux, 'Fight against the Extractive Industries Transparency Initiative, The' (2013) 11 Loy. U. Chi. Int'l L. Rev. 65.

[123] Alexandra Gillies and Antoine Heuty, 'Does Transparency Work: The Challenges of Measurement and Effectiveness in Resource-Rich Countries' (2011) 6 Yale J. Int'l Aff. 25, 37–39; Benjamin K Sovacool and others, 'Energy Governance, Transnational Rules, and the Resource Curse: Exploring the Effectiveness of the Extractive Industries Transparency Initiative (EITI)' (2016) 83 World Development 179.

[124] 'Countries' (*Extractive Industries Transparency Initiative*) <https://eiti.org/countries> accessed 12 August 2020.

[125] 'History of the EITI' (n 120).

[126] EITI International Secretariat, 'The EITI Standard 2016' (EITI 2016) Requirement 2.5; EITI International Secretariat, 'EITI Standard 2019' Requirement 2.5.

[127] EITI International Secretariat, 'EITI Standard 2019' (n 126) Requirement 6.1 and 6.4.

[128] ibid Requirements 1.4, 6.3, 7.1, 7.4.

[129] ibid Requirement 4.2.

[130] ibid Requirement 2.4.

[131] ibid Requirement 1.4 and 1.5.

[132] Zorka Milin, 'Mapping Recent Developments in Transparency of Extractive Industries' (2016) 1 BHRJ 321, 322.

industries and obliges countries to disclose and explain the rules and practices that govern the relationship between the government and SOE, as well as needing detailed information about their level of ownership, going all the way down to subsidiary and joint venture levels.[133] Any changes in the level of ownership or any other related transactions must be disclosed as provided in Requirements 2.6(a). According to Requirement 2.6(b), SOEs are expected to disclose their audited financial reports or main financial items where financial statements are not available. Furthermore, Requirement 2.6(c) encourages implementing States to 'describe the rules and practices related to SOEs' operating and capital expenditures, procurement, subcontracting and corporate governance' (e.g., the procedures related to the appointment, composition and code of conduct for the board of directors). For the purposes of the EITI, an SOE is defined as a 'wholly or majority government-owned company that is engaged in extractive activities on behalf of the government'.[134] Nevertheless, requirement 2.6(a)(i) acknowledges the scope of definitional variation at the domestic level and suggests that national laws and government structures are taken into account in the scope of the definition. The disclosure of information related to social expenditures, and the impact of the extractive sector on the economy, is covered by Requirement 6 and covers both POEs and SOEs. For example, under Requirement 6.2, implementing countries must include disclosures from SOEs on their quasi-fiscal expenditures.[135] The application of this requirement has potentially wide ramifications. For example, the top ten major Chinese companies[136] operating in EITI implementing countries are State owned, with a recent EITI report showing that there is not much difference in reporting between Chinese companies and companies from other countries and that in 2016 Chinese companies reported in at least twenty-four implementing countries.[137]

---

[133] Barnes, 'State-Owned Entities as Key Actors in the Promotion and Implementation of the Agenda 2030 for Sustainable Development: Examples of Good Practices' (n 113) 9.

[134] EITI International Secretariat, 'EITI Standard 2019' (n 126) Requirement 6.2.

[135] In accordance with Requirement 6.2 quasi-fiscal expenditures include 'arrangements whereby SOEs undertake public social expenditure such as payments for social services, public infrastructure, fuel subsidies and national debt servicing, etc. outside of the national budgetary process'.

[136] China Metallurgical Group Corporation, China Minmetals, China Nonferrous Metal Mining Group, China Railway Corporation, China National Offshore Oil Corporation, China National Petroleum Corporation, PetroChina Company, Sinochem, Sinopec, Zijn Mining. All of those companies are either fully or in majority State owned.

[137] EITI International Secretariat, 'Chinese Companies Reporting in EITI Countries: Review of the Engagement of Chinese Firms in Countries Implementing the EITI' (EITI 2016) 4–5.

3.3.6 *UN Global Compact*

The UN Global Compact has its roots in a speech given on 31 January 1999 by former UN Secretary General Kofi Annan at the World Economic Forum in Davos.[138] In that speech, Annan envisaged a partnership between business and the UN, which would be 'mutually supportive' with the aim of giving a 'human face to the global market'. After this speech, the UN Global Compact debuted in year 2000 with a set of 9 Principles, to which a 10th Principle, dealing with corruption, was added in 2004. The UN Global Compact is a multi-stakeholder initiative composed of the UN, governments, civil society organisations and businesses, whose main aim is to prompt 'companies to align their strategies and operations with universal principles on human rights, labour, environment and anti-corruption and [to] take actions that advance societal goals'.[139] The 10 Principles are derived from the UDHR, the ILO Declaration on Fundamental Principles and Rights at Work, the Rio Declaration on Environment and Development and the UN Convention against Corruption. The Principles are brief and they address human rights concerns (Principles 1–2), labour issues (Principles 3–6), responsible environmental practices (Principles 7–9) and the need to take measures against corruption (Principle 10).[140] To join, a company must pledge to 'operate responsibly, in alignment with universal sustainability principles', 'take actions that support society', commit to push sustainability deep 'into the company's DNA', report annually on ongoing efforts and engage locally.[141] At the time of writing, 11,183 businesses and 156 States have joined this initiative.[142] The UN supports the UN Global Compact initiative through several General Assembly Resolutions.[143]

The UN Global Compact seeks to achieve its goals mainly through engagement mechanisms that focus on leadership, dialogues, learning, outreach and

---

[138] 'Secretary-General Proposes Global Compact on Human Rights, Labour, Environment, in Address to World Economic Forum in Davos | Meetings Coverage and Press Releases' <https://www.un.org/press/en/1999/19990201.sgsm6881.html> accessed 12 August 2020.

[139] 'Homepage | UN Global Compact' <https://www.unglobalcompact.org/> accessed 12 August 2020.

[140] 'The Ten Principles | UN Global Compact' <https://www.unglobalcompact.org/what-is-gc/mission/principles> accessed 12 August 2020.

[141] 'What's the Commitment? | UN Global Compact' <https://www.unglobalcompact.org/participation/join/commitment> accessed 26 August 2020.

[142] 'Homepage | UN Global Compact' (n 140).

[143] Towards global partnerships: A principle-based approach to enhanced cooperation between the United Nations and all relevant partners (A/RES/73/254) 2019.

networking, but this initiative is voluntary in nature and there are no means to measure or monitor the performance of its participants.[144] The companies that have joined must make an annual disclosure that is called Communication on Progress (COP). The aim of this disclosure is to show how 'business informs stakeholders about its efforts to implement the UN Global Compact'.[145] Failure to submit a COP results in a change in the status of the participant, which can eventually lead to expulsion. A COP must contain a statement by the chief executive officer of the business expressing continued support for the UN Global Compact, a description of practical actions taken to support this initiative and a measurement of outcomes.[146] COPs that do not meet those minimum requirements are given a twelve-month 'learner' grace period. If a company does not submit their yearly report on time, they will be designated as 'non-communicating'[147] and will be expelled at the end of one year from when it was given this status. Although the UN Global Compact does not expressly refer to State corporate ownership in any of its 10 Principles, the commentary to Principle 2 states that 'State-owned enterprises should be aware that because they are part of the State, they may have direct responsibilities under human rights law'.[148] The UN Global Compact initiative is the 'world's largest corporate sustainability initiative', which has brought together the largest number of business ever assembled for this purpose. However, it also suffers from several weaknesses: the language of the Principles is so vague that companies can 'circumvent or not comply' with most of its requirements, there is no enforcement mechanism and its COP has been described as largely a 'mere ritual or a public relations exercise'.[149]

3.3.7 *The Application of Other Relevant Instruments*

The instruments analysed above have been selected for their application to SOEs. As discussed, some of those instruments are specifically designed for

---

[144] Deva, *Regulating Corporate Human Rights Violations* (n 19) 93.

[145] 'UN Global Compact Policy on Communicating Progress' <https://www.unglobalcompact.org/participation/report/cop>.

[146] ibid.

[147] Andreas Rasche and others, 'Which Firms Leave Multi-Stakeholder Initiatives? An Analysis of Delistings from the United Nations Global Compact' [2020] Regulation and Governance.

[148] 'Principle 2 | UN Global Compact' <https://www.unglobalcompact.org/what-is-gc/mission/principles/principle-2> accessed 12 August 2020.

[149] Deva, *Regulating Corporate Human Rights Violations* (n 19) 97–99; Surya Deva, 'Global Compact: A Critique of the UN's Public-Private Partnership for Promoting Corporate Citizenship' (2006) 34 Syracuse J. Int'l L. & Com. 107.

SOEs (the OECD Guidelines on the Corporate Governance of State-Owned Enterprises, the OECD Common Approaches for Officially Supported Export Credits and Environmental and Social Due Diligence and the Santiago Principles), with others only having specific provisions that apply to SOEs (the UNGPs and the Extractive Industries Transparency Initiative), while some instruments do not have any specific provisions that apply to SOEs, but because it has been specifically clarified by the relevant bodies that they apply to SOEs in equal measure (e.g., the OECD Guidelines for Multinational Enterprises and the ILO Tripartite Declaration concerning Multinational Enterprises and Social Policy) they have been included in the analysis. Consequently, the instruments selected above are not an exhaustive list of international soft law instruments that may be applicable to the activities of SOEs. By way of example, the OECD Common Approaches for Officially Supported Export Credits and Environmental and Social Due Diligence refer to other standards that may be applicable to ECAs during the environmental and social review, such as the International Finance Corporation Performance Standards;[150] the World Bank Guidelines for Environment, Health and Safety;[151] the World Bank Safeguard Policies[152] and the Environmental and Social Framework.[153] Furthermore, at any given time, other sector standards (e.g., some SWFs are signatories to the Principles for Responsible Investment which may also be applicable concomitantly with the Santiago Principles) or industry-specific standards (e.g., OECD Due Diligence Guidance for Responsible Supply Chains of Minerals from Conflict-Affected and High-Risk Areas,[154] OECD Due Diligence Guidance for Meaningful Stakeholder Engagement in the Extractive Sector[155]) may be applicable to SOEs, as well as the standards that are found in host States. Due to space constraints, it is not possible to address all of them in this monograph, but the reader should be aware that they may also be applicable.

---

[150] IFC Performance Standards on Environmental and Social Sustainability (2012).
[151] World Bank Group Environmental, Health, and Safety Guidelines (30 April 2007).
[152] 'Environmental and Social Policies' (World Bank) <http://www.worldbank.org/en/projects-operations/environmental-and-social-policies> accessed 10 July 2018.
[153] ibid.
[154] OECD Due Diligence Guidance for Responsible Supply Chains of Minerals from Conflict-Affected and High-Risk Areas (17 July 2012).
[155] OECD Due Diligence Guidance for Meaningful Stakeholder Engagement in the Extractive Sector (4 December 2015).

3.4 REGIONAL APPROACHES TO THE REGULATION
OF STATE-OWNED ENTITIES

This section will briefly examine several selected[156] international and regional instruments regulating public procurement with the end aim of determining to what extent those frameworks allow or restrict the integration of human rights in public procurement supply chains.[157] The main focus in this section is on the EU Public Procurement Directives[158] as an example of a regional approach to the regulation of SOEs; however, for completeness, several international instruments that regulate public procurement will also be analysed. It should also be noted that although significantly less expansive in scope, the United States has also recently adopted public procurement rules that seek to specifically target human trafficking.[159] Public procurement refers to the 'acquisition by public bodies, such as government departments and municipalities of the various goods and services that they need for their activities'.[160] States are some of the largest purchasers of goods and services and overall, public procurement amounts to EUR 1 trillion a year in world

---

[156] International Labour Organisation, 'Report III (Part 1B): General Survey Concerning the Labour Clauses (Public Contracts) Convention 1949 (No. 84)' (International Labour Office 2008) 62–99. (See chapter III for a thorough examination of recent developments in the field of public procurement. There are a multitude of international and regional programmes and initiatives being developed by different institutions – such as the UNCITRAL's Model Law on Procurement, the WTO Agreement on Government Procurement, the World Bank, the International Finance Corporation, the Asian Development Bank, the Inter-American Development Bank, the European Bank for Reconstruction and Development, the OECD, the European Union, the Common Market for Eastern and Southern Africa, the West African Economic and Monetary Union, the Asia-Pacific Economic Cooperation, the Southern Common Market (MERCOSUR), the North-American Free Trade Agreement (NAFTA), the Equator Principles for Financial Institutions and the International Federation of Consulting Engineers (FIDIC) – seeking to harmonise not only their own procurement practices, but also those of their national partners.).

[157] It must be recalled that at the domestic level, public procurement is largely regulated though contract and/or administrative law.

[158] Directive 2014/23/EU of the European Parliament and of the Council of 26 February 2014 on the award of concession contracts [OJ L 94/1 (28 March 2014) (the 'Concessions Directive').]; Directive 2014/24/EU of the European Parliament and of the Council of 26 February 2014 on public procurement and repealing Directive 2004/18/EC [OJ L 94/65 (28 March 2014) (the 'Public Sector Directive').]; Directive 2014/25/EU of the European Parliament and of the Council of 26 February 2014 on procurement by entities operating in the water, energy, transport and postal services sectors and repealing Directive 2004/17/EC [OJ L 94/243 (28 March 2014) (the 'Utilities Directive').].

[159] Federal Acquisition Regulation; Ending Trafficking in Persons [Federal Register Vol. 8, No 19].

[160] Sue Arrowsmith, John Linarelli and Don Wallace, *Regulating Public Procurement – National and International Perspectives* (Kluwer Law International BV 2000) 1.

trade flows, while in the EU alone its value is about EUR 425 billion, or approximately 3.4 per cent of EU Gross Domestic Product (GDP).[161] Even in OECD countries, public procurement amounts to between 15 and 25 per cent of GDP.[162] Consequently, it has been suggested that governments should harness this enormous purchasing power for good by integrating human rights 'via the terms of purchase contracts, by exercising leverage over their immediate suppliers and, through supply chain requirements, in turn over other companies involved in the production process'.[163] Nevertheless, across most regulatory regimes, the primary policy aims of public procurement continue to remain efficiency, non-discrimination between tenderers and open competition, while social, environmental or other societal goals remain secondary in nature.[164]

The importance of establishing minimum standards for workers directly employed in public works was recognised as early as 1936, when the International Labour Organisation produced the Reduction of Hours of Work (Public Works) Convention (No. 51) applying to those 'directly employed on building or civil engineering works financed or subsidized by central governments' and which provided 'for a weekly average of working hours not exceeding 40 hours, overtime work up to a limit of 100 hours in any year (in exceptional cases of pressure of work) and overtime wage rates of not less than 25 per cent in excess of normal rate'.[165] The Conference in the Public Works (National Planning) Recommendation 1937 (No. 51) followed in 1937 and it addressed 'minimum standards of conditions of recruitment and wage rates of workers directly employed in public works'.[166] Although

---

[161] Institute for Human Rights and Business, 'Protecting Rights by Purchasing Right: The Human Rights Provisions, Opportunities and Limitations under the 2014 EU Public Procurement Directives' (2015) 8.

[162] John Morrison and Haley St Dennis, 'State of Play: Human Rights in the Political Economy of States: Avenues for Application' (Institute for Human Rights and Business 2014) 53 <https://www.ihrb.org/pdf/2014-03-18_State-of-Play_HR-Political-Economy-States.pdf>.

[163] Claire Methven O'Brien and Olga Martin-Ortega, 'The Role of the State as Buyer under UN Guiding Principle 6 (Submission to UN Working Group on Business and Human Rights Consultation on "The State as an Economic Actor: The Role of Economic Diplomacy Tools to Promote Business Respect of Human Rights")' [2018] University of Groningen Faculty of Law Research Paper Series No. 14/2018; Olga Martin-Ortega and Claire Methven O'Brien, *Public Procurement and Human Rights* (Edward Elgar 2019); Olga Martin-Ortega and Claire Methven O'Brien, 'Advancing Respect for Labour Rights Globally through Public Procurement' (2017) 5 Politics Gov. 69.

[164] Claire Methven O'Brien and Olga Martin-Ortega, 'Human Rights and Public Procurement of Goods and Services' in Surya Deva and David Birchall (eds), *Research Handbook on Human Rights and Business* (Edward Elgar 2020) 247.

[165] International Labour Organisation (n 156) 2.

[166] ibid.

Convention No. 51 was never ratified and Recommendation 1937 (No. 51) was withdrawn, both instruments paved the way for ILO Labour Clauses (Public Contracts) Convention (No. 94)[167] which was later supplemented by Recommendation No. 84. Both instruments sought to ensure that public authorities observe 'socially acceptable standards in work performed on the public account' and it was 'recognised that fair labour clauses in public contracts may play a useful role in attaining and maintaining a high standard of social protection at the national level'.[168] Other significant international instruments are the WTO Agreement on Government Procurement,[169] the UNCITRAL Model Law on Public Procurement[170] and the UNGPs. The WTO Agreement on Government Procurement is a plurilateral agreement, whose purpose is to mutually open government procurement among its parties by establishing rules that require 'open, fair and transparent conditions of competition'. With the focus being largely on competition rules, the 1994 WTO Agreement on Government Procurement had limited scope for the advancement of secondary objectives, such as environmental and social policy, an issue that has been addressed, to a certain extent, in the 2012 Revised WTO Agreement on Government Procurement. The 2012 Revised WTO Agreement on Government Procurement does not make express reference to human rights but it allows for the following derogations from its general regime: where it is 'necessary in order to protect human, animal, or plant life or health' (Art. III.2.b), for measures designed to advance environmental protection (Art. X. 6) and where procurement is conducted 'for the specific purpose of providing international assistance' (Art. II. 3). The 2011 UNCITRAL Model Law on Public Procurement (UNCITRAL Model Law) aims to harmonise national procurement laws and is currently used as a model by twenty-three States, various international organisations and institutions such as the Organisation for Security and Cooperation in Europe, the World Bank, the African, Asian and Inter-American Development Banks and the European Bank for Reconstruction and Development.[171] Overall, the UNCITRAL Model Law has a similar focus on competition rules, but it allows for the integration of socio-economic policies in the procurement

---

[167] Convention Co94 – Labour Clauses (Public Contracts) Convention, 1949 (No. 94).
[168] International Labour Organisation (n 156) 5–7.
[169] WTO Agreement on Government Procurement (1994); Revised WTO Agreement on Government Procurement (2012).
[170] UNCITRAL Model Law on Public Procurement (2011).
[171] ibid; 'Status: UNCITRAL Model Law on Public Procurement (2011) | United Nations Commission on International Trade Law' <https://uncitral.un.org/en/texts/procurement/modellaw/public_procurement/status> accessed 16 August 2020.

process (Article 9(2)(b)) while the Guide to Enactment expressly states that human rights are covered under the term 'sustainable procurement', which is an umbrella term for the 'pursuit of social, economic and environmental policies through procurement'.[172] The UNGPs address public procurement as part of the 'State-business nexus'[173] in Principle 6, which provides that 'States should promote respect for human rights by business enterprises with which they conduct commercial transactions'.[174] The Commentary to Principle 6 further clarifies that States conduct a 'variety of commercial transactions with business enterprises not at least through their procurement activities',[175] thus recognising the important linkages between public procurement and human rights. States thus have 'unique opportunities to promote awareness of and respect for human rights by those enterprises, including through the terms of contracts, with due regard to States' relevant obligations under national and international law'.[176]

The EU Public Procurement Directives[177] do provide several opportunities for the integration of human rights considerations into all phases of EU public procurement processes such as the pre-tender and market engagement phase, the technical specifications phase, the exclusion phase, the selection phase, the award phase and the contracting phase. As an illustration, the exclusion phase addresses specific instances and provides, among others, that procurers must exclude bidders which are in breach of the social security contribution payments[178] or have been convicted of child labour or other forms of trafficking,[179] or where there is no compliance with environmental, social or labour

---

[172] Guide to Enactment of the UNCITRAL Model Law on Public Procurement 2014 5.

[173] Mihaela M Barnes, 'The United Nations Guiding Principles on Business and Human Rights, the State Duty to Protect Human Rights and the State-Business Nexus' (2018) 15 Brazilian J. Int. Law 42, 47–52.

[174] Ruggie, 'Guiding Principles on Business and Human Rights: Implementing the United Nations "Protect, Respect and Remedy" Framework (Report of the Special Representative of the Secretary-General on the Issue of Human Rights and Transnational Corporations and Other Business Enterprises, John Ruggie)' (n 17) 10.

[175] ibid.

[176] ibid.

[177] Directive 2014/23/EU of the European Parliament and of the Council of 26 February 2014 on the award of concession contracts (n 158); Directive 2014/24/EU of the European Parliament and of the Council of 26 February 2014 on public procurement and repealing Directive 2004/18/EC (n 158); Directive 2014/25/EU of the European Parliament and of the Council of 26 February 2014 on procurement by entities operating in the water, energy, transport and postal services sectors and repealing Directive 2004/17/EC (n 158).

[178] Public Sector Directive Art. 57(2); Recital 105 and 106 of the Utilities Directive; Art. 38(5) of the Concessions Directive.

[179] Public Sector Directive Art. 57(1)(f); Utilities Directive Art. 80; Art. 38(4)(f) of the Concessions Directive.

law obligations.[180] There are also several cross-cutting issues that are present in all the EU Public Procurement Directives such as the overarching 'social clause', the label and certification requirements and subcontracting issues. The overarching social clause provides that Member States must take 'appropriate measures' to ensure that the performance of a contract requires compliance with the environmental, social and labour law obligations by economic operators.[181] As a novel issue, the EU Procurement Directives state that social labels can be used in the technical specifications, award criteria or the contract performance conditions,[182] while procurers can require that economic actors prove their suitability by providing certifications.[183] The overarching social clause and the exclusion and selection criteria apply in equal measure to subcontractors.[184] Despite the generally progressive stance of the EU Public Procurement Directives on the protection of human rights, one of their main weaknesses is that, in terms of human rights instruments, they only make specific reference to the eight ILO Conventions and several other instruments such as the Vienna Convention for the protection of the Ozone Layer and its Montreal Protocol on substances that deplete the Ozone Layer, the Basel Convention on the Control of Transboundary Movements of Hazardous Wastes and their Disposal, the Stockholm Convention on Persistent Organic Pollutants and the Convention on the Prior Informed Consent Procedure for Certain Hazardous Chemicals and Pesticides in International Trade (and its three regional Protocols).[185] There is no mention in any of the Annexes to the EU Public Procurement Directives of the UDHR and the ICCPR or the ICESCR, which cumulatively make up the International Bill of Human Rights. Consequently, the EU Public Procurement directives do not appear to recognise the full international human rights framework. It has been speculated that this might be likely due to an oversight on the part of the EU, rather than an intentional omission, and in any event this oversight will only likely have an effect in the small number of EU Member States that have not signed and ratified those

---

[180] Public Sector Directive Art. 57(4)(a); Utilities Directive Art. 80; Art. 38(7)(a) of the Concessions Directive.

[181] Public Sector Directive Art. 18(2); Utilities Directive Art. 36(2); Art. 30(3) of the Concessions Directive.

[182] Public Sector Directive Art. 43(1); Utilities Directive Art. 61(1).

[183] Public Sector Directive Art. 64(1)–(4); Utilities Directive Art. 62(1).

[184] Public Sector Directive Arts. 63 and 71(1); Utilities Directive Arts. 88(1) and 88(6); Arts. 42(1) and 42(4) of the Concessions Directive.

[185] Public Sector Directive Annex X; Utilities Directive Annex XIV; Annex X of the Concessions Directive.

instruments.[186] However, from a policy point of view, it has been argued that 'the absence of these international human rights instruments points to incoherence across the EU's commitments to human rights, and to the implementation of the UNGPs within public procurement processes in particular'.[187]

3.5 DOMESTIC APPROACHES TO THE REGULATION OF STATE-OWNED ENTITIES

States have a duty to take a variety of measures in order to provide against corporate abuse of human rights, regardless whether they occur in the public or private sphere. The UN Human Rights Council has summarised this issue in the following way:

> States are required to take a variety of measures in order to effectively protect against corporate abuse. They must generally monitor compliance by third parties and in most cases introduce legislative measures to prohibit and proscribe certain behaviour; establish administrative and juridical mechanisms to effectively and impartially investigate all companies and bring perpetrators to justice; and facilitate the provision of effective remedies, including the provision of reparation to victims, where appropriate.[188]

Following a survey organised by the Working Group on Business and Human Rights and sent to all the UN Member States in 2015, which focused expressly on the role of States as economic actors, and which specifically queried whether States had policies, regulations or guidance in place that addressed the need for SOEs to implement respect for human rights throughout their operations, twenty Member States replied with answers:[189] Brazil, Chile, Colombia, Cuba, Cyprus, Denmark, France, Georgia, Ghana, Italy, Kenya, Republic of Korea, Sweden, Switzerland, the Kyrgyz Republic, Norway, the Netherlands, the Russian Federation, the United Kingdom, and the United States of America. Some States did not have a specific regulatory regime for SOEs, which were instead covered by the provisions of

---

[186] Institute for Human Rights and Business (n 161) 24.
[187] ibid.
[188] Ruggie, 'State Responsibilities to Regulate and Adjudicate Corporate Activities under the United Nations' Core Human Rights Treaties (Report of the Special Representative of the Secretary-General on the Issue of Human Rights and Transnational Corporations and Other Business Enterprises)' (John F Kennedy School of Government 2007) 3.
[189] 'OHCHR | Working Group Surveys on Implementation of the UN Guiding Principles on Business and Human Rights' <https://www.ohchr.org/EN/Issues/Business/Pages/ImplementationGP.aspx> accessed 18 August 2020.

the Constitution and other pertinent legislation such as corporate or labour laws and they included Cyprus,[190] Cuba,[191] France,[192] Georgia,[193] Ghana,[194] Italy,[195] the Kyrgyz Republic,[196] Kenya,[197] Russia,[198] Switzerland,[199] the Netherlands,[200] the United Kingdom[201] and the United States.[202] Chile's reply was that it did not have a specific policy or regulation that focused specifically on the need for SOEs to implement and respect human rights, but that it had social sustainability policies that covered SOEs and which addressed, among

[190] 'Cyprus' Response to the Survey on the Implementation of the Guiding Principles on Business and Human Rights: The Role of States as Economic Actors' <https://www.ohchr.org/EN/Issues/Business/Pages/2015Survey.aspx>.

[191] 'Cuba's Response to the Survey on the Implementation of the Guiding Principles on Business and Human Rights: The Role of States as Economic Actors' <https://www.ohchr.org/EN/Issues/Business/Pages/2015Survey.aspx>.

[192] 'France's Response to the Survey on the Implementation of the Guiding Principles on Business and Human Rights: The Role of States as Economic Actors' <https://www.ohchr.org/EN/Issues/Business/Pages/2015Survey.aspx>.

[193] 'Georgia's Response to the Survey on the Implementation of the Guiding Principles on Business and Human Rights: The Role of States as Economic Actors' <https://www.ohchr.org/EN/Issues/Business/Pages/2015Survey.aspx>.

[194] 'Ghana's Response to the Survey on the Implementation of the Guiding Principles on Business and Human Rights: The Role of States as Economic Actors' <https://www.ohchr.org/EN/Issues/Business/Pages/2015Survey.aspx>.

[195] 'Italy's Response to the Survey on the Implementation of the Guiding Principles on Business and Human Rights: The Role of States as Economic Actors' <https://www.ohchr.org/EN/Issues/Business/Pages/2015Survey.aspx>.

[196] 'The Kyrgyz Republic's Response to the Survey on the Implementation of the Guiding Principles on Business and Human Rights: The Role of States as Economic Actors' <https://www.ohchr.org/EN/Issues/Business/Pages/2015Survey.aspx>.

[197] 'Kenya's Response to the Survey on the Implementation of the Guiding Principles on Business and Human Rights: The Role of States as Economic Actors' <https://www.ohchr.org/EN/Issues/Business/Pages/2015Survey.aspx>.

[198] 'Russia's Response to the Survey on the Implementation of the Guiding Principles on Business and Human Rights: The Role of States as Economic Actors' <https://www.ohchr.org/EN/Issues/Business/Pages/2015Survey.aspx>.

[199] 'Switzerland's Response to the Survey on the Implementation of the Guiding Principles on Business and Human Rights: The Role of States as Economic Actors' <https://www.ohchr.org/EN/Issues/Business/Pages/2015Survey.aspx>.

[200] 'Netherland's Response to the Survey on the Implementation of the Guiding Principles on Business and Human Rights: The Role of States as Economic Actors' <https://www.ohchr.org/EN/Issues/Business/Pages/2015Survey.aspx>.

[201] 'UK's Response to the Survey on the Implementation of the Guiding Principles on Business and Human Rights: The Role of States as Economic Actors' <https://www.ohchr.org/EN/Issues/Business/Pages/2015Survey.aspx>.

[202] 'USA's Response to the Survey on the Implementation of the Guiding Principles on Business and Human Rights: The Role of States as Economic Actors' <https://www.ohchr.org/EN/Issues/Business/Pages/2015Survey.aspx>.

others, issues of gender, age, nationality and diversity in the composition of their boards.[203] Countries that did have specific policies, regulations and guidances that expressly integrated human rights and/or the UNGPs throughout the operations of their SOEs included Norway,[204] Sweden,[205] Colombia,[206] Cyprus[207] and Denmark.[208] India, Spain, New Zealand, Australia and Finland also have specific requirements for SOEs that are generally framed in 'corporate social responsibility' (CSR) and 'sustainable economy' terminology, rather than 'business and human rights'.

For example, India has issued the Guidelines on Corporate Social Responsibility and Sustainability for Central Public Sector Enterprises.[209] Spain's Sustainable Economy Law of 2011 requires SOEs to file annual corporate governance reports and sustainability reports.[210] New Zealand incorporates SOEs within in the wider public sector and the pertinent legislation in this regard is contained in the State Sector Act 1988,[211] the Public Finance Act 1989[212] and the Crown Entities Act 2004.[213] Finland, which has the largest market capitalization of SOEs relative to GDP, has recently issued a Government Resolution on State Ownership Policy, requiring SOEs listed

---

[203] 'Chile's Response to the Survey on the Implementation of the Guiding Principles on Business and Human Rights: The Role of States as Economic Actors' <https://www.ohchr.org/EN/Issues/Business/Pages/2015Survey.aspx>.

[204] 'Norway's Response to the Survey on the Implementation of the Guiding Principles on Business and Human Rights: The Role of States as Economic Actors' <https://www.ohchr.org/EN/Issues/Business/Pages/2015Survey.aspx>.

[205] 'Sweden's Response to the Survey on the Implementation of the Guiding Principles on Business and Human Rights: The Role of States as Economic Actors' <https://www.ohchr.org/EN/Issues/Business/Pages/2015Survey.aspx>.

[206] 'Colombia's Response to the Survey on the Implementation of the Guiding Principles on Business and Human Rights: The Role of States as Economic Actors' <https://www.ohchr.org/EN/Issues/Business/Pages/2015Survey.aspx>. Colombia's responded that it was in the process or reviewing all its legislation in order to bring it in line with the UNGPs.

[207] 'Cyprus' Response to the Survey on the Implementation of the Guiding Principles on Business and Human Rights: The Role of States as Economic Actors' (n 190).

[208] 'Denmark's Response to the Survey on the Implementation of the Guiding Principles on Business and Human Rights: The Role of States as Economic Actors' <https://www.ohchr.org/EN/Issues/Business/Pages/2015Survey.aspx>.

[209] Guidelines on Corporate Social Responsibility and Sustainability for Central Public Sector Enterprises (Guidelines on Corporate Social Responsibility and Sustainability for Central Public Sector Enterprises (DPE F No. 15 (13)/2013-DPE (GM)).

[210] Ley N° 2/2011 de 4 de marzo de 2011 sobre Economía Sostenible (modificada por la Ley N° 2/2012 de 29 de junio de 2012) paras 35–39.

[211] State Sector Act 1988.

[212] Public Finance Act 1989.

[213] Crown Entities Act 2004.

or unlisted to report on their sustainability performance,[214] while the Finnish National Action Plan on Business and Human Rights provides that SOEs 'are required to observe human rights responsibly and transparently both in their own organisations and in subcontractor chains, in full accordance with the UNGPs' and draws attention to the fact that the Finish State uses a separate accountability mechanism for dealing with human rights violations committed by SOEs.[215] Portugal requires SOEs to include in their annual report a sustainability analysis including the adoption of gender equality plans,[216] while Switzerland has recognised that it is the 'special responsibility of the State to safeguard human rights' through SOEs and notes that 'federal enterprises are required to play an exemplary role'.[217]

Sweden has changed its official State Ownership Policy and Guidelines for State-Owned Enterprises (the Policy) in 2016. The Policy emphasises the fact that State-owned enterprises should work towards achieving a healthy work environment, respect for human rights, decent working conditions, environmental sustainability and high standards of business ethics, particularly through the prevention of corruption as well as responsible conduct with respect to the payment of taxes.[218] Furthermore, 'State-owned enterprises should act as role models within the area of sustainable business and should otherwise behave in a manner that promotes public confidence'.[219] The Policy forms an inherent part of the legal framework for the regulation of State-owned enterprises and compliance is mandatory for all companies that are State owned (e.g., it applies in cases of full, majority and minority interest ownership).[220] Sweden's SWF (Swedfund International AB) and the Swedish Export Credit Corporation are also required to comply with the Policy.

[214] Morrison and St Dennis (n 162) 52; Government of Finland, 'Government Ownership Steering: Financial Annual Report 2015' (2015) 18–20 <vnk.fi/government-ownership-steering>.

[215] Finnish Ministry of Employment and the Economy (46/2014), 'National Action Plan for the Implementation of the UN Guiding Principles on Business and Human Rights' 5.

[216] Portugal, Council of Ministers Resolution 49/2007 approving the Principles of Good Governace of Public Companies.

[217] 'Report of the Working Group on the Issue of Human Rights and Transnational Corporations and Other Business Enterprises (A/HRC/32/45)' 13.

[218] Government of Sweden, Ministry of Enterprise and Innovation, 'The State's Ownership Policy and Guidelines for State-Owned Enterprises 2017' 4 <https://www.government.se/reports/2017/06/the-states-ownership-policy-and-guidelines-for-state-owned-enterprises-2017/>.

[219] ibid; Rasmus KløCker Larsen and Sandra Atler, 'Applying the First Pillar of the UN Guiding Principles to Development Cooperation: The Performance of Swedish Agencies and State-Owned Enterprises' (2018) 3 BHRJ 131.

[220] Barnes, 'State-Owned Entities as Key Actors in the Promotion and Implementation of the Agenda 2030 for Sustainable Development: Examples of Good Practices' (n 113) 12.

The latest version of the Policy expressly integrates the UN Global Compact, the UNGPs, the OECD Guidelines for Multinational Enterprises and the goals of the Agenda 2030 for Sustainable Development.[221] The ultimate responsibility for the integration of sustainable business practices into State-owned enterprises falls onto the board of directors. All State-owned enterprises have mandatory reporting obligations, and the board of directors must ensure that sustainability reporting is done in a comprehensive and transparent manner, as required in the reporting guidelines from the Global Reporting Initiative. The reports include, among others, materiality analyses, appropriate sustainability disclosures and clear information about stakeholder engagement.[222]

Norway has adopted similar policies[223] and the aim of the Norwegian government is for State-ownership 'to be an example of best practice internationally'.[224] The main legal framework for State ownership is provided for by constitutional arrangement, but it ultimately delegates the administration of the various SOEs to the corresponding ministry, with the ministry's administration of ownership being exercised under constitutional and parliamentary responsibility.[225] The OECD Guidelines for SOEs and the UNGPs are incorporated and apply to all companies that are State owned, and SOEs are required to carry out human rights due diligence.[226] The Norwegian Export Credit Guarantee Agency (GIEK) assesses all applications for social and environmental risks and expressly follows the OECD Common

---

[221] Government of Sweden, Ministry of Enterprise and Innovation (n 218) 4.

[222] ibid 8–9. Ministry of Enterprise and Innovation: Sweden, 'Response to Working Group Survey on Implementation of the Guiding Principles – Business Enterprises Owned or Controlled by the State' (2016) <https://www.ohchr.org/EN/Issues/Business/Pages/2015Survey.aspx>; Barnes, 'State-Owned Entities as Key Actors in the Promotion and Implementation of the Agenda 2030 for Sustainable Development: Examples of Good Practices' (n 113) 12.

[223] Norwegian Government, 'Response to Working Group Survey on Implementation of the Guiding Principles – Business Enterprises Owned or Controlled by the State' (2016) <https://www.ohchr.org/EN/Issues/Business/Pages/2015Survey.aspx>.

[224] 'Diverse and Value-Creating Ownership' (2014) Meld. St. 27 (2013–2014) Report to the Storting (white paper) Recommendation of the Ministry of Trade, Industry and Fisheries of 20 June 2014, approved in the Council of State the same day. (The Solberg Government) 60 <https://www.regjeringen.no/en/dokumenter/meld.-st.-27-2013-2014/id763968/>; 'Opportunities for All: Human Rights in Norway's Foreign Policy and Development Cooperation' (2014) Meld. St. 10 (2014–2015) Report to the Storting (white paper) 60–61.

[225] 'Diverse and Value-Creating Ownership' (n 224) 61; Barnes, 'State-Owned Entities as Key Actors in the Promotion and Implementation of the Agenda 2030 for Sustainable Development: Examples of Good Practices' (n 113) 15.

[226] 'Diverse and Value-Creating Ownership' (n 224) 65; 'The State's Direct Ownership of Companies: Sustainable Value Creation' The State's Direct Ownership of Companies Meld. St. 8 (2019–2020) Report to the Storting (white paper) 66–74.

Approaches for Export Credit Agencies, the UNGPs and other relevant standards such as the IFC Performance Standards (2012) and the World Bank Guidelines for Environment, Health and Safety.[227] Later initiatives, such as the creation of the Norwegian National Action Plan for Business and Human Rights[228] and the integration of human rights generally and the UNGPs expressly into the investment policy of Norges Bank, the world's largest sovereign wealth fund,[229] are further illustrations of the commitment that Norway has made in this area.[230]

In China, all SOEs are supervised and administered by the State-Owned Assets Supervision and Administration Commission of the State Council (SASAC), an institution under the direct management of the State Council, charged with the supervision and management of all centrally administered State-owned enterprises, excluding financial enterprises.[231] The SASAC has issued 'Guidelines to the State-Owned Enterprises, directly under the Central Government, on fulfilling Corporate Social Responsibilities' (Guidelines)[232] and has issued a third National Human Rights Action Plan of China (2016–2020).[233] Within China, SOEs have pioneered corporate social responsibility reporting and the adoption of corporate social responsibility reporting standards, such as the Global Reporting Initiative Sustainability Reporting

---

[227] 'Sustainability – GIEK' <https://www.giek.no/sustainability/> accessed 31 August 2020.

[228] Norwegian Ministry of Foreign Affairs, 'Business and Human Rights National Action Plan for the Implementation of the UN Guiding Principles' <https://www.regjeringen.no/en/dokumenter/business_hr/id2457944/>.

[229] Norges Bank Investment Management, 'Human Rights Expectations towards Companies' <https://www.nbim.no/contentassets/3258fe10181544cc8e02566c7237fa5f/human-rights-expectations-document2.pdf>.

[230] Barnes, 'State-Owned Entities as Key Actors in the Promotion and Implementation of the Agenda 2030 for Sustainable Development: Examples of Good Practices' (n 113) 15.

[231] 'SASAC' <http://en.sasac.gov.cn/index.html> accessed 18 August 2020; 'What We Do' <http://en.sasac.gov.cn/2018/07/17/c_7.htm> accessed 18 August 2020. SASAC performs the following functions: 'supervises and manages the State-owned assets of centrally administered State-owned enterprises'; it is responsible for the supervision and for ensuring the increase in the value of State-owned assets; it takes charge of the reform and restructuring of State-owned enterprises; it appoints and removes the top executives of the entities supervised; it manages the day-to-day operation of the supervisory panels; takes charge of the State-owned capital operational budget and ensures that surplus capital is returned to the State; it ensures that the supervised enterprises apply relevant legislation, regulation and principles; and it takes charge of the "fundamental management" of those entities'".

[232] 'Guidelines to the State-Owned Enterprises Directly under the Central Government' <http://en.sasac.gov.cn/2011/12/06/c_313.htm> accessed 18 August 2020; Barnes, 'State-Owned Entities as Key Actors in the Promotion and Implementation of the Agenda 2030 for Sustainable Development: Examples of Good Practices' (n 113) 12–14.

[233] 'National Human Rights Action Plan of China (2016–2020)' <http://english.gov.cn/archive/publications/2016/09/29/content_281475454482622.htm> accessed 18 August 2020.

Guideline, the ISO 2600 Standards and other similar industry-specific initiatives since the mid-2000s.[234] Certain measures have also been taken with regard to the investment activities of all Chinese businesses. The Ministry of Commerce and the Ministry of Environmental Protection have issued a Guidance on Environmental Protection in Foreign Investment Cooperation, which requires enterprises operating abroad to 'establish' the concept of environmental protection internally, to fulfil social responsibility for environmental protection, to respect the religions and customs of the host country, to pay adequate consideration to labour concerns, to respect the environmental protection laws of the host country, to perform environmental impact assessments throughout the project and to 'study and learn' from the standards and practices of international organizations and multilateral financial institutions.[235] The Green Credit Guidelines issued by the China Banking and Regulatory Commission are another relevant measure and requires banks that finance overseas investment to strengthen environmental and corporate social responsibility requirements.[236] Other sector specific measures, such as the Guidelines for Social Responsibility in Outbound Mining Investment, expressly incorporate the UNGPs and state that those companies need to 'observe the UN Guiding Principles on Business and Human Rights during the entire lifecycle of the mining project'.[237]

3.6 WEAVING THE THREADS TOGETHER: IMPLICATIONS FOR INTERNATIONAL LAW

This chapter has so far examined various instruments that regulate State corporate ownership on three levels: international, regional and domestic. It can be recalled from the above discussion that one of the main features of the

---

[234] Teng Li and Ataur Belal, 'Authoritarian State, Global Expansion and Corporate Social Responsibility Reporting: The Narrative of a Chinese State-Owned Enterprise' (2018) 42 Account. Forum 199, 199, 202–204.

[235] 'MOFCOM and MEP Jointly Issued Guidance on Environmental Protection in Foreign Investment and Cooperation' <http://english.mofcom.gov.cn/article/newsrelease/significantnews/201303/20130300043146.shtml> accessed 18 August 2020; Barnes, 'The United Nations Guiding Principles on Business and Human Rights, the State Duty to Protect Human Rights and the State-Business Nexus' (2018) 15 Brazilian J. Int. Law 42, 56–57.

[236] 'Notice of the CBRC on Issuing the Green Credit Guidelines' <http://www.cbrc.gov.cn/EngdocView.do?docID=3CE646AB629B46B9B533B1D8D9FF8C4A> accessed 18 August 2020.

[237] China Chamber of Commerce of Metals, Minerals & Chemicals Importers & Exporters, 'CCMCMC Guidelines for Social Responsibility in Outbound Mining Investments' (2014) 34–36.

great majority[238] of those instruments, particularly those found at the international level, is that they are not binding, that they exist in the realm of soft
law, a concept that lacks an exact definition,[239] but which stands to describe
an almost 'infinite variety'[240] 'of non-legally binding instruments used in
contemporary international relations by States and international organizations'.[241] Consequently, the main question that arises is what effect, do non-
binding instruments have on international law? In order to answer this
question, one is drawn into a similar – and to a certain extent interconnected –
debate to that concerning the concept of legal personality in international law
encountered in Chapter 2. If, in Chapter 2, the question was '*Who* can be a
legal person in international law?'; the questions in this chapter are '*What
forms part* of international law and *who has a say in deciding* this?'; Is soft law

---

[238] However, the WTO Agreement on Global Procurement, the EU Procurement Directives ILO
Convention No. 94 are binding on State parties to those instruments. The OECD Guidelines
provide 'voluntary principles and standards for responsible business conduct consistent with
applicable laws and internationally recognised standards. States adhering to the Guidelines
make a binding commitment to implement them in accordance with the Decision of the
OECD Council on the OECD Guidelines for Multinational Enterprises. Furthermore,
matters covered by the Guidelines may also be the subject of national law and
international commitments'.

[239] RR Baxter, 'International Law in "Her Infinite Variety"' (1980) 29 Int'l & Comp. L.Q. 549, 550;
CM Chinkin, 'The Challenge of Soft Law: Development and Change in International Law'
(1989) 38 Int'l & Comp. L.Q. 850, 851; Pierre-Marie Dupuy, 'Soft Law and the International
Law of the Environment' (1991) 12 Mich. J. Int'l L. 428. (Baxter states that 'soft law' is
represented by 'norms of various degrees of cogency, persuasiveness, and consensus which are
incorporated in agreements between States but do not create enforceable rights and duties'.
Baxter understands 'international agreements' in a broad sense to include 'treaties, in the strict
sense, through to declarations of policy, joint communiqués, or resolutions of the General
Assembly, to commitments of varying character made from the highest levels of government
down to the lowest'. According to Chinkin: 'Soft law instruments range from treaties, but
which include only soft obligations ("legal soft law") to non-binding or voluntary resolutions
and codes of conduct formulated and accepted by international and regional organisations
("non-legal soft law"), to statements prepared by individuals in a non-governmental capacity,
but which purport to lay down international principles.' Dupuy explains that: '[M]uch of soft
law is incorporated within "soft" (i.e. non-binding) instruments such as recommendations and
resolutions of international organisations, declarations and "final acts" published at the
conclusion of international conferences and even draft proposals elaborated by groups of
experts. It is thus generally understood that "soft" law creates and delineates goals to be
achieved in the future rather than actual duties, programs rather than prescriptions, guidelines
rather than strict obligations.').

[240] Christine Chinkin, 'Normative Development in the International Legal System' in Dinah
Shelton (ed), *Commitment and Compliance: The Role of Non-binding Norms in the
International Legal System* (Oxford University Press 2003) 25–29.

[241] Alan Boyle, 'Soft Law in International Law-Making' in Malcolm D Evans (ed), *International
Law* (4th edn, Oxford University Press 2014) 119.

part of international law?[242] In this context, 'soft' law has been regarded as a 'trouble maker', 'because it is either *not yet* or *not only* law'.[243] This has led some commentators to argue that a bright line exists between law and non-law: something is either law or is not.[244] Although the relevance of this stance in contemporary international law has been questioned,[245] it is important to come to this debate with the realisation that 'whenever we come to approach an object of intellectual inquiry we all carry our professional presuppositions, cultural biases, and personal experience with us' and that 'there is no such thing as a neutral view from "nowhere" as traditional legal scholarship wants us to believe'.[246]

---

[242] Matthias Goldmann, 'Relative Normativity' in Jean d'Aspremont and Sahib Singh (eds), *Concepts for International Law* (Edward Elgar 2019). Goldmann provides an immersive account of the history and evolution of the concept of 'relative normativity' in international law, from classical, to modern international law, to contemporary approaches to this phenomenon.

[243] Dupuy, 'Soft Law and the International Law of the Environment' (n 240) 420. (Emphasis added).

[244] Prosper Weil, 'Towards Relative Normativity in International Law' (1983) 77 Am. J. Int. Law 417, 417–418. ('[T]he threshold does exist: on the one side of the line, there is born a legal obligation that can be relied on before a court or arbitrator, the flouting of which constitutes an internationally unlawful act giving rise to international responsibility; on the other side, there is nothing of the kind.').

[245] Karen Knop, 'Introduction to the Symposium on Prosper Weil, "Towards Relative Normativity in International Law?"' (2020) 114 AJIL Unbound 67; Mónica García-Salmones Rovira, 'What Is Positivism Today?' (2020) 114 AJIL Unbound 87; Sienho Yee, 'The International Law of Co-Progressiveness as a Response to the Problems Associated with "Relative Normativity"' (2020) 114 AJIL Unbound 97; John Tasioulas, 'Prosper Weil and the Mask of Classicism' (2020) 114 AJIL Unbound 92; Paola Gaeta, 'The Super-Normativity of International Criminal Law' (2020) 114 AJIL Unbound 82; José E Alvarez, 'The Relativity Apocalypse Is Nigh' (2020) 114 AJIL Unbound 77; Pierre-Marie Dupuy, 'Prosper Weil's Article: A Stimulating Warning' (2020) 114 AJIL Unbound 72. (See in particular Pierre-Marie Dupuy p. 76: 'Faced with the obvious erosion of the authority of international obligations in the eyes of some governments, we cannot overlook this question in contemporary times. Nevertheless, international society can no longer be reduced to the individualized expression of the will of juxtaposed sovereigns. On the contrary, the irreversible rise of globalisation suggests that the *Lotus* has definitely sunk. Moreover, the truly global challenges affecting the entire international community, in both its social and legal sense, will encourage it to strengthen its cooperation, whatever the current blindness of some governments. The purpose of international law is, of course, always to organise the coexistence of sovereign states, but one cannot limit it to that single purpose. In particular, as demonstrated by practice, this system of law, which is also a legal *order* in the sense of Hans Kelsen, H. L. A. Hart, Georges Scelle, and Santi Romano, is also characterised by the affirmation that a set of rules and principles with a *universal* dimension, some of which are of such importance to all that cannot be denied by anyone.').

[246] Andrea Bianchi, 'Reflexive Butterfly Catching: Insights from a Situated Catcher' in Joost Pauwelyn, Ramses A Wessel and Jan Wouters (eds), *Informal International Lawmaking* (Oxford University Press 2012) 203.

In the view of bright line scholars, the concept of soft law is effectively redundant[247] and is nothing more than a 'self-serving quest' by international lawyers for new legal materials.[248] To this end, various criteria – such as sanction, form, intent, effect, substance and belief – have been put forward to assist in distinguishing between law and non-law.[249] An actor's capacity to make law and the consequences that follow from categorising something as either law and non-law (e.g., the ability to enforce a norm before a forum, the application of the secondary rules of international law, the respect or legitimacy that comes with the status of being law and its impact on power relations) have all been considered as relevant factors in this analysis.[250] Other commentators[251] understand legal normativity 'as a matter of degree with varying scales

---

[247] Jan Klabbers, 'The Redundancy of Soft Law' (1996) 65 Nord. J. Int. Law 181. ('[L]aw can be more or less, specific, more or less exact, more or less determinate, more or less wide in scope, more or less pressing, more or less serious, more or less far-reaching, the only thing it cannot be is more or less binding.').

[248] Jean d'Aspremont, 'Softness in International Law: A Self-Serving Quest for New Legal Materials' (2008) 19 Eur. J. Int. Law 1088, 1088–1093; Jean d'Aspremont, 'Bindingness' in Jean d'Aspremont and Sahib Singh (eds), *Concepts for International Law* (Edward Elgar 2019).

[249] Joost Pauwelyn, 'Is It International Law or Not, and Does It Even Matter?' in Joost Pauwelyn, Ramses A Wessel and Jan Wouters (eds), *Informal International Lawmaking* (Oxford University Press 2012) 131–141.

[250] ibid 141–152; Thomas Schultz, *Transnational Legality: Stateless Law and International Arbitration* (Oxford University Press 2014).

[251] Chinkin, 'The Challenge of Soft Law' (n 239) 866; R Higgins, *Problems and Process: International Law and How We Use It* (Clarendon Press 1994) 17–38; Dupuy, 'Soft Law and the International Law of the Environment' (n 239) 435; Alain Pellet, 'The Normative Dilemma: Will and Consent in International Law-Making' (1992) 12 AYBIL 22, 52–53. (As Chinkin argues: 'The use of soft law instruments has presented a challenge to the normative structure, the traditional sources, the subjects and subject matter of international law. The international legal order is an evolving one that requires a wide range of modalities for change and development, especially into new subject areas. The participants within the decentralised international legal system do not have available for use the legislative processes or other sophisticated techniques for change that typically exist in domestic legal systems. They must draw upon the entire continuum of mechanisms ranging from the traditional international legal forms to the soft law instruments. Labeling those instruments as law or non-law disguises the realty that both play a major role in the development of international law and both are needed for the regulation of States' activities and for the creation of expectations. Soft law instruments allow for the incorporation of conflicting standards and goals and provide States with the room to manoeuvre in the making of claims and counterclaims. While this process inevitably causes normative confusion and uncertainty in terms of the traditional sources of international law, it is probably the inevitable consequence of unresolved pressures for change in international law'. According to Dupuy: "Soft" law is not merely a new term for an old (customary) process; it is both a sign and a product of the permanent state of multilateral cooperation and competition among the heterogeneous members of the contemporary world community. The existence of "soft" law compels us to re-evaluate the general international law-making process and, in doing so, illuminates the difficulty of explaining this phenomenon by referring solely to the classical

of normativity and a large grey zone between what is law and what is not law'.[252] The proponents of soft law have pointed out that 'the use of a treaty does not itself ensure a hard obligation', there being many treaties that are devoid of legal content.[253] Soft law instruments are concluded by States to combine collective regulation and restraint with flexibility and freedom to respond to 'events and changing circumstances'.[254] From this angle, 'drawing a formal distinction between hard and soft obligations is less important than understanding the process at work within the law-making environment and the products that flow from it'.[255] It would thus be a mistake to dismiss soft law 'as not law and therefore of no importance': soft law is 'an element in the law-making process precisely *because it leads to law*, not to something less than law'[256] and overall, soft law norms make an important contribution towards the progressive development of international law.[257]

In light of the above discussion, the argument made here is not that the soft instruments examined in this chapter already *are* international law, as envisaged in Article 38(a), (b) and (c) of the Statute of the International Court of Justice, the argument is that those instruments, taken cumulatively, *can influence* the development international law. The way new legal principles emerge in international law is either by treaty, custom or as a general principle of

---

theory of formal sources of public international law.' Pellet states that 'the evil comes from the incapacity – or unwillingness – of lawyers to accept law as it is – to consent to it, "in her infinite variety"'.).

[252] Pauwelyn (n 249) 128; Dinah Shelton, 'Law, Non-Law and the Problem of "Soft-Law"' in Dinah Shelton (ed), *Commitment and Compliance: The Role of Non-binding Norms in the International Legal System* (Oxford University Press 2003) 10.

[253] Boyle (n 241) 126–128; Chinkin, 'The Challenge of Soft Law' (n 239) 851; Oscar Schachter, 'The Twilight Existence of Nonbinding International Agreements' (1977) 71 Am. J. Int. Law 296.

[254] Chinkin, 'The Challenge of Soft Law' (n 239) 853; Chinkin, 'Normative Development in the International Legal System' (n 240) 22; GC Shaffer and MA Pollack, 'Hard vs. Soft Law: Alternatives, Complements, and Antagonists in International Governance' (2010) 94 Minn. L. Rev. 706.

[255] Chinkin, 'Normative Development in the International Legal System' (n 240) 23; H Hillgenberg, 'A Fresh Look at Soft Law' (1999) 10 Eur. J. Int. Law 499.

[256] Boyle (n 241) 119. (Emphasis added).

[257] Shelton (n 252) 1; Mauro Barelli, 'The Role of Soft Law in the International Legal System: The Case of the United Nations Declaration on the Rights of Indigenous Peoples' (2009) 58 Int'l & Comp. L.Q. 957; Elena Baylis, 'The International Law Commission's Soft Law Influence' (2019) 13 Fla. Int'l U. L. Rev. 1007. (Shelton argues that 'non-binding norms have complex and potentially large impact in the development of international law. Customary law, for example, one of the main sources of international legal obligation, requires compliance (state practice) not only as a result of the obligation, but as a constitutive, essential part of the process by which law is formed'.).

law.[258] Those are the primary sources of international law, as defined in Article 38(a), (b) and (c) of the Statute of the International Court of Justice.[259] Since there is no treaty yet that deals with the issue of SOEs and human rights,[260] this task would fall onto the development of custom:

> Once a prospective norm has been formulated in soft form it can become a catalyst for the development of customary international law. To many commentators this is the *raison d'etre* of soft law and its entry point into the traditional sources of law.[261]

Consequently, there is a clear possibility that customary norms *could* form in this area. For example, custom could develop to the effect that States have specific obligations – as a matter of international law – to take additional steps to ensure that the entities they own or control respect human rights. The advantage of customary international law is that it would be applicable to all States, which ultimately gives a wider coverage of the subject matter in question.[262] The development of new legal principles by way of custom is explained in Article 38(1)(b) of the Statute of the International Court of Justice as 'international custom, as evidence of a general practice accepted as law'. The first element in the formation of customary international law is 'general practice', while the second entails that the general practice must have been 'accepted as law'.[263] In *Nicaragua*, the ICJ made the following remark with regard to the formation of customary international law:

---

[258] H Thirlway, *The Sources of International Law* (Oxford University Press 2014) 3–8.

[259] Statute of the International Court of Justice 1946. The secondary sources of international law (judicial decisions and the teaching of most highly qualified publicists) are addressed in Article 38(d).

[260] For example, references to 'State-owned enterprises' only appeared in the Second Revised Draft of the Legally Binding Instrument to Regulate, in International Human Rights Law, the Activities of Transnational Corporations and Other Business Enterprises (6 August 2020). The two earlier versions (Revised Draft, Legally Binding Instrument to Regulate, in International Human Rights Law, the Activities of Transnational Corporations and Other Business Enterprises (16 July 2019) and the Legally Binding Instrument to Regulate, in International Human Rights Law, the Activities of Transnational Corporations and Other Business Enterprises (Zero Draft 16 July 2018)) made no reference whatsoever to State-owned enterprises.

[261] Chinkin, 'Normative Development in the International Legal System' (n 240) 32.

[262] Thirlway (n 258) 56.

[263] International Law Commission, 'Draft Conclusions on Identification of Customary International Law, with Commentaries, 2018 (A/73/10)' (2018) 124–129, 133. (Conclusion 6: Forms of Practice states that '(1) Practice may take a wide range of forms. It includes both physical and verbal acts. It may, under certain circumstances, include inaction. (2) Forms of State practice include, but are not limited to: diplomatic acts and correspondence; conduct in connection with resolutions adopted by an international organization or at an

[T]he Court has to emphasize that, as was observed in the *North Sea Continental Shelf* cases for a new customary rule to be formed, not only must the acts concerned 'amount to a settled practice', but they must be accompanied by the *opinio juris sive necessitatis*. Either the States taking such an action or other States in a position to react to it, must have behaved so that their conduct is 'evidence of a belief that the practice is rendered obligatory by the existence of a rule of law requiring it. The need for such a belief, i.e. the existence of a subjective element, is implicit in the very notion of the *opinio juris sive necessitatis*.[264]

In the *Colombian – Peruvian Asylum Case* the ICJ further stated that

the party which relies on a custom of this kind must prove that this custom is established in such a manner that it has become binding on the other Party ... [it must be proven that] the rule invoked by it is in accordance with a *constant and uniform usage practiced by the States in question*, and that this usage is the *expression of a right appertaining to the State* ... and a *duty*.[265]

As can be observed, the standards for the formation of customary international law are strict and while it cannot be presently argued that the various regulatory approaches discussed above represent customary international law, neither can it be denied that those instruments demonstrate an evolution in State practice in the area of State corporate ownership (e.g., State practice being the first element of customary law).[266] For example, unlike many standards, codes of conduct and other similar guidelines that stem from

---

intergovernmental conference; conduct in connection with treaties; executive conduct, including operational conduct "on the ground"; legislative and administrative acts; and decisions of national courts. (3) There is no predetermined hierarchy among the various forms of practice.').

[264] *Military and Paramilitary Activities in and against Nicaragua (Nicaragua v United States of America)* (International Court of Justice, Merits, Judgment ICJ Reports 1986, p 14) [207].

[265] *Colombian-Peruvian Asylum Case* (International Court of Justice, Judgment, ICJ Reports 1950, p 266) 276. (Emphasis added).

[266] International Law Commission, 'Draft Conclusions on Identification of Customary International Law, with Commentaries, 2018 (A/73/10)' (n 263) 130–131. (The commentary to Conclusion 4 'Requirement of Practice' clarifies that 'it is primarily the practice of States that is to be looked at in determining the content and rules of customary international law'. However, 'in certain cases' the practice of international organisations also contributes to the formation and expression of rules of customary international law ... international organisations serving as arenas or catalysts for the practice of States'. The words 'in certain cases' in paragraph 2 indeed serve to indicate that the practice of international organizations will not be relevant to the identification of all rules of customary international law, and further that it may be the practice of only some, not all, international organizations that is relevant'.).

informal sources,[267] the UNGPs have been unanimously endorsed by the UN Human Rights Council, an inter-governmental body within the UN system that is made up of forty-seven States that are responsible for the promotion and protection of all human rights worldwide. As discussed at the outset of this chapter, the influence of the UNGPs across various areas of international and domestic law is unquestionable and 'if ever a UN document has made that mystical journey from policy to soft law, it is the UNGPs'.[268] In terms of 'norm targets',[269] it is also telling that the State-business nexus (UNGPs 4, 5 and 6) can be found in Pillar I, which focuses on the State duty to protect human rights. Similarly, the OECD Guidelines for Multinational Enterprises and the OECD Guidelines on the Corporate Governance of SOEs are equally known standards that stem from the OECD, an international organisation with thirty-seven member States. The OECD Guidelines on the Corporate Governance of SOEs are recommendations that are directed *to* governments. The EITI

---

[267] See in general Joost Pauwelyn, Ramses A Wessel and Jan Wouters (eds), *Informal International Lawmaking* (1st edn, Oxford University Press 2012); Eyal Benvenisti, *The Law of Global Governance* (Brill Nijhoff 2014); Martti Koskenniemi, 'Global Governance and Public International Law' (2004) 37 Kritische Justiz 241; Chinkin, 'Normative Development in the International Legal System' (n 240) 30; International Law Commission, 'Draft Conclusions on Identification of Customary International Law, with Commentaries, 2018 (A/73/10)' (n 263) 132. (The Draft Conclusions on Identification of Customary International Law make it clear that 'the conduct of entities other than States and international organizations – for example, non-governmental organizations (NGOs) and private individuals, but also transnational corporations and non-State armed groups – is neither creative nor expressive of customary international law. As such, their conduct does not contribute to the formation, or expression, of rules of customary international law, and may not serve as direct (primary) evidence of the existence and content of such rules. The paragraph recognizes, however, that such conduct may have an indirect role in the identification of customary international law, by stimulating or recording the practice and acceptance as law (*opinio juris*) of States and international organizations. For example, the acts of private individuals may sometimes be relevant to the formation or expression of rules of customary international law, but only to the extent that States have endorsed or reacted to them'.) (Footnotes omitted).

[268] Ratner (n 34) 164.

[269] Chinkin, 'Normative Development in the International Legal System' (n 240) 35–36. ('The targets of soft law are equally diverse. They include states, businesses and trade institutions, NGOs, IGOs, officials of IGOs, government officials, and individuals. Soft law that is targeted at private actors cannot be transformed into customary international law as it has no intended impact upon state behaviour. It may be used specifically to target private actors, including corporations, in ways that would not be possible through treaties, especially in legal systems that have no doctrine of self-executing treaties. Soft law thus straddles, international (traditionally targeted at states) and national (traditionally targeted at individuals) regulation and fills gaps. In this way, it can be seen as a "bridge" between international legality and legitimacy. The response of the target is all important in establishing that legitimacy and, where states are the target, in transforming the principles into binding international obligations.') (Footnotes omitted).

standard to promote transparency and accountability in the extractive industries is implemented directly by States, which need to meet certain requirements on transparency and accountability in order to achieve satisfactory
progress. The ILO Tripartite Declaration is the outcome of a negotiated
solution between governments, employers and workers' organisations, which
was first adopted in 1977. Since then, it has undergone significant revisions in
2000, 2006 and 2017 and it is largely based on principles contained in the ILO
Conventions and Recommendations. The Santiago Principles promote transparency, good governance, accountability and prudent investment practices in
SWFs and are endorsed by leading sovereign wealth funds from 34 States,
while the UN Global Compact, the world's largest sustainability initiative, has
been joined by 157 States. The WTO Agreement on Government
Procurement is binding on State parties, while the EU Public Procurement
Directives are binding on EU Members States. Furthermore, particular notice
must be taken of the measures that States have taken to regulate their own
SOEs: Sweden's State Ownership Policy and Guidelines for SOEs, Norway's
State Ownership Policy and the 10 Principles for Corporate Governance,
China's Guidelines to SOEs on fulfilling Corporate Social Responsibility
and the Guidelines for Social Responsibility in Outbound Mining
Investment (which expressly incorporate the UNGPs) and Spain's,
Portugal's, New Zealand's, Australia's and Finland's corporate social responsibility requirements for SOEs demonstrate how a specific State practice is
currently developing in this area. Even in the context of the corporate social
responsibility of multinationals in general, it has been suggested that there is
clear evidence that customary law principles may be already emerging in
respect of several issues such as minimum international health, safety and
environmental standards, supply chain responsibility, sustainable development, obligations to warn and to consult, environmental impact assessments,
openness and transparency and external monitoring.[270] Zerk argues that

> although most of the 'soft law' initiatives . . . are explicitly non-binding, they
> are still legally significant . . . as a way of testing attitudes, developing consen-
> sus around an issue and shaping future norms. Already, a number of themes
> are emerging from international 'soft law' initiatives, which could well form
> the foundations of future international rules on CSR. Some of these could
> possibly emerge as customary principles, though others are more likely to be
> features of treaty-based regimes.[271]

---

[270] Jennifer A Zerk, *Multinationals and Corporate Social Responsibility: Limitations and
Opportunities in International Law* (1st pbk. edn, Cambridge University Press 2011) 262–277.
[271] ibid 263.

The ICJ made the following comments in relation to the emergence of new norms and standards relating to the environment:

> [N]ew norms and standards have been developed, set forth in a great number of instruments during the last two decades. Such new norms have to be taken into consideration, and such new standards given proper weight, not only when States contemplate new activities but also when continuing with activities begun in the past.[272]

Another point that must be considered is 'whose practice, and whose *opinio juris* is relevant to the inquiry?'[273]

> One thing that can be stated with certainty is that unanimity among all States is not a requirement, either in the sense that all States must have been shown to have participated in it, or in the sense that there is evidence that the *opinio*, the view that it is a binding custom is held by all States.[274]

Just as in the law of maritime delimitation, States that do not possess a coastline are unable to participate in the practice of maritime delimitation, nor would States that do not have SOEs or those that do not receive sovereign investment. What does seem to be important, however, is that States 'whose interests are particularly affected'[275] participate (e.g., the home and host State of the SOE) in this process. Furthermore, as Boyle argues, there is at least an element of good faith commitment, 'evidencing in some cases a desire to influence State practice or expressing some measure of law-making and progressive development'.[276] As such, there is at least a reasonable expectation that States that do endorse certain soft law instruments should comply with them.[277]

---

[272] *Gabčíkovo-Nagymaros Project (Hungary/Slovakia)* (International Court of Justice, Judgment, ICJ Reports 1997, p 7) [140].

[273] Thirlway (n 258) 59.

[274] ibid 64.

[275] *North Sea Continental Shelf* (International Court of Justice, Judgment, ICJ Reports 1969, p 3) [74]; International Law Commission, 'Draft Conclusions on Identification of Customary International Law, with Commentaries, 2018 (A/73/10)' (n 263) 136. ('The requirement that the practice be "widespread and representative" does not lend itself to exact formulations, as circumstances may vary greatly from one case to another (for example, the frequency with which circumstances calling for action arise . . . . Thus, in assessing generality, an indispensable factor to be taken into account is the extent to which those States that are particularly involved in the relevant activity or are most likely to be concerned with the alleged rule ("specially affected States") have participated in the practice.').

[276] Boyle (n 241) 120. (Quoting the Separate Opinion of Judge Lauterpacht in *Voting Procedure on Questions relating to Reports and Petitions concerning the Territory of South West Africa, Advisory Opinion*, ICJ Reports 1955 4, 118 ('The State in question, while not bound to accept the recommendation, is bound to give it due consideration in good faith.').

[277] Barelli (n 257) 960.

3.7 INTERIM CONCLUSION

This chapter has demonstrated that SOEs inhabit a complex and dynamic regulatory landscape. To this extent, various types of instruments, with different degrees of 'legal significance and effectiveness'[278] and at various levels (e.g., international, regional and domestic) have been used to address the human rights challenges associated with State corporate ownership. While it is important to assess each instrument on its own merits in order to discover its particular strength and weaknesses, most will be gained by taking in a broad view that looks beyond the formal aspects of each instrument. For this purpose, the context, the challenges that it sought to address, its content and the institutional background of each particular instrument are overall more important than whether an instrument is classified as hard or soft law. Another factor that must be considered is the interplay between the various hard and soft instruments and also between the various levels of regulation. For example, it has been shown that international instruments (e.g., the UNGPs) have been incorporated not only in other international standards (e.g., the OECD Guidelines for Multinational Enterprises, the ILO Tripartite Declaration, etc.) but have also influenced the overall practice of several States and the development of other hard and soft instruments. Cumulatively taken, the soft law instruments and the evolution and change in State practice can be expected to have an impact on the development of customary international law in this area. To be sure, soft law being the 'trouble maker' that it is, poses serious challenges to the traditional structure of international law, but at the same time it offers opportunities for evolution, change and expansion into new subject areas.[279] While Chapter 2 has shown that the conceptualisation of *who* can be a 'subject' of international law is not static, but that it depends 'upon the needs of the community', it would be logical to say that *what* can become part of international law reflects the same needs.

---

[278] ibid 983.
[279] Chinkin, 'The Challenge of Soft Law' (n 239) 866. For example, Chinkin argues that soft law challenges the normative structure, the traditional sources, the subjects and subject matter of international law.

4

Fundamental Change in International Law

State Immunity and State-Owned Entities

4.1 INTRODUCTION

State immunity presents itself as a unique challenge with respect to SOEs because if an SOE pleads immunity, a domestic court could be barred from either adjudicating the dispute in question or from enforcing a judgment that has been obtained against an SOE. State immunity could thus leave victims without a method to access justice, or without an effective remedy, if the judgment that was obtained cannot be enforced. With a focus on immunity from adjudication, this chapter begins with an introduction to the doctrine of State immunity and the evolution from absolute immunity to restrictive immunity. Since the privileges associated with immunity are only accorded to States, the chapter examines next the circumstances in which SOEs will be assimilated into the State and the related issue of piercing the corporate veil. While, in general, courts respect the separate legal personality of an entity, the corporate veil will be pierced when an entity is an *alter ego* of the government or when the separateness of an entity would result in fraud or injustice. The analysis then turns to an examination of some of the techniques devised for distinguishing between acts *jure imperii* and acts *jure gestionis* such as the 'purpose', 'nature' or 'context' of a particular transaction. Next, the chapter deals with the exceptions to immunity and commences by looking at some of the 'established' exceptions to immunity such as the commercial transactions exception and the non-commercial tort exception and their relevance to SOEs, then continues by asking whether there is a human rights exception to State immunity. The overall purpose of this chapter is to demonstrate how the increased participation of States in economic activities, through their SOEs, has fundamentally changed the fabric of international law through a 'redefinition' of the functions of the State and ultimately that of the concept of sovereignty itself.[1]

4.2 GENERAL COMMENTS ON STATE IMMUNITY

State immunity is a principle of international law whereby a State and its emanations are presumed to enjoy 'exemption from or non-amenability to any outside authority, be it national or international, and whether legislative, administrative or judicial'.[2] Immunities are conferred in order to 'ensure an orderly allocation and exercise of jurisdiction in accordance with international law in proceedings concerning States, to respect the sovereign equality of States and to permit the effective performance of the functions of persons who act on behalf of States'.[3] Although this very issue – whether under international law States are generally entitled to immunity – has been debated for a long time,[4] in the *Jurisdictional Immunities Case*, the ICJ settled this matter by clarifying that State immunity is part of customary international law.[5] State immunity is a plea which, when invoked, acts as a bar to the adjudicatory and enforcement powers of a court or other adjudicatory body. Immunity from jurisdiction acts as a bar to the adjudicatory powers of a court, while immunity from enforcement relates to the enforcement of judgments against the property of a State. In the case of immunity from jurisdiction, the

[1] Xiaodong Yang, *State Immunity in International Law* (Cambridge University Press 2012) 8.
[2] ibid 1–2.
[3] Hazel Fox, 'Resolution on the Immunity from Jurisdiction of the State and of Persons Who Act on Behalf of the State in Case of International Crimes (Napoli Session)' (Institut de Droit International 2009) 1.
[4] H Lauterpacht, 'The Problem of Jurisdictional Immunities of Foreign States' (1951) 28 Brit. YB Int'l L. 220, 228. ('The view that there is at present no rule of international law which obliges states to grant jurisdictional immunity to other states is, admittedly, unorthodox and, being at variance with the view almost uniformly expressed in textbooks, at first sight startling.').
[5] *Jurisdictional Immunities of the State (Germany v Italy : Greece intervening)* (International Court of Justice, Judgment, ICJ Reports 2012, p 99) [57]. ('The Court considers that the rule of State immunity occupies an important place in international law and international relations. It derives from the principle of sovereign equality of States, which, as Article 2, paragraph 1 of the Charter of the United Nations makes clear, is one of the fundamental principles of the international legal order. This principle has to be viewed together with the principle that each State possesses sovereignty over its own territory and that there flows from that sovereignty the jurisdiction of the State over events and persons within that territory. Exceptions to the immunity of the State may represent a departure from the principle of sovereign equality. Immunity may represent a departure from the principle of territorial sovereignty and the jurisdiction which flows from it.'). For a more nuanced view of the legal basis for immunity see Yang (n 1) 44–58.

ICJ clarified the preliminary nature of this plea in the *Jurisdictional Immunities Case*:

> Immunity from jurisdiction is an immunity not merely from being subjected to an adverse judgment but from being subjected to the trial process. *It is, therefore, necessarily preliminary in nature.* Consequently, a national court is required to determine whether or not a foreign State is entitled to immunity as a matter of international law before it can hear the merits of the case brought before it and before the facts have been established. If immunity were to be dependent upon the State actually having committed a serious violation of international human rights law or the law of armed conflict, then it would become necessary for the national court to hold an enquiry into the merits in order to determine whether it had jurisdiction. If, on the other hand, the mere allegation that the State had committed such wrongful acts were to be sufficient to deprive the State of its entitlement to immunity, immunity could, in effect be negated simply by skillful construction of the claim.[6]

The characterisation of State immunity as preliminary and procedural in nature, has been criticised in some of the dissenting opinions[7] in the *Jurisdictional Immunities Case*, as well as in academic commentary.[8] The crux of the argument is that by regarding immunity as preliminary in nature, there is a disconnect from the substantive rules that govern the existence and nature of the wrongful act in question. Overall, the adoption of this technique has supported a finding that State immunity trumps even the rules of *jus cogens*.[9] However, as Orakhelashvili clarifies, the preliminary or procedural

---

[6] ibid 82. (Emphasis added).

[7] *Jurisdictional Immunities of the State (Germany v Italy: Greece intervening)* (n 5) (Dissenting Opinion of Judge Cançado Trindade at [294, 295]: 'To me the separation between procedural and substantive law is not ontologically or deontologically viable: *la forme conforme le fond.* Legal procedure is not an end in itself, it is a means to the realization of justice. And the application of substantive law is *finaliste*, it purports to have justice done.').

[8] A Bianchi, 'Gazing at the Crystal Ball (Again): State Immunity and Jus Cogens beyond *Germany v Italy*' (2013) 4 J. Int. Dispute Settl. 457, 460.

[9] *Jurisdictional Immunities of the State (Germany v Italy: Greece intervening)* (n 5). (Dissenting Opinion of Judge Cançado Trindade at [296]: 'In the present Judgment, the Court's majority starts from the wrong assumption that no conflict exists, or can exist, between the substantive "rules of *jus cogens*" (imposing the prohibitions of the "murder of civilian in occupied territory, the deportation of civilian inhabitants to slave labour and the deportation of prisoners of war to slave labour") and the "procedural rules of State immunity". This tautological assumption leads the Court to its upholding of State immunity even in the grave circumstances of the present case. There is thus a material conflict, even though a formalist one may not be discernable. The fact remains that a conflict does exist, and the Court's reasoning leads to what I perceive as a groundless deconstruction of *jus cogens*, depriving the latter of its effects and legal consequences.') (Footnotes omitted).

nature of State immunity is still dependent 'on the substantive characterisation of the act in question as sovereign or non-sovereign'.[10] This is because the 'distinction between sovereign and non-sovereign acts cannot be affected by the "procedural" nature of immunities', since it is the substantive nature of the act that brings the bar into effect that must be identified before it can be determined whether the bar can be applied in the first place.[11]

State immunity has a long history and the writings on it are 'prolific'.[12] Initially a personal privilege that was afforded only to kings, who were free from suit and prosecution in their own courts, immunity went through a period of transformation, later becoming the immunity of the Crown.[13] The foundations of State immunity, as understood today, stem from the principles concerning the territorial jurisdiction and sovereign equality of States. Territorial jurisdiction and State immunity are interconnected in that State immunity reinforces the principle of exclusive territorial jurisdiction that States have over their own territory. In *The Schooner Exchange v M'Faddon*, one of the earliest cases addressing sovereign equality, Marshall CJ, of the US Supreme Court stated that

> perfect equality and absolute independence of sovereigns, and this common interest impelling them to mutual intercourse and an exchange of good offices with each other, have given rise to a class of cases in which every sovereign is understood to wave the exercise of a part of that complete exclusive territorial jurisdiction, which has been stated to be attributable of every nation.[14]

Initially, bar several exceptions,[15] State immunity had an 'absolute' character. Unless it consented to jurisdiction, a State was fully immune from the jurisdiction or enforcement powers of a court in all circumstances.[16] Absolute State immunity was *de rigueur* during the nineteenth and the first half of the

---

[10] Alexander Orakhelashvili, 'Jurisdictional Immunities of the State' (2012) 106 Am. J. Int. Law 609, 613–614.

[11] ibid.

[12] H Fox and P Webb, *The Law of State Immunity* (3rd edn, Oxford University Press 2013) 2.

[13] George W Pugh, 'Historical Approach to the Doctrine of Sovereign Immunity' (1953) 13 La. L. Rev. 476, 476–478.

[14] *The Schooner Exchange v M'Fadden* (United States, Supreme Court, 11 US (7 Cranch) 116 (1812)).

[15] For instance, exceptions to State immunity have always existed in the case of immovable property, which has been regarded as forming part of the territory of the forum State. Furthermore, States could always wave immunity, if they so desired.

[16] *The Parlement Belge* (United Kingdom (1880) LR 5 PD 197). (According to Brett LJ, sovereign immunity came from 'the character of the sovereign authority, its high dignity, whereby it is not subject to any authority of any kind'.).

twentieth century.[17] In the second half of the twentieth century, however, a shift occurred, whereby as a result in the increase in State trading, it was considered that, by virtue of adherence to absolute State immunity, SOEs may have an advantage over POEs.[18] Consequently, many States had started to adhere to the restrictive view of State immunity:

> The growing participation of States in international economic activities fundamentally transformed the functions of the State and that transformation resulted in a vastly different conception of the State. With the steadily increasing volume of commercial and other dealings between States and foreign private persons on an equal footing came the gradually diminishing justifiability of a State's assertion of immunity vis-à-vis a valid claim based on such dealings in a foreign court. In this sense, the evolution of the doctrine of restrictive immunity has witnessed and to a certain extent contributed to a redefinition of sovereign activities and therefore of sovereignty, and has ultimately even led to an encroachment of the area traditionally regarded as typically sovereign.[19]

Under the 'restrictive' approach, immunity is still available for acts which involve the exercise of governmental authority (*acta jure imperii*), but not, among others, for those acts where the State is engaging in commercial activities (*acta jure gestionis*).[20] Nevertheless, the current trend towards restrictive immunity from adjudication is not entirely reflected in the case of immunity from enforcement. The Yukos saga is an illustrative case in this area[21] and 'short of resort to war, there is therefore little alternative even today

---

[17] Yang (n 1) 3, 19–20.

[18] Hazel Fox, 'The Restrictive Rule of State Immunity: The 1970s Enactment and Its Contemporary Status' in Tom Ruys and Nicolas Angelet (eds), *The Cambridge Handbook of Immunities and International Law* (Cambridge University Press 2019) 22; Yang (n 1) 20; Wenhua Shan and Peng Wang, 'Divergent Views on State Immunity in the International Community', in Nicolas Angelet and Luca Ferro (eds), *The Cambridge Handbook of Immunities and International Law* (Cambridge University Press 2019).

[19] Yang (n 1) 3, 8, 19.

[20] MN Shaw, *International Law* (Cambridge University Press 2008) 509.

[21] Tom Ruys, Nicolas Angelet and Luca Ferro, 'Introduction – International Immunities in a State of Flux?', in Nicolas Angelet and Luca Ferro (eds), *The Cambridge Handbook of Immunities and International Law* (Cambridge University Press 2019) 2; Fox, 'The Restrictive Rule of State Immunity: The 1970s Enactment and Its Contemporary Status' (n 18) 32. (Following the arbitral award in Yukos, the Russian Federation was required to pay $50 billion to former stockholders of the Yukos oil company. The enforcement proceedings have brought changes to laws in France and Russia. In France, through the Sapin II law (Loi 2016-1691), the French Code of Civil Enforcement Procedures is amended by the introduction of Articles L. 111-1-1–111-1-3. The net effect of the new measures is that it is more difficult to enforce against State property. For example, Article L.111-1-1 states that 'Provisional or enforcement measures cannot be applied to the property of a foreign State unless there is a prior authorization from a

but to make settlement of judgment debts with the cooperation of the debtor State and by diplomatic means'.[22] Thus, even if an injured party manages to bring a State before a court or other international adjudicatory body, the challenge of enforcing the resulting judgment could make the whole process a 'pyrrhic' victory. The practice of States demonstrates that the turn towards restrictive State immunity has started as a 'slow, gradual and yet irreversible'[23] shift, rather than an overnight change and that it has taken many years to accomplish.[24] Restrictive State immunity is now 'on its way to becoming a significant principle of customary international law',[25] although some commentators have questioned whether this development reflects general international law. Orakhelashvili argues that

> the 'general rule versus specific exceptions' approach is endorsed in national statutes on State immunity and in treaties that are either not in force or have a rather low ratification status, but it has not been recognised as being part of general international law. UK courts have repeatedly recognised that the State Immunity Act of 1978 does not represent the restrictive immunity doctrine, but instead endorses the absolute doctrine of State immunity which is then qualified by exceptions stated in the statutory text. National statues

---

judge in an *ex parte* order'. Article L. 111-1-2 states that enforcement measures may only be granted if 'the State concerned has expressly consented to the application of such a measure ... reserved or affected this property to the satisfaction of the claim which is the purpose of the proceedings', or if 'the property in question is specifically in use or intended to be used by the State concerned for purposes unrelated to non-commercial public service and is linked to the entity against which the proceedings are initiated'. Article L.111-1-3 further states that diplomatic property is immune from enforcement *unless* a special and express waiver was given to enforce against it. The 2016 Russian Law on Jurisdictional Immunity of a Foreign State and a Foreign State's Property (Federal Law No. 297-FZ (2015) deals with the application of rules pertaining to immunity from jurisdiction and immunity from enforcement over property owned by foreign States in Russia and it largely operates through reciprocity.).

[22] Fox and Webb (n 12) 479, 481. ('Whilst the restrictive doctrine has laid open a wide area of procedural and substantive law to enable national courts to exercise jurisdiction over foreign States in respect of commercial transactions, State immunity continues to bar to a very large extent the enforcement of judgments given by such courts against foreign States. In the absence of the consent of the State, UNCSI Part IV sets out in respect of State property a rule of immunity from execution in respect of both pre-judgment and post-judgment enforcement save in respect of narrowly defined categories of property. Again and again thwarted judgment creditors have sought to attach assets of foreign States within the forum State territory, only to be refused orders for execution by national courts. Not surprisingly, Professor Sucharitkul, the ILC's first Special Rapporteur, described immunity from execution as 'the last fortress, the last bastion of State sovereignty.').

[23] Yang (n 1) 32.

[24] ibid 11–19.

[25] Fox, 'The Restrictive Rule of State Immunity: The 1970s Enactment and Its Contemporary Status' (n 18) 30.

apply only within national legal systems and do not, as such, indicate what the position under international law is. There are currently only a few States that have national legislation on State immunity, and thus the 'general immunity versus special exceptions' pattern those statues adhere to cannot be seen as representative of the international legal position on this matter.[26]

The earliest recorded case where a court endorsed restrictive State immunity is from Belgium in 1879, with Italy following in 1903, Austria in 1907, Switzerland in 1918, Greece in 1928, Germany in 1963, France in 1969, the United States in 1952 as a result of the Tate letter[27] and the UK in 1977 with the decision in the *Philippine Admiral*[28] which was followed in 1978 by the State Immunity Act.[29] Thus, 'when discussing the rule of State immunity during the twentieth century, one should always describe the situation in terms of two opposing practices: some courts would grant absolute immunity to foreign States whereas others would limit that immunity to a greater or lesser degree'.[30] Most States now adopt restrictive immunity with the notable exceptions, among others, of China,[31] Brazil,[32] Bulgaria, the Czech Republic, Poland, Romania[33] and Russia.[34] Nevertheless, it must be recalled that even in cases where a State still adheres to absolute immunity,

> it is national courts that determine the theory and practice of State immunity; and at present it is their unanimous position that foreign States only enjoy limited or restricted immunity. What is under debate is only the extent to which that immunity ought to be restricted. That is, a State enjoys immunity

---

[26] Alexander Orakhelashvili, 'Jurisdictional Immunities of States and General International Law: Explaining the Jus Gestionis v. Jus Imperii Divide' in Tom Ruys and Nicolas Angelet (eds), *The Cambridge Handbook of Immunities and International Law* (Cambridge University Press 2019) 109.

[27] RM Jarvis 'The Tate Letter: Some Words Regarding Its Authorship' (2015) 55 Am. J. Legal Hist. 465.

[28] *The Philippine Admiral* (United Kingdom, [1977] AC 373) 402. ('In this country – and no doubt in most other countries in the western world – the state can be sued in its own courts on commercial contracts into which it has entered and there is no apparent reason why foreign states should not be equally liable to be sued in respect of such transactions.').

[29] State Immunity Act 1978.

[30] Yang (n 1) 3.

[31] *Democratic Republic of Congo v FG Hemisphere Associates LLC* (Hong Kong Special Administrative Region, Court of Final Appeal, [2011] HKCFA 43 (8 June 2011)); *Russell Jackson et al v People's Republic of China* (United States District Court for the Northern District of Alabama 794 F2d 1490 (11th Cir 1986)); Shan and Wang (n 18) 63.

[32] Shaw (n 20) 514.

[33] Fox and Webb (n 12) 161.

[34] Law on Jurisdictional Immunity of a Foreign State and a Foreign State's Property (2016) (Federation Federal Law No. 297-FZ (2015)).

from legal proceedings before national courts in some cases but not in others; what matters now is not *whether* State immunity should be limited, but *when* and *how*.[35]

Initially, State immunity emerged mainly from domestic case law, but later on other sources such as treaties, national legislation, statements by governments and scholarly opinions became equally important to the development of this doctrine.[36] One of the most interesting aspects of State immunity is that there is a high degree of cross-fertilization in the practice of courts across the world with 'constant references to cases decided by foreign national courts, arbitral tribunals and other authorities'.[37] Consequently, overall, the sources of the law of State immunity are mixed and both domestic and international law are relevant,[38] but international law 'leaves national law (and judicial practice) a wide measure of discretion as to the specific circumstances in which foreign State immunity is to be given effect'.[39] This is because immunity

> is a doctrine of international law which is applied in accordance with national law in local courts. Its requirements are governed by international law but the individual national law of the State before whose courts a claim another State is made determines the precise extent and manner of application .... Consequently, the law of State immunity is a mix of international and national law. This interaction complicates the law relating to State immunity and creates considerable tensions.[40]

At the international level, the main sources of the law of State immunity are custom;[41] treaties, such as the UN Convention on the Jurisdictional

---

[35] Yang (n 1) 3.
[36] ibid 26.
[37] ibid 27.
[38] Lori Fisler Damrosch, 'The Sources of Immunity Law: Between International and Domestic Law' in Tom Ruys and Nicolas Angelet (eds), *The Cambridge Handbook of Immunities and International Law* (Cambridge University Press 2019); Orakhelashvili, 'Jurisdictional Immunities of States and General International Law' (n 26) 111–112. (Orakhelashvili cautions that in cases where the practice of domestic courts 'openly and professedly' place domestic 'legal standards over the criteria elaborated under international comity or international law, cannot sensibly be seen as part of State practice that contributes to the development of international legal aspects of State immunity'. The practice of a group of States in this area might, nevertheless, still be seen as 'contributing to the creation of a new rule of customary international law'.).
[39] Yang (n 1) 43.
[40] Fox and Webb (n 12) 1.
[41] Damrosch (n 38) 46–47. ('National practice relevant to ascertaining rules of customary international law on immunities can emanate from the judicial, executive or legislative organs of States .... *Opinio juris*, the subjective belief as to whether a given practice entails legal obligation, can equally emanate from judicial, executive or legislative organs.').

Immunities of States and their Property (UNCSI),[42] which although it has not yet entered into force, has codified the existing customary international law in this area;[43] the European Convention on State Immunity (ECSI);[44] the practice of international courts and tribunals and the contributions of bodies such as the International Law Commission, the Institut de Droit International and the International Law Association.[45] The ICJ has dealt with immunities four times since 2002: in the *Arrest Warrant of 11 April 2000 (Democratic Republic of the Congo v Belgium)*,[46] in the *Obligation to Prosecute or Extradite (Belgium v Senegal)*,[47] in the *Jurisdictional Immunities of the State Case (Germany v Italy, Greece Intervening)*[48] and in the *Immunities and Criminal Proceedings (Equatorial Guinea v France)*,[49] with another case currently pending in the ICJ.[50] Notable domestic legislation includes the US Foreign Sovereign Immunities Act 1976 (US FSIA),[51] the United Kingdom State Immunity Act 1978 (UK SIA)[52] and Australia's Foreign States Immunities Act 1985 (AU FSIA) which will be analysed in Section 4.3.[53] Where present, immunity statutes are likely to provide the exclusive basis for the commencement of legal action against a foreign State.[54]

4.3 SEPARATE ENTITIES AND STATE IMMUNITY

Since the privileges associated with immunity are only accorded to a State, this section will examine in what circumstances SOEs will be assimilated into the State. This analysis is necessary because a State can be 'brought before a

---

[42] United Nations Convention on Jurisdictional Immunities of States and Their Property 2004.

[43] UNCSI has been ratified by twenty-two States: Austria, Equatorial Guinea, Czech Republic, Finland, France, Iran, Iraq, Italy, Japan, Kazakhstan, Latvia, Lebanon, Liechtenstein, Mexico, Norway, Portugal, Romania, Saudi Arabia, Slovakia, Spain, Sweden and Switzerland.

[44] European Convention on State Immunity 1972.

[45] Damrosch (n 38).

[46] *Arrest Warrant of 11 April 2000 (Democratic Republic of the Congo v Belgium)* (International Court of Justice, Judgment, ICJ Reports 2002, p 3). Hereinafter the *Arrest Warrant Case*.

[47] *Questions relating to the Obligation to Prosecute or Extradite (Belgium v Senegal)* (International Court of Justice, Judgment, ICJ Reports 2012, p 422).

[48] *Jurisdictional Immunities of the State (Germany v Italy: Greece intervening)* (n 5). Hereinafter the *Jurisdictional Immunities Case*.

[49] *Immunities and Criminal Proceedings (Equatorial Guinea v France)* (International Court of Justice, General List No 163, 2016).

[50] *Certain Iranian Assets (Islamic Republic of Iran v United States of America)* (International Court of Justice, General List No 164, 2016).

[51] Foreign Sovereign Immunities Act 1976 (United States).

[52] State Immunity Act 1978.

[53] Foreign States Immunities Act 1985 (Cth).

[54] Yang (n 1) 42–44.

court in various legal capacities and as several different entities'.[55] For example, from the point of view of international law, States are permitted to organise themselves, internally, as they see fit. On this point, the International Law Commission has stated that 'without a fixed prescription for State authority, international law has to accept, by and large, the actual systems adopted by States'.[56] The ICJ has expressly acknowledged this in the *Western Sahara Advisory Opinion* where it stated that 'no rule of international law ... requires the structure of a State to follow any particular pattern, as is evident from the diversity of the forms of States found in the world today'.[57] UNCSI defines a 'State' in Article 2(1)(b) as follows:

> (i) the State and its various organs of government; (ii) constituent units of a federal State or political subdivisions of the State which are entitled to perform acts in the exercise of the sovereign authority of the State, and are acting in that capacity; (iii) *agencies* or *instrumentalities* of the State and *other entities*, to the extent that they are entitled to perform and are actually performing acts in the exercise of the sovereign authority of the State; (iv) representatives of the State acting in that capacity. (Emphasis added.)

Domestic law also acknowledges that States may be composed of various political subdivisions, agencies or instrumentalities. The US FSIA defines in section 1603(b) a 'foreign State' to include a 'political subdivision of a foreign State or an *agency* or *instrumentality* of a foreign State'. The UK SIA states in section 14(1)(2) that any references to a State includes references to the 'sovereign or other head of that State in its public capacity', the government and any department of that State, but not any other separate entity, which is distinct from the executive organs of the government of that State and is capable of suing or being sued, *unless* that entity is exercising acts *jure imperii*. Australia adopts a similar approach to the UK in sections 1 and 11 of the AU FSIA and defines a 'foreign State' to include an 'independent sovereign State' or a separate territory, covering not only the head of the foreign State, and the executive government, but also all manner of political subdivisions such as provinces, states and self-governing territories. One could then imagine the organisation of a State as a structure, where at the very top there is the head of the State and the central government. Immediately below the pinnacle there is the middle of the structure, which is composed by political subdivisions,

---

[55] Fox and Webb (n 12) 336.

[56] International Law Commission, 'First Report on State Responsibility, by Mr. James Crawford, Special Rapporteur' (1998) DOCUMENT A/CN.4/490 and Add. 1–7* para 154.

[57] *Western Sahara (Advisory Opinion)* 12 (International Court of Justice, Advisory Opinion, ICJ Reports 1975, p 12) [94].

departments of State with separate legal personality and dependent territories. The last layer of the structure is composed of entities that have a separate legal personality such as State agencies, instrumentalities and SOEs.[58] This means that

> the availability of immunity turns on the identification or connection with the State: only the State itself, or an organ or individual identified or connected with the State can be entitled to immunity. One can at once see that immunity becomes more derivative in nature, the further away one moves from the State proper. Seen in this light, it is not difficult to conclude that an entity separate from the State itself enjoys immunity only when it is, or can be considered as being, endowed with certain attributes of the State, such as structurally forming part of the State apparatus and/or exercising certain functions normally entrusted only to a governmental department of the State.[59]

With this background in mind, the remainder of this section will examine two interconnected issues: first, in what circumstances can SOEs be assimilated into the State in order to enjoy immunity; and second, the circumstances under which the corporate veil will be pierced, resulting also in an SOE being assimilated into the State.

4.3.1 *Assimilating State-Owned Entities into the State*

According to US FSIA section 1603,

(a) A 'foreign State', except as used in section 1608 of this title, includes a political subdivision of a foreign state or an agency or instrumentality of a foreign state as defined in subsection (b).

(b) An 'agency or instrumentality of a foreign State' means any entity: (1) which is a separate legal person, corporate or otherwise, and (2) which is an organ of a foreign state or political subdivision thereof, or a majority of whose shares or other ownership interest is owned by a foreign state or political subdivision thereof, and (3) which is neither a citizen of a State of the United States as defined in section 1332 (c) and nor created under the laws of any third country.

---

[58] Joseph W Dellapenna, *Suing Foreign Governments and Their Corporations* (2nd edn, Transnational Publishers 2003).

[59] Yang (n 1) 230–231.

Under section 14 of the UK SIA,

(1) The immunities and privileges conferred by this Part of the Act apply to any foreign or commonwealth State other than the United Kingdom; and references to a State include references to: (a) the sovereign or other head of that State in his public capacity; (b) the government of that State; and (c) any department of that government, but not to any entity (hereafter referred to as a 'separate entity') which is distinct from the executive organs of the government of the State and capable of suing or being sued.

(2) A separate entity is immune from the from the jurisdiction of the courts of the United Kingdom, if and only if: (a) the proceedings relate to anything done by it in the exercise of sovereign authority; and (b) the circumstances are such that a State (or, in the case of proceedings to which section 10 above applies, a State which is not a party to the Brussels Convention) would have been so immune.

Section 3(3) of the AU FSIA states that a reference to a foreign State includes a reference to

(a) a province, state, self-governing territory or other political subdivision (by whatever name known) of a foreign State; (b) the head of a foreign State, or of a political subdivision of a foreign State in his or her public capacity; and (c) the executive government or part of the executive government of a foreign State or of a political subdivision of a foreign State, including a department or organ of the executive government of a foreign state or subdivision; but does not include a reference to a separate entity of a foreign State.

Section 3(1) of the AU FSIA defines the term 'separate entity' as follows:

In relation to a foreign State, means a natural person (other than an Australian citizen), or a body corporate or corporation sole (other than a body corporate or corporation sole that has been established by or under a law of Australia), who or that: (a) is an agency or instrumentality of the foreign State; and (b) is not a department or organ of the executive government of the foreign State.

It follows from the above that, on the one hand, under the US FSIA the presumption of immunity extends not only to the State itself, but also to its 'agencies and instrumentalities'. It is clear that the definition of 'agency or instrumentality' is broad enough to cover all manner of SOEs. Consequently, a US court will, as a first step, examine the *status* of the entity in question, then, as a second step it will look into the *conduct* or *the transaction* that has given rise to the lawsuit in order to determine if that particular conduct or transaction falls within one of the exceptions to immunity.[60] If the entity in question is found to be a State entity, then for immunity to be denied, the conduct in question must fall within one of the exceptions to immunity. On the other hand, the situation under the UK SIA, and to a certain extent under the AU FSIA, is the opposite. If an entity has a separate status, then it will be denied immunity, unless that entity can prove that it was in the exercise of an act *jure imperii*. An SOE will thus be denied immunity under the UK SIA and the AU FSIA *unless* it could prove that it was in the exercise of sovereign authority. Thus, if in the US FSIA the inquiry starts with the focus being on the *status* of the entity in question, under UK SIA and, to a certain extent, the AU FSIA, the focus is on the *separateness* of the entity and of the *act* in question. Despite this apparent divergence in approaches,

> in the final analysis, however, there does not seem to be much difference; for in all cases involving separate entities the courts must, and in practice do, consider all the relevant circumstances of the case before a sensible decision can be reached. A multifactor analysis thus seems to be the only viable test, regardless of the approaches purportedly taken in the practice of individual States.[61]

During the process of determining the *status* of an entity, courts have performed a detailed analysis of the constitution, functions, powers and activities of the entity in question. In addition, the following factors have also been taken into consideration: whether the entity in question was created by special law which prescribed its powers and duties; whether the board was selected by the government in accordance with a special law; whether the entity has separate legal personality; whether the entity had powers to hold or sell property and to sue and be sued; whether the entity was run as a distinct economic enterprise; whether the entity was subjected to the same budgetary and personnel requirements as government agencies; whether the entity was entirely or in majority owned by the foreign State; whether its status as a State entity was assumed or undisputed; whether the entity came from an economic system where State corporate ownership was common.[62] For example, in order to determine the status of the Central Bank of Nigeria in *Trendtex Trading Corporation v Central Bank of Nigeria*, Lord Denning MR stated that

---

[60] ibid 279.
[61] ibid 232.
[62] ibid 234.

I confess that I can think of no satisfactory test except that of looking to the functions and control of the organisation. I do not think that it should depend on foreign law alone. I would look at all the evidence to see whether the organisation was under governmental control and exercised governmental functions.[63]

According to Shaw LJ, the following features of the Central Bank of Nigeria supported his finding that it was not a department of the government of Nigeria:

It is, in the first place, a statutory corporation whose personality, powers and legal attributes are determined by the Central Bank of Nigeria Act 1958 and the amending enactments which followed. The totality of that legislation represents the intention and objectives of those who created and moulded it for the performance of its contemplated functions. If it was designed as a department of state, many titles indicative of that status come readily to mind. What was conferred upon it was the title of a bank. Nowhere in that legislation is it called anything but a bank; and not a 'Federal' or 'National' or 'State' bank but a 'Central' bank. The 52 sections of the principal Act and the several amending orders and enactments contain no direct indication that the bank is a department of the government and there are many indications which deny it that status. The very name has a commercial ring. Its powers do not identify it with the government and in some respects preclude identification with the government.[64]

In cases where it is clear that an entity is separate from the State, the inquiry turns to whether the entity in question has performed an act *jure imperii*. It must be emphasised that even in cases where an act is done by a separate State entity according to directions of the State, that entity will only be entitled to immunity if that particular act is characterised as *jure imperii*.[65] Since under the US FSIA the presumption of immunity is extended and expanded to include various 'agencies and instrumentalities', the first question that must be answered by the courts is whether that particular entity is actually an 'agency or an instrumentality', as defined under section 1603(b). Under section 1603(b), an entity classifies as an 'agency or instrumentality of a foreign State' if it is 'a separate legal person corporate or otherwise', which has close links with the State either as 'an organ of a foreign State', or as an entity whose 'majority shares or other ownership interest is owned by a foreign State' and

---

[63] *Trendtex Trading Corporation v Central Bank of Nigeria* (United Kingdom [1977] QB 529) 561.
[64] ibid 574–575. Per Shaw LJ.
[65] *Kuwait Airways Corp v Iraqi Airways Co (No. 1)* (United Kingdom, House of Lords, [1995] 1 WLR 1147) 1160. Per Lord Goff.

'which is neither a citizen of a State of the United States nor created under the laws of any third country'. Prima facie, the requirement for incorporation generally results in a presumption of separate judicial status, but the corporate veil can be pierced, as Section 4.3.2 shows, in cases of abuse, when the entity in question is in fact an *alter ego* of the government or where the maintenance of separate legal personality would result in fraud and injustice.[66] In *Transaero, Inc. v La Fuerza Aerea Boliviana*,[67] one of the main issues in dispute was whether the Bolivian Air Force was to be classified as a 'foreign State' or as an 'agency or instrumentality' under section 1608 of the US FSIA, which deals with the service of process. The classification under section 1608 ultimately depended upon whether the Bolivian Air Force was a 'separate legal person, corporate or otherwise' under section 1603(b)(1) of the US FSIA. To this end, the court developed the 'categorical approach' to distinguish between a 'foreign State' and an 'agency or instrumentality', by looking at whether the defendant is the type of entity that is an 'integral part of a foreign State's political structure [or rather] an entity whose structure is predominantly commercial'. After the application of this test, the court concluded that the Bolivian Air Force was a 'foreign State or political subdivision' of Bolivia.[68] The close links between an entity and the State were examined in the *Arbitration Between Trans Chem. Ltd. and China Nat. Machinery Import and Export Corp.*, where the court had to determine whether China National Machinery Import and Export Corporation (CNMC) could be considered an 'agency or instrumentality' of China. After a detailed analysis of the framework for State-owned industrial enterprises in China, as well as CNMC's documents, the court concluded that 'Chinese industrial enterprises "owned by the whole people", including CNMC, are "state-owned", with proprietary rights exercised by the State Council on behalf of the state'. Consequently, CNMC was an 'agency or instrumentality' of China, within the meaning of US FSIA section 1603(b)(2).[69] However, opposite conclusions on this issue have also been reached.[70] The special links between a State and

---

[66] Fox and Webb (n 12) 521.

[67] *Transaero, Inc v La Fuerza Aerea Boliviana* (United States, Court of Appeals, District of Columbia, 30 F3d 148 (DC Cir 1994)).

[68] ibid; *Segni v Commercial Office of Spain* (United States, District Court, ND Illinois, ED, 650 F Supp 1040 (ND Ill 1986)). (In *Transaero* the court stated that 'it is hard to see what would count as the 'foreign state' if its armed forces do not'.).

[69] *Arbitration between Trans Chem Ltd and China Nat Machinery Import and Export Corp* (United States, District Court for the Southern District of Texas, 978 F Supp 266 (1997)).

[70] *Proctor Gamble v Viskoza-Loznica* (United States, District Court, WD Tennessee, Western Division 33 F Supp 2d 644 (WD Tenn 1998)).

its national oil companies was addressed by US courts in several cases.[71] For example, in *Corporacion Mexicana de Servicios Maritimos, S.A. de C.V. v The M/T Respect*, the court concluded that Pemex Refining was an 'organ' for the purposes of US FSIA since

> as the district court explained, [Pemex-Refining] is an integral part of the United Mexican States. [Pemex-Refining] was created by the Mexican Constitution, Federal Organic Law, and Presidential Proclamation; it is entirely owned by the Mexican Government; is controlled entirely by government appointees; employs only public servants; and is charged with the exclusive responsibility of refining and distributing Mexican government property. Thus Pemex-[Refining] is a subdivision of the United Mexican States and therefore qualifies for foreign sovereign immunity under FSIA.[72]

In so far as majority ownership is concerned, while 'pooling' appears to be allowed,[73] this is not the case with regard to 'tiering' and the US Supreme Court has clarified that a particular shareholding must be directly held by the State:

> The Dead Sea Companies, as indirect subsidiaries of the State of Israel, were not instrumentalities of Israel under the FSIA at any time. Those companies cannot come within the statutory language which grants status as an instrumentality of a foreign state to an entity a 'majority of whose shares or other ownership interest is owned by a foreign state or political subdivision thereof'. §1603(b)(2). We hold that only direct ownership of a majority of shares by the foreign state satisfies the statutory requirement.[74]

---

[71] *US Fidelity and Guar v Braspetro Oil Services* (United States, District Court for the Southern District of New York, 219 F Supp 2d 403 (SDNY 2002)); *Corporacion Mexicana de Servicios Maritimos, SA de CV v The M/T Respect* (United States, Court of Appeals, 89 F3d 650 (9th Cir 1996)). (In *US Fidelity and Guar v Braspetro Oil Services*, the court emphasised that 'Petrobras, directly and indirectly through Braspetro employees who serve as Brasoil officers, controls the day-to-day operations of Brasoil to such an extent that Brasoil is the alter ego of Petrobras, which is an "agency or instrumentality" of Brazil, which qualifies as a foreign state under section 1603(b)'.).

[72] *Corporacion Mexicana de Servicios Maritimos, S.A. de C.V. v The M/T Respect* (United States, Court of Appeals, 89 F3d 650 (9th Cir 1996)) 655.

[73] *Mangattu v M/V Ibn Hayyan* (United States, Court of Appeals, Fifth Circuit 35 F3d 205 (5th Cir 1994)); *In re Air Crash Disaster* (United States, Court of Appeals, Seventh Circuit, 96 F3d 932 (7th Cir 1996)); *Concesionaria DHM, SA v International Finance Corp* (United States, District Court, SD New York, 03 Civ 845 (JGK) (SDNY Mar 6, 2004)). ('The ownership interests of more than one foreign government may be combined to reach the majority ownership required by section 1603(b)(2).' In *Mangattu*, the plaintiffs/appellants worked as merchant seamen on *M/V Ibn Hayyan*, a vessel that was owned by six foreign sovereigns: Saudi Arabia, Kuwait, Qatar, United Arab Emirates, Iraq (each owning a 19.3 per cent share) and Bahrain (owning a 3.335 per cent share).).

[74] *Dole Food Co v Patrickson* (United States, Supreme Court, 538 US 468, 2003) 474.

This section has shown that SOEs can be and often are assimilated into the State for the purpose of State immunity. While some domestic jurisdictions extend the presumption of immunity to various 'agencies and instrumentalities', other jurisdictions start from the presumption that if an entity is separate from the government, it should not be entitled to immunity, unless it is in the exercise of acts *jure imperii*. However, in the end this difference in approach does not matter that much, since in all cases that deal with separate entities, courts will engage in a multi-factor analysis and will consider all the relevant circumstances of a particular case before reaching a decision.

4.3.2 *Piercing the Corporate Veil of State-Owned Entities*

According to a basic principle of corporate law, a corporation has separate personality, rights and obligations that are distinct from its shareholders.[75] Generally, courts respect the separate legal personality of a corporate entity, including an SOE, and the corporate veil will only be pierced in certain limited circumstances, such as, for instance, when it can be proven that the entity in question is an *alter ego* of the government or when maintaining the corporate veil would result in fraud or injustice.[76] This status quo is also recognised in international law:

> [T]he process of 'lifting the corporate veil' or 'disregarding the legal entity' has been found justified and equitable in certain circumstances or for certain purposes. The wealth of practice already accumulated on the subject in municipal law indicates that the veil is lifted, for instance, to prevent the misuse of the privileges of legal personality, as in certain cases of fraud or malfeasance, to protect third persons such as a creditor or purchaser, or to prevent the evasion of legal requirements or of obligations. Hence the lifting of the veil is more frequently employed from without, in the interest of those dealing with the corporate entity. However, it has also been operated from within, in the interest of – among others – the shareholders, but only in exceptional circumstances. In accordance with the principle expounded above, the process of lifting the veil, being an exceptional one admitted by municipal law in respect of an institution of its own making, is equally admissible to play a similar role in international law. It follows that on the

---

[75] *Salomon v Salomon Salomon* (United Kingdom, House of Lords [1897] AC 22).
[76] Albert Badia, *Piercing the Veil of State Enterprises in International Arbitration* (Kluwer Law International 2014).

international plane also there may in principle be special circumstances which justify the lifting of the veil in the interest of shareholders.[77]

Also, the Annex to the UNCSI further provides in relation to Article 10 that

the term 'immunity' in article 10 is to be understood in the context of the present Convention as a whole. Article 10, paragraph 3, does not prejudge the question of 'piercing the corporate veil', questions relating to a situation where a State entity has deliberately misrepresented its financial position or subsequently reduced its assets to avoid satisfying a claim, or other related issues.

The analysis now turns to the consideration of several cases from domestic jurisdictions on the veil piercing. In the process of piercing the veil, UK courts start from the presumption that if a State creates an SOE as a separate legal personality, it will enjoy its status as such and the limited liability that flows from this status, even in cases where there is a high degree of interference by the State in the operations of the SOE. For example, in *I Congreso del Partido* Lord Wilberforce stated that

State-controlled enterprises, with legal personality, ability to trade and to enter into contract of private law, though wholly subject to the control of their state, are a well-known feature of the modern commercial scene. The distinction between them, and their governing state, may appear artificial: but it is an accepted distinction in the law of England and in other states.[78]

As already discussed in *Trendtex Trading Corporation v Central Bank of Nigeria*, the Court of Appeal had to decide whether the Central Bank of Nigeria was the *alter ego* of the Nigerian government.[79] The Central Bank of Nigeria was an incorporated entity that performed governmental functions such as the issuing of legal tender and was largely under government control.[80] The court held that in making a determination whether the Central Bank of Nigeria was a separate and distinct entity from the Government of Nigeria, the municipal law of the State in which the entity was created should also be examined. Although the difficulty of deciding this issue was recognised, it was ultimately held that 'on the whole' the Central Bank of Nigeria was not an *alter ego* government.[81] Similarly, in *C. Czarnikow Ltd. v Centrala*

---

[77] *Case Concerning Barcelona Traction, Light and Power Company, Limited (Belgium v Spain)* (International Court of Justice, Judgment, ICJ Reports 1970, p 3) paras 57–58.
[78] *I Congreso del Partido* (United Kingdom, [1983] 1 AC 244) 258.
[79] *Trendtex Trading Corporation v Central Bank of Nigeria* (n 63).
[80] ibid 529. Per Lord Denning MR.
[81] ibid 560.

Handlu Zagranicznego 'Rolimpex', the House of Lords was asked to determine if a Polish SOE was an *alter ego* of the Polish government.[82] Rolimpex sought to rely on the issuance of a government ban on the export of sugar as a defence against a claim of default by C. Czarnikow Ltd, a UK company. Rolimpex argued that although it was fully owned by the government, it was a separate entity and it made its own business decisions. The House of Lords agreed with Rolimpex and, despite the fact that it had to comply with all the directions of the Minister of Foreign Trade, as well as with the Polish national economic plan, it made its own commercial decisions and was thus not an *alter ego* of the Polish State.[83] The US takes a similar approach on this issue. In *First National City Bank v Banco Para el Comercio Exterior de Cuba*,[84] the US Supreme Court was asked to determine whether Banco Para el Comercio Exterior de Cuba (Bancec), a Cuban State-owned bank which had separate legal personality, was truly independent from the Cuban government, or merely its *alter ego*. The Supreme Court stated that, while generally 'duly created instrumentalities of a foreign state are to be accorded presumption of independent status', in this case

> it was clear that Bancec lacked an independent existence, and was a mere arm of the Cuban Government, performing a purely governmental function. The control of Bancec was exclusively in the hands of the Government, and Bancec was established solely to further Governmental purposes. Moreover, Bancec was totally dependent on the Government for financing, and required to remit all of its profits to the Government .... Bancec is not a mere private corporation, the stock of which is owned by the Cuban Government, but an agency of the Cuban Government in the conduct of the sort of matters which, even in a country characterized by private capitalism, tend to be supervised and managed by Government.[85]

---

[82] *C Czarnikow Ltd v Centrala Handlu Zagranicznego 'Rolimpex'* (United Kingdom, House of Lords [1979] AC 351) 195. ('The respondents are an organisation of the state. Under Polish law they have a legal personality. Though subject to directions by the appropriate minister who can tell them "what to do and how to do it", as a state enterprise they make their own decisions about their commercial activities. They decide with whom they will do business and on what terms and they have considerable freedom in their day-to-day activities. They are managed on the basis of economic accountability and are expected to make a profit. The arbitrators in my opinion rightly found as a fact that the respondents were not so closely connected with the government of Poland as to be precluded from relying on the ban imposed by the decree as government intervention.').

[83] ibid.

[84] *First National City Bank v Banco Para el Comercio Exterior de Cuba* (United States, Supreme Court, 462 US 611 (1983)).

[85] ibid 618.

Furthermore, the Court emphasised the fact that it declined to 'adhere blindly' to the corporate form, if doing so would cause an injustice. In this case, injustice would be caused since Cuba would have been able to escape liability for breaches of international law 'simply by transferring the assets to separate juridical entities':

> To hold otherwise would permit governments to avoid the requirements of international law simply by creating juridical entities whenever the need arises. We therefore hold that Citibank may set off the value of its assets seized by the Cuban Government against the amount sought by Bancec. Our decision today announces no mechanical formula for determining the circumstances under which the normally separate juridical status of a government instrumentality is to be disregarded. Instead, it is the product of the application of internationally recognized equitable principles to avoid the injustice that would result from permitting a foreign state to reap the benefits of our courts while avoiding the obligations of international law.[86]

In *Bridas v Government of Turkmenistan (Bridas I)*,[87] a case that arose out of an arbitration conducted under the auspices of the International Chamber of Commerce concerning a joint venture agreement (JVA) between the Government of Turkmenistan and Bridas, an Argentinian company, for the exploitation of oil and gas resources in Turkmenistan, the US Court of Appeals of the 5th Circuit, offered an extended list of factors that may be taken into consideration in determining whether an entity is an *alter ego* of a State. Those circumstances will be discussed in detail further in this section, but what seems to be important is the *whole context* of the transactions in question. There does not seem to be one factor that has precedence over the other. In *Bridas I*, the arbitration tribunal held that Turkmenistan was liable for the repudiation of the joint venture agreement. Reaching the enforcement stage, Turkmenistan challenged the award in the Houston District Court by arguing that it had never agreed to the arbitration in the first place, so the arbitral tribunal did not have jurisdiction over the dispute. The history of the joint venture itself is somewhat complex, whereby the initial 'Turkmenian Party' to the joint venture agreement was a fully owned SOE, whose identity was changed during the lifetime of the contract several times. For instance, after Bridas filed its arbitration complaint, Turkmenistan dissolved the 'Turkmenian Party' and replaced it with Turkmenneft, another fully owned SOE. Subsequently, Turkmenistan decided to completely abolish its Ministry

---

[86] ibid 633–634. (References omitted).
[87] *Bridas SAPIC v Government of Turkmenistan (Bridas I)* (United States, Court of Appeals for the Fifth Circuit, 345 F3d 347 (5th Cir 2003)).

for Oil and Gas, which was in charge of the supervision of Turkmenneft, and
decreed that all proceedings from the oil and gas exports were to be directed
into a special State Oil and Gas Development Fund. Those assets were
declared immune from seizure. Ultimately, the proceedings reached the
Court of Appeals for the 5th Circuit, who was called to determine how a
non-signatory to an arbitration agreement could be still bound by it. In this
inquiry, the court considered several theories, such as agency, *alter ego*,
estoppel and third-party beneficiary, but it ultimately held that only the *alter
ego* theory was applicable. In its determination, the Court said that agency
could not be applicable because although Turkmenneft was controlled by
Turkmenistan, there was not enough evidence to establish that it 'had the
apparent authority to bind the Government'.[88] The argument on estoppel
failed because it did not appear that the Government had 'exploited' the JVA
to the 'degree' that 'estoppel requires'.[89] The third-party beneficiary argument
also failed because it was not enough that the Government benefitted from
the existence of the JVA 'other than to the degree ordinarily expected when an
instrumentality of a sovereign enters into a contract to develop the country's
natural resources'.[90] The arguments that Turkmenneft was an *alter ego* of
Turkmenistan did succeed, and in this context the Court said that

> this is not to say that the decision to apply the alter ego doctrine to bind a
> parent is made routinely. 'Courts do not lightly pierce the corporate veil even
> in deference to the strong policy favoring arbitration'. The corporate veil may
> be pierced to hold an alter ego liable for the commitments of its instrumental-
> ity only if (1) the owner exercised complete control over the corporation with
> respect to the transaction at issue and (2) such control was used to commit a
> fraud or wrong that injured the party seeking to pierce the veil .... The
> district court erred in premising its conclusion solely upon the existence of
> corporate formalities and an absence of comingling of funds and directors.
> Alter ego determinations are highly fact-based and *require considering the
> totality of the circumstances in which the instrumentality functions*. No single
> factor is determinative. This should be apparent from the extensive list of
> circumstances that courts have developed to guide alter ego determinations.[91]

This extensive list of circumstances contains, among other, the following:

(1) the parent and subsidiary have common stock ownership; (2) the parent
and subsidiary have common directors or officers; (3) the parent and

[88] ibid [24–31].
[89] ibid [38–44].
[90] ibid [45–50].
[91] ibid 33. (Emphasis added). References omitted.

subsidiary have common business departments; (4) the parent and subsidiary file consolidated financial statements; (5) the parent finances the subsidiary; (6) the parent caused the incorporation of the subsidiary; (7) the subsidiary operated with grossly inadequate capital; (8) the parent pays salaries and other expenses of subsidiary; (9) the subsidiary receives no business except that given by the parent; (10) the parent uses the subsidiary's property as its own; (11) the daily operations of the two corporations are not kept separate; (12) the subsidiary does not observe corporate formalities.[92]

The case was remanded back to the District Court, who was instructed 'to take into account all of the aspects of the relationship between the Government and Turkmenneft',[93] but it ultimately found that there was an 'insufficient showing of complete domination or extensive control so as to warrant a finding that Turkmenneft was the *alter ego* of the Government of Turkmenistan'.[94] Nevertheless, the District Court added further factors that may be taken into consideration when one deals with the relationship between SOEs and the States that control them:

> (1) whether the directors of the 'subsidiary' act in the primary and independent interest of the 'parent'; (2) whether others pay or guarantee debts of the dominated corporation; and (3) whether the alleged dominator deals with the dominated corporation at arm's length; (4) whether state statutes and case law view the entity as an arm of the state; (5) the source of the entity's funding; (6) the entity's degree of local autonomy; (7) whether the entity is concerned primarily with local, as opposed to statewide, problems; (8) whether the entity has the authority to sue and be sued in its own name; and (9) whether the entity has the right to hold and use property.[95]

Bridas appealed this decision back to the Court of Appeals of the 5th Circuit. In *Bridas II*, the Court discussed this issue once more, and it reiterated that 'in making an *alter ego* determination, a court *is concerned with reality and not form* and with how the corporation operated' and that this doctrine operated only if (a) owner exercised full control over the entity in question with respect to the transaction at issue and (b) if the control was used to 'commit a fraud or wrong that injured the party seeking to pierce the veil'.[96]

---

[92] ibid footnote 11.
[93] ibid [37].
[94] *Bridas SAPIC v Government of Turkmenistan (Bridas II)* (United States, Court of Appeals, Fifth Circuit, 21 April 2006).
[95] ibid.
[96] Ibid. (Emphasis added).

Based on this, the Court of Appeal held that Turkmenneft was an *alter ego* of Turkmenistan and in reaching this determination, the Court said that

> although the balance of 'formalities factors' and some of the 'operational factors' may be consistent with Turkmenneft's existence as an independent and self-supporting entity, the court's skepticism about Turkmenneft's arm's-length status is critical. The Government manipulated Turkmenneft legally and economically to repudiate the contract with Bridas and then render it impossible for Bridas to collect damages .... Despite some indicia of separateness, the reality was that when the Government's export ban forced Bridas out of the joint venture, the Government then exercised its power as a parent entity to deprive Bridas of a contractual remedy. Intentionally bleeding a subsidiary to thwart creditors is a classic ground for piercing the corporate veil.[97]

Under domestic and international law, a corporation has separate legal personality and its rights and obligations are distinct from its shareholders. This principle applies regardless whether that particular entity is privately or publicly owned. Nevertheless, courts will pierce the corporate veil in circumstances where the entity in question is nothing but an *alter ego* of a government or where maintaining separateness would result in fraud or injustice. However, in both cases, the threshold for lifting the veil is set high and courts will generally look at the whole context of a given case.

4.4 DISTINGUISHING BETWEEN ACTS *JURE IMPERII* AND ACTS *JURE GESTIONIS*

In general, for an exception to State immunity to stand scrutiny three requirements must be fulfilled: first, the plea must be procedural in nature; second, due regard must be given to the tension between the principle of sovereign equality and the principle of territoriality of the forum State and third, the act or acts that are at the basis of the inquiry must be properly characterised as either *jure imperii* or *jure gestionis*.[98] This section will deal with the third requirement only, since the first requirement has already been discussed in the introduction to this chapter, while the second will be dealt in Sections 4.5.2 and 4.5.3.

The distinction between acts *jure imperii* and acts *jure gestionis* is 'inextricably linked with the development of the rationale and rules on State immunity

---

[97] ibid.
[98] Fox and Webb (n 12) 396.

over the past century, especially the demise of the absolute immunity doctrine and the emergence of the restrictive immunity doctrine'.[99] At its core, the distinction between acts *jure imperii* and acts *jure gestionis* embodies the capitalist conception of the liberal state and its inherent distinction between the public and the private spheres, concepts addressed in Chapter 2, with the consequence that economic transactions would have a private character and would not be protected by the veil of immunity.[100] As discussed elsewhere, the rationale for the development of the restrictive doctrine has been the increasing involvement of States, through their SOEs, in commercial transactions.[101] States that adopt the restrictive approach generally recognise a commercial or private law exception to immunity, but its application is 'so diverse and the criterion by which it is determined so differently formulated as to prevent the articulation of the exception in terms acceptable to all'.[102] This state of affairs is largely due to the fact that all domestic legal systems classify acts *jure gestionis* and acts *jure imperii* differently, and to a certain extent, this is a situation that raises similar difficulties to those that will be encountered in Chapter 5, concerning the meaning of 'governmental authority' for the purpose of attribution under Article 5 of the ILC Articles.

The process of distinguishing between acts *jure imperii* and acts *jure gestionis* is 'central' to the law of State immunity.[103] The ICJ did not directly address this issue in the *Jurisdictional Immunities Case*, but it stated that this distinction was important because it determines whether the exception to immunity can or cannot be claimed.[104] It follows that the classification of an act as either *jure imperii* or *jure gestionis* is a determination that must be made before jurisdiction can actually be exercised.[105] While no State has elaborated

---

[99] Orakhelashvili, 'Jurisdictional Immunities of States and General International Law' (n 26) 105.

[100] J Finke, 'Sovereign Immunity: Rule, Comity or Something Else?' (2010) 21 Eur. J. Int. Law 853, 865.

[101] *Victory Transport Inc v Comisaría General* (United States, District Court for the Southern District of New York, 232 F Supp 294 (SDNY 1963)). ('Growing concern for individual rights and public morality coupled with the increasing entry of governments into what had previously been regarded as private pursuits, has led a substantial number of nations to abandon the absolute theory of sovereign immunity in favour of a restrictive theory.').

[102] Fox and Webb (n 12) 395.

[103] ibid 398.

[104] *Jurisdictional Immunities of the State (Germany v Italy: Greece intervening)* (n 5) para 60. ('The Court is not called upon to address the question of how international law treats the issue of State immunity in respect of *acta jure gestionis*. The acts of the German armed forces and other State organs which were subject to the proceedings in Italian courts clearly constituted *acta jure imperii*.').

[105] ibid. ('To the extent that the distinction between acts *jure imperii* and acts *jure gestionis* is significant for determining whether or not a State is entitled to immunity from the jurisdiction

a 'list' of acts *jure imperii* or *jure gestionis* in legislation, this being an area of the law that has been largely left for the courts to develop,[106] in the *Jurisdictional Immunities Case*, the Court has suggested that, as way of distinguishing between acts *jure imperii* and acts *jure gestionis*, one could look at 'whether the acts in question fail to be assessed by reference to the law governing the exercise of sovereign power *(jus imperii)* or the law concerning non-sovereign activities of a State, especially private and commercial activities *(jus gestionis)*'.[107] Nevertheless, domestic courts[108] as well as academic commentators[109] have suggested that, among others, the following acts are highly likely fall into the *jure imperii* category: (a) transactions of the State in terms of international law; (b) internal, administrative and legislative acts of the State; (c) issues the resolution of which has been allocated to another remedial context; (d) the content or implementation of the foreign, defence and security policies of the State and (e) intergovernmental agreements creating agencies, institutions, or funds subject to the rule of public international law.

Overall, the situation is similar in the case of acts *jure gestionis*. While no comprehensive list could be found in either legislation or case law, the following activities have been classified by courts as *jure gestionis*: leasing or purchasing of immovable property, issuance of government bonds, banking activities, carriage of goods and people, operation of an airline, ownership of patents in the forum State, construction of oil production platforms, contract negotiations and contractual obligations, purchase of medical and scientific materials etc.[110] To this end, there are several techniques that have been

---

of another State's courts in respect of a particular act, it has to be applied before that jurisdiction can be exercised, whereas the legality or illegality of the act is something which can be determined only in the exercise of that jurisdiction. Although the present case is unusual in that the illegality of the acts at issue has been admitted by Germany at all stages of the proceedings, the Court considers that this fact does not alter the characterization of those acts as *acta jure imperii*.').

[106] Fox and Webb (n 12) 399.

[107] *Jurisdictional Immunities of the State (Germany v Italy: Greece intervening)* (n 5) para 60.

[108] *Claim against the Empire of Iran Case* (German Federal Constitutional Court, 45 ILR 57 (1963)); *I Congreso del Partido* (n 78) 264; *Rahimtoola v Nizam of Hyderabad* (United Kingdom, House of Lords [1958] AC 379) 422; *Victory Transport Inc. v Comisaría General* (United States, District Court for the Southern District of New York, 232 F Supp 294 (SDNY 1963)) 360; *Saudi Arabia v Nelson* (United States, Supreme Court, 507 US 349 (1993)).

[109] Fox and Webb (n 12) 399–402; Yang (n 1) 81–85.

[110] Yang (n 1) 76–79. (While Yang provides quite an extensive list, he further clarifies that while it is 'impossible for any legislator or judge to provide an all-encompassing list of commercial activities ... it seems far more preferable to have no list at all, or to have an open-ended list coupled with the broadest guidelines, thereby leaving the matter largely to the discretion of the judge, who can then decide the issue on a case-by-case basis'.).

developed by courts, which have been incorporated into the legislation of States with immunity statutes, for determining whether a particular act is to be classified as *jure gestionis*. Some of the most common techniques have been to conduct an inquiry into either the 'purpose' or 'nature' of the act in question, or to look at the whole 'context' of the transaction. Before addressing those three techniques in detail, it must be clarified that, for the purposes of State immunity, the notion of a commercial transaction contains three elements: it relates to an activity concerning business and trade, which arises from a voluntary transaction between two parties and which is made by reference to the domestic private law of a given State, either expressly or implicitly.[111] Another issue that must be noted is that the *jure imperii* / *jure gestionis* distinction is not made 'by reference to the lawfulness or unlawfulness of a particular act but on whether that act can also be performed by a private person in furtherance of a private-law relationship'.[112]

According to the purpose test, an act will be classified as *jure imperii* if that particular act serves a sovereign purpose. Since all State activities ultimately serve a sovereign purpose, the purpose test favors the State and enlarges immunity,[113] and although it may have been highly relevant at a time when State functions were limited largely to the maintenance of State defences and internal public order, it has lost much of its significance once State involvement in commercial activities became de rigueur in the second half of the twentieth century.[114] Nevertheless, jurisprudence from Italy and France shows that the purpose test has not been entirely abandoned. For example, in *Arab Republic of Libya v SpA Imprese Marittime Frassinetti and SpA Italiana Lavori Marittimi e Terrestri*, the Italian Court of Cassation held that when dealing with the question of immunity it is essential to determine whether the 'nature of the activities of the foreign State … were intended to achieve public, institutional ends'.[115] In *X v Saudi School in Paris and Kingdom of Saudi Arabia*, the French Court of Cassation held that States 'enjoy jurisdictional immunity in so far as the act giving rise to the dispute between the parties, by its nature or purpose' is an exercise of the sovereignty and not a 'normal act of administrative management'.[116]

---

[111] Fox and Webb (n 12) 403.
[112] Yang (n 1) 438.
[113] Fox and Webb (n 12) 406.
[114] Yang (n 1) 98.
[115] *Arab Republic of Libya v SpA Imprese Marittime Frassinetti and SpA Italiana Lavori Marittimi e Terrestri* (Italy (1979) 78 ILR 91) 92.
[116] *X v Saudi School in Paris and Kingdom of Saudi Arabia* (France (2003) 127 ILR 163) 166.

Immunity is lost under the nature test if the particular act is commercial in nature. This is currently the predominant position adopted by many States.[117] The nature test restricts the scope of immunity and is 'more protective of third parties entering into commercial transaction with a State', but its application 'can sometimes lead to outcomes that may appear arbitrary and blur the line between sovereign and commercial conduct'.[118] As expected, contrary to the purpose test, the nature test does not take into consideration the purpose of the act. On this issue, in the *Empire of Iran* case, the German Constitutional Court stated that

> the distinction between sovereign and non-sovereign acts of State cannot be drawn according to the purpose of the State's action, nor whether the action is recognizably connected with sovereign functions of the State. For ultimately the State's activity will if not entirely then at least in by far the greater part serve sovereign purposes and functions and be in some still recognizable connection with them. Nor can it depend on whether the State has acted commercially. Commercial activity of States does not differ in essence from other non-sovereign activity of States. The criterion for distinguishing between acts *iure imperii* and *iure gestionis* can instead only be the nature of the State's action or the legal relationship that has arisen, but not the motive or purpose of the State's act. It therefore depends on whether the foreign State has acted in exercise of the sovereign power inherent in it, that is in public law, or as a private person, that in private law.[119]

Similarly, in *Saudi Arabia v Nelson*, the US Supreme Court further clarified that

> a state engages in commercial activity under the restrictive theory where it exercises 'only those powers that can also be exercised by private citizens', as distinct from those 'powers peculiar to sovereigns'. Put differently, a foreign state engages in commercial activity for purposes of the restrictive theory only where it acts 'in the manner of a private player within the market . . . . [W]hether the State acts 'in the manner of' a private party is a question of behaviour not motivation.[120]

---

[117] Yang (n 1) 86–98. (Among others, Belgium, Germany, Greece, Kenya, the Netherlands, Nigeria, Portugal, South Africa, Switzerland and Zimbabwe have adopted the nature approach.)

[118] Yas Banifatemi, 'Jurisdictional Immunity of States: Commercial Transactions' in Nicolas Angelet and Luca Ferro (eds), *The Cambridge Handbook of Immunities and International Law* (Cambridge University Press 2019) 141.

[119] *Claim against the Empire of Iran Case* (n 108) 80.

[120] *Saudi Arabia v Nelson* (n 108) 360.

Nevertheless, difficulties remain in the application of the nature test and 'the purpose of an act may just sneak into the picture in one guise or another'.[121] This means that, in reality, both the purpose and nature of an act would ultimately be relevant in making a determination. This leads us to the third type of technique used to distinguish between acts *jure imperii* and acts *jure gestionis*: the context approach, which is particularly relevant for the purposes of the UK SIA, since that particular immunity statute is silent about the criteria for determining a commercial activity. As the name implies, in an attempt to avoid the challenges posed by the nature/purpose tests, the context approach takes a broader approach to this matter. Lord Wilberforce, in *I Congreso del Partido*, succinctly clarified this position as follows:

> The conclusion which emerges is that in considering, under the 'restrictive' theory whether state immunity should be granted or not, the court must consider the whole context in which the claim against the state is made, with a view to deciding whether the relevant act(s) upon which the claim is based, should, in that context, be considered as fairly within an area of activity, trading or commercial, or otherwise of a private law character, in which the state has chosen to engage, or whether the relevant act(s) should be considered as having been done outside that area, and within the sphere of governmental or sovereign activity.[122]

The determination of whether an act is *jure gestionis* or *jure imperii* is to be done by looking at the whole context of the case, in order to isolate the 'exact' act(s) which forms the basis of the plea, then once the relevant act(s) is/are isolated, it is necessary to ask whether a private citizen might have been able to perform that act.[123] In the UK, this position was confirmed by the House of Lords in *Kuwait Airways Corporation v Iraqi Airways Corporation (No. 1)*.[124] Canadian courts have taken a similar approach and generally apply the context approach.[125] A variety of acts have been deemed to be commercial,

---

[121] Yang (n 1) 87.

[122] *I Congreso del Partido* (n 78) 267.

[123] ibid 262. ('When . . . a claim is brought against a state . . . and state immunity is claimed, it is necessary to consider what is the relevant act which forms the basis of the claim: is this, under the old terminology and act "*jure gestionis*" or is it an act "*jure imperii*": is it . . . a "private act" or is it a "sovereign or public act" a private act meaning in this context an act of a private law character such as a private citizen might have entered into?' Per Lord Wilberforce) (References omitted).

[124] *Kuwait Airways Corp v Iraqi Airways Co (No. 1)* (n 65) 1157. ('The ultimate test is not just the purpose or the motive of the act is to serve the purposes of the state, but that the act is of its own character a governmental act, as opposed to an act which any private citizen can perform.' Per Lord Goff.).

[125] *Re The Canada Labour Code* (Canada (1992) 86 IRL 626) 278. ('It seems to me that a contextual approach is the only reasonable basis of applying the doctrine of restrictive immunity. The alternative is to attempt the impossible – an antiseptic distillation of a

even if the purpose for which they were undertaken was ultimately sovereign, such as contracts for the sale or purchase of goods that ultimately benefitted the government, the activities of State airlines and even the issuance of bonds.[126] In France, a distinction is made between *actes de commerce* and *actes de puissance publique* (this distinction being supported by the separation between administrative and civil courts).[127]

Overall, difficulties will always remain in determining which acts are ultimately *jure gestionis* and which remain *jure imperii*.[128] Hersch Lauterpacht noted that because the State cannot act but as a public person, all acts *jure gestionis* are in fact acts *jure imperii*.[129] James Crawford has also called the distinction between *acta jure imperii* and *acta jure gestionis* 'radically deficient and cannot claim to represent general international law'.[130] Other scholars further underline the difficulties in this area by asking the question whether a contract between a foreign State entity and a private manufacturer for the purchase of army boots, or 'a warship, or of munitions or the foodstuff necessary for the maintenance of the national economy' is a public or private act?[131] Cristoph Schreuer noted the issue of 'borderline cases' and suggested a list of criteria to be considered, including the participants in the activity or transaction, the claimant's legitimate expectations, whether the contract is typically commercial, whether sovereign prerogative is involved, the legal forms and methods of the transaction and whether a denial of

---

"once-and-for-all" characterisation of the activity in question, entirely divorced from its purpose. It is true that purpose should not predominate, as this approach would convert virtually every act by commercial agents of the state into an act *jure imperii*. However, the converse is also true. Rigid adherence to the 'nature' of an act to the exclusion of purpose would render innumerable government activities *jure gestionis*. Neither of these extremes offers and appropriate resolution of the problem.').

[126] Shaw (n 20) 522–527.

[127] Fox and Webb (n 12) 405.

[128] *Claim against the Empire of Iran Case* (n 108) 79; *Holland v Lampen-Wolfe* (United Kingdom, House of Lords [2000] UKHL 40). (In the *Empire of Iran Case* the German Constitutional Court stated that 'the fact that it is difficult to draw the line between sovereign and non-sovereign State activities is no reasoning for abandoning the distinction'. Lord Clyde in *Holland v Lampen-Wolfe* also noted that 'difficult as the distinction may be at common law, we have to do the best we can to apply it'.).

[129] Lauterpacht (n 4) 224. ('[T]here is force in the view that, at least in modern conditions, the distinction between acts *jure gestionis* and *jure imperii* cannot be placed on a sound logical basis.').

[130] James Crawford, 'International Law and Foreign Sovereigns: Distinguishing Immune Transactions' (1984) 54 Br. Yearb. Int. Law 75, 89.

[131] Lee M Caplan, 'State Immunity, Human Rights, and Jus Cogens: A Critique of the Normative Hierarchy Theory' (2003) 97 Am. J. Int. Law 741, 758; Lauterpacht (n 4) 225.

immunity would involve a political backlash.[132] As far as SOEs are concerned, the general accepted approach is that those entities should not be able to plead immunity solely by virtue of being owned by the government, as long as the acts in which that SOE engages are of a commercial nature, which can be performed by any other private party. This has clearly helped to ensure that SOEs are more accountable, at least towards their partners in commercial transactions. The situation of SWFs is somewhat peculiar, and some commentators have argued that the current rules of sovereign immunity 'do not provide satisfactory results for cases involving SWFs due to the fact that they are 'overly favourable towards sovereign immunity'.[133]

4.5 EXCEPTIONS TO STATE IMMUNITY

UNCSI Article 5 states that 'a State enjoys immunity, in respect of itself and its property, from the jurisdiction of the courts of another State, subject to the provisions of the present Convention'. Part III Articles 10–17 of the same instrument lists the exceptions to sovereign immunity. Those exceptions cover commercial transactions, contracts of employment, personal injuries and damage to property, ownership of property situated in the State of the forum, intellectual and industrial property, ships that are owned by the State and which are used for commercial purposes and an arbitration agreement, which was entered into by the State with a foreign person. Similar approaches exist in Article 15 of the ECSI, in section 1 of the UK SIA, section 1604 of the US FSIA and section 9 of the AU FSIA, with the exceptions listed in sections 11–20 of the AU FSIA, Articles 7–12 ECSI, sections 3–11 of the UK SIA and section 1605 of the US FSIA. There being a general presumption in favour of immunity, if a particular set of facts fits within one of the expressly specified exceptions to immunity, then immunity is lifted, if they do not, then immunity remains intact. It must also be noted that the exceptions to immunity apply only in the case of civil proceedings, with States enjoying absolute immunity in criminal proceedings. Nevertheless, express or implied waivers of immunity[134] and, in

---

[132] Christoph H Schreuer, *State Immunity: Some Recent Developments*, vol 8 (Grotius 1988) 41–43.

[133] Victorino Tejera, 'The Interaction of the Jurisdictional Immunities of the State and the Sovereign Wealth Funds: The Case of the US FSIA Vis-à-Vis the 2004 UN Convention' (Graduate Institute of International and Development Studies 2017) 237–258; Victorino Tejera, 'The US Law Regime of Sovereign Immunity and the Sovereign Wealth Funds' (2016) 25 U. Miami Bus. L. Rev. 1.

[134] Larry C Backer, 'Human Rights Responsibilities of State-Owned Enterprises' in Surya Deva and David Birchall (eds), *Research Handbook on Human Rights and Business* (Edward Elgar 2020) 228.

some jurisdictions, the engagement in terrorist activities or the provision of material support to entities that engaged in terrorist activities are also exceptions to this general rule.

4.5.1 *State-Owned Entities and the Commercial Transactions Exception*

The main exception to the jurisdictional immunity of States is contained in the commercial transaction exception which is reflected in international and domestic instruments on State immunity.[135] For example, in the UNCSI, the commercial activities exception is covered in Article 10, which states that

> 1. If a State engages in a commercial transaction with a foreign natural or juridical person and, by virtue of the applicable rules of private international law, differences relating to the commercial transaction fall within the jurisdiction of a court of another State, the State cannot invoke immunity from that jurisdiction in a proceeding arising out of that commercial transaction. 2. Paragraph 1 does not apply: (a) in the case of a commercial transaction between States; or (b) if the parties to the commercial transaction have expressly agreed otherwise. 3. Where a State enterprise or other entity established by a State which has an independent legal personality and is capable of: (a) suing or being sued; and (b) acquiring, owning or possessing and disposing of property, including property which that State has authorized it to operate or manage, is involved in a proceeding which relates to a commercial transaction in which that entity is engaged, the immunity from jurisdiction enjoyed by that State shall not be affected.

Article 2(1)(c) of UNCSI states that a 'commercial transaction' is understood as

> (i) any commercial contract or transaction for the sale of goods or supply of services; (ii) any contract for a loan or other transaction of a financial nature, including any obligation of guarantee or of indemnity in respect of any such loan or transaction; (iii) any other contract or transaction of a commercial, industrial or professional nature, but not including a contract of employment of persons.
>
> (2) In determining whether a contract or transaction is a "commercial transaction" under paragraph 1(c), reference should be made primarily to the nature of the contract of transaction, but its purpose should also be taken into account if the parties to the contract or transaction have so agreed, or if in the practice of the State of the forum, that purpose is relevant to determining the non-commercial character of the contract or transaction.

---

[135] Banifatemi (n 118) 125.

Consequently, under the UNSCI, the criterion for determining the nature of a transaction would be made by adopting a dual nature/purpose test which embodies the long debate and ultimate political compromise that was made between liberal and welfare States on this issue,[136] with one commentator noting that the reason for the modified 'nature test was to protect developing countries that sought to promote their national development'.[137] Article 7(1) of ECSI does not expressly provide for a method for determining the commerciality of the act, but the requirement that the engagement in a particular activity must be done in a similar manner to a 'private person' appears to imply that the criterion for making this determination is indeed the 'nature' test:

> A Contracting State cannot claim immunity from the jurisdiction of a court of another Contracting State if it has on the territory of the State of the forum an office, agency or other establishment through which it engages, in the same manner as a private person, in an industrial, commercial or financial activity, and the proceedings relate to that activity of the office, agency or establishment.[138]

A criterion approach is also adopted in some domestic immunity statutes. For example, Article 1603(d) of the FSIA states that

> a 'commercial activity means either a regular course of commercial conduct or a particular commercial transaction or act. The commercial character of an activity shall be determined by reference to the nature of the course of conduct or particular transaction or act, rather than by reference to its purpose.

That the nature test is relevant for making a determination under the US FSIA was further cemented by the US Supreme Court in *Republic of Argentina v Weltover*[139] and *Saudi Arabia v Nelson*.[140] In contrast, rather than

---

[136] Fox and Webb (n 12) 411, 415–417.
[137] Shaw (n 20) 516.
[138] European Convention on State Immunity Article 7(1).
[139] *Republic of Argentina v Weltover Inc* (United States, Supreme Court, 504 US 607 (1992)) 614. ('[W]hen a foreign government acts, not as regulator of a market, but in the manner of a private player within it, the foreign sovereign's actions are "commercial" within the meaning of the FSIA. Moreover, because the Act provides that the commercial character of an act is to be determined by reference to its "nature" rather than its "purpose", the question is not whether the foreign government is acting with a profit motive or instead with the aim of fulfilling uniquely sovereign objectives. Rather, the issue is whether the particular actions that the foreign state performs (whatever the motive behind them) are the type of actions by which a private party engages in "trade and traffic or commerce".') (References omitted).
[140] *Saudi Arabia v Nelson* (n 108) 361.('Unlike Argentina's activities that we considered in *Weltover*, the intentional conduct alleged here (the Saudi Government's wrongful arrest,

making a reference to the nature or purpose test, the UK SIA and the AU FSIA list a broad suite of activities that are considered commercial. Section 3(1) and (3)UK SIA state that

> 3(1) A State is not immune as respects proceedings relating to – (a) a commercial transaction entered into by a State; (b) an obligation of the State which by virtue of a contract (whether a commercial transaction or not) falls to be performed wholly or partly in the United Kingdom;
> 3(3) In this section 'commercial transaction' means: (a) any contract for the supply of goods or services; (b) any loan or other transaction for the provision of finance and any guarantee or indemnity in respect of any such transaction or of any other financial obligation; and (c) any other transaction or activity (whether of a commercial, industrial, financial, professional or other similar character) into which a State enters or in which it engages otherwise than in the exercise of sovereign authority.

Similarly, section 11(3) of the AU FSIA states that

> (3)In this section, commercial transaction means a commercial, trading, business, professional or industrial or like transaction into which the foreign State has entered or a like activity in which the State has engaged and, without limiting the generality of the foregoing, includes: (a) a contract for the supply of goods or services; (b) an agreement for a loan or some other transaction for or in respect of the provision of finance; and (c) a guarantee or indemnity in respect of a financial obligation; but does not include a contract of employment or a bill of exchange.

By including a residual category of 'commercial activities', either expressly as the UK SIA does in section 3(3)(c) or by implied reference as is the case of the AU FSIA (e.g., section 11(3) uses the wording 'without limiting the generality of the foregoing') the statutes leave it to the discretion of the courts to determine what those commercial activities might be, by going to the purpose or nature test.[141] Another important point is the requirement for a jurisdictional nexus between the territory of the State in question and the act upon which the claim was based. For instance, under the US FSIA, a jurisdictional nexus is required by section 1605(a)(2) which clarifies that

---

imprisonment, and torture of Nelson) could not qualify as commercial under the restrictive theory. The conduct boils down to abuse of the power of its police by the Saudi Government, and however monstrous such abuse undoubtedly may be, a foreign state's exercise of the power of its police has long been understood for purposes of the restrictive theory as peculiarly sovereign in nature.').

[141] Banifatemi (n 118) 127.

a foreign state shall not be immune from the jurisdiction of the court of the United States or of the State in any case – in which the action is based upon commercial activity carried on in the United States by the foreign State; or upon an act performed in the United States in connection with a commercial activity of the foreign State elsewhere; or upon an act outside the territory of the United States in connection with a commercial activity of the foreign state elsewhere and that act causes a direct effect in the United States.

The phrase 'based upon' should be given its natural meaning.[142] US courts adopt a two-part test to determine if a foreign State's commercial activities are sufficient to deprive it of sovereign immunity:

[T]he initial inquiry is whether there is a sufficient jurisdictional connection or nexus between the commercial activity and the United States. The second inquiry is whether there exists a substantive connection or nexus between the commercial activity and the subject matter of the cause of action.[143]

Three types of nexus are envisaged under section 1605(a)(2). The first type of nexus requires that the commercial activity is carried on in the United States and contemplates 'doing business or maintaining a permanent establishment in the US'.[144] The second type of activity requires the 'performance in the US of either contractual acts in pursuance of that foreign-based activity or some element of a tortious act connected with that foreign activity'.[145] The third type of nexus concerns the situation where the act is performed outside of the US but which requires the causation of a 'direct effect' in the United States, which is more than 'trivial'.[146]

The commercial transaction exception is well entrenched in the law of State immunity; in essence, commercial transactions being the cause of the shift from absolute immunity to restrictive immunity. While certain immunity statutes spell out the categories of commercial transactions for which immunity is lifted, the reality is that courts are given a wide margin of discretion when deciding this issue. In addition, some immunity statutes require a

---

[142] *Saudi Arabia v Nelson* (n 108) 357.
[143] *Federal Ins Co v Richard I Rubin Co* (United States, Court of Appeals, Third Circuit 12 F3d 1270, 1993) 1286.
[144] Fox and Webb (n 12) 264.
[145] ibid.
[146] *Republic of Argentina v Weltover Inc.* (United States, Supreme Court, 504 US 607 (1992)) 618. ('[W]e reject the suggestion that section 1605(a)(2) contains any unexpressed requirement of "substantiality" or "foreseeability". As the Court of Appeals recognised, an effect is "direct" if it follows "as an immediate consequence of the defendant's ... activity".').

jurisdictional nexus between the transaction and the territory of the State where immunity is pleaded.

4.5.2 State-Owned Entities and the Non-commercial Tort Exception

States are generally unable to claim immunity from jurisdiction in cases of tortious conduct that has resulted in personal injury or damage to property in the territory of the forum State. The non-commercial tort exception could thus become relevant with regard to breaches of certain human rights, environmental damage and other damage to property caused by SOEs. In the UNCSI this exception can be found in Article 12:

> Unless otherwise agreed between the States concerned, a State cannot invoke immunity from jurisdiction before a court of another State which is otherwise competent in a proceeding which relates to pecuniary compensation for death or injury to the person, or damage to or loss of tangible property, caused by an act or omission which is alleged to be attributable to the State, if the act or omission occurred in whole or in part in the territory of that other State and if the author of the act or omission was present in that territory at the time of the act or omission.

Similar provisions are present in ECSI Article 11,[147] US FSIA section 1605 (a)(5),[148] UK SIA section 5[149] and AU FSIA section 13.[150] The commentary to the UNSCI states that the non-commercial tort exception is applicable only in

---

[147] Article 11: 'A Contracting State cannot claim immunity from the jurisdiction of a court of another Contracting State in proceedings which relate to redress for injury to the person or damage to tangible property, if the facts which occasioned the injury or damage occurred in the territory of the State of the forum, and if the author of the injury or damage was present in that territory at the time when those facts occurred.'

[148] Section 1605(a)(5) provides that 'a foreign State shall not be immune from the jurisdiction of the courts of the United States or of the States in any case: not otherwise encompassed in paragraph (2) above, in which money damages are sought against a foreign state for personal injury or death, or damage to or loss of property, occurring in the United States and caused by the tortious act or omission of that foreign state or of any official or employee of that foreign state while acting within the scope of his office or employment; except this paragraph shall not apply to: (A) any claim based upon the exercise or performance or the failure to exercise or perform a discretionary function regardless of whether the discretion be abused, or (B) any claim arising out of malicious prosecution, abuse of process, libel, slander, misrepresentation, deceit, or interference with contract rights'.

[149] According to section 5, 'a State is not immune as respects proceedings in respect of: (a) death or personal injury; or (b) damage to or loss of tangible property, caused by an act or omission in the United Kingdom'.

[150] Under section 13, 'a foreign State is not immune in a proceeding in so far as the proceeding concerns: (a) the death of, or personal injury to, a person; or (b) loss of or damage to tangible property; caused by an act or omission done or omitted to be done in Australia'.

cases when the State would have been liable under the *lex loci delicti commissi*, and although 'as a rule' the State is immune from the jurisdiction of the courts of another State, in those circumstances, immunity would be withheld:

> The exception contained in this article is therefore designed to provide relief or possibility of recourse to justice for individuals who suffer personal injury, death or physical damage to or loss of property caused by an act or omission which might be intentional, accidental or caused by negligence attributable to a foreign State. Since the damaging act or omission has occurred in the territory of the State of the forum, the applicable law is clearly the *lex loci delicti commissi* and the most convenient court is that of the State where the delict was committed. A court foreign to the scene of the delict might be considered as a *forum non conveniens*. The injured individual would have been without recourse to justice had the State been entitled to invoke its jurisdictional immunity.[151]

According to Sucharitkul Sompong, special rapporteur on the issue of jurisdictional immunities of States and their property, since a State is 'bound to afford a reasonable measure of legal protection' to persons that are found in its territory, the main purpose of this exception is to protect injured parties, regardless of their status in the forum State (e.g., nationals, residents, foreigners or tourists).[152] Consequently, 'the sovereignty of the State responsible or liable for the damage incurred by the injured individual is not directly at stake in most cases. A State conducting activities in the territory of another State is obliged to respect local laws and regulations and to abide by all ground rules'.[153] While this exception was initially designed to cover death, personal injuries and damage to property, it has nevertheless been considered broad enough to also cover a 'panoply of acts and omissions',[154] including 'intentional physical harm such as assault and battery, malicious damage to property, arson, homicide, political assassination',[155] war crimes and terrorist

---

[151] 'Draft Articles on Jurisdictional Immunities of States and Their Property, with Commentaries' (1991) Yearbook of the International Law Commission, 1991, vol. II, Part Two. (A/46/10) 44.

[152] Sompong Sucharitkul, 'Fifth Report on Jurisdictional Immunities of States and Their Property (UN Doc. A/CN.4/363 and Add.1*, 22 March and 11 April 1983)' (Yearbook of the International Law Commission 1983) para 72.

[153] ibid 73.

[154] Sally El Sawah, 'Jurisdictional Immunity of States and Non-Commercial Torts' in Tom Ruys and Nicolas Angelet (eds), *The Cambridge Handbook of Immunities and International Law* (Cambridge University Press 2019) 142.

[155] 'Draft Articles on Jurisdictional Immunities of States and Their Property, with Commentaries' (n 151) 45.

attacks. Furthermore, the exception bypasses the *forum non conveniens* limitations to jurisdiction, which would have left individuals injured without recourse to justice. Another issue to consider is that the non-commercial tort exception does not cover cases where there is no physical damage, such as damage to reputation, interference with contractual rights, defamation, misrepresentation or nuisance.[156]

Nevertheless, from an international law perspective, the *Jurisdictional Immunities Case* has called into question whether, as a matter of international law, one can argue that an exception from absolute sovereign immunity still exists for non-contractual personal injuries and tangible loss to property.[157] First, it is worth noting from the outset that the *Jurisdictional Immunities Case* dealt with circumstances that involved armed conflict between the parties, a situation different to the usual operation of SOEs. Second, in this context, Hazel Fox and Phillipa Webb note that

> in respect to tortious acts arising out of commercial transactions the exception in UNCSI, Article 10 might be applicable. Both the US and the UK Acts envisage the possibility that *proceedings in tort may be brought within the commercial exception*; 'activity' as defined in the FSIA is broad enough to remove immunity from torts arising out of commercial activity and the inclusion of 'activity in which the State engages' in the residuary clause of subsection 3 of the commercial transaction exception in the SIA embraces and has been held to embrace tortious activity. Where such 'commercial tortious conduct' can be alleged, the more relaxed jurisdictional requirements of the commercial exception may apply, with the result that claims for economic loss resulting from tortious conduct may be claimed.[158]

In general, two conditions must be satisfied for the non-commercial tort exception to apply. First, the act or omission in question must occur in whole or in part in the territory of the State of the forum; and second, the perpetrator must have been physically present there at the time of the act or the omission, in order to establish a nexus between the two. It is important to note that under the non-commercial tort exception the *jure imperii / jure gestionis* debate is to a certain extent sidelined, with the focus of the inquiry instead turning to the territorial nexus between the tort and the forum State.[159] On the one hand, both the UNCSI in Article 12 and the ECSI in Article 11 require a dual territorial link requirement: the act or omission must have occurred in the

---

[156] ibid; El Sawah (n 154) 144.
[157] Fox and Webb (n 12) 475.
[158] ibid 478. (Emphasis added).
[159] Yang (n 1) 199, 207–215.

territory of the forum State *and* the perpetrator must have been physically present in the territory of that particular State. The requirement for the actor to be present in the forum State has the effect of excluding cases of trans-boundary tort or damage. On the other hand, the UK SIA requires only a single territorial link: the act or omission must have occurred in the UK and courts have routinely declined to exercise jurisdiction when this condition was not met.[160] The Australian approach is similar to that of the UK. While a textual interpretation of section 1605(a)(5) US FSIA appears to suggest that only the injury or damage is needed to occur on US territory, the courts have clarified that the act or omission must have a link with the United States.[161] Nevertheless, the United States has enacted specific legislation, which, in certain circumstances, allows for exceptions to sovereign immunity to bypass the strict territorial nexus requirements, for example, in cases where a plaintiff can prove that a State has sponsored terrorism.[162] Provisions of this kind exist in the Antiterrorism and Effective Death Penalty Act[163] and in the Justice against Sponsors of Terrorism Act (JASTA).[164] The Antiterrorism and Effective Death Penalty Act added Section 1605A to the US FSIA, whereby State 'sponsors of terrorism' are denied immunity for 'money damages' for 'personal injury or death that was caused by an act of torture, extrajudicial killing, aircraft, sabotage, hostage taking or the provision of material support or resources' for such an act. JASTA amends the US FSIA by inserting a new section 1605B in this legislation and thus supplements the existing US FSIA terrorist exception that was already present in Section 1605A. Section 1605B gives federal courts jurisdiction over civil claims against a State for physical injury to persons or property or death occurring in the United States and caused by an act of terrorism in the United States *and* a 'tortious act or acts of the foreign State, or of any official employee, or agent of that foreign state while acting within the scope of his or her office, employment or agency, *regardless* where the tortious act or acts of the foreign state occurred'.[165] Section 4 of JASTA imposes civil liability on a person who 'aids, abets by knowingly providing substantial assistance, or who conspires with the person

---

[160] *Al-Adsani v Government of Kuwait (No. 2)* (United Kingdom, Court of Appeal (1996) 107 ILR 536); *Jones v Saudi-Arabia* (United Kingdom, [2006] UKHL 26).
[161] *Argentine Republic v Amerada Hess Shipping Corp et al* (United States Supreme Court (1989) 488 US 428) 441.
[162] David P Stewart, 'Immunity and Terrorism' in Tom Ruys and Nicolas Angelet (eds), *The Cambridge Handbook of Immunities and International Law* (Cambridge University Press 2019).
[163] Antiterrorism and Effective Death Penalty Act 1996 (US).
[164] Justice against Sponsors of Terrorism Act (2016).
[165] ibid section 3.

who committed' an act of international terrorism. JASTA has been criticised 'for dangerously disrupting the principle of sovereign immunity and the separation of powers doctrine by limiting the executive's control over foreign policy'.[166] Nevertheless, commentators have pointed out that this legislation has some serious limitations.[167] First, it does not overturn prior decisions, which rejected personal jurisdiction over past defendants; second, section 5 gives the executive branch powers to intervene in judicial proceedings by requesting a stay in pending litigation, which could undermine the very purpose of the legislation; third, the legislation does not appear to affect the broader immunity from enforcement provisions found in the US FSIA sections 1609, 1610 and 1611, meaning that the immunity of State-owned assets will be largely preserved.

Overall, SOEs should not be able to claim immunity for non-commercial torts as long as the requirements for this exception, as set out by statute or common law in the case of States that do not have immunity legislation, are met. This means that certain human rights claims, such as those concerning money damages for intentional infliction of bodily injury, or environmental damage due to negligence, that took place in the territory of the forum State would not be barred from adjudication as a result of the application of immunity. Furthermore, in such cases, human rights law and domestic criminal law provisions would also be applicable.

4.5.3 *State-Owned Entities and Human Rights Violations: An Exception to Immunity?*

The doctrine of State immunity, however, becomes truly challenging in cases that have elements of extraterritoriality, as Yang limpidly remarks:

> The problems … arise where human rights litigation is instituted against an alleged perpetrator when that person remains outside the territory of the forum State, and/or with respect to human rights violations committed outside that territory. Thus, the crux of the matter, when it comes to immunity with regard to human rights violations is the exercise of *extraterritorial jurisdiction* and the exemption therefrom. As international law currently stands, there are insuperable obstacles to an ideally unhampered exercise of jurisdiction (and denial of immunity) over human rights violations

---

[166] Katherine Holcombe, 'JASTA Straw Man: How the Justice against Sponsors of Terrorism Act Undermines Our Security and Its Stated Purpose' (2017) 25 Am. U.J. Gender Soc. Pol'y & Law; Yang (n 1) 227–228.

[167] Holcombe (n 166) 369–372.

committed abroad . . . . The pitfall lies in the fact that normally State immunity issues arise within the territorial jurisdiction; so the issue of whether or not the court has jurisdiction is often superfluous and of little practical import: the court simply *has* jurisdiction by virtue of the territoriality principle. In the context of human rights litigation, however, the claimant in many cases has to argue for extraterritorial jurisdiction, which may or may not exist.[168]

What transpires is that elements pertaining to jurisdiction often get conflated with those relating to immunity, despite the fact that the availability of the plea of immunity has the effect of affirming jurisdiction.[169] The following paragraphs will describe one of the preferred techniques for addressing the challenges associated with extraterritorial jurisdiction in human rights litigation. After this necessary diversion, the section continues on the topic of State immunity and *jus cogens* violations.

Until recently, litigation under the US Alien Tort Statute (ATS)[170] has proven to be one of the preferred avenues through which multinational corporations in general could be brought to justice for human rights abuses abroad.[171] The ATS could be applicable to all corporations, regardless of whether their ownership is public or private, but as discussed throughout this chapter, certain limitations imposed by State immunity would come into play in the case of SOEs. The ATS contains a single sentence, which states that 'the district courts shall have original jurisdiction of any civil action by an alien for a tort only, committed in violation of the law of nation or a treaty of the United States'. Consequently, such actions can be brought in US courts *by an alien* for compensation for a *tort* in *violation of the law of nations*. The scope of the ATS has been restricted, however, since the decision in *Kiobel v Royal Dutch Petroleum* where a group of Nigerian citizens, residing in the US, filed a suit in the federal court against certain Dutch, British and Nigerian corporations for aiding and abetting the Nigerian military to commit gross human rights violations in order to support the development of oil concessions.[172] Ultimately, the Supreme Court of the United States said that the ATS did not

---

[168] Yang (n 1) 423, 425.
[169] ibid 426. ('[I]mmunity precludes the exercise of an otherwise exercisable jurisdiction.').
[170] Alien Tort Statute.
[171] *Filártiga v Peña-Irala* (United States, Court of Appeals (1980) 630 F2d 876); *Kadic v Karadžic* (United States, Court of Appeals, Second Circuit (1995) 70 F3d 232); *Doe v Unocal* (United States, Court of Appeals, 9th Circuit (2002) 395 F3d 932); *Sosa v Alvarez-Machian* (United States, Supreme Court (2004) 542 US 692); *Wiwa v Royal Dutch Petroleum* (United States, Court of Appeals (2000) 226 F3d 88); *Presbyterian Church of Sudan v Talisman Energy* (United States, Court of Appeals, Second Circuit (2009) 582 F3d 244).
[172] *Kiobel v Royal Dutch Petroleum Co.* ((United States Supreme Court, 2013)133 S Ct 1659).

rebut the presumption against extraterritoriality and that a plaintiff is unable to file a suit under the ATS unless the claim 'touches and concerns the territory of the United States'.[173] The Supreme Court did not go into any details about what those requirements may mean in *Kiobel*,[174] but commentators have argued that, for a claim to 'touch and concern' the United States, the wrongful conduct must have occurred in the United States and must also be a violation of international law.[175] *Kiobel* thus represents a significant departure from previous ATS case law in this area. In *Filartiga v Peña Irala*, the US Court of Appeals for the Second Circuit held that a Paraguayan police officer, who tortured another Paraguayan in Paraguay, could be held accountable in the US for violation of customary international law. The Court said that 'the torturer has become – like the pirate and slave trader before him – *hostis humani generis*, an enemy of all mankind'.[176] Following *Filártiga*, in 1995, Ms Kadic (on her own behalf and on behalf of her son and other Croat and Muslim citizens that were in similar circumstances) brought a suit in the Federal Court against Radovan Karadzic, the president of the Republika Srpska – who happened to be in the United States at the time at the invitation of the UN – for war crimes, genocide, torture, rape, summary execution and other atrocities committed by troops under his command. The United States Court of Appeals, Second Circuit, held that Karadzic was not immune and that the law of nations applied not only to States, but also to non-State actors.[177] In *Doe v Unocal*, four Burmese villagers commenced suit against Unocal and its US parent company, alleging various human rights violations, including slavery, false imprisonment, assault and negligence in relation to the construction of the Yadana gas pipeline in Myanmar. The US Court of Appeals for the Ninth Circuit held that the application of customary international law extended to multinational corporations.[178] In *Sosa v Alvarez – Machian*, however, the Supreme Court held that extraterritorial jurisdiction under the ATS was only permissible in a limited number of circumstances

---

[173] ibid 1669.

[174] ibid.

[175] 'Clarifying Kiobel's "Touch and Concern" Test' <https://harvardlawreview.org/2017/05/clarifying-kiobels-touch-and-concern-test/> accessed 12 August 2020; PS Morris, 'Lex Internationalis: Kiobel, Empires, and the Color of Human Rights' (2015) 7 Geo. J.L. & Mod. Critical Race Persp. 71; R McCorquodale, 'Waving Not Drowning: Kiobel Outside the United States' (2013) 107 Am. J. Int. Law 846; C Kaeb and D Scheffer, 'The Paradox of Kiobel in Europe' (2013) 107 Am. J. Int. Law 852; SH Cleveland 'After Kiobel' (2014) 12 J. Int. Crim. Justice 551.

[176] *Filártiga v Peña-Irala* (n 171).

[177] *Kadic v Karadžic* (n 171).

[178] *Doe v Unocal* (n 171).

which were 'specific, universal, and obligatory',[179] thus likely pointing to norms *jus cogens*. Returning to *Kiobel*, while the Supreme Court did not elaborate precisely what the 'touch and concern' test involved, it ultimately clarified that 'on these facts' – all the relevant conduct complained of having taken place outside the US – 'it would reach too far to say that mere *corporate presence* suffices'.[180] The Court further stated that even if claims 'touch and concern' the territory of the US 'they must do so with sufficient force to displace the presumption against extraterritorial application'.[181] Ultimately, the Court concluded that it was up to Congress to determine otherwise, by passing a statute that was more comprehensive than the ATS. Nevertheless, despite this setback, jurisdiction under the ATS is still available if a claim 'touches and concerns' the territory of the US with sufficient force to displace the presumption against extraterritoriality. In theory, such a claim could 'touch and concern' the United States with sufficient force, as explained by Justice Breyer – who concurred with the Court's judgment, although he rejected its reasoning – if

(1) the alleged tort occurred on American soil, (2) the defendant is an American national, or (3) if the defendant's conduct substantially and adversely affects an important American national interest, and that includes a distinct interest in preventing the United States from becoming a safe harbor (free of civil as well as criminal liability) for a torturer or other common enemy of mankind.[182]

Despite the setback in *Kiobel*, the US Supreme Court was asked again to make a determination whether corporations can be sued for human rights violations under the ATS in *Joseph Jesner v Arab Bank*.[183] In this case, the plaintiffs alleged that the Arab Bank financed terrorist activities in Israel, the West Bank and Gaza through its US subsidiaries. In the oral arguments, the Supreme Court Justices clarified that they were concerned about the 'foreign entanglements' and 'international repercussions' that litigation under the ATS may bring and wondered whether 'extending it to corporate liability' would have the same problematic result of increasing 'entanglements, as it obviously

---

[179] *Sosa v Alvarez-Machian* (n 171). ('Federal courts should not recognise private claims under federal common law for violations of any international law norm with less definite content and acceptance among civilised nations than the historical paradigm.' Thus, arbitrary detention for a day could not be equated with piracy or crimes against humanity for instance.).

[180] *Kiobel v Royal Dutch Petroleum Co.* (n 172) 14. (Emphasis added).

[181] ibid.

[182] *Kiobel v Royal Dutch Petroleum Co.* (n 172). Breyer J at pp. 1–2.

[183] *Joseph Jesner v Arab Bank* (United States, Supreme Court (2018) 138 S Ct 1386).

had here with respect to the government of Jordan'.[184] Unsurprisingly, the Supreme Court decision maintains the status quo established in *Kiobel*. In a 5-4 decision, the Supreme Court (Justice Kennedy, writing for the majority) held that the plaintiffs' claims could not proceed against the Arab Bank and that 'foreign corporations may not be defendants in suits brought under the ATS'.[185] The decision explained that the ATS 'was intended to promote harmony in international relations' and not 'significant diplomatic tension' as this litigation had already caused for the past thirteen years, given that Jordan was a critical ally of the United States in the Middle East.[186] Furthermore, in the opinion of the Supreme Court, 'foreign corporate defendants create unique problems' and 'courts were not well suited to make the required policy judgements' in this context, a task which was best left to Congress.[187] Justice Sotomayor, joined by Justices Ginsburg, Breyer and Kagan, delivered the dissenting opinion and said that

> in categorically barring all suits against foreign corporations under the ATS, the Court ensures that foreign corporations – entities capable of wrongdoing under our domestic law – remain immune from liability for human rights abuses, however egregious they may be . . .. Immunizing corporations that violate human rights from liability under the ATS undermines the system of accountability for law-of-nations violations that the First Congress endeavored to impose. It allows these entities to take advantage of the significant benefits of the corporate form and enjoy fundamental rights, without having to shoulder attendant fundamental responsibilities.[188]

Returning to the issue of State immunity, since the general presumption favours immunity in cases of human rights violations perpetrated by SOEs, claimants would be successful in lifting the veil of immunity only when a particular set of circumstances fits within one of the expressly specified exceptions to immunity. Since no broad exception to State immunity for violations of human rights in general could be located in legislation or jurisprudence, the question that follows is whether this situation is any different in cases of *jus cogens* violations. The remainder of this section will first deal with the jurisprudence in this area, followed by a brief review of some of the theories that have been proposed by various commentators for bypassing the challenge of immunity.

---

[184] ibid. Oral Arguments 11 October, 2017 per Justice Roberts at page 7 and Justice Alito at page 10.
[185] ibid 27.
[186] ibid 25–26.
[187] ibid 27–29.
[188] ibid 33–34.

In the *Jurisdictional Immunities Case* the ICJ authoritatively stated that 'under customary international law as it presently stands, a State is not deprived of immunity by reason of the fact that it is accused of serious violations of international human rights law or the international law of armed conflict'.[189] Consequently, the plea of sovereign immunity is available to a State even for violations of *jus cogens* norms. This issue was considered before the *Jurisdictional Immunities Case* by other courts, which reached similar conclusions. For example, in *Saudi Arabia v Nelson*, the US Supreme Court held that torture acts could not be classified as a 'commercial activity' and dismissed the case for 'lack of subject matter jurisdiction'.[190] The court clarified that Nelson's claims (unlawful arrest, imprisonment and torture) were actually sovereign acts performed by the Saudi police in their official capacity. Even though Nelson was recruited in the United States, this activity did not amount to a commercial activity carried out in the United States for the purposes of the US FSIA. *Jones v Saudi Arabia* concerned the Jones' allegations that he was tortured while in prison in Saudi Arabia. The arguments of the House of Lords, ultimately upholding immunity, although lengthy, are worth reproducing in full:

In countering the claimants' argument the Kingdom, supported by the Secretary of State, is able to advance four arguments which in my opinion are cumulatively irresistible. First, the claimants are obliged to accept, in the light of the *Arrest Warrant* decision of the International Court of Justice that state immunity *ratione personae* can be claimed for a serving foreign minister accused of crimes against humanity. Thus, even in such a context, the international law prohibition of such crimes, having the same standing as the prohibition of torture, does not prevail. It follows that such a prohibition does not automatically override all other rules of international law. The International Court of Justice has made plain that breach of a *jus cogens* norm of international law does not suffice to confer jurisdiction .... Secondly, article 14 of the Torture Convention does not provide for universal civil jurisdiction. It appears that at one stage of the negotiating process the draft contained words, which mysteriously disappeared from the text, making this clear. But the natural reading of the article as it stands in my view conforms with the US understanding noted above, that it requires a private right of action for damages only for acts of torture committed in territory under the jurisdiction of the forum state. This is an interpretation shared by Canada, as its exchanges with the Torture Committee make clear. The correctness of this reading is confirmed when comparison is made between

---

[189] *Jurisdictional Immunities of the State (Germany v Italy: Greece intervening)* (n 5) para 91.
[190] *Saudi Arabia v Nelson* (n 108) 355–363.

the spare terms of article 14 and the much more detailed provisions governing the assumption and exercise of criminal jurisdiction . . . . Thirdly, the UN Immunity Convention of 2004 provides no exception from immunity where civil claims are made based on acts of torture. The Working Group in its 1999 Report makes plain that such an exception was considered, but no such exception was agreed. Despite its embryonic status, this Convention is the most authoritative statement available on the current international understanding of the limits of state immunity in civil cases, and the absence of a torture or *jus cogens* exception is wholly inimical to the claimants' contention . . . . Fourthly, there is no evidence that states have recognised or given effect to an international law obligation to exercise universal jurisdiction over claims arising from alleged breaches of peremptory norms of international law, nor is there any consensus of judicial and learned opinion that they should. This is significant, since these are sources of international law. But this lack of evidence is not neutral: since the rule on immunity is well-understood and established, and no relevant exception is generally accepted, the rule prevails.[191]

The ECHR reached similar conclusions. In *Al-Adsani v United Kingdom* the court held that

the Court, while noting the growing recognition of the overriding importance of the prohibition of torture, does not accordingly find it established that there is yet acceptance in international law of the proposition that States are not entitled to immunity in respect of civil claims for damages for alleged torture committed outside the forum State. The 1978 Act, which grants immunity to States in respect of personal injury claims unless the damage was caused within the United Kingdom, is not inconsistent with those limitations generally accepted by the community of nations as part of the doctrine of State immunity.[192]

Academic commentators have proposed several justifications for a *jus cogens* exception to State immunity, such as the implied waiver theory, the normative hierarchy theory and the right to a judge or a remedy theory.[193] According to the implied waiver theory, when a State 'violates one of a core

---

[191] *Jones v Saudi-Arabia* (n 160) paras 24–28. (Footnotes omitted).
[192] *Al-Adsani v United Kingdom* (European Court of Human Rights, Grand Chamber, Merits, Application No 35763/97) [66].
[193] Pierre d'Argent and Pauline Lesaffre, 'Immunities and Jus Cogens Violations' in Nicolas Angelet and Luca Ferro (eds), *The Cambridge Handbook of Immunities and International Law* (Cambridge University Press 2019) 615; Markus Krajewski and Christopher Singer, 'Should Judges Be Front-Runners? The ICJ, State Immunity and the Protection of Fundamental Human Rights' in A Bogdandy von and R Wolfrum (eds), *Max Planck Yearbook of United Nations Law*, vol 16 (Brill 2012) 23–26.

group of fundamental norms [such as norms *jus cogens*], it impliedly waives its immunity from the jurisdiction of a US court under the FSIA'[194] with section 1605(a)(1) becoming operative. That section states that a State shall not benefit from immunity when it 'has waived its immunity either explicitly or by implication'. The implied waiver theory has, however, been ultimately rejected by courts in the US and Europe.[195] For example, in *Ferrini v Germany*, the Italian Supreme Court of Cassation clarified that

> it should be noted that there exist no actions that necessarily imply a specific will. A waiver cannot be conceived of in the abstract, but can only established *in concreto* if the facts ascertained make it possible to describe specific conduct as 'abdicative'. Besides, it seems unlikely that a party that is guilty of such serious violations would intend to waive the benefit deriving from jurisdictional immunity, this being a prerogative that (if it does not entirely prevent it), certainly makes it more difficult to investigate their responsibility.[196]

The normative hierarchy theory purports that a State's jurisdictional immunity is abrogated for violations of norms *jus cogens*.[197] Although initially this theory appeared to have gained traction for instance in Greece's Supreme Court,[198] and in Italy,[199] immunity was ultimately upheld by the Greek Special Supreme Court[200] as well as by the ECHR,[201] so the Italian courts

---

[194] Adam C Belsky, Mark Merva and Naomi Roht-Arriaza, 'Implied Waiver under the FSIA: A Proposed Exception to Immunity for Violations of Peremptory Norms of International Law' (1989) 77 Cal. L. Rev. 365, 366.

[195] d'Argent and Lesaffre (n 193) 616–617. (Reviews the jurisprudence where the implied waiver theory has been argued as an exception to immunity.).

[196] *Ferrini v Germany* (Italy, Supreme Court of Cassation, Case No 5044/04, ILDC 19 (IT 2004), 11 March 2004) [8.2.]; Pasquale De Sena and Francesca De Vittor, 'State Immunity and Human Rights: The Italian Supreme Court Decision on the Ferrini Case' (2005) 16 Eur. J. Int. Law 89.

[197] Bianchi, 'Gazing at the Crystal Ball (Again)' (n 8); A Bianchi, 'Immunity versus Human Rights: The Pinochet Case' (1999) 10 Eur. J. Int. Law 237.

[198] *Prefecture of Voiotia v Federal Republic of Germany* ((Greece) 4 May 2000, 129 ILR 513); d'Argent and Lesaffre (n 193).

[199] *Ferrini v Germany* (n 196).

[200] *Margellos and Others v Federal Republic of Germany* (Greece, Special Supreme Court, 17 September 2002, 129 ILR 525).

[201] *Kalogeropoulou v Greece and Germany* (European Court of Human Rights, Application No 59021/00, 12 December 2002); *Jones and others v The United Kingdom* (European Court of Human Rights, Fourth Section, Applications Nos 34356/06 and 40528/06, 14 January 2014). For a review of the jurisprudence of the ECHR, see [186]–[192]. For a justification whether the Court should depart from the approach taken by the Grand Chamber in *Al-Adsani*, see [193]–[197].

appear to have been outliers on this issue.[202] In *Kalogeropoulou v Greece and Germany* the ECHR stated that

> the Court does not find it established, however, that there is yet acceptance in international law of the proposition that States are not entitled to immunity in respect of civil claims for damages brought against them in another State for crimes against humanity. The Greek Government cannot therefore be required to override the rule of State immunity against their will. This is true at least as regards the current rule of public international law, as the Court found in the aforementioned case of *Al-Adsani*, but does not preclude a development in customary international law in the future.[203]

The right to a judge or to a remedy would be restricted if immunity was upheld for *jus cogens* violations.[204] Regional human rights courts[205] and domestic courts[206] have, nevertheless, clarified that the right of access to a court can be subjected to limitations. For example, on this issue the ECHR stated that

> the Minister of Justice's refusal to give the applicants leave to apply for expropriation of certain German property situated in Greece cannot be regarded as an unjustified interference with their right of access to a tribunal, particularly as it was examined by the domestic courts and confirmed by a judgment of the Greek Court of Cassation.[207]

While leaving the door open for the possibility that immunity may be lifted in cases where there may not be any other 'reasonable alternative means' to

---

[202] d'Argent and Lesaffre (n 193) 618–619; *Ferrini v Germany* (n 196) para 9.1. (In *Ferrini*, the Court clarified that 'the recognition of immunity from jurisdiction for States that are responsible for such offences is in blatant contrast with the normative framework outlined above, since this recognition obstructs rather than protects such values, the protection of which is rather to be considered, in accordance with such norms and principles, essential for the entire international community, so that in the most serious cases it should justify mandatory forms of response. Moreover, there can be no doubt that this antinomy must be resolved by giving precedence to the higher-ranking norms, as pointed out in the dissenting opinions expressed by the minority judges (eight against nine) appended to the *Al-Adsani* decision. This therefore rules out the possibility that in such hypotheses the State could enjoy immunity from foreign jurisdiction. This would appear to be borne out by the *Furundzija* decision, which lists the possibility of victims "bringing civil suits for compensation before the Courts of a foreign state" among the effects of the violation of norms of this type at 'an inter-State level'.).

[203] *Kalogeropoulou v Greece and Germany* (n 201) 9.

[204] d'Argent and Lesaffre (n 193) 620–623.

[205] *Kalogeropoulou v Greece and Germany* (n 201); *Al-Adsani v United Kingdom* (n 192).

[206] d'Argent and Lesaffre (n 193) 621.

[207] *Kalogeropoulou v Greece and Germany* (n 201) 9.

effectively protect an applicant's rights under the Convention,[208] the ECHR has reached a similar conclusion in *Al-Adsani v United Kingdom*:

The right of access to a court is not, however, absolute, but may be subject to limitations; these are permitted by implication since the right of access by its very nature calls for regulation by the State. In this respect, the Contracting States enjoy a certain margin of appreciation, although the final decision as to the observance of the Convention's requirements rests with the Court. It must be satisfied that the limitations applied do not restrict or reduce the access left to the individual in such a way or to such an extent that the very essence of the right is impaired. Furthermore, a limitation will not be compatible with Article 6(1) if it does not pursue a legitimate aim and if there is no reasonable relationship of proportionality between the means employed and the aim sought to be achieved. The Court must first examine whether the limitation pursued a legitimate aim. It notes in this connection that sovereign immunity is a concept of international law, developed out of the principle *par in parem non habet imperium*, by virtue of which one State shall not be subject to the jurisdiction of another State. The Court considers that the grant of sovereign immunity to a State in civil proceedings pursues the legitimate aim of complying with international law to promote comity and good relations between States through the respect of another State's sovereignty.[209]

Section 4.5.3 has shown how international, regional and domestic courts have tackled human rights and State immunity in cases with extraterritorial elements. The overall conclusion that can be drawn is that at present one cannot speak of a human rights exception to State immunity. Under customary international law, as it currently stands, immunity is not lifted if, in the exercise of acts *jure imperii*, a State is accused of human rights violations, including *jus cogens* norms. The situation is similar at the domestic level. Ultimately, however, foreign States are entitled to immunity only to the extent that the forum State grants them that privilege. In the legal frameworks pertaining to State immunity that are currently in place at international and

---

[208] *Waite and Kennedy v Germany* (European Court of Human Rights, Application Number 26083/94) [68–74]; *Beer and Regan v Germany* (European Court of Human Rights, Grand Chamber, Application Number 28934/95) [58–63]; Philippa Webb, 'A Moving Target: The Approach of the Strasbourg Court to Immunity' in Anne van Aaken and Iulia Motoc (eds), *The European Convention on Human Rights and General International Law* (Oxford University Press 2018) 255; Lorna McGregor, 'State Immunity and Human Rights: Is There a Future after Germany v. Italy?' (2013) 11 J. Int. Crim. Justice 125, 133–136.

[209] *Al-Adsani v United Kingdom* (n 192) para 53.

domestic levels, the point of departure is a presumption of immunity, which will be set aside only in a limited set of circumstances. No such exception currently exists in cases of human rights violations, despite several solutions on how to reconcile State immunity and human rights having been proposed in academic commentary and by courts. Consequently, assuming that assimilation into the State is actually possible, an SOE could plead immunity in cases of human rights violations, with the ultimate effect that a domestic court could be barred from adjudicating the dispute in question or from enforcing a judgment against State property. State immunity could thus leave victims without a method to access justice, or without an effective remedy, if the judgment that was obtained cannot be enforced. The imposition of restrictions in the application of domestic legislation conferring jurisdiction, such as the ATS, adds additional hurdles in cases that have extraterritorial elements, but it also emphasises the sovereign right that States have to regulate access to their own courts. No doubt the expansion of human rights is a development that poses a new set of challenges to traditional doctrines of international law such as State immunity. However, as Philippa Webb has pointed out, State immunity has proved to be a 'moving target'[210] over the past fifty years or so, having evolved from a system that provided benefits only for States to a system that is increasingly expected to take into consideration the protection of individuals. It is thus not far-fetched to assume that this area could further develop in a way that could accommodate developments in human rights law. Since the rules of State immunity are largely customary in nature, they can always evolve through State practice. Furthermore, immunity statutes, where present, could be amended to include a human rights exception to immunity. Nevertheless, in spite of the challenges, the rules on immunities have proven to be 'rather resilient',[211] as demonstrated by jurisprudence such as the *Arrest Warrant Case*[212] and the *Jurisdictional Immunities Case*.[213] Nevertheless, a further issue that must be emphasised is the 'profoundly reciprocal character'[214] of the rules of immunity, an aspect which to a certain extent limits the development of this area of the law, since if a State limits immunity by creating a new exception, for instance, then it can expect the same treatment in return.

---

[210] Webb (n 208) 251.
[211] d'Argent and Lesaffre (n 193) 614.
[212] *Arrest Warrant of 11 April 2000 (Democratic Republic of the Congo v Belgium)* (International Court of Justice, Judgment, ICJ Reports 2002, p 3).
[213] *Jurisdictional Immunities of the State (Germany v Italy: Greece intervening)* (n 5).
[214] d'Argent and Lesaffre (n 193) 614.

4.6 INTERIM CONCLUSION

This chapter bears certain similarities to Chapter 2 in that they both deal with the same undercurrent: a divergence among different conceptualisations of international law. If the emphasis in Chapter 2 was on the different conceptualisations of international legal personality, the focus in this chapter has been on the different conceptualisations of sovereignty, as embodied by the shift from absolute to restrictive immunity. What can be observed in both instances, however, is that international law has an inherent flexibility and ability to adapt to change. The creation of legal frameworks to assimilate all manners of SOEs into the State, the possibility to pierce the corporate veil when required, the establishment of various techniques to distinguish between acts *jure imperii* and acts *jure gestionis* and the creation of exceptions to immunity bears witness to the continuous process of dialogue that exists between the domestic and international spheres. The adoption of those frameworks and concepts in international law ultimately demonstrates the inherent flexibility of this discipline. Prompted by an increase in the trading and commercial activities of States, the shift from absolute to restrictive immunity was gradual but irreversible and continues to this day. Overall, the development of the restrictive doctrine of sovereign immunity has had the role of increasing the accountability of SOEs, as far as their commercial transactions are concerned, and those entities cannot generally claim to be immune as a way to bypass their contractual obligations. Furthermore, SOEs should not be able to claim immunity for non-commercial torts, as long as the requirements for this exception are met. While there is no general human rights exception to State immunity, certain human rights claims, such as those concerning money damages for intentional infliction of bodily injury, or environmental damage due to negligence that took place in the territory of the forum State, would not be barred from adjudication. Nevertheless, difficulties arise in cases of human rights violations that have extraterritorial elements, with the rules of immunity proving to be incredibly resilient. Under customary international law, as it currently stands, immunity is not lifted if, in the exercise of acts *jure imperii*, a State has violated human rights, including *jus cogens* norms. Nevertheless, since the rules of State immunity are largely customary in nature, future State practice can develop to include a human rights exception to immunity. Overall, this chapter aimed to show how the emergence of SOEs and their engagement in commercial activities on the international plane have fundamentally altered the very fabric of international law as clearly demonstrated by the shift from the absolute to the restrictive doctrine of immunity.

5

The Continued Relevance of General International Law

State Responsibility and State-Owned Entities

5.1 INTRODUCTION

This chapter examines the responsibility of States for the acts and omissions of their SOEs. The chapter first analyses responsibility by attribution of conduct, then looks at responsibility for lack of due diligence. The starting point is an introduction to the nature and scope of State responsibility as well as the three elements that must be satisfied for State responsibility to exist: (a) the existence of a breach (b) which is attributable and (c) the absence of any valid justification for non-performance. Particular emphasis will be placed on the role and process of attribution and why a State should be allowed to shield themselves from liability for the acts and omissions of an entity that it owns or controls. The analysis starts by examining the current status of the rules of attribution in general international law applicable to SOEs, as found in Articles 4, 5 and 8 of the ILC Articles. It will be shown that, in certain circumstances, the high threshold for attribution found in general international law may lead to a great majority of the conduct of SOEs being unattributable. Several solutions will be offered to address this challenge. For example, a lower threshold for attribution, such as that expressed by the concept of 'overall control' rather than 'effective control', may be required to address this challenge. As a further solution to the challenges posed by the rules of attribution, Section 5.3 focuses on the responsibility of States for lack of due diligence. The concept of due diligence becomes relevant when certain acts and omissions cannot be attributed to the State, because, for instance, they are not perpetrated by State organs, by actors that are exercising governmental authority or those that are not under the 'effective control' of the State. In such circumstances, a State can nevertheless be held responsible for failure to act diligently to take all the necessary measures available to prevent the occurrence of a specific act. The chapter starts with a brief history of the concept of due diligence and progresses by arguing that in certain circumstances States have due diligence obligations – as a matter of international law – to ensure that SOEs do not violate human rights. Some suggestions about how States could discharge their obligations will also be made, in light of recent State practice. The overall aim of the chapter is to demonstrate the continued relevance and importance of customary international law rules in the context of State corporate ownership.

5.1.1 *The Scope and Nature of State Responsibility*

Since the subjects under study are SOEs, not States, the question that arises is under what circumstances and to what extent can States be responsible for the acts and omissions of their SOEs? The recognition that States often delegate some of their functions to entities that are not part of the State was addressed by the International Law Commission (ILC), when it acknowledged the significance of this issue and said that 'it is important that the State should not be able to evade its international responsibility in certain circumstances solely because it has entrusted the exercise of some governmental functions of authority to entities that are separate from the State'.[1] The rules of State responsibility have been said to have a 'logic similar to that of vicarious liability in domestic law', their main purpose being to provide third parties with 'incentives to control the behaviour of wrongdoers whom they can monitor and influence'.[2] As in any domestic legal order, the principle of responsibility is also central to the international legal system.[3] State responsibility is a

---

[1] International Law Commission, 'Yearbook of the International Law Commission: Documents of the Twenty-Sixth Session: Reports of Special Rapporteurs, Other Documents Submitted by Members of the Commission and Report of the Commission to the General Assembly' (1974) A/CN.4/SER.A/1974/Add.l (Part 1) 282, para 17.

[2] EA Posner and AO Sykes, 'An Economic Analysis of State and Individual Responsibility under International Law' (2007) 9 Am. L. & Econ. Rev. 72, 72, 77, 86–96. ('Neither states nor corporations commit harmful acts – people do. The acts may be committed by prime ministers, CEOs, soldiers, or employees. Corporate liability involves the imposition of liability on the owners of a corporation for the harmful acts of some actual or apparent agent of the corporation. So too, state responsibility under international law involves the imposition of some penalty on the citizenry of a nation as a whole for the harmful act of individual government agents or citizens. In both cases, individuals with no direct connection to the harmful act, other than their status as part owner or citizen in the entity to be sanctioned, bear a cost. That cost may be termed "vicarious liability", by which we mean the imposition of a sanction on one party simply by virtue of that party's status in relation to the individual who commits the harmful act.').

[3] Pierre-Marie Dupuy, 'The International Law of State Responsibility: Revolution or Evolution?' (1989) 11 Mich. J. Int'l L 126. ('In every system of law, responsibility as a legal institution plays a leading part, because it both organizes and reveals the level of integration of this system, as well

fundamental principle of international law, which arises out of two other interconnected fundamental doctrines: State sovereignty and the equality of States.[4]

The concept of responsibility can be traced back to Roman law, which had a well-developed principle of collective responsibility that remained relatively unchanged until the early Middle Ages.[5] In the late Middle Ages, the principle of collective responsibility softened, largely due to the increase in the number and size of the various human collectives and a 'tribe could avoid collective responsibility by withdrawing community protection from the individual actor and evicting the person from the community'.[6] During the seventeenth century, further distancing from the notion of collective responsibility took place and responsibility for the acts or omissions of the members of a given community was viewed to be the fault of the king. This type of responsibility was narrowly defined to include what would now be considered as only outright acts of the State.[7] Following the peace of Westphalia, there was a gradual shift and expansion in the concept of responsibility which now rested with the State – as a subject of international law – rather than with the person of the king.[8] However, those early conceptualisations of the State were still based on 'the notion of the state as a tribal unit, defined by personal membership rather than a territorial entity' and it was not until the nineteenth and early twentieth century that those old notions were completely discarded

---

as the prevailing conceptions inside it regarding the nature of rights and of obligations, the consequences of their infringement and, perhaps more deeply, the ethical and social foundations of the whole. The establishment of a certain type of responsibility requires contemplation of the relationship it defines between the subjects of law, their acts and the community to which they belong.').

[4] Malcom N Shaw, *International Law* (Cambridge University Press 2008) 566; Alain Pellet, 'The Definition of Responsibility in International Law' in James Crawford and others (eds), *The Law of International Responsibility* (Oxford University Press 2010) 4. (Pellet argues that 'far from constituting "an abandonment of its sovereignty"', the possibility for a State to incur responsibility 'is an attribute of State sovereignty'. In the same way that the responsibility of the individual is the consequence of his or her liberty, it is *because* the State is sovereign, and as a result, coexists with other entities which are equally sovereign, that the State can engage its own responsibility and invoke the consequences of the responsibility of others: 'if it is the prerogative of sovereignty to be able to assert its rights, the counterpart of that prerogative is the duty to discharge its obligations'.) (Footnotes omitted).

[5] Jan Arno Hessbruegge, 'The Historical Development of the Doctrines of Attribution and Due Diligence in International Law' (2003) 36 NYUJ Int'l. L. & Pol. 265, 276–281.

[6] ibid 280.

[7] ibid 281–287.

[8] ibid 287–292.

to make way for the emergence of the current system, where responsibility is based on control over territory or persons.[9]

There are two broad principles in international law that deal with the responsibility of a State for the acts of non-State actors. First, States will be responsible for the acts or omissions of non-State actors that can be *attributed* to the State. For example, the acts of State organs – de jure or de facto – are automatically attributable to the State, as are the acts of non-State actors if they are performed in the exercise of governmental authority, or if the non-State actor is under the instruction, direction or control of the State. Second, outside of those circumstances, the acts or omissions of non-State actors are generally not attributable to the State, unless the State was required to exercise *due diligence* in preventing or reacting to those acts and omissions and it has failed to do so. Some commentators have referred to the two principles as 'responsibility by attribution' and 'responsibility due to failure to exercise due diligence'.[10]

Also, an important point to distinguish at this stage is the difference between the primary rules and secondary rules of State responsibility. The primary rules are concerned with the relevant substantive obligation – be it a norm of customary international law or a specific treaty provision – while the secondary rules are concerned with defining the general rules *through which* States can be responsible.[11] The 'rapid and continuous developments in both custom or treaty', led the 'corpus of primary rules beyond the reach of codification' and has been the main cause of the split between primary and secondary rules.[12] As such, an identification of the primary rule would require one to discover the norm, which has allegedly been breached by looking at customary norms or treaty provisions. Another key point is that while the basic approach to the law of State responsibility is that of objective responsibility – which does not generally require an element of fault – there may be substantive obligations which indeed include an element of fault as a prerequisite. In such cases, the existence of fault is a necessary condition for responsibility to arise. To put it simply – in the words of James Crawford – 'if the primary rules require fault (of a particular character) or damage (of a particular kind) then they do; if not, then not'.[13] Furthermore, the secondary rules of State

---

[9] ibid 292, 295.
[10] ibid 268–269.
[11] James Crawford, *State Responsibility: The General Part* (1st pbk. edn, Cambridge University Press 2014) 64–66.
[12] ibid 65.
[13] James Crawford, 'Revising the Draft Articles on State Responsibility' (1999) 10 Eur. J. Int. Law 435, 438.

responsibility do not deal with the concept of due diligence in detail, so any argument that such an obligation exists in a particular case would have to be made by reference to the primary rules.[14]

State responsibility, as a distinct field of legal study, is a creation of the late nineteenth century.[15] The disastrous aftermaths of the two world wars put this topic high on the agenda of both the Hague Codification Conference of 1930 and of the ILC in 1947.[16] The ILC worked on this issue for over half a century until 2001, when under the stewardship of the Special Rapporteur James Crawford, the ILC adopted the ILC Articles. At the end of 2001, the United Nations General Assembly 'took note' of the ILC Articles and annexed the text to the General Assembly Resolution 56/83, thereby recommending them to all governments for appropriate action 'without prejudice to the question of their future adoption'.[17] The ILC Articles have not been adopted to the status of convention, but they are, nevertheless, considered to represent an accurate codification of the customary international law on State responsibility.[18] Some commentators have emphasised that despite the fact that the ILC Articles have not been adopted into a convention, it is unlikely to ultimately affect their success, and it is possible that they will have more influence as an ILC text, rather than as a multilateral treaty.[19] As such, when one enquires about the sources of the law on State responsibility, while the ILC Articles present an accurate codification of the customary international law on State responsibility, they are not the only source where such obligations may be found. In addition to the ILC Articles, certain States may have specific treaty arrangements that create either completely or partially different regimes in this area. This fact is acknowledged in Article 55, which states that the ILC Articles are not applicable 'to the extent that the conditions for the existence of an internationally wrongful act or the content or implementation of the international responsibility of a State are governed by special rules of

---

[14] V Chetail 'The Legal Personality of Multinational Corporations, State Responsibility and Due Diligence: The Way Forward' in Denis Alland and others (eds), *Unity and Diversity of International Law: Essays in Honour of Professor Pierre-Marie Dupuy* (Brill 2014) 124–125; Robert P Barnidge Jr, 'The Due Diligence Principle under International Law' 8 ICLR 81, 87.
[15] Crawford, *State Responsibility* (n 11) 3–44.
[16] ibid 28–44.
[17] Articles on Responsibility of States for Internationally Wrongful Acts (November 2001, Supplement No. 10 (U.N. Doc. A/56/10 (2001) 2.
[18] *Application of the Convention on the Prevention and Punishment of the Crime of Genocide (Bosnia and Herzegovina v Serbia and Montenegro)* (International Court of Justice, Judgment, ICJ Reports 2007, p 43) [401].
[19] David D Caron, 'The ILC Articles on State Responsibility: The Paradoxical Relationship between Form and Authority' (2002) 96 Am. J. Int. Law 857, 857.

international law'. By way of example, such rules can be found for instance in the SCM Agreement.[20]

It follows that, as Douglas argues:

International law does not contain a single body of secondary rules of State responsibility for all wrongful acts committed by a State. This is particularly evident in the case of international treaties that confer rights directly upon non-State actors, such as the European Convention Human Rights, the Algiers Accords establishing the Iran/US Claims tribunals, bilateral investment treaties, NAFTA, the Energy Charter Treaty, and the ICSID Convention. These treaties create mechanisms for non-State actors to invoke the international responsibility of contracting States which transcend the traditional dichotomy between public and private international law. The secondary obligations generated by the implementation of State responsibility in these cases are different in juridical character from secondary obligations that arise on the inter-State plane. It is thus appropriate to consider them as sub-systems of State responsibility that share a distinctive feature in that the new legal relationship which arises upon the commission of the wrongful act is between a State and a non-State actor rather than between two or more States. Unlike in the traditional domains of public international law, the obligations created in special regimes involving non-State actors, such as in the investor/State sphere of the ICSID Convention, 'are not simply based on the separation of States, and consequently not focused on the anti-parallel exercise of sovereignty by interference of one State in the sovereignty of another State'.[21]

Nevertheless, even in such circumstances, the ILC Articles may be partially applicable, as a fallback mechanism,[22] alongside any *lex specialis* responsibility

---

[20] *United States – Definitive Anti-Dumping and Countervailing Duties on Certain Products from China (Appellate Body Report)*) (World Trade Organisation (WT/DS379/AB/R 11 March 2011)) para 316. ('The question in the present case, however, is not whether certain of the ILC Articles are to be *applied*, that is, whether attribution of conduct of the SOEs and SOCBs at issuc to the Government of China is to be assessed pursuant to the ILC Articles instead of Article 1.1(a)(1) of the *SCM Agreement*. There is no doubt that the provision being applied in the present case is Article 1.1(a)(1)').

[21] Zachary Douglas, 'Other Specific Regimes of Responsibility: Investment Treaty Arbitration and ICSID' in James Crawford and others (eds), *The Law of International Responsibility* (Oxford University Press 2010) 819.

[22] Robert Kolb, *The International Law of State Responsibility: An Introduction* (Edward Elgar 2018) 73. ('The presumption is that these special regimes derogate from the general rules only to the extent stipulated for or else necessary for the implementation of the object and purpose of the special regime.').

regime.[23] For example, as Article 304 of the UN Convention on the Law of the Sea states:

The provisions of this Convention regarding responsibility and liability for damage are without prejudice to the application of existing rules and the development of further rules regarding responsibility and liability under international law.[24]

Overall, the principles of State responsibility have wide application and are regularly used across many branches of international law such as investment law,[25] trade law,[26] human rights[27] and humanitarian

---

[23] Brunno Simma, 'Of Planets and the Universe: Self-Contained Regimes in International Law' (2006) 17 Eur. J. Int. Law 483; Bruno Simma and Dirk Pulkowski, 'Leges Speciales and Self-Contained Regimes' in James Crawford and others (eds), *The Law of International Responsibility* (Oxford University Press 2010) 140; J Crawford, *Chance, Order: The Course of International Law* (Hague Academy of International Law 2014) 303–309. (Simma and Pulkowski clarify that 'the ILC introduced a tool for connecting the rules on State responsibility with other regimes of international law. However, the application of the principle is controversial with regard to subsystems that have attained a particularly high degree of autonomy. The more system's operation is "closed" towards its international law environment, the less likely is it to fall back on the rules on State responsibility . . . [However,] to avoid confusion, the term "self-contained regime" should not be used to circumscribe the unrealistic hypothesis of a fully autonomous legal subsystem'.).

[24] United Nations Convention on the Law of the Sea 1994 Article 304.

[25] Luca Schicho, 'Attribution and State Entities: Diverging Approaches in Investment Arbitration' (2011) 12 JWIT 283; Srilal M Perera, 'State Responsibility: Ascertaining the Liability of States in Foreign Investment Disputes' (2005) 6 JWIT 499; Jean-Marc Loncle and Jean-Baptiste Morel, 'Emanations of States and ICSID Arbitration' [2008] Int'l Bus. L.J. 29; Paul Blyschak, 'State-Owned Enterprises and International Investment Treaties: When Are State-Owned Entities and Their Investments Protected?' (2011) 6 J. Int'l L. & Int'l Rel. 1, 35–51; Guillermo J. Garcia Sanchez, 'The Hydrocarbon Industry's Challenge to International Investment Law: A Critical Approach' (2016) 57 Harv. Int'l L.J. 475, 513–518; Nick Gallus, 'State Enterprises as Organs of the State and BIT Claims' (2006) 7 JWIT 761; Michael Feit, 'Responsibility of the State under International Law for the Breach of Contract Committed by a State-Owned Entity' (2010) 28 Berkeley J. Int'l L. 142; Michael Feit, 'Attribution and the Umbrella Clause: Is There a Way out of the Deadlock' (2012) 21 Minn. J. Int'l L. 21; Deborah Russo, 'The Attribution to States of the Conduct of Public Enterprises in the Fields of Investment and Human Rights Law', *The Italian Yearbook of International Law 2019* (Brill Nijhoff 2020) 93.

[26] Santiago Villapando, 'Attribution of Conduct to the State: How the Rules of State Responsibility May Be Applied within the WTO Dispute Settlement System' (2002) J. Int. Econ. Law 393, 408; Jaemin Lee, 'State Responsibility and Government-Affiliated Entities in International Economic Law: The Danger of Blurring the Chinese Wall between "State Organ" and "Non-State Organ" as Designed in the ILC Draft Articles' (2015) 49 JWIT 117. (Generally, the rules of the WTO agreements do not normally depart from the solutions offered by international law, except in some rare cases.).

[27] Melissa E Crow, 'Smokescreens and State Responsibility: Using Human Rights Strategies to Promote Global Tobacco Control' (2004) 29 Yale J. Int'l L. 209; Danwood Mzikenge Chirwa,

law,[28] international criminal law,[29] environmental law and more recently in the context of cyber security.[30] A State that has breached an international obligation must 'make reparation in an adequate form'.[31] A finding that a State is internationally responsible rests on the fulfillment of three conditions: (a) the existence of a breach (b) which is attributable to the State and (c) the absence of any valid justification for non-performance.[32] This chapter deals with points (a) and (b) and only to the extent that they may relate to SOEs.

'The Doctrine of State Responsibility as a Potential Means of Holding Private Actors Accountable for Human Rights' (2004) 5 Melb. J. Int'l L. 1; Robert Dufresne, 'The Opacity of Oil: Oil Corporations, Internal Violence, and International Law' (2003) 36 NYUJ Int'l. L. & Pol. 331; Robert McCorquodale and Penelope Simons, 'Responsibility Beyond Borders: State Responsibility for Extraterritorial Violations by Corporations of International Human Rights Law' (2007) 70 Mod. L. Rev. 598; Deborah Russo, 'The Attribution to States of the Conduct of Public Enterprises in the Fields of Investment and Human Rights Law', *The Italian Yearbook of International Law 2019* (Brill Nijhoff 2020) 93.

[28] Katerina Galai, 'Companies of Past and Present: Lessons from the East Indian Company on the Use and Regulation of Private Forces Today' (2016) 4 Legal Issues J. 1, 11–15.

[29] *Prosecutor v Du[Ko Tadi] a/k/a 'Dule'* (ICTY (IT-94-1-T), 7 May 1990, Trial Chamber); *Prosecutor v Du[Ko Tadi]* (ICTY (IT-94-1-A), 15 July 1999, Appeals Chamber); *Application of the Convention on the Prevention and Punishment of the Crime of Genocide (Bosnia and Herzegovina v Serbia and Montenegro)* (International Court of Justice, Judgment, ICJ Reports 2007, p 43).

[30] Jessica Zhanna Malekos Smith, 'No State Is an Island in Cyberspace' (2016) 5 J.L. & Cyber Warfare 4; Michael Schmitt and Liis Vihul, 'Proxy Wars in Cyberspace: The Evolving International Law of Attribution' (2014) 1 Fletcher Sec. Rev. 53; Thomas Payne, 'Teaching Old Law New Tricks: Applying and Adapting State Responsibility to Cyber Operations' (2016) 20 Lewis & Clark L. Rev. 683; Scott J Shackelford, Scott Russell and Andreas Kuehn, 'Unpacking the International Law on Cybersecurity Due Diligence: Lessons from the Public and Private Sectors' (2016) 17 Chi. J. Int'l L. 1; Griffin M Barnett, 'Combating Trade Secret Theft by Foreign State-Owned Entities: An International Law Approach' (2016) 5 J. Int. & Comp. Law 2; Zachary P Augustine, 'Cyber Neutrality: A Textual Analysis of Traditional Jus in Bello Neutrality Rules through a Purpose-Based Lens' (2014) 71 AFL Rev. 69.

[31] *Case Concerning the Factory at Chorzów (Germany v Poland)(Jurisdiction)* (Permanent Court of International Justice, Series A No 9 (Judgment of 26 July 1927)) 21.

[32] James Crawford and Simon Olleson, 'The Character and Forms of International Responsibility', *International Law* (4th edn, Oxford University Press 2014) 453. (Although Article 2 of the ILC only outlines two elements of what might constitute an 'internationally wrongful act of a State' – that is, attribution and breach – the Commentaries to the Draft Articles clarify that 'Article 2 introduces and places in the necessary legal context the questions dealt with in subsequent chapters of Part One. Subparagraph (a) – which states that conduct attributable to the State under international law is necessary for there to be an internationally wrongful act – corresponds to chapter II, while chapter IV deals with the specific cases where one State is responsible for the internationally wrongful act of another State. Subparagraph (b) – which states that such conduct must constitute a breach of an international obligation – corresponds to the general principles stated in chapter III, while chapter V deals with cases where the wrongfulness of conduct, which would otherwise be a breach of an obligation, is precluded'. Consequently, the introduction of the third element, which deals with the circumstances that preclude wrongfulness, is more a matter of logic rather than a strict legal

5.1.2 *Breach of an International Obligation*

The element of breach sits at the heart of State responsibility, since as Article 1 of the ILC Articles states, 'every internationally wrongful act of a State entails the international responsibility of that State'. Article 2 clarifies that an internationally wrongful act consists of either an act or omission that has two elements: it is attributable to the State under international law and constitutes a breach of an international obligation. Article 12 of the ILC Articles defines a breach as an 'act of a State', which 'is not in conformity with what is required of it by that obligation, regardless of its origin or character'. The Commentaries further elaborate on the meaning of this issue in the following manner:

> The expression 'not in conformity with what is required of it by that obligation' is the most appropriate to indicate what constitutes the essence of a breach of an international obligation by a State. It allows for the possibility that a breach may exist even if the act of the State is only partly contrary to an international obligation incumbent upon it. In some cases precisely defined conduct is expected from the State concerned; in others the obligation only sets a minimum standard above which the State is free to act. Conduct proscribed by an international obligation may involve an act or omission or a combination of acts and omissions . . . .. The phrase 'not in conformity with' is flexible enough to cover the many different ways in which an obligation can be expressed, as well as the various forms which a breach may take.[33]

Another factor to consider in the interpretation of Article 12 is the clarification that the origin or character of the obligations is unimportant and this 'formula refers to all possible sources of international obligations' regardless whether they have their origin in treaty, custom or a decision made by an international judicial body, tribunal or an organ of an international organisation.[34] This principle has also been confirmed in the *Rainbow Warrior*

---

requirement under Article 2. Crawford and Olleson further note on this issue that 'in principle, the fulfillment of these conditions is a sufficient basis for international responsibility, as has been consistently affirmed by international courts and tribunals. In some cases, however, the respondent State may claim that it is justified in its non-performance, for example, because it was acting in self-defence or was subject to a situation of force majeure. In international law such defences or excuses are termed "circumstances precluding wrongfulness". They will be a matter for the respondent State to assert and prove, not for the claimant State to negate'.) (Footnotes omitted).

[33] International Law Commission, *Draft Articles on Responsibility of States for Internationally Wrongful Acts, with Commentaries* (Yearbook of the International Law Commission, Vol II, Part Two 2001) 55.

[34] ibid.

arbitration, where the tribunal stated that 'any violation by a State of any obligation of whatever origin, gives rise to State responsibility and consequently to the duty of reparation'.[35] The term 'obligation' is limited to those obligations that a State has under international law and a breach of contractual obligations are not enough to engage responsibility.[36] Furthermore, as Article 3 of the ILC Articles clarifies, the 'characterization of an act of State as internationally wrongful is governed by international law', meaning that the internal law of the State in question does not have a role to play in this determination.[37]

The question whether the rules of State responsibility found in general international law are actually applicable to human rights violations has been debated in the literature. Chirwa, for instance, points to some limitations in this regard, such as the difficulty of establishing a connection between the State in question and the conduct that constitutes a violation of international law and the fact that the general principles of State responsibility do not recognise the rights of individuals to enforce international law generally.[38] However, Crawford has clarified that Article 12 of the ILC Articles

> make it clear that the origin and character of an obligation are irrelevant to the question whether a breach has occurred for the purposes of establishing responsibility. Subject to the *lex specials* principle the general provisions on breach apply to all forms of breach across all fields of international law – even though breaches themselves may fall into different categories for the purpose of establishing when a breach has occurred.[39]

Furthermore,

> human rights law and the general international law principles of state responsibility should be regarded as forming part of a single whole. They are complimentary and mutually reinforcing...the difference in history and

---

[35] *Case concerning the difference between New Zealand and France concerning the interpretation or application of two agreements concluded on 9 July 1986 between the two States and which related to the problems arising from the Rainbow Warrior Affair (New Zealand v France)* (Decision of 30 April 1990, United Nations, Reports of International Awards, Volume XX pp 215–284) [75].

[36] Feit, 'Responsibility of the State under International Law for the Breach of Contract Committed by a State-Owned Entity' (n 25); Feit, 'Attribution and the Umbrella Clause: Is There a Way out of the Deadlock' (n 25).

[37] International Law Commission, *Draft Articles on Responsibility of States for Internationally Wrongful Acts, with Commentaries* (n 33) 36.

[38] Chirwa (n 27) 10.

[39] Crawford, *State Responsibility* (n 11) 219–220. (Footnotes omitted.)

in jurisprudential origins between the two should not conceal their essential affinity and their increasing convergence.[40]

The chapter does not attempt to catalogue every single wrong that could be committed by SOEs and for which the State may ultimately be responsible because, as it has been recognised by several commentators,[41] there may be a wide range of such activities which may ultimately render States responsible for those acts and omissions:

> This facilitation may range from the provision of financing and other services by export credit agencies to the negotiation and ratification of bilateral investment agreements that assist extraterritorial investment by corporate nationals. It also includes the failure by a state to prevent actions by its corporate nationals (including privatized state corporations) that violate human rights both within and outside its territory.[42]

5.2 RESPONSIBILITY BY ATTRIBUTION OF CONDUCT

5.2.1 *General Comments on the Concept of Attribution*

For a State to be found responsible, three elements must be satisfied: there must be an internationally *wrongful act or omission* that constitutes a *breach of an international obligation* which is *attributable* to the State under

---

[40] Chirwa (n 27) 10. (Footnotes omitted).

[41] McCorquodale and Simons (n 27); J Schönsteiner 'Attribution of State Responsibility for Actions or Omissions of State-Owned Enterprises in Human Rights Matters' (2019) 40 U. Pa. J. Int'l L. 895, 898–899. (Schönsteiner clarifies that 'typical human rights violations will depend on the sector in which the SOE works. SOEs are usually to be found in the extractive and energy sectors; in the services sector, especially banking and passenger transportation; and in telecommunications. As has been documented in case studies, violations in these sectors include, violations of indigenous land rights, including eviction or resettlement without free, prior, and informed consent; violations of the right to health, the right to water; or the right to live in a healthy environment in relation to emissions, spills, rupture of tailing dams, or similar environmental damage due to contamination; violations of individual and collective labour rights; and violations of the right to life, integrity, freedom of assembly, or freedom of expression in relation to social protest against business projects. Finally, there might be violations of the right to information or the right to participation in the project planning, design, exploration, operation, and closure phases. With regard to community and client relations in the service sector, violations may additionally occur through discrimination, be it due to race, ethnicity, gender, sexual orientation, national origin, religion, participation in a trade union, or socio-economic condition, among other grounds'.) (Footnotes omitted).

[42] McCorquodale and Simons (n 27) 599.

international law and for which there is *no valid justification for non-perform-ance*. Attribution thus forms a critical part in the law on State responsibility:

> The State being a moral person without any physical existence, can act only through persons whose conduct is performed on behalf of the State. The notion of attribution thus concerns this 'attachment' of a legal position from one individual to another subject: the legal fact that the action of one is considered to be the action of another. Hence, attribution can be defined as a legal operation through which acts and omissions of individuals performed on behalf of the State are considered legally to be the acts and omissions of the latter, in view of a certain legal function (here the one of responsibility).[43]

Attribution has the function of limiting the responsibility of States to conduct which 'engages the State as an organisation'.[44] Since, in theory, 'the conduct of all human beings, corporations or collectivities linked to the State by nationality, habitual residence or incorporation might be attributed to the State, whether or not they have any connection to the Government',[45] if no such limitation would exist, the task of governing would become impossible. As States can 'only act through "agents" in control of the State or some part of its apparatus, it is only the acts of those individuals that can be attributed to the State if done under actual or apparent authority of the State.'[46] Since private conduct is generally not attributable, the main principle that underlies the doctrine of attribution is that States must be held responsible for the official actions of those that are in fact controlling the State. In this context, questions thus arise in relation to the attribution of conduct of SOEs, an issue on which the ILC made the following remarks:

> If such corporations act inconsistently with the international obligations of the State concerned the question arises whether such conduct is attributable to the State. In discussing this issue it is necessary to recall that international law acknowledges the general separateness of corporate entities at the national level, except in those cases where the 'corporate veil' is a mere device or a vehicle for fraud or evasion. The fact that the State initially establishes a corporate entity, whether by a special law or otherwise, is not a sufficient basis for the attribution to the State of the subsequent conduct of

---

[43] Robert Kolb, *The International Law of State Responsibility: An Introduction* (Edward Elgar 2018) 70; Marko Milanovic, 'Special Rules of Attribution of Conduct in International Law' (2020) 96 Int. Law Stud. 303.

[44] International Law Commission, *Draft Articles on Responsibility of States for Internationally Wrongful Acts, with Commentaries* (n 33) 38.

[45] ibid.

[46] Gordon A Christenson, 'Attributing Acts of Omission to the State' (1991) 12 Mich. J. Int'l L 60, 312.

that entity. Since corporate entities, although owned by and in that sense subject to the control of the State, are considered to be separate, prima facie their conduct in carrying out their activities is not attributable to the State unless they are exercising elements of governmental authority within the meaning of article 5. This was the position taken, for example, in relation to the de facto seizure of property by a State-owned oil company, in a case where there was no proof that the State used its ownership interest as a vehicle for directing the company to seize the property. On the other hand, where there was evidence that the corporation was exercising public powers, or that the State was using its ownership interest in or control of a corporation specifically in order to achieve a particular result, the conduct in question has been attributed to the State.[47]

The three rules of attribution that are relevant to this chapter can be found in Articles 4, 5 and 8 of the ILC Articles.[48] The first rule of attribution is found in Article 4, which deals with the situation where the conduct of a State organ can be attributed to the State based on the status of that entity being an *organ* of that State, either because that entity is deemed as such in the domestic law of the State in question, or because it was actually acting in this manner, even if its status as a State organ was not acknowledged in domestic law.[49] This situation is triggered by the principle of the unity of the State, and it operates by *renvoi* to the domestic law of the relevant State, as explained by the ILC:

> International law makes no distinction between different components of the State for the purposes of the law of responsibility, even if the State does so, for example by treating different organs as distinct legal persons under its own law. The relevant international principle is that of the 'unity of State'. In this respect, the process of attribution is an autonomous one under international law, as stipulated in Article 4.[50]

---

[47] International Law Commission, *Draft Articles on Responsibility of States for Internationally Wrongful Acts, with Commentaries* (n 33) 48.

[48] In addition to Articles 4, 5 and 8, chapter II of the ILC Articles – titled 'Attribution of Conduct to a State' – further deals with attribution in Article 6 (covering the special case where on organ of one State is placed the disposal of another State and empowered to exercise the governmental authority of that State); Article 7 (deals with excess of authority or contravention of instructions); Article 9 (attribution of conduct that was carried out in the absence or default of the official authorities); Article 10 (conduct of an insurrectional or other movement) and Article 11 (addresses conduct that was acknowledged and adopted by a State as its own).

[49] International Law Commission, *Draft Articles on Responsibility of States for Internationally Wrongful Acts, with Commentaries* (n 33) 42.

[50] International Law Commission, 'First Report on State Responsibility, by Mr James Crawford, Special Rapporteur' (1998) DOCUMENT A/CN.4/490 and Add. 1–7* 34.

The second rule of attribution is contained in Article 5 and is based on the *exercise of governmental authority* by the entity in question. The main purpose of Article 5 is to ensure that States do not abuse the delegation of governmental authority in order to evade responsibility. The critical and separate issues under Article 5 are whether the functions or powers exercised by the entity in question could actually constitute governmental authority *and* whether that governmental authority was *in fact* exercised. For instance, while many entities may be endowed with functions that constitute governmental authority generally, the conduct in question may not amount to an exercise of that authority,[51] a situation that is relevant particularly in cases where SOEs have so-called mixed functions. In cases where an entity has mixed functions it will be only the acts that are deemed as being the exercise of 'governmental authority', *in that particular instance*, that will be attributed to the State, with all other acts falling outside the scope of attribution. Under Article 8, it is assumed that by virtue of the extensive control exercised by the State over a given entity, that entity is akin to an *alter ego* of the State.[52] While Article 8 starts from the premise that private conduct is not attributable to the State, its provisions are applicable to two circumstances. First, Article 8 deals with the situation where private persons are acting under the *instructions* of the State as auxiliaries to police or army forces. This circumstance has a relatively narrow sphere of application. The second circumstance deals with State *direction* or *control* over a particular entity. It is in the second circumstance that most SOEs would fit. As far as the relationship between the three rules of attribution covered by Articles 4, 5 and 8 is concerned, dispute settlement bodies have addressed the rules separately, which is considered to be the orthodox approach.[53]

Consequently, recalling that the subjects of this monograph are SOEs, the questions that must be asked are different under each rule of attribution. Under Article 4, the crucial question will be whether the SOE has the status of a 'State organ' de jure or de facto.[54] Under Article 5, the pertinent question is this: Are the actions of the SOE of such nature that they can be deemed to be an exercise of governmental authority *and* was that governmental authority

---

[51] *EDF (Services) Limited v Romania* (ICSID Case No ARB/05/13) [195]; *Bayindir Insaat Turizm Ticaret Ve Sanayi AS v Islamic Republic of Pakistan* (ICSID Case No ARB/03/29) [123].

[52] Galai (n 28) 11–15.

[53] *Jan de Nul NV and Dredging International NV v Arab Republic of Egypt* (ICSID Case No ARB/04/13 (Award)) [143, 155]; *Bayindir Insaat Turizm Ticaret Ve Sanayi A.S. v Islamic Republic of Pakistan* (ICSID Case No ARB/03/29) paras 111–124; *EDF (Services) Limited v Romania* (ICSID Case No ARB/05/13) paras 187–214; Schicho (n 25) 289.

[54] Crawford, *State Responsibility* (n 11) 124–126.

in fact exercised? For the purposes of this question the existence (or not, as the case may be) of separate legal personality will be less important, as long as it can be proved that the entity in question *did in fact* exercise elements of governmental authority. Thus, the main inquiry in this instance turns on the character and forms of governmental authority by asking what exactly is meant by an exercise of governmental authority by a State organ? In the third instance, which is covered by Article 8 of the ILC Articles, the existence of separate legal personality is a given. However, because the State controls to such an extent the affairs of that entity, the entity is in fact considered to be under the 'effective control' of that State. While this situation is indeed encountered usually in the case of SOEs, it does not exclude the possibility of a fully private actor being completely controlled by a State in order to achieve a certain end. All three situations will be examined in detail below, first from a general perspective, then from the perspective of SOEs through relevant examples applicable to each rule.

5.2.2 *Attribution Based on Status: When Does a State-Owned Entity Have the Status of a 'State Organ'?*

Article 4 of the ILC Articles states that

> (1) The conduct of any State organ shall be considered an act of that State under international law, whether the organ exercises legislative, executive, judicial or any other functions, whatever position it holds in the organisation of the State, and whatever its character as an organ of the central government or of a territorial unity of the State. (2) An organ includes any person or entity, which has that status in accordance with the internal law of the State.

Consequently, the question that must be asked for the purposes of Article 4 is under what circumstances will an SOE be considered as having the status of a 'State organ'? This is because 'once it is established that an entity is an organ of the State, the presumption is that all of its acts are attributable to the State unless the contrary is proven'.[55] Attribution under Article 4 is the most direct, in comparison to Article 5 and Article 8, which can be considered as auxiliary forms of responsibility. Another unique aspect of attribution under Article 4 is that it is only in the context of this article that the terminology of 'State organ' is actually permitted, rendering the use of the word 'organ' in the context of attribution under Article 5 or Article 8 'inapposite'.[56] If an SOE cannot be

---

[55] *EDF (Services) Limited v Romania* (n 53) para 188.
[56] Crawford, *State Responsibility* (n 11) 126.

considered as having the status of a 'State organ', then attribution under Article 4 is not possible. According to the Commentaries to the ILC Articles 'a "State organ" covers all the individual or collective entities which make up the organisation of the State and act on its behalf.[57] Judicial decisions have confirmed that the legislative,[58] executive[59] and the judicial branch,[60] as well as federal[61] and other similar internal subdivisions[62] are indeed State organs, and the State is responsible for their actions, thus reflecting the principle of the unity of the State.[63] This rule has achieved the status of customary international law.[64]

While, to a certain extent, it might be obvious that the legislative, executive and the judiciary as well as any constituent territorial subdivisions or federal units form the essential structure of a State, at least where the internal organisation of the State in question is based on principles such as the separation of powers, this is not the case with SOEs. For instance, a State could function equally well without the existence of any SOEs integrated in its formal structure, and this situation is often encountered, for example, in economic systems which are based on capitalism. Article 4 thus looks at the structure of the State, and the criteria that will be discussed below seek to determine *if* and *where* a 'State organ' would fit within the structure of the State. Consequently, the tests that determine whether an entity is a State organ or not can be said to be structural in nature.[65] The structural test is composed of elements that overall seek to determine the public nature of the entity in

---

[57] International Law Commission, *Draft Articles on Responsibility of States for Internationally Wrongful Acts, with Commentaries* (n 33) 40.
[58] *Case Concerning Certain German Interests in Polish Upper Silesia* (Permanent Court of International Justice, 1926, Series A, No 7 (The Merits)) 19).
[59] *Armed Activities on the Territory of the Congo (Democratic Republic of the Congo v Uganda)* (International Court of Justice, Judgment, ICJ Reports 2005, p 168) [213].
[60] *United States – Import Prohibition of Certain Shrimp and Shrimp Products* (World Trade Organisation, WT/DS58/AB/R 12 October 1998) [173].
[61] *Metalclad Corporation v The United Mexican States* (ICSID Case No ARB(AF)/97/1) [73].
[62] *Compañiá de Aguas del Aconquija SA and Vivendi Universal SA v Argentine Republic* (ICSID Case No ARB/97/3 (formerly Compañía de Aguas del Aconquija, SA and Compagnie Générale des Eaux v Argentine Republic)) [49].
[63] *United States – Measures Affecting the Cross-Border Supply of Gambling and Betting Services (Report of the Panel)* (World Trade Organisation, WT/DS285/R) (e.g. para 6.128).
[64] *Difference Relating to Immunity from Legal Process of a Special Rapporteur of the Commission on Human Rights* (International Court of Justice, Advisory Opinion, ICJ Reports 1999, p 62) 87.
[65] *Salini Costruttori S.pA and Italstrade S.pA v Kingdom of Morocco* (ICSID Case No ARB/00/4 Decision on Jurisdiction (French Original: 129 Journal du droit international 196 (2002)) (English translation: 42 ILM 609 (2003), 6 ICSID Rep 400 (2004))) [32]; *Emilio Agustín Maffezini v The Kingdom of Spain* (ICSID Case No ARB/97/7, Decision of the Tribunal on

question. For example, in the application of the structural test, dispute settlement bodies may look at elements such as whether the entity in question is set up through special law, or under general corporations law; the procedure for the appointment of the management of the entity; the degree of State involvement in the day-to-day management of the business; whether the entity has a separate budget; whether its employees have status as public officials and whether the entity is subject to public law provisions.[66] Mere ownership alone is not sufficient to make an entity a State organ, and some commentators believe that, while any inquiry with regard to ownership may be relevant in the context of Articles 5 and 8, this is not the case in the context of Article 4, because a 'governmental agency cannot maintain a shareholding in another agency, nor can a governmental agency own another agency'.[67] Yet this view does not appear to leave any room for some relatively novel forms of State ownership that could very well fit within the architecture of Article 4, such as SWFs. While ownership alone is not enough to make an SOE an organ of the State, it is nevertheless a criterion that could be taken into consideration where there is no internal law of the State that bestows the status of organ upon an entity, but factual circumstances show that in fact that entity behaves as a State organ. In such a situation, the entity could be regarded as a de facto State organ. In this context, the Commentaries to the ILC Articles further clarify this issue by stating that the State 'cannot avoid responsibility for the conduct of a body which does *in truth act* as one of its organs merely by denying it that status under its own law' and consequently, 'each case will have to be dealt with on the basis of its own facts and circumstances'.[68]

For example, the arbitral tribunal in *EDF (Services) Limited v Romania* (*EDF*), a case which involved a dispute concerning certain investments made by the Claimant in duty free commercial areas around various airports in Romania, and which were allegedly effectively expropriated from the Claimant through the actions of Romania,[69] concluded that a State's mere ownership of an SOE was not sufficient to make that SOE an organ of the

Objections to Jurisdiction, 17 July 2003) [77]; *Noble Ventures, Inc v Romania* (ICSID Case No ARB/01/11, Award, 2005) [70–78].

[66] *Jan de Nul N.V. and Dredging International N.V. v Arab Republic of Egypt* (ICSID Case No ARB/04/13 (Award)) para 146; *Gustav F W Hamester GmbH & Co KG v Republic of Ghana* (ICSID Case No ARB/07/24) [182–187].

[67] Lee (n 26) 130.

[68] International Law Commission, *Draft Articles on Responsibility of States for Internationally Wrongful Acts, with Commentaries* (n 33) 42. (Emphasis added).

[69] In this case, EDF claimed that the passage of the Government Ordinance No. 104 resulted in the bankruptcy for one of EDF's joint venture companies.

State. In this particular case, both SOEs (AIBO and TAROM) were 'possessing legal personality under Romanian law, separate and distinct from that of the State' and as such they 'could not be considered a State organ'.[70] The approach taken by the arbitral Tribunal in *EDF* seems to confirm the strong presumption that exists in international law, that the separateness of corporate entities must be observed, unless the corporate entity was set up as a vehicle for fraud. The Commentaries to the ILC Articles also clarify that States cannot 'avoid responsibility for the conduct of a body which does in truth act as one of its organs merely by denying it that status under its own law'.[71]

The door is thus still left open for the possibility of attribution under Article 4(2) which makes *renvoi* to domestic law, and which clarifies that an 'organ includes any person or entity which has that status in accordance with the internal law of the State'. First, the Commentaries to the ILC Articles have made it clear that the term 'person or entity' is used in the broadest sense to 'include any natural or legal person',[72] so there is no doubt that an SOEs would be covered by this provision. Second, if the internal law of a State deems 'any natural or legal person' to be an organ of that particular State, then this issue will be regarded as conclusive and that entity will be treated as a State organ. The functions performed by the State organ are inconsequential, as long as internal law has bestowed the 'status' of organ on that particular entity. In *EDF*, the arbitral Tribunal noted that, since there was no law granting AIBO or TAROM, the 'status of a body of the Romanian State, the two entities may not be considered State bodies' within the meaning of Article 4 of the ILC Articles.[73] Nevertheless, even if the internal law of a State does not expressly bestow the status of organ upon an entity, but factual circumstances indicate that in fact that entity behaved as a State organ, under the rules of State responsibility, that entity will be deemed to be a de facto State organ. This emphasises the flexibility of Article 4(2) and also the fact that international law looks generally at substance rather than form.[74] It follows that if an SOE is not given the status of a State organ through domestic law,

---

[70] *EDF (Services) Limited v Romania* (n 53) 190.
[71] International Law Commission, *Draft Articles on Responsibility of States for Internationally Wrongful Acts, with Commentaries* (n 33) 42; *Case Concerning Barcelona Traction, Light and Power Company, Limited (Belgium v Spain)* (International Court of Justice, Judgment, ICJ Reports 1970, p 3) para 56.
[72] International Law Commission, *Draft Articles on Responsibility of States for Internationally Wrongful Acts, with Commentaries* (n 33) 42.
[73] *EDF (Services) Limited v Romania* (n 53) para 190; *Bayindir Insaat Turizm Ticaret Ve Sanayi A.S. v Islamic Republic of Pakistan* (n 53) paras 111–123.
[74] Crawford, *State Responsibility* (n 11) 125.

but if that SOE acts as a State organ, its actions will be considered to be those of the State and will be attributed to the State.

Nevertheless, high degree of dependence on the State is required for an entity to be considered as an organ of the State. The ICJ dealt with this issue first in *Nicaragua*[75] and several decades later in the *Bosnian Genocide Case*.[76] In *Nicaragua*, the ICJ held that for an entity to become a State organ, the relationship between the entity and the State had to be 'so much one of dependence on the one side and control on the other that it would be right to equate the *contras*, for legal purposes with an organ of the United States government, or as acting on behalf of the Government'.[77] Some of the following circumstances may be relevant in a determination that an entity is a State organ: whether that entity was created by the State (the *contras* were independent), the exact degree and type of influence exercised by the State over the entity (in this case it was the simple cessation of financial aid), the payment of the leaders was made by the State and whether the control was full and complete.[78] The Court seemed to require that this dependence is not only *full* but also *continuous*, and any periods of time where the degree of dependence is lessened seems to have an impact on the final outcome.[79] The ICJ reaffirmed this state of affairs in the *Bosnian Genocide Case* where, to criticism from the dissenting members of the Bench,[80] it ultimately held that neither the Republika Srpska nor the VRS (the Army of the Republika Srpska) could be regarded as mere instruments through which the FRY (Federal Republic of Yugoslavia) acted.[81]

The high degree of dependence required for a determination that an SOE is a State organ would thus make attribution under Article 4 of the ILC Articles extremely unlikely, in that it would occur in only a handful of situations. Nevertheless, it might indeed be possible for attribution to occur for the acts SWFs or other entities that have been created by special law or those SOEs that do not have separate legal personality, as long as the criterion

---

[75] *Military and Paramilitary Activities in and against Nicaragua (Nicaragua v United States of America)* (International Court of Justice, Merits, Judgment ICJ Reports 1986, p 14).
[76] *Application of the Convention on the Prevention and Punishment of the Crime of Genocide (Bosnia and Herzegovina v Serbia and Montenegro)* (n 29).
[77] *Military and Paramilitary Activities in and against Nicaragua (Nicaragua v United States of America)* (n 75) para 109.
[78] ibid paras 109–112.
[79] ibid para 111.
[80] For this purpose, see Declaration of Judge Bennouna (p. 364); Dissenting Opinion of Judge ad hoc Mahiou (paras 101–112); Dissenting Opinion of Vice-President Al-Khasawneh (para 54).
[81] *Application of the Convention on the Prevention and Punishment of the Crime of Genocide (Bosnia and Herzegovina v Serbia and Montenegro)* (n 29) paras 394–395.

of *complete dependence* on the State is also satisfied as outlined in the *Bosnian Genocide Case*. This issue becomes however more challenging, however, in cases where the entity in question has a separate legal personality,[82] independent board members or where the State does not hold 100 per cent ownership of an entity, unless that particular entity is a State organ as provided for by domestic law.

5.2.3 Attribution Based on the Exercise of 'Governmental Authority': Was the State-Owned Entity in Exercise of 'Governmental Authority'?

Attribution based on the exercise of 'governmental authority' is addressed in Article 5 of the ILC Articles:

> The conduct of a person or entity which is not an organ of the State under article 4 but which is empowered by the law of that State to exercise elements of the governmental authority shall be considered an act of the State under international law, provided the person or entity is acting in that capacity in the particular instance.

The wording of Article 5 clarifies that the focus of this article is entirely different to that of Article 4, which looked into the structure of the State in order to determine status as a State organ; instead, Article 5 focuses on the inquiry whether the particular function exercised by an entity is governmental in nature. The particular function exercised by the entity in question is thus the main issue that matters for the purposes of attribution under Article 5, and neither the public or private character of the entity nor the degree of control by the State is relevant. The relevance of Article 5 has recently increased, particularly due to the fact that the modern State is outsourcing an increasing number of functions that have been traditionally provided by the State, such as policing and security.[83] In the words of the ILC, the purpose of Article 5 is to

---

[82] *Eureko BV v Republic of Poland* (Ad-hoc Arbitration seated in Brussels, Partial Award 2005) [130–134].(This case concerned the status of the Polish State Treasury, an entity that had separate legal personality under Polish law (see paras 119–121). The Tribunal said in paragraph 134: '[W]hatever may be the status of the State Treasury in Polish law, in the perspective of international law, which this Tribunal is bound to apply, the Republic of Poland is responsible to Eureko for the actions of the State Treasury. These actions, if they amount to an internationally wrongful act, are clearly attributable to the Respondent and the Tribunal so finds.').

[83] Crawford, *State Responsibility* (n 11) 127.

take account of the increasingly common phenomenon of parastatal entities, which exercise elements of governmental authority in the place of State organs, as well as situations where former State corporations have been privatized but retain certain public or regulatory functions . . . . The fact that an entity can be classified as public or private according to the criteria of a given legal system, the existence of a greater or lesser State participation in its capital, or more generally, in the ownership of its assets, the fact that it is not subject to executive control – these are not decisive criteria for the purposes of attribution of the entity's conduct to the State. Instead, article 5 refers to the true common feature, namely that these entities are empowered, if only to a limited extent or in a specific context, to exercise specified elements of governmental authority.[84]

Thus, the overall policy argument for attribution under Article 5 of the ILC Articles is that States should not be allowed to evade their responsibility by delegating to other entities functions that are normally exercised by the State. The ILC has acknowledged that doing otherwise would create a 'dangerous loophole'.[85] In the case of an SOE, for attribution under Article 5 to be possible, two cumulative requirements need to be satisfied. The first requirement is to identify whether any law of the State in question empowers the given entity to exercise elements of 'governmental authority', and the second step is to determine if 'governmental authority' was in fact exercised in that particular instance. The Commentaries to the ILC Articles acknowledge the difficulty and complexity of interpreting the concept of governmental authority and explain that what is regarded, as governmental authority will depend on the 'particular society, its history and traditions'.[86] Thus, a wide margin of discretion seems to be given to dispute settlement bodies as decision-makers in a given case. However, the fundamental concept that underpins attribution under Article 5 is, in essence, a search for agency in the relationship between the State and the SOE. For example, arbitration tribunals have used structural as well as functional tests in order to determine the existence of governmental authority in a particular instance.[87] In line with the Commentaries to the ILC

---

[84] International Law Commission, *Draft Articles on Responsibility of States for Internationally Wrongful Acts, with Commentaries* (n 33) 42.

[85] International Law Commission, 'Report of the International Law Commission on the Work of Its Twenty-Sixth Session, 6 May–26 July 1974, Official Records of the General Assembly, Twenty-Ninth Session, Supplement No. 10' (1974) A/9610/Rev.1 278.

[86] International Law Commission, *Draft Articles on Responsibility of States for Internationally Wrongful Acts, with Commentaries* (n 33) 43.

[87] *Emilio Agustín Maffezini v The Kingdom of Spain* (n 65) para 78.

Articles,[88] the functional test looks at the content of the powers conferred on the entity,[89] the method of conferral,[90] the purpose for which the entity has to exercise them[91] and the extent to which the entity is accountable for their exercise.[92]

An illustration of the overall operation of attribution under Article 5 of the ILC Articles can be observed from *Noble Ventures v Romania*,[93] where the arbitral Tribunal had to determine if the actions of the Romanian State Ownership Fund (SOF),[94] an 'institution of public interest' with separate legal personality under Romanian law established in 1992 and which had the task of privatising Romanian State-owned enterprises, were attributable to Romania. The Claimant, Noble Ventures, was a US company, which invested in Combinatul Siderurgic Resita (CSR). The privatisation agreement concluded between Noble Ventures and SOF included collateral agreements and a Share Purchase Agreement by which Noble Ventures acquired almost all of CSR's share capital.[95] The Claimant alleged that certain conduct by Romania fell short of the requirements of the United States – Romania BIT, on which the investment was based. Specifically, Noble Ventures alleged that Romania failed to provide full protection and security during a period of extreme labour unrest, that it had effectively expropriated the investor's property through a 'colorable use of bankruptcy laws' and that it has also made certain misrepresentations about key assets.[96] While ultimately the arbitral Tribunal rejected all the allegations of breach of the BIT, in its Award it also considered the legal question whether the actions of State privatisation agencies could be attributed to the Romanian State for the purposes of assessing liability under the Romania-US BIT. The Tribunal noted that while SOF and the associated Authority for the Protection and Management of State Ownership (APAPS) could not be regarded as State organs under Article 4 of the ILC Articles, since

---

[88] International Law Commission, *Draft Articles on Responsibility of States for Internationally Wrongful Acts, with Commentaries* (n 33) 43.
[89] *Sergei Paushok, CJSC Golden East Company and CJSC Vostokneftegaz Company v The Government of Mongolia* (Award on Jurisdiction and Liability (Uncitral 1976)) [574–597].
[90] *Jan de Nul N.V. and Dredging International N.V. v Arab Republic of Egypt* (n 66).
[91] *Ceskoslovenska Obchodni Banka, AS v The Slovak Republic* (Decision on Objections to Jurisdiction, ICSID Case No ARB/97/4, 24 May 1999) 23; *Noble Ventures, Inc. v Romania* (ICSID Case No ARB/01/11, Award, 2005) paras 73–79.
[92] *Hyatt Corporation International v Iran* (Iran-US CTR 72, 89) 89–92; Crawford, *State Responsibility* (n 11) 131.
[93] *Noble Ventures, Inc. v Romania* (n 91).
[94] SOF was later renamed 'The Authority for Privatization and Management of the State Ownership' (APAPS).
[95] *Noble Ventures, Inc. v Romania* (n 91) para 2.
[96] ibid paras 12–17.

they were legal entities separate from Romania, they did act 'at all relevant times on the basis of Romanian law which defined their competence'.[97] For example, among others, the Romanian Privatisation Law (which empowered SOF and APAPS) provided in Article 5(1) that SOF was 'an institution of public interest, a legal person, subordinated to Government, acting for a diminished involvement of the State and the local public administration authorities in the economy, by selling their shares'. The control of the SOF was in the hands of the prime minister who effectively had the power to appoint and remove the whole Board. Furthermore, the organisational and operational regulation of the SOF was entirely approved by the government. Based on those facts, the Tribunal concluded the following:

> In the judgment of the Tribunal, no relevant legal distinction is to be drawn between SOF/APAPS, on the one hand, and a government ministry, on the other hand, when the one or the other acted as the empowered public institution under the Privatization Law. All the acts allegedly committed by SOF/APAPS were related to the investment of the Claimant. There is no indication from the parties, and there is no reason to believe, that any act by these institutions was outside the scope of their mandate. Consequently, the Tribunal concludes that SOF and APAPS were entitled by law to represent the Respondent and did so in all of their actions as well as omissions. The acts allegedly in violation of the BIT are therefore attributable to the Respondent for the purposes of assessment under the BIT.[98]

Overall, what can be observed from the above is that attribution under Article 5 of the ILC Articles is narrow and also likely to cover a handful of cases only. For instance, the first requirement – the identification of a domestic law that expressly empowers a given entity to exercise elements of governmental authority[99] – would cover only a few SOEs, given that in a large proportion of cases such entities are usually created under general commercial law. The wide margin of discretion given to dispute settlement bodies in interpreting the elusive concept of 'governmental authority' adds further challenges in this area. Consequently, Section 5.2.4 will analyse the provisions of Article 8 of the ILC Articles in order to determine what are the boundaries

---

[97] ibid paras 70–78.
[98] ibid paras 78–80.
[99] International Law Commission, *Draft Articles on Responsibility of States for Internationally Wrongful Acts, with Commentaries* (n 33) 43. ('The internal law in question must specifically authorize the conduct as involving the exercise of public authority; it is not enough that it permits activity as part of the general regulation of the affairs of the community.').

for attribution in instances when SOEs act on the instructions of or are under the direction and control of the State.

5.2.4 Attribution Based on Control: Is the State-Owned Entity under the 'Direction or Control' of the State?

The third type of attribution is based on control and is contained in Article 8 of the ILC Articles:

> The conduct of a person or group of persons shall be considered an act of State under international law if the person or group of persons is in fact acting on the *instructions* of, or under the *direction* or *control* of, that State in carrying out the conduct.[100]

Article 8 starts from the premise that the conduct of private persons is not generally attributable to the State. This general principle is confirmed in the Commentaries to the ILC Articles which also clarify that Article 8 deals with two circumstances: the first involves private persons acting on the *instructions* of the State in carrying out the wrongful act or omission, while the second deals with 'a more general situation where private persons act under the State's *direction* or *control*'.[101] This section deals mainly with the second circumstance, since the first circumstance has a relatively narrow scope of application, as was noted in the Commentaries:

> Most commonly, cases of this kind will arise where State organs supplement their own action by recruiting and instigating private persons or groups who act as 'auxiliaries' while remaining outside the official structure of the State. These include, for example, individuals or groups of private individuals who, though not specifically commissioned by the State and not forming part of its police or armed forces, are employed as auxiliaries or are sent as 'volunteers' to neighboring countries, or who are instructed to carry out particular missions abroad.[102]

A practical application of attribution based on control, where the private persons are acting on the instruction of the State, arises in the context of private military or security companies that have been contracted by the State

---

[100] Articles on Responsibility of States for Internationally Wrongful Acts (November 2001, Supplement No. 10 (U.N. Doc. A/56/10 (2001). (Emphasis added).
[101] International Law Commission, *Draft Articles on Responsibility of States for Internationally Wrongful Acts, with Commentaries* (n 33) 47.
[102] ibid.

to conduct certain activities on its behalf.[103] Given this relatively narrow field of application for attributing acts and omissions based on State instructions, in the context of SOEs, the possibility still exists for attribution based on State direction or control. For instance, in many SOEs, the State is often, if not the only shareholder, a majority one, and, as such, it has the power to set the strategy of the company in question, to appoint and dismiss the executive management and to generally set the trajectory of SOEs, despite the separate legal personality of the entity in question. Certain States have even designated governmental agencies whose only purpose is to supervise and set the strategy for its SOEs, which are, for all practical purposes, set up as separate entities. For example, in China, SASAC has this role. In this context, the policy that underpins attribution under Article 8 is that States should not be able to avoid accountability just because certain acts and omissions were performed by entities or persons that are completely separate from the government. While the second circumstance has a broader sphere of application, its practical application is also more challenging, particularly with regard to the application of the tests for determining whether the acts or omissions were in fact performed under the direction or control of the State in question. As far as the possibility of a distinction between direction or control, the Commentaries clarify that those terms are disjunctive and that it is sufficient to establish any one of them.[104]

Due to the fact that Article 8 does not actually specify or make any comment with regard to the actual level of control that the State has to have over the entity in question, there are two tests that have been used by dispute settlement bodies to determine whether the required level of control actually exists: the 'effective control' test and the 'overall control' test. The remainder of this section will analyse the two tests and will also attempt to evaluate them on their merits. The effective control test was developed by the ICJ in the *Nicaragua*[105] case, where the Court held that the conduct of the *contras* could not be attributed to the United States. The question of the degree of control required was discussed as follows:

> The Court has taken the view ... that United States participation, even if preponderant or decisive, in the financing, organizing, training, supplying and equipping of the contras, the selection of its military or paramilitary

---

[103] Crawford, *State Responsibility* (n 11) 145.

[104] International Law Commission, *Draft Articles on Responsibility of States for Internationally Wrongful Acts, with Commentaries* (n 33) 48.

[105] *Military and Paramilitary Activities in and against Nicaragua (Nicaragua v United States of America)* (n 75).

targets, and the planning of the whole of its operation, is still insufficient in itself, on the basis of the evidence in the possession of the Court, for the purpose of attributing to the United States the acts committed by the contras in the course of their military or paramilitary operations in Nicaragua. All the forms of United States participation mentioned above, and even the general control by the respondent State over a force with a high degree of dependency on it, would not in themselves mean, without further evidence, that the United States directed or enforced the perpetration of the acts contrary to human rights and humanitarian law alleged by the applicant State. Such acts could well be committed by members of the *contras* without the control of the United States. For this conduct to give rise to legal responsibility of the United States, it would in principle have to be proved that that State had *effective control* of the military or paramilitary operations of which the alleged violations were committed.[106]

The Court did not elaborate any further on the meaning of this phrase, but it held that in this particular instance, this threshold was not met. Two main conclusions can thus be gathered from *Nicaragua*: first, for the purpose of attribution under Article 8 of the ILC Articles, the effective control test is applicable; and second, the effective control test advanced by *Nicaragua* has a very high threshold for determining the required level of control necessary for attribution.

The International Criminal Tribunal for the former Yugoslavia (ICTY) had the opportunity to consider the effective control test in the *Tadić* case at both the Trial Chamber stage and at the Appeal stage.[107] In order to determine the international nature of the conflict, the Trial Chamber looked at the relationship between the parties that were engaged in the conflict, on one side were the Bosnian parties (Bosnian Muslims, Serbs and Croats) and on the other side were the Federal Republic of Yugoslavia (FRY) and Croatia. The Tribunal looked in particular at the acts of the Republika Srpska, an entity which was opposed to the independence of Bosnia and Herzegovina and stated that its acts could be imputable to FRY 'if those forces were acting as de facto organs or agents of that state for that purposes or more generally'. In its determination whether the acts of Republika Srpska could be attributable to the FRY, the Tribunal turned to *Nicaragua*, and while recognising that the facts of the two cases were 'very different', it concluded that the ultimate question that needed to be answered was whether after 19 May 1992 the FRY, 'by its withdrawal from the territory of the Republic of Bosnia and

---

[106] ibid 116. (Emphasis added).
[107] *Prosecutor v Du[Ko Tadi] a/k/a 'Dule'* (n 29) 200–217.

Herzegovina and notwithstanding its continuing support for the VRS,[108] had sufficiently distanced itself from the VRS so that those forces could not be regarded as de facto organs or agents of the VJ[109] and hence of FRY'.[110] While drawing parallels to *Nicaragua*, the Tribunal held that since there was no 'effective control' over the military forces, the FRY could not be held responsible for the acts of the Republika Srpska.[111] It is worthy of note that the Tribunal did not clarify the meaning of 'effective control' as was discussed in *Nicaragua*, nor did it make any comments on the various thresholds required by Article 8 of the ILC Articles. In her dissenting opinion, Presiding Judge McDonald advanced the view that in fact the *Nicaragua* case establishes two distinct tests for attributability: the first was based on agency; and the second one, when the issue of agency was not applicable, involved the situation where the party in question is 'specifically charged' to carry out a particular act on its behalf[112] Judge McDonald further said that if the standard of proof required in *Nicaragua* for a determination of agency was that of effective control, that finding should be limited to the facts of *Nicaragua* and that in the *Tadić* case no such high threshold was required.[113]

The Appeals Chamber had the opportunity to reconsider both the question of the correctness of the application of the rules of State responsibility for the purposes of determining whether the conflict was international and the relevance of the effective control test as established by *Nicaragua*. On the first question, the Appeals Chamber noted that the approach taken by the Trial Chamber was correct because, since international humanitarian law does not contain any criteria unique to this body of law for establishing when a person may be regarded as being under the control of a State, 'it is necessary to examine the notion of control by a State over individuals [as was] laid down in general international law ... [and] this notion can be found in those general international rules on State responsibility'.[114] Insomuch as the applicability of the *Nicaragua* test was concerned, the Appeals Chamber dismissed the Prosecution's arguments that two different classes of responsibility exist in international law: one for purposes of general international law and the other for determining individual criminal responsibility. The test applicable in both situations was that based on the general principles for attribution and which

---

[108] The VRS was the army of Republika Srpska.
[109] The VJ was the army of the FRY.
[110] *Prosecutor v Du[Ko Tadi] a/k/a 'Dule'* (n 29) para 587.
[111] ibid para 605.
[112] ibid 296.
[113] ibid.
[114] *Prosecutor v Du[Ko Tadi]* (n 29) para 98.

are contained in the rules of State responsibility.[115] While the Appeals Chamber confirmed the existence of two tests for attribution under Article 8 of the ILC Articles, it dismissed and criticised the interpretation of the Trial Chamber and held that the effective control test from *Nicaragua* was unpersuasive in that it went not only 'against the logic' of the law of State responsibility, but also against judicial practice.[116] In the words of the Appeals Chamber, this determination was based on the following reasoning:

> The principles of international law concerning the attribution to States of acts performed by private individuals are not based on rigid and uniform criteria. These principles are reflected in Article 8 of the Draft on State Responsibility adopted on first reading by the United Nations International Law Commission and, even more clearly, in the text of the same provisions as provisionally adopted in 1998 by the ILC Drafting Committee. Under this Article, if it is proved that individuals who are not regarded as organs of a State by its legislation nevertheless do in fact act on behalf of that State, their acts are attributable to the State. The rationale behind this rule is to prevent States from escaping international responsibility by having private individuals carry out tasks that may not or should not be performed by State officials, or by claiming that individuals actually participating in governmental authority are not classified as State organs under national legislation and therefore do not engage State responsibility. In other words, States are not allowed on the one hand to act de facto through individuals and on the other to disassociate themselves from such conduct when these individuals breach international law. The requirement of international law for the attribution to States of acts performed by private individuals is that the State exercises control over the individuals. *The degree of control may, however, vary according to the factual circumstances of each case. The Appeals Chamber fails to see why in each and every circumstance international law should require a high threshold for the test of control. Rather, various situations may be distinguished.*[117]

In order to give meaning to this interpretation, the Appeals Chamber drew the distinction between a *private individual* or other *non-organised groups* and *organised and hierarchically structured groups*, and it acknowledged that in the first instance it was 'necessary to prove not only that the State exercised some measure of authority over those individuals but also that it issued specific instructions to them concerning the performance of those acts', while in the second instance 'overall control' was enough.[118] The Appeals Chamber

---

[115] ibid para 105.
[116] ibid paras 113, 115–145.
[117] ibid para 117. (Citations omitted. Emphasis added).
[118] ibid paras 118–120.

considered that the difference between an organised group, such as a military unit, was of the outmost importance because

> the former normally has a structure, a chain of command and a set of rules as well the outward symbols of authority. Normally a member of the group does not act on its own but conforms to the standards prevailing in the group and is subject to the authority of the head of the group. Consequently, for the attribution to a State of acts of these groups it is sufficient to require that the group as a whole be under the *overall control* of the State.[119]

While the overall control test endorsed by the Appeals Chamber eases attribution, it has met strong opposition from the ICJ in the *Bosnian Genocide* case, where the Court had the opportunity to consider again, not only the general application of the *Nicaragua* test, but also the ICTY's Appeals Chamber decision in *Tadić*. The Court clarified that the effective control test formulated in *Nicaragua* was not only the 'correct' test as far as attribution under Article 8 of the ILC Articles was concerned, but also clarified the differences between the requirements of Article 4 and those of Article 8 in the following words:

> The test thus formulated differs in two respects from the test – described above – to determine whether a person or entity may be equated with a State organ even if not having that status under internal law. First, in this context it is not necessary to show that the persons who performed the acts alleged to have violated international law were in general in a relationship of 'complete dependence' on the respondent State; it has to be proved that they acted in accordance with that State's instructions or under its 'effective control'. It must however be shown that this 'effective control' was exercised, or that the State's instructions were given, in respect of each operation in which the alleged violations occurred, not generally in respect of the overall actions taken by the persons or groups of persons having committed the violations.[120]

The Court continued its analysis and said that not even the 'particular characteristics of genocide' could justify a deviation from the effective control test elaborated in *Nicaragua*[121] and criticised the departure from this test by the

---

[119] ibid para 122.
[120] *Application of the Convention on the Prevention and Punishment of the Crime of Genocide (Bosnia and Herzegovina v Serbia and Montenegro)* (n 29) para 400.
[121] ibid para 401. ('The rules for attributing alleged internationally wrongful conduct to a State do not vary with the nature of the wrongful act in question in the absence of a clearly expressed lex specialis. Genocide will be considered as attributable to a State if and to the extent that the physical acts constitutive of genocide that have been committed by organs or persons other than the State's own agents were carried out, wholly or in part, on the instructions or directions of

Appeals Chamber in *Tadić*.[122] Yet this statement is problematic, because the concept of norms *jus cogens* is maintained in ILC Articles 40 and 41, which could mean that when a breach of such norms is an issue for consideration, the rules of attribution may require 'subtle variations' as Judge Al-Khasawneh noted in his Dissenting Opinion.[123] The Court justified its opinion on the basis that the overall control test has the 'major drawback' of broadening too much the scope of State responsibility by bringing it to a 'breaking point, the connection which must exist between the conduct of a State's organs and its international responsibility'.[124]

What can be observed from the above is that the overall control test significantly eases attribution, which could ultimately lead to a wider range of acts and omissions being attributed to the State, when compared to those that would be attributable under the effective control test. In the context of SOEs, on the one hand, the adoption of the effective control test would mean that most of the conduct of a given entity would not be attributable to the State, unless it could be proven that 'each activity' of the SOE that resulted in a violation of human rights was in fact performed under the instructions of the State. It is thus likely that the presence of separate legal personality, the presence of independent managers or any degree of autonomy – even if insignificant – would be fatal for the purpose of attribution. The adoption of the overall control would, on the other hand, allow for 'various situations to be distinguished' as the Appeals Court in *Tadic* and academic commentary have clarified.[125] This could ultimately mean that a given State policy concerning SOEs, the adequate supervision of the State of those entities and the reality of 'what the State should have known' in the context of the operation of those entities, would all be matters that could be taken into consideration when making a determination on the issue of attribution.

---

the State, or under its effective control. This is the state of customary international law, as reflected in the ILC Articles on State Responsibility.').

[122] ibid paras 402–406.

[123] *Application of the Convention on the Prevention and Punishment of the Crime of Genocide (Bosnia and Herzegovina v Serbia and Montenegro)* (n 29). (Dissenting Opinion of Vice-President Al-Khasawneh [39]: 'Unfortunately, the Court's rejection of the standard in the Tadic case fails to address the crucial issue raised therein – *namely that different types of activities, particularly in the ever-evolving nature of armed conflict, may call for subtle variations in the rules of attribution.*') (Emphasis added. Footnotes omitted).

[124] ibid paras 406.

[125] *Prosecutor v Du[Ko Tadi]* (n 29) para 117; Nicholas Tsagourias and Michael Farrell, 'Cyber Attribution: Technical and Legal Approaches and Challenges' (2020) 31 Eur. J. Int. Law 941, 962–965.

5.2.5 *An Assessment of the Rules of Attribution Found in General International Law and Their Applicability to Other Regimes*

Sections 5.2.2–5.2.4 have explored the three classic rules of attribution: attribution due to status as a State organ, attribution as a consequence of exercising governmental authority and attribution based on direction or control. All three rules of attribution find their source in customary international law as codified by the ILC Articles. It can be observed, however, that the high thresholds required in each case would make attribution problematic in the case of SOEs. For instance, the high degree of dependence required to show that an entity is a de facto State organ makes attribution under Article 4 extremely unlikely. The elusive nature of the meaning of 'governmental authority' in the context of Article 5 demonstrates further challenges is this area. The situation is not much different under Article 8, whereby the effective control test first laid out in *Nicaragua* was later confirmed in the *Bosnian Genocide Case*, despite the ground being laid out for a more flexible rule of attribution in *Tadić*. Yet, as Judge McDonald argued in the *Tadić* case, the effective control test goes completely 'against the logic' of the law of State responsibility and creates the very 'dangerous loophole' that the ILC was keen to avoid through the codification efforts undertaken in the law of State responsibility. While some commentators have argued that the ICJ's decision in the *Bosnian Genocide Case* 'effectively ends the debate as to the correct standard of control', others have argued that the emergence of alternative techniques for allocating responsibility, such as lowering the threshold of control, attribution for omissions and the establishing of a due diligence process, 'may foretell the eclipse of general secondary rules of attribution and cast further doubt on the notion that the effective control test is an objective, portable, general concept of law'.[126] Some commentators have argued that a lower threshold in relation to attribution may even be applicable altogether in the field of human rights:

> This does not mean that human rights treaty monitoring bodies cannot themselves require a lower level of control by a state over a non-state actor than that found in general international law. Indeed, the ICJ in *Democratic Republic of Congo v Uganda* indicated that international human rights law applies to a state's conduct extraterritorially even when the level of control is less than that of an occupying power. In reaching this conclusion, the ICJ is appearing to allow the possibility of there being a lower test of control under

---

[126] Kristen E Boon, 'Are Control Tests Fit for the Future: The Slippage Problem in Attribution Doctrines' (2014) 15 Melb. J. Int'l L. 330, 332.

international human rights law, while not adopting it under general international law. This approach could become even more important since the beginning of the (illegal) action by the 'occupying' forces in Iraq, where it is clear that many private corporations were contracted by the states involved to provide a variety of services – from providing intelligence to recreating state infrastructure to support such military action – and that some of those corporations abused human rights. So international human rights law could be accepted as taking a different approach – due to its subject matter and aim – from the general application of the international law of state responsibility in relation to aspects of attribution.[127]

Although it has been claimed that the special character of human rights treaties make the international principles of State responsibility irrelevant to their operation,[128] the reality is that, as discussed at the outset of this chapter, the ILC Articles will still come into play as a fallback mechanism.[129] This much was implied, for instance, by the ECHR – whose jurisprudence will be used as an example for the remainder of this section – in *Banković* where it stated the following:

> The Court must also take into account any relevant rules of international law when examining questions concerning its jurisdiction and, consequently, determine State responsibility in conformity with the governing principles of international law, although it must remain mindful of the Convention's special character as a human rights treaty. The Convention should be interpreted as far as possible in harmony with other principles of international law of which it forms part.[130]

Crawford and Keene have also noted in the context of the EConHR, for instance, that the real question is whether the Court has departed from the ILC Articles and if those departures are necessary given the special character of the Convention.[131] Overall, it appears that that while there are certain

---

[127] Robert McCorquodale, 'The Impact of International Human Rights Law on State Responsibility' in Menno T Kamminga and M Scheinin (eds), *The Impact of Human Rights on General International Law* (Oxford University Press 2009) 235–254.

[128] Malcolm Evans, 'State Responsibility and the European Convention on Human Rights: Role and Realm' in Malgosia Fitzmaurice and Dan Sarooshi (eds), *Issues of State Responsibility before International Judicial Institutions* (Hart 2004) 159.

[129] Iulia Motoc and Johann Justus Vasel, 'The ECHR and Responsibility of the State: Moving Towards Judicial Integration' in Anne van Aaken and Iulia Motoc (eds), *The European Convention on Human Rights and General International Law* (Oxford University Press 2018).

[130] *Banković and Others v Belgium and Others* (European Court of Human Rights, Application No 52207/99, Decision on Admissibility) [57]. (References omitted).

[131] James Crawford and Amelia Keene, 'The Structure of State Responsibility under the European Convention on Human Rights' in Anne van Aaken and Iulia Motoc (eds), *The European*

general discernable trends[132] concerning the ECHR's engagement with the ILC Articles, what can be generally observed is that the ILC Articles are fully applicable 'in the human rights context as the relevant secondary rules on State responsibility'.[133] Furthermore, recent research demonstrates that the general rules for the attribution of conduct that are found in international law are equally applicable in other areas of international law such as international humanitarian law, the law on the use of force and European human rights law.[134] Of particular relevance in this context is the ECHR's jurisprudence concerning SOEs,[135] considered by Milanovic as 'candidates for special rules of attribution'.[136] A significant number of those cases[137] arise under Article 6 of

---

Convention on Human Rights and General International Law (Oxford University Press 2018) 178–179.

[132] ibid 197–198. (Overall, the jurisprudence of the ECHR 'presents a ragged and unsystematic appearance' concerning its engagement with the ILC Articles. For example, in some instances the ECHR has not applied the ILC Articles, but instead has developed 'a novel "acquiescence or connivance" rule to hold a third State responsible for the acts of another State on its territory (*El- Masri*), a rule that has no place in Article 16 of ARISWA. It also refused to apply the ARIO in finding that an "ultimate authority" test was to be preferred to the "effective control" rule set out in what is now Article 7 of the ARIO (*Behrami*). Moreover, the Court has broadly interpreted Article 3 of the EConHR so as to engage States' direct responsibility for the acts of private actors without reference to the attribution rules under the ARISWA (*Costello-Roberts*). More recently, the Court relied heavily on positive obligations under the EConHR to avoid difficult State responsibility questions in the *Sargsyan* and *Chiragov* cases. But there are other indications that the Court has more fully applied the rules on State responsibility and has pulled back from some of its earlier departures. It is also making its own contribution to the rules on the responsibility of States for the Acts of IOs, influencing the drafting of the ARIO'.) (Footnotes omitted).

[133] ibid; Motoc and Vasel (n 129).

[134] Milanovic, 'Special Rules of Attribution of Conduct in International Law' (n 43).

[135] ibid 376. ('There have been three basic types of cases in which the Court has dealt with the relationship between States and State-owned companies. First, there are the Article 34 EConHR cases, starting with *Radio France*, in which the Court is deciding whether a State-owned enterprise has standing to bring an application. Second, there are the cases in which the Court is deciding whether a State is liable for the debts of a State-owned company and the non-execution of any domestic judgment about such a debt. In such cases, the Court applies the *Mykhaylenky* presumption that a State is liable for the debts of such companies unless it can demonstrate that the company enjoys "sufficient institutional and operational independence" from the State. That test is applied with varying degrees of contextual sensitivity and corresponding detail in the reasoning. Third, there are a very small number of cases, such as *Kotov*, in which the sufficient institutional and operational independence test is (in some variant) used to attribute conduct rather than a debt.').

[136] ibid 366.

[137] *Ališić and Others v Bosnia and Herzegovina, Croatia, Serbia, Slovenia and 'The former Yugoslav Republic of Macedonia'* (European Court of Human Rights (Application No 60642/08)) [114–118]; *Mykhaylenky and Others v Ukraine* (European Court of Human Rights (Application Nos 35091/02, 35196/02, 35201/02, 35204/02, 35945/02, 35949/02, 35953/02, 36800/02, 38296/02 and 42814/02)) [43–46]; *Cooperativa Agricola Slobozia-Hanesei v Moldova*

the EConHR (the right to a fair trial) and Article 1 of Protocol 1 of the EConHR (the right to property) and deal with the liability of States for the unpaid debts of their SOEs:

[A] State has the positive obligation to ensure that the judgments of its domestic courts are executed and that any outstanding debts under these judgments are paid. That obligation will, however, have a different intensity depending on whether the debt is owed by a private entity or by the State itself. In the former scenario, the State only has to take reasonable steps and act diligently to ensure that the private debts are paid. In the latter, the State must pay the debt in full, or there will be a violation of Article 1 of Protocol 1; lack of funds does not excuse the State, although it might exceptionally justify a delay in payment.[138]

The criteria used by the ECHR to determine whether a State would be held responsible for the debts of its SOEs have included the company's legal status (whether it was set up under public or private law); the nature of its activity (public function or ordinary commercial transaction); the context of its operation (monopoly or heavily regulated business); its institutional and operational independence; whether the state was directly responsible for the company's financial difficulties and whether the State syphoned corporate funds to the detriment of the company and its stakeholders and whether the State failed to keep an arm's-length relationship with the company or otherwise abused the corporate form.[139] Sometimes, although not explicitly stated,[140] the ECHR does appear to go through an exercise that could be considered as being similar to that of attribution in general international law.[141]

(European Court of Human Rights, Application No 39745/02) [17–19]; *Yershova v Russia* (European Court of Human Rights (Application No 1387/04)) [54–63]; *Kotov v Russia* (European Court of Human Rights (Application No 54522/00)) [92–107].

[138] Milanovic, 'Special Rules of Attribution of Conduct in International Law' (n 43) 369–370.

[139] *Ališić and Others v Bosnia and Herzegovina, Croatia, Serbia, Slovenia and 'The former Yugoslav Republic of Macedonia'* (n 137) paras 114–115; *Yershova v Russia* (n 137) paras 55–62.

[140] Milanovic, 'Special Rules of Attribution of Conduct in International Law' (n 43) 372.

[141] *Saliyev v Russia* (European Court of Human Rights (Application No 35016/03)) [69]. ('The next question to answer is whether an act by a municipal institution can entail the responsibility of the State under the Convention. The Government argued that Magadan municipality was not a "State authority" within the Convention meaning. However, the Court is not convinced by that argument. Firstly, in a number of cases the Court has regarded the debts of municipal enterprises as State debts (see, for example, *Gizzatova v Russia*, no. 5124/03, 13 January 2005). In a very recent case, also concerning State responsibility for the debts of a municipal enterprise, the Court held that local (that is, municipal) authorities were linked to the State administration (see *Yershova v Russia*, no. 1387/04, §§ 54 et seq., 8 April 2010). The Court's reasoning in *Yershova* clearly implied that it did not regard municipalities as not being part of the State authorities in the broad sense, even if in domestic terms municipal authorities were

At other times, the ECHR's engagement with the ILC Articles is more explicit.[142] Overall, however, it appears that although the ECHR's approach to attribution is 'highly contextual, inconsistent and frequently unreasoned', it cannot be said with any certainty that any special rules of attribution have been developed by the Court.[143] Consequently, a lack of clarity in reasoning or a failure to extensively engage with the ILC Articles cannot be taken to mean that the general rules of attribution are no longer applicable. After all, as Milanovic clarifies, one 'might disagree with how the ILC has formulated any given attribution rule, but then the disagreement is about the scope of the *generally* applicable rules of attribution, not about the existence of a special rule'.[144] This is not to say that special rules of attribution cannot develop as envisaged in Article 55 of the ILC Articles. They clearly can, however, as discussed elsewhere, the development of any such rules must be clearly expressed.[145] For instance, one would expect that in such cases, the adjudicative body in question would commence its inquiry by looking at the general rules of attribution as codified by the ILC Articles and any following departures, reflecting a given *lex specialis*, clearly reasoned and justified. Such an approach would ultimately promote consistency between existing or emerging specialised fields of international law and general international law.

---

independent from regional and federal government. In Russian law municipal authorities are treated on the same footing as federal or regional bodies for many purposes (see, for example, the full text of Article 1070 of the Civil Code of the Russian Federation concerning strict liability of State bodies for certain types of civil wrongs, quoted in *Matveyev v Russia*, no. 26601/02, § 30, 3 July 2008; see also the analysis of the word "State body" employed in section 57(4) of the Media Act in *Romanenko and Others v Russia*, no. 11751/03, § 45, 8 October 2009). The municipal bodies are formed by the local population; they have wide-ranging powers in various areas of life, examples of which can be found in the Court's case-law concerning Russia (see, for example, *Kimlya and Others v Russia*, nos. 76836/01 and 32782/03, § 53, ECHR 2009– ...; *Kuimov v Russia*, no. 32147/04, § 30, 8 January 2009; and *Kukalo v Russia*, no. 63995/00, § 33, 3 November 2005). Even if their competence is limited (see, mutatis mutandis, *Cherepkov v Russia* (dec.), no. 51501/99, ECHR 2000-I, where the Court analysed whether municipal bodies had "legislative power" within the meaning of Article 3 of Protocol No. 1 of the Convention), their powers cannot be characterised as anything other than "public".').

[142] *Kotov v Russia* (n 137) paras 30–32; *Liseytseva and Maslov v Russia* (European Court of Human Rights (Application Nos 39483/05 and 40527/10)) 128–130.

[143] Milanovic, 'Special Rules of Attribution of Conduct in International Law' (n 43) 379.

[144] ibid 388–389.

[145] *Application of the Convention on the Prevention and Punishment of the Crime of Genocide (Bosnia and Herzegovina v Serbia and Montenegro)* (n 29) para 406.

5.3 RESPONSIBILITY FOR LACK OF DUE DILIGENCE

5.3.1 *General Comments on the Concept of Due Diligence in International Law*

The concept of due diligence becomes relevant when certain acts and omissions cannot be attributed to the State, because, for example, they are not perpetrated by State organs, by actors that are exercising governmental authority or those that are not under the effective control of the State. In such circumstances, a State can nevertheless be held responsible for failure to act diligently to take all the necessary measures available to prevent or punish the occurrence of a specific act. This section starts with a brief introduction to the concept of due diligence and progresses by arguing that in certain circumstances States have due diligence obligations – as a matter of international law – to ensure that SOEs do not violate human rights. Some suggestions about how States could discharge their obligations will also be made in light of recent State practice.

Due diligence is an ongoing standard of conduct that is required to discharge an obligation. As such, due diligence is a 'best efforts' obligation 'to do all in one's power to achieve a result, but without ultimate commitment'.[146] Best efforts obligations must be distinguished from 'obligations of result', which 'involve a guarantee of the outcome'.[147] Overall, due diligence aims to supply a standard of reasonable care against which fault can be assessed.[148] Consequently, in the words of the International Law Association (ILA) due diligence

---

[146] P Dupuy, 'Reviewing the Difficulties of Codification: On Ago's Classification of Obligations of Means and Obligations of Result in Relation to State Responsibility' (1999) 10 Eur. J. Int. Law 371, 378.

[147] ibid 375, 378–379. ('In the civil law tradition, an obligation of conduct is, as rightly pointed out by Combacau, "*une obligation de s'efforcer*", i.e. an obligation to endeavour or to strive to realize a certain result. Typical in this respect is the obligation of a doctor in relation to a patient. He or she must do everything that a reasonable person and competent physician can do in order to look after a patient. But a doctor has no obligation, in the strict meaning of the term, to heal or cure the patient. In contrast, in the case of an obligation of result, as it is commonly understood, there is a burden on the person who owes such an obligation to attain a precise result. When I buy a car, the seller has the obligation, after I have paid for it, to provide me with the car.' Dupuy further notes that 'in the classical conception of the distinction . . . the statement of a damage . . . suffered by State A, in case of state responsibility for negligence as well as in other cases of state responsibility, invites *consideration of the conduct which was at its origin*. If a) it consists of a lack of diligence, and b) this lack is attributable to the organs of State B, the latter will be held responsible'.) (Footnotes omitted). Obligations of conduct are also known as 'best efforts' obligations or 'obligations of means'.

[148] Duncan French and Tim Stephens, 'ILA Study Group on Due Diligence in International Law (Second Report)' (International Law Association 2016) 2.

can be seen as a technique of proceduralisation, deferring controversial inquiries as to the content of substantive rules regulating wrongdoing to less controversial questions relating to informed decision-making and process. Rather than posing answers to questions of breach, due diligence instead tends to inquire whether States have taken reasonable and appropriate steps to avoid or mitigate injury to other States.[149]

The concept of due diligence can be traced back to Roman law, where a person could be held liable for accidental harm caused to others as a consequence of that person's failure to meet an objective standard of care that a reasonable person (*diligens paterfamilias*) would have adopted in that particular case. The concept of *diligens paterfamilias* has influenced the development of the tort of negligence in many domestic legal systems.[150] In international law, due diligence 'functions primarily as a standard of conduct that defines and circumscribes the responsibility of a State *in relation to the conduct of third parties*'.[151] In its present form, in international law, the concept of due diligence can be viewed as one of the limits to State sovereignty. As such, States 'acknowledge a series of case specific obligations of conduct, aimed at preventing an undesired effect, harmful to other members of the international community or foreign individuals' – or to put it differently – 'State sovereignty stops where the obligation to diligently protect the rights and interests of others starts'.[152] A State's obligations of due diligence are assessed by reference to the primary rules (e.g., the substantive obligation itself) and not by reference to the secondary rules of State responsibility. In the history of international law, Grotius laid the intellectual foundations for the concept during the seventeenth century, but it was not until the nineteenth century that due diligence, as it is understood today, emerged as a concept to mediate interstate relations.[153] The increase in the movement of people across borders, which led States to accept that they had an obligation to protect aliens that were in their territory, and the consolidation in the concept of State sovereignty, whereby States were required to protect the security of other States in both times of peace and war, are likely to have been the most

---

[149] ibid 3.
[150] Jonathan Bonnitcha and Robert McCorquodale, 'The Concept of "Due Diligence" in the UN Guiding Principles on Business and Human Rights' (2017) 28 Eur. J. Int. Law 899, 903.
[151] ibid. (Emphasis added).
[152] Joanna Kulesza, *Due Diligence in International Law* (Brill Nijhoff 2016) 57–58.
[153] Duncan French and Tim Stephens, 'ILA Study Group on Due Diligence in International Law (First Report)' (International Law Association 2014) 2–3.

important early contributions to the evolution of the concept of due diligence in international law.[154] The ILC Articles do not mention the term 'due diligence'[155] in their text, although codification efforts have been attempted since the early twentieth century.[156] On the evolution of the standard of due diligence, the ILA further notes the following:

> Although the issue of fault attracted significant attention in the development of the Articles on State Responsibility, it is to primary rules of conduct, rather than secondary rules of responsibility, that we must look to determine the applicable standard of behaviour. As the Commentaries explain, the Articles lay down no general standard, whether it involves 'some degree of fault, culpability, negligence or want of due diligence' . . . . In the second-half of the twentieth century, the development of the 'due diligence' standard has been dominated by practice in the field of international environmental law . . . . The omission of due diligence from the Articles on State Responsibility in relation to state wrongs generally, led the Commission to take up the concept in other contexts, most notably in the Draft Articles on the Prevention of Transboundary Harm from Hazardous Activities where the Commentaries explained that the duty to take 'preventing or minimization activities measures is one of due diligence', and that '[t]he standard of due diligence against which the conduct of the State of origin of [transboundary environmental harm] should be examined is that which is generally considered to be appropriate and proportional to the risk of transboundary harm in the particular instance'.[157]

General obligations of due diligence exist in customary international law – which should be regarded as the common standard for this concept[158] – as well as in many other specialised fields of international law, such as, among

---

[154] ibid 2.
[155] 'Report of the International Law Commission' (International Law Commission 1999) A/54/10 para 420. (The ILC Special Rapporteur James Crawford noted that 'defining the precise nature of due diligence could not be done in the context of the draft articles without spending many more years on the topic and, even if the problem were resolved, that would in effect be based on the presumption that any primary rule, or most primary rules, contained a qualification of due diligence'.).
[156] 'First Report Submitted to the Council by the Preparatory Committee for the Codification' (Preparatory Committee for the Codification Conference (Conference for the Codification of International Law) 1930).
[157] French and Stephens, 'ILA Study Group on Due Diligence in International Law (First Report)' (n 153).
[158] French and Stephens, 'ILA Study Group on Due Diligence in International Law (Second Report)' (n 148) 6.

others, the law of neutrality, diplomatic protection, human rights and environmental law, the law of the sea, the law of international watercourses, international investment law, cyber security, national security and business and human rights.[159] In principle, there is 'no contradiction between the general standard and the more specific expressions of due diligences in sub-branches of international law'.[160] For example, in the *S.S. Lotus* case, the Permanent Court of International Justice stated that '[i]t is well settled that a State is bound to use due diligence to prevent the commission within its dominions of criminal acts against another nation or its people'.[161] In *Trail Smelter Arbitration*, the Tribunal stated that 'a State owes at all times a duty to protect other States against injurious acts by individuals from within its jurisdiction'.[162] In the *Corfu Channel Case*, the ICJ emphasised that States have an obligation 'not to allow knowingly its territory to be used for acts contrary to the rights of other States'.[163] Due diligence was also considered a key element in determining State responsibility in the case of the *United States Diplomatic and Consular Staff in Tehran*, where the ICJ stated that the Iranian authorities were aware of their 'obligations to protect the United States Consulate . . . and

[159] Kulesza (n 152); Riccardo Pisillo-Mazzeschi, 'The Due Diligence Rule and the Nature of the International Responsibility of States' 35 Ger. Yearb. Int. Law 9, 22–41; Draft Articles on Prevention of Transboundary Harm from Hazardous Activities, with commentaries 2001; Basic Principles and Guidelines on the Right to a Remedy and Reparation for Victims of Gross Violations of International Human Rights Law and Serious Violations of International Humanitarian Law (A/RES/60/147); *Military and Paramilitary Activities in and against Nicaragua (Nicaragua v United States of America)* (n 75) para 57; *Application of the Convention on the Prevention and Punishment of the Crime of Genocide (Bosnia and Herzegovina v Serbia and Montenegro)* (n 29) para 430; *Armed Activities on the Territory of the Congo (Democratic Republic of the Congo v Uganda)* (n 59) paras 179, 189, 228, 232, 233, 246, 247, 250–300; *Corfu Channel (United Kingdom of Great Britain and Northern Ireland v Albania)* (International Court of Justice, Judgment of April 9th 1949, ICJ Reports 1949, p 4); French and Stephens, ILA Study Group on Due Diligence in International Law (First Report)' (n 153); French and Stephens, 'ILA Study Group on Due Diligence in International Law (Second Report)' (n 148); Chetail (n 14) 126; Markus Krajewski, 'The State Duty to Protect against Human Rights Violations through Transnational Business Activities' (2018) 23 Deakin L. Rev. 13.

[160] French and Stephens, 'ILA Study Group on Due Diligence in International Law (Second Report)' (n 148) 6. ('The broader obligation of due diligence underlies the more specific instances of due diligence, which will become operational if they apply in a given situation. As there is no norm-conflict between the very general due diligence and these more specific manifestations, it seems also justified to say that no conflict of law rules are needed to resolve these (such as *lex generalis* and *lex specialis* rules).').

[161] *S.S. Lotus (France v Turkey)* (Permanent Court of International Justice, 1927 PCIJ (ser A) No 10 (Sept 7)) para 269.

[162] *Trail Smelter Arbitration (United States v Canada)* (Reports of International Awards (Award 16 April 1938 and 11 March 1941) Volume III, pp 1905–1982) 1963.

[163] *Corfu Channel (United Kingdom of Great Britain and Northern Ireland v Albania)* (n 159) 22.

of the need for action on their part, and similarly failed to use the means which were at their disposal to comply with their obligations'.[164] Arbitration tribunals in international investment law have reached similar conclusions.[165] Some commentators have even asserted that the obligation of due diligence exists as a basic principle of international law:[166]

> By asserting the responsibility of a state because of a lack of due diligence, one is not affirming that the state itself has committed the unlawful act that occurred. Rather, the state's responsibility is engaged because it committed a separate violation of international law by not taking all of the necessary measures available to prevent or to punish the occurrence of a specific act.[167]

The concept of due diligence can be found to various extents in all the core human rights treaties.[168] Due diligence is important in the context of international human rights law because it defines the 'extent of a State's obligations to prevent and respond to infringements of human rights by private actors within its territory or jurisdiction'.[169] For example, in the well-known case of *Velàsquez – Rodriguez v Honduras*, the Inter-American Court of Human Rights stated the following:

> Thus, in principle, any violation of rights recognized by the Convention carried out by an act of public authority or by persons who use their position of authority is imputable to the State. However, this does not define all the circumstances in which a State is obligated to prevent, investigate and punish human rights violations, nor all the cases in which the State might be found responsible for an infringement of those rights. *An illegal act which violates human rights and which is initially not directly imputable to a State (for example, because it is the act of a private person or because the person responsible has not been identified) can lead to international responsibility of*

---

[164] *United States Diplomatic and Consular Staff in Tehran* (International Court of Justice, Judgment, ICJ Reports 1980, p 3) [68].

[165] *Asian Agricultural Products Ltd v Republic of Sri Lanka* (ICSID Case No ARB/87/3) 562. ('Accordingly, the Tribunal considers that the Respondent through said inaction and omission violated its due diligence obligation which requires undertaking all possible measures that could be reasonably expected to prevent the eventual occurrence of killings and property destructions.').

[166] Kulesza (n 152) 19; Barnidge (n 14) 92.

[167] Chetail (n 14) 125; French and Stephens, ILA Study Group on Due Diligence in International Law (First Report)' (n 153) 31–32.

[168] French and Stephens, ILA Study Group on Due Diligence in International Law (First Report)' (n 153) 14.

[169] Bonnitcha and McCorquodale, 'The Concept of "Due Diligence" in the UN Guiding Principles on Business and Human Rights' (n 150) 904.

the State, not because of the act itself, but because of the lack of due diligence
to prevent the violation or to respond to it as required by the Convention.'[170]

Similar comments have been made by the Committee on the Elimination
of Discrimination against Women[171] and by the United Nations Human
Rights Committee in General Comment Number 31:

> [T]he positive obligations on States Parties to ensure Covenant rights will
> only be fully discharged if individuals are protected by the State, not just
> against violations of Covenant rights by its agents, but also against acts
> committed by private persons or entities that would impair the enjoyment
> of Covenant rights in so far as they are amenable to application between
> private persons or entities. There may be circumstances in which a failure to
> ensure Covenant rights ... would give rise to violations by States Parties of
> those rights, as a result of States Parties' permitting or failing to take appro-
> priate measures or to exercise due diligence to prevent, punish, investigate or
> redress the harm caused by such acts by private persons or entities.[172]

As far as the content of due diligence is concerned, there are four inter-
related issues that must be addressed: first, there is the issue of the degree of
diligence required; second, whether due diligence has an objective or subjective content; third, whether the concept is rigid or flexible and finally, the
limits applicable to this concept.[173] As a general rule, in international law, due
diligence is expected to confirm to a 'minimum standard' that would reasonably be expected in that particular circumstances, rather than by reference to a
standard of diligence that a State 'normally uses in its own internal affairs'.[174]
Due diligence has an objective content, that is, 'what counts is not the
subjective attitude of fault on the part of the individuals acting as State organs,
but the breach of an *objective standard* of conduct by the State *considered as a*

---

[170] *Velàsquez Rodríguez v Honduras* (Inter-American Court of Human Rights, Judgment of July
29, 1988 (Ser C) No 4 (1988)) [172]. (Emphasis added).
[171] General Recommendation No. 19 (UN Doc. A/47/38, 1992) para [9]. ('It is emphasized,
however, that discrimination under the Convention is not restricted to action by or on behalf of
Governments (see articles 2 (e), 2 (f) and 5). Under article 2 (e) the Convention calls on States
parties to take all appropriate measures to eliminate discrimination against women by any
person, organization or enterprise. *Under general international law and specific human rights
covenants, States may also be responsible for private acts if they fail to act with due diligence to
prevent violations of rights or to investigate and punish acts of violence, and for providing
compensation.*') (Emphasis added).
[172] UN Human Rights Committee (HRC), General comment no. 31, The nature of the general
legal obligation imposed on States Parties to the Covenant, 26 May 2004, CCPR/C/21/Rev.1/
Add.13 31.
[173] Pisillo-Mazzeschi (n 159) 41–46.
[174] ibid 41.

whole'.[175] An Advisory Opinion of the International Tribunal for the Law of
the Sea has clarified that due diligence is a 'variable concept' which may
change over time 'as measures considered sufficiently diligent at a certain
moment may become not diligent enough in light, for instance, of new
scientific or technological knowledge'.[176] The relevant 'factors in determining
whether a State's conduct in a particular scenario has met the standard of due
diligence include the degree of the risk of harm and the resources, both
economic and technological, available to the State'.[177] Similar variables have
been proposed in academic commentary, which examined the 'degree of the
State's control over certain areas of its territory', 'the importance of the interest
protected' and the 'degree of predictability of the harm'.[178] The threshold for
the limit of due diligence is high and responsibility is only excluded 'if the
damage could not have been avoided, not even by using all necessary due
diligence', States being expected to exercise due diligence even in situations of
force majeure.[179] However, it must also be recalled, as noted by the ICJ in the
Bosnian Genocide Case, that States are not 'under an obligation to succeed
whatever the circumstances' and that the obligation was 'to employ all means
reasonably available to them' to prevent a violation of international law.[180] In
international human rights law,[181] particularly in the jurisprudence of the
ECHR,[182] due diligence obligations are often expressed through the concept

---

[175] ibid 42.
[176] *Responsibilities and obligations of States sponsoring persons and entities with respect to activities
in the Area (Advisory Opinion of 1 February 2011)* (International Tribunal for the Law of the
Sea, ITLOS Reports 2011, p 10) [117].
[177] Bonnitcha and McCorquodale, 'The Concept of "Due Diligence" in the UN Guiding
Principles on Business and Human Rights' (n 150) 906.
[178] Pisillo-Mazzeschi (n 159) 44.
[179] ibid 45–46.
[180] *Application of the Convention on the Prevention and Punishment of the Crime of Genocide
(Bosnia and Herzegovina v Serbia and Montenegro)* (n 29) para 430.
[181] UN Human Rights Committee (HRC), General comment no. 31, The nature of the general
legal obligation imposed on States Parties to the Covenant, 26 May 2004, CCPR/C/21/Rev.1/
Add.13 para 8. ('[T]he positive obligations on States Parties to ensure Covenant rights will only
be fully discharged if individuals are protected by the State, not just against violations of the
Covenant rights by its agents, but also against acts committed by private persons or entities.
There may be circumstances in which a failure to ensure Covenant rights as required by article
2 would give rise to violations by States Parties of those rights, as a result of States Parties'
permitting or failing to take appropriate measures or to exercise due diligence to prevent,
punish, investigate or redress the harm caused by such acts by private persons or entities.').
[182] *A v United Kingdom* (European Court of Human Rights (Application No 25599/94)) [22];
Z and others v United Kingdom (European Court of Human Rights (Application No 29392/95))
[72]; *Edwards v United Kingdom* (European Court of Human Rights (Application No 46477/
99)) [54].

of 'positive obligations', which are 'obligations not simply to refrain from denying human rights, but to take specific measures to protect them'.[183] The due diligence obligation of States to 'employ all means available to them' in order to fulfill their duty to protect – such as the passing of legislative, administrative, judicial, financial and educational measures to achieve this end – should not be confused with the newer concept of 'human rights due diligence', which targets enterprises generally and which has generally been defined as a 'process of investigation' to 'identify and manage commercial risks'.[184] States' due diligence obligation is an ongoing 'standard of conduct' that arises under international law, while human rights due diligence[185] is largely a voluntary mechanism that targets enterprises as a result of the application of the UNGPs or other soft law instruments.[186] Human rights due diligence has been defined in the following manner:

> [H]uman rights due diligence is a means by which business enterprises can identify, prevent, mitigate and account for the harms that they may cause, and through which judicial and regulatory bodies can assess an enterprise's respect for human rights.[187]

States' due diligence obligations, as a matter of international law, are also separate from the various concepts of due diligence that States use in their day-to-day regulatory functions. While it is ultimately through the process of enacting legislative, administrative and judicial measures that States comply with their varied international obligations, including those found in the field of international human rights – there are four other separate circumstances in which States have been found to use the concept of due diligence in their day-

---

[183] Susan Marks and Fiorentina Azizi, 'Responsibility for Violations of Human Rights Obligations: International Mechanisms' in James Crawford and others (eds), *The Law of International Responsibility* (Oxford University Press 2010) 731; Vladislava Stoyanova, 'Fault, Knowledge and Risk within the Framework of Positive Obligations under the European Convention on Human Rights' [2020] Leiden J. Int. Law 1.

[184] Bonnitcha and McCorquodale, 'The Concept of "Due Diligence" in the UN Guiding Principles on Business and Human Rights' (n 150) 901; John Gerard Ruggie and John F Sherman, 'The Concept of "Due Diligence" in the UN Guiding Principles on Business and Human Rights: A Reply to Jonathan Bonnitcha and Robert McCorquodale' (2017) 28 Eur. J. Int. Law 921; Jonathan Bonnitcha and Robert McCorquodale, 'The Concept of "Due Diligence" in the UN Guiding Principles on Business and Human Rights: A Rejoinder to John Gerard Ruggie and John F. Sherman, III' (2017) 28 Eur. J. Int. Law 929; Chetail (n 14) 128.

[185] Bonnitcha and McCorquodale, 'The Concept of "Due Diligence" in the UN Guiding Principles on Business and Human Rights' (n 150); Robert McCorquodale and others, 'Human Rights Due Diligence in Law and Practice: Good Practices and Challenges for Business Enterprises' (2017) 2 BHRJ 195.

[186] Chetail (n 14) 128.

[187] De Schutter and others, 'Human Rights Due Diligence: The Role of States' (2012) 1.

to-day regulatory functions.[188] The first approach makes due diligence a requirement 'as *a matter of regulatory compliance*' with specific laws, such as consumer protection and anti-corruption. The second approach seeks to give *incentives* such as export credit, for instance, to companies that already have strong due diligence processes in place. In the third approach, States seek to *encourage due diligence* through transparency and disclosure measures. The fourth approach is a combination of the above. This demonstrates that, despite the recent increase in the usage of the concept of human rights due diligence, this practice is 'not a creation of the UN Human Rights Council' nor is it an exclusively 'voluntary measure for corporate social responsibility', but that it 'originates from the legal tools that States are already using to ensure that business behaviour meets social expectations, including standards set in law'.[189]

5.3.2 *State Corporate Ownership and the Concept of Due Diligence in International Law*

In the UNGPs, SOEs can be encountered in Pillar 1 (under the State duty to protect human rights) and in Pillar 2 (under the corporate responsibility to protect human rights). As discussed in Chapter 1, under the State duty to protect human rights, the UNGPs offer three perspectives on the 'State-business nexus'.[190] First, Principle 4 addresses the State ownership function directly, through direct ownership or control of a business enterprise by the State, as well as indirectly, when the State does not own or control a given business, but instead provides that business with support and services.[191] Second, Principle 5 of the UNGPs provides that 'States must exercise adequate oversight in order to meet their international human rights obligations when they contract with, or legislate for, business enterprises to provide services that may impact on upon the enjoyment of human rights'. Principle 5 thus seeks to address the situation when, as a result of the privatisation of certain services, there may be a negative effect on the enjoyment of human

---

[188] ibid 5.
[189] ibid 4.
[190] Mihaela M Barnes, 'The United Nations Guiding Principles on Mihaela M Barnes, 'The United Nations Guiding Principles on Business and Human Rights, the State Duty to Protect Human Rights and the State-Business Nexus' (2018) 15 Brazilian J. Int. Law 42, 47–51.
[191] John G Ruggie, 'Guiding Principles on Business and Human Rights: Implementing the United Nations "Protect, Respect and Remedy" Framework (Report of the Special Representative of the Secretary-General on the Issue of Human Rights and Transnational Corporations and Other Business Enterprises)' (2011) A/HRC/17/31 9.

rights.[192] The third and last perspective on the State-business nexus is offered by Principle 6, which provides that 'States should promote respect for human rights by businesses with which they conduct commercial transactions'[193] and covers the significant public procurement activities conducted by States.[194]

As far as the State duty to protect human rights in the context of the State-business nexus is concerned, UNGP Principle 4 provides that States must take '*additional steps* to protect against human rights abuses' by SOEs 'including, where appropriate, by requiring *human rights due diligence*'.[195] The State duty to protect under the UNGPs is thus composed of two elements: the requirement to take 'additional steps' and the requirement to perform due diligence.[196] The requirement to take additional steps has been discussed by the United Nations Working Group on Business and Human Rights (UN Working Group), primarily from the point of view of ensuring adequate corporate governance mechanisms inside SOEs. In this context, States are required to set the expectations that they have from SOEs in the area of human rights, provide clarification of the relationship between the company boards and the State, ensure that there are appropriate oversight and follow-up mechanisms for capacity-building and require human rights due diligence as well as disclosure, transparency and reporting mechanisms and effective remedy.[197] The second element, which requires States to ensure that their SOEs perform human rights due diligence must, however, be viewed in the broader context of the State's own due diligence obligations under international law.[198] The reason for this approach is the element of *knowledge*[199]

---

[192] ibid 10.

[193] ibid.

[194] Institute for Human Rights and Business, 'Protecting Rights by Purchasing Right: The Human Rights Provisions, Opportunities and Limitations under the 2014 EU Public Procurement Directives' (2015); Olga Martin-Ortega, 'Public Procurement as a Tool for the Protection and Promotion of Human Rights: A Study of Collaboration, Due Diligence and Leverage in the Electronics Industry' (2018) 3 BHRJ 75.

[195] Ruggie, 'Guiding Principles on Business and Human Rights: Implementing the United Nations "Protect, Respect and Remedy" Framework (Report of the Special Representative of the Secretary-General on the Issue of Human Rights and Transnational Corporations and Other Business Enterprises)' (n 191) 9. (Emphasis added).

[196] Barnes, 'The United Nations Guiding Principles on Business and Human Rights, the State Duty to Protect Human Rights and the State-Business Nexus' (2018) 15 Brazilian J. Int. Law 42, 52–57.

[197] 'Leading by Example: The State, State-Owned Enterprises and Human Rights (Report of the Working Group on the Issue of Human Rights and Transnational Corporations and Other Business Enterprises)' (2016) A/HRC/32/45 12–19.

[198] Barnes, 'The United Nations Guiding Principles on Business and Human Rights, the State Duty to Protect Human Rights and the State-Business Nexus' (2018) 15 Brazilian J. Int. Law 42, 54–57.

[199] Stoyanova (n 183) 4 ('As to knowledge, it is necessary first to underscore that the state as an organizational entity cannot actually have this psychological and cognitive attitude. Rather,

that is present in the relationship between the State and its SOEs. Consequently, it is 'only reasonable to assume that State *should be aware* about how their SOEs operate, given that it is the State that ultimately sets out the operational strategy for its SOEs'.[200] Support for this assertion can be gathered from jurisprudence as well as from State practice.

For example, the element of *knowledge* was considered key by the ICJ in the *Corfu Channel Case*.[201] In that case, the ICJ had to determine whether the mines had been laid with the *knowledge* of Albania. The Court started its inquiry by laying down a general principle:

> [I]t cannot be concluded from the mere fact of the control exercised by a State over its territory and waters that that State necessarily knew, or ought to have known, of any unlawful act perpetrated therein, nor yet that it necessarily knew, or should have known, the authors. This fact, by itself and apart from other circumstances, neither involves prima facie responsibility nor shifts the burden of proof.[202]

The Court further continued:

> On the other hand, the fact of this exclusive territorial control exercised by a State within its frontiers has a bearing upon the methods of proof available to establish the knowledge of that State as to such events. By reason of this exclusive control, the other State, the victim of a breach of international law, is often unable to furnish direct proof of facts giving rise to responsibility. Such a State should be allowed a more liberal recourse to *inferences of fact* and *circumstantial evidence*. This indirect evidence is admitted in all systems of law, and its use is recognized by international decisions. It must be regarded as of special weight when it is based on a series of facts linked together and leading logically to a single conclusion.[203]

responsibility for omission can be established by comparing the actual state conduct with a conduct that one can legitimately expect from a normally directed and diligent state. This suggests that the standard of fault is negligence, and the type of negligence applied is objective. However, what conduct can be expected from a diligent state can be dependent on the actual availability of relevant information about the risk of harm, which ought to not only be objectively assessed, but also subjectively appreciated. It follows that actual knowledge and subjective appreciation of information by specific individuals who are part of the institutional structures of the state might be of relevance.').

[200] Mihaela M Barnes, 'The United Nations Guiding Principles on Business and Human Rights, the State Duty to Protect Human Rights and the State-Business Nexus' (2018) 15 Brazilian J. Int. Law 42, 56.

[201] *Corfu Channel (United Kingdom of Great Britain and Northern Ireland v Albania)* (n 159) 17–18.

[202] ibid 18.

[203] ibid. (Emphasis added).

Circumstantial evidence and factual inferences must, however, leave 'no room for reasonable doubt', and by examining Albania's attitude before the incident and the feasibility of observing the mines from its own coast, the Court concluded that Albania was responsible for the explosions and the damage caused to the UK.[204] This conclusion was reached through evidence that Albania 'kept a close watch' over the waters of the North Corfu Channel and by the expert evidence which indicated that it would have been possible for Albania to observe the laying of the mines from its coast.[205] In the context of positive obligations, the jurisprudence of the ECHR has also long since distinguished between the obligations of taking protective operational measures and the obligation of adopting an effective regulatory framework to provide general protection to the society at large.[206]

In the context of SOEs, State practice supports the conclusion that States are aware how their SOEs operate. For example, the Swedish State Ownership Policy and Guidelines for State-Owned Enterprises expressly integrates the Global Compact, the UNGPs, the OECD Guidelines as well as the Agenda 2030 in its ambit and forms an integral part of the legal framework for the regulation of SOEs in Sweden as was discussed in Chapter 3.[207] Compliance is mandatory for all fully or majority-owned Swedish SOEs and a process of dialogue has been commenced to ensure compliance even in the case of entities where the State holds a minority shareholding. China – often criticised for its poor environmental and human rights records – has also undertaken considerable efforts to establish a 'responsible public image' as an owner.[208] As discussed elsewhere, in China all SOEs

---

[204] ibid 23.

[205] ibid 19–22.

[206] Stoyanova (n 183) (The article provides a review of the jurisprudence in this area and concludes that 'the ECtHR has consistently referred to the standard of "knew or ought to have known" in its analysis, reflecting actual or putative knowledge by the state about risk of harm. This standard is applied to establish a breach of the positive obligation to take operational measures to protect a concrete individual who might have been at "real and immediate risk" of harm. The standard of "knew or ought to have known" is also applied for the establishment of a breach of the positive obligation of ensuring an effective regulatory framework aimed at providing general protection. Any deficiencies in this regulatory framework have to be causally linked to the harm sustained by the specific applicant'.).

[207] Government of Sweden, Ministry of Enterprise and Innovation, 'The State's Ownership Policy and Guidelines for State-Owned Enterprises 2017' <https://www.government.se/reports/2017/06/the-states-ownership-policy-and-guidelines-for-state-owned-enterprises-2017/>.

[208] Jing Zhu, 'The 2030 Agenda for Sustainable Development and China's Implementation' (2017) 15 CJPRE 142; Danyun Xu, Lei Wang and Junchang Liu, 'Assessing the Social Performance of State-Owned Forest Farms in China: Integrating Forest Social Values and Corporate Social Responsibility Approaches' (2017) 32 Scand. J. For. Res. 338; Yasir Shahab, Collins G Ntim and Farid Ullah, 'The Brighter Side of Being Socially Responsible: CSR

are supervised and administered by the State-Owned Assets Supervision and Administration Commission of the State Council (SASAC), an institution under the direct management of the State Council that is tasked with the supervision and management of all SOEs (excluding financial enterprises).[209] SASAC has issued a set of 'Guidelines to State-Owned Enterprises Directly under the Supervision of the Central Government on Fulfilling Corporate Social Responsibilities'.[210] Of particular importance is the statement that SOEs are 'the backbone' of China's economy and that fulfilling corporate social responsibility is not only their mission, but also an 'ardent expectation and requirement' from the public'.[211] China's Ministry of Commerce and the Ministry of Environmental Protection have also issued a Guidance on Environmental Protection in Foreign Investment Cooperation, which requires entities that operate abroad to address the concept of environmental protection internally, to pay adequate consideration to environmental and labour concerns and to 'study and learn' from the standards and practices of

Ratings and Financial Distress among Chinese State and Non-State Owned Firms' [2018] Applied Economics Letters 1; Jennifer Qiu, 'Quality of CSR Reporting in China: A Comparative Analysis Between State- and Privately-Owned Real Estate Companies' [2017] Social Impact Research Experience (SIRE) 38; Christopher Marquis, Juelin Yin and Dongning Yang, 'State-Mediated Globalization Processes and the Adoption of Corporate Social Responsibility Reporting in China' (2017) 13 Manag. Organ. Rev. 167; Christopher Marquis and Cuili Qian, 'Corporate Social Responsibility Reporting in China: Symbol or Substance?' (2014) 25 Organ. Sci. 127; Dan Guttman and others, 'Environmental Governance in China: Interactions between the State and "Nonstate Actors"' (2018) 220 J. Environ. Manage. 126; Richard Aidoo and others, 'Footprints of the Dragon: China's Oil Diplomacy and Its Impacts on Sustainable Development Policy in Ecuador and Ghana' (2017) 8 Revue internationale de politique de développement; Mihaela M Barnes, 'State-Owned Entities as Key Actors in the Promotion and Implementation of the Agenda 2030 for Sustainable Development: Examples of Good Practices' (2019) Laws 8, 10. <doi:10.3390/laws8020010>.

[209] 'SASAC'. <http://en.sasac.gov.cn/index.html> accessed 18 August 2020; 'SASAC About SASAC – SASAC Main Functions – SASAC'. <http://en.sasac.gov.cn/n1408028/n1408521/index.html> accessed 4 February 2019. SASAC 'supervises and manages the State-owned assets of centrally administered State-owned enterprises'; it is responsible for the supervision and for ensuring the increase in the value of State-owned assets; it takes charge of the reform and restructuring of State-owned enterprises; it appoints and removes the top executives of the entities supervised; it manages the day-to-day operation of the supervisory panels; takes charge of the State-owned capital operational budget and ensures that surplus capital is returned to the State; it ensures that the supervised enterprises apply relevant legislation, regulation and principles; and it takes charge of the 'fundamental management' of those entities.

[210] 'Guidelines to the State-Owned Enterprises Directly under the Central Government'. <http://en.sasac.gov.cn/2011/12/06/c_313.htm> accessed 18 August 2020.

[211] ibid.

international organisations and multilateral financial institutions.[212] Similar measures have been taken in the financial sector by China's Banking and Regulatory Commission through the issuance of a set of Green Credit Guidelines.[213] Other States such as Spain (in the Sustainable Economy Law of 2011),[214] Finland (in the Government Resolution on State Ownership)[215] and Norway[216] are also heading on this path.

The State practice discussed in the preceding paragraph demonstrates that it is ultimately States that determine how well SOEs are regulated. Consequently, even if, as a result of corporate structuring, it may not be possible to attribute the acts or omissions of an SOE back to the State, States may still have due diligence obligations, as a matter of international law, to ensure that the entities that they own or control do not violate human rights. It follows that the approach taken in UNGP Principle 4, which requires States to ensure that SOEs perform human rights due diligence only 'where appropriate' is questionable.[217] Under international law, States have an obligation to ensure that they exercise appropriate diligence to prevent, punish, investigate and redress human rights violations caused by all non-State actors. For example, human rights due diligence, could be viewed as a procedural aspect, which all States must take in order to operationalise their broader obligations of due diligence under international law. Human rights due diligence can be viewed in a similar manner to that of an environmental impact assessment which was deemed necessary in *Pulp Mills on the River*

---

[212] 'MOFCOM and MEP Jointly Issued Guidance on Environmental Protection in Foreign Investment and Cooperation'. <http://english.mofcom.gov.cn/article/newsrelease/significantnews/201303/20130300043146.shtml> accessed 18 August 2020.

[213] 'Notice of the CBRC on Issuing the Green Credit Guidelines'. <http://www.cbrc.gov.cn/EngdocView.do?docID=3CE646AB629B46B9B533B1D8D9FF8C4A> accessed 18 August 2020.

[214] Ley N° 2/2011 de 4 de marzo de 2011 sobre Economía Sostenible (modificada por la Ley N° 2/2012 de 29 de junio de 2012) Articles 35–39.

[215] Government of Finland, 'Government Ownership Steering: Financial Annual Report 2015' (2015) <vnk.fi/government-ownership-steering>.

[216] 'Diverse and Value-Creating Ownership' (2014) Meld. St. 27 (2013–2014) Report to the Storting (white paper) Recommendation of the Ministry of Trade, Industry and Fisheries of 20 June 2014, approved in the Council of State the same day. (The Solberg Government) 60. <https://www.regjeringen.no/en/dokumenter/meld.-st.-27-2013-2014/id763968/>; 'Opportunities for All: Human Rights in Norway's Foreign Policy and Development Cooperation' (2014) Meld. St. 10 (2014–2015) Report to the Storting (white paper) 60–61.

[217] Ruggie, 'Guiding Principles on Business and Human Rights: Implementing the United Nations "Protect, Respect and Remedy" Framework (Report of the Special Representative of the Secretary-General on the Issue of Human Rights and Transnational Corporations and Other Business Enterprises)' (n 191) 9.

Uruguay (Argentina v Uruguay).[218] Human rights due diligence, in the context of the State-business nexus, must thus be viewed as part of States' broader due diligence obligations under international law.[219] Furthermore, ensuring that a rigorous process of human rights due diligence is in place could also assist in addressing questions connected to complicity.[220] Overall, States have continuous due diligence obligations to ensure that the entities that they own or control do not violate human rights. Furthermore, the principle of due diligence is flexible enough to be 'restrictively or expansively interpreted, as the particular facts and circumstances' require to hold States responsible for their actions and omissions related to non-State actors'.[221] Overall, this demonstrates that international law can provide adequate answers to a lot of the challenges associated with States and their SOEs and that sometimes 'quite ironically general international law can be more *avant-garde* than the most recent soft law instrument'.[222]

5.3.3 A State's Due Diligence Obligations Apply Extraterritorially

This section argues that States have a general obligation, as a matter of international law, to regulate the extraterritorial activities of their SOEs, as an exception to the general principle of international law, which purports that a State's jurisdiction is primarily territorial. The *nexus* between the State and its SOEs as well as the *control* by the State over its SOEs supports this argument. Often SOEs internationalise their activities due to State policy, which shows that a *nexus* can be found between the home State and the SOEs

---

[218] *Pulp Mills on the River Uruguay (Argentina v Uruguay)* (Judgment, ICJ Reports 2010, p 14) [68–158, 204]; O McIntyre, 'The Proceduralisation and Growing Maturity of International Water Law: Case concerning Pulp Mills on the River Uruguay (Argentina v Uruguay), International Court of Justice, 20 April 2010' (2010) 22 J. Environ. Law 475; Akiko Takano, 'Due Diligence Obligations and Transboundary Environmental Harm: Cybersecurity Applications' (2018) 7 Laws 36. See also *Certain Activities Carried out by Nicaragua in the Border Area (Costa Rica v Nicaragua)* and *Construction of a Road in Costa Rica along the San Juan River (Nicaragua v Costa Rica)* Judgment, I.C.J. Reports 2015, p. 665.

[219] Barnes, 'The United Nations Guiding Principles on Business and Human Rights, the State Duty to Protect Human Rights and the State-Business Nexus' (2018) 15 Brazilian J. Int. Law 42, 54–57.

[220] Sabine Michalowski, 'Due Diligence and Complicity: A Relationship in Need of Clarification' in Surya Deva and David Bilchitz (eds), *Human Rights Obligations of Business: Beyond the Corporate Responsibility to Respect?* (Cambridge University Press 2013); Florian Wettstein, 'Making Noise about Silent Complicity: The Moral Inconsistency of the "Protect, Respect and Remedy" Framework' in Surya Deva and David Bilchitz (eds), *Human Rights Obligations of Business: Beyond the Corporate Responsibility to Respect?* (Cambridge University Press 2013).

[221] Barnidge (n 14) 81.

[222] Chetail (n 14) 129.

that is not *usually* encountered in the case of POEs. For instance, the element of nexus can be found either based on the *direct control* that the State has over the SOE in question, or on an element of *knowledge* that States *should have* about the businesses that they own. This section proceeds by analysing, in turn, nexus based on control and nexus based on knowledge.

5.3.3.1 The Challenge of Extraterritoriality

It is a generally accepted principle of international law that the jurisdiction of a State is primarily territorial and that States are permitted to exercise universal jurisdiction only in an extremely limited number of instances, such as for crimes against humanity, genocide, war crimes, piracy, torture and forced disappearance.[223] The territorial basis for jurisdiction arises from the interconnected principles of sovereign equality and non-intervention.[224] Nevertheless, States have long since exercised extraterritorial jurisdiction by mutual consent in various domains such as anti-corruption, anti-trust, securities regulation, environmental protection and general civil and criminal jurisdiction.[225] It has also long been recognised that States are the primary duty bearers with regard to the protection of human rights[226] and that the human rights obligations of States are not necessarily 'territorially confined'.[227] The ICJ has confirmed this

---

[223] Shaw (n 4) 471, 485–499. (There are some other exceptions to the rule that a State's jurisdiction is primarily territorial. Those exceptions relate principally to the establishment of criminal jurisdiction over persons and are based on *nationality* (the offender is a national of the State), *passive personality* (aliens have committed offences abroad that may have affected the nationals of that particular State), *the protective principle* (aliens that have committed acts abroad as a result of which the national security of that State is impaired).

[224] *Banković and Others v Belgium and Others* (n 130) paras 59–60.

[225] John G Ruggie, 'Business and Human Rights: Further Steps toward the Operationalization of the "Protect, Respect and Remedy" Framework (Report of the Special Representative of the Secretary-General on the Issue of Human Rights and Transnational Corporations and Other Business Enterprises, John Ruggie' (2010) A/HRC/14/27 11.

[226] Malcolm D Evans (ed), *International Law* (4th edn, Oxford University Press 2014) 196.

[227] UN Committee on Economic, Social and Cultural Rights, General comment No. 24 (2017) on State obligations under the International Covenant on Economic, Social and Cultural Rights in the context of business activities, 10 August 2017, E/C.12/GC/24 paras 25–37; McCorquodale and Simons (n 27) 606.(In paragraph 27, the General Comment 24 clarifies that the 'extraterritorial obligations of States under the covenant follow from the fact that the obligations of the Covenant are expressed without any restriction linked to territory or jurisdiction . . . . It would be contradictory . . . to allow a State to remain passive where an actor domiciled in its territory and/or under its jurisdiction, and thus under its control or authority, harmed the rights of others in other States, or where conduct by such an actor may lead to foreseeable harm being caused'.).

line of reasoning in the Advisory Opinion concerning the *Legal Consequences of the Construction of a Wall in the Occupied Palestinian Territory*:

The Court would observe that, while the jurisdiction of States is primarily territorial, it may sometimes be exercised outside the national territory. Considering the object and purpose of the International Covenant on Civil and Political Rights, it would seem natural that, even when such is the case, State parties to the Covenant should be bound to comply with its provisions...The *travaux préparatoires* of the Covenant confirm the Committee's interpretation of Article 2 of that instrument . . .. In conclusion the Court considers that the International Covenant on Civil and Political Rights is applicable in respect of acts done by a State in the exercise of its jurisdiction outside its own territory.[228]

A similar conclusion was reached in the *Armed Activities Case (Democratic Republic of the Congo v Uganda)*, where the Court held that the core international human rights and international humanitarian law instruments were applicable to Ugandan forces while they were in the territory of the Democratic Republic of the Congo,[229] and in the *Application of the International Convention on the Elimination of all Forms of Racial Discrimination (Georgia v Russia)*[230] where it was noted that 'there is no restriction of a general nature in CERD relating to its territorial application . . . these provisions generally appear to apply to the actions of a State party when it acts beyond its territory'.[231] The ECHR has reached similar conclusions in a string of cases,[232] while academic commentators and international organisations also have largely similar views on this issue.[233] On the

---

[228] *Legal Consequences of the Construction of a Wall in the Occupied Palestinian Territory* (International Court of Justice, Advisory Opinion, ICJ Reports 2004, p 136) paras 109–111. (Footnotes and paragraph numbers omitted).

[229] *Armed Activities on the Territory of the Congo (Democratic Republic of the Congo v Uganda)* (n 59) paras 179–180, 215–221.

[230] *Application of the International Convention on the Elimination of All Forms of Racial Discrimination (Georgia v Russian Federation)* (International Court of Justice, Provisional Measures (No 2008/35) 15 October 2008).

[231] ibid 3.

[232] *Loizidou v Turkey* (European Court of Human Rights, Grand Chamber, Application No 15318/89) [52]; *Case of Cyprus v Turkey* (European Court of Human Rights, Grand Chamber, Application no 25781/94) [61, 76]; *Case of Issa and Others v Turkey* (European Court of Human Rights, Second Section (Application no 31821/96) [68].

[233] McCorquodale and Simons (n 27); Sara L Seck, 'Home State Responsibility and Local Communities: The Case of Global Mining' (2014) 11 Yale Hum. Rts. & Dev. L.J. 10; Marko Milanovic, *Extraterritorial Application of Human Rights Treaties: Law, Principles, and Policy* (Oxford University Press 2011); WM Henry Jr, 'Litigating Global Warming: Substantive Law in Search of a Forum' (2004) 16 Fordham Envtl. L. Rev. 371; Expert meeting on the role of states

one hand, commentators believe that States have an obligation – under the principle of due diligence – to regulate extraterritorially all the businesses incorporated in their territory.[234] On the other hand, jurisprudence[235] has reached this conclusion based on the notion of the *control* of military forces over an area or over a population – a situation that arguably has different characteristics to the extraterritorial regulation of business activities.[236] In the case law coming from the ECHR, there seem to be two models for extending the extraterritorial application of the EConHR.[237] In the first model, jurisdiction is based on the spatial control over a territory, while in the second model, jurisdiction is based on the assertion of powers and control over individuals. The *Banković* decision referred to at the beginning of this chapter is an example of the first model. The territorial focus of the *Banković* reasoning was reinforced by the Court in other cases such as *Al-Skeini v UK*,[238] but there the ECHR also said that jurisdiction can arise by virtue of the exercise of powers over individuals:

> It is clear that, whenever the State, through its agents, exercises control and authority over an individual, and thus jurisdiction, the State is under an obligation under Article 1 to secure to that individual the rights and freedoms under Section I of the Convention that are relevant to the situation of that individual.[239]

in regulating and adjudicating the activities of corporations with respect to human rights, organized by the Special Representative of the UN Secretary-General on Business and Human Rights and the Danish section of the International, and Commission of Jurists, 'The Role of States in Effectively Regulating and Adjudicating the Activities of Corporations with Respect to Human Rights'.

[234] McCorquodale and Simons (n 27); Seck (n 233); Henry (n 233); Expert meeting on the role of states in regulating and adjudicating the activities of corporations with respect to human rights, organized by the Special Representative of the UN Secretary-General on Business and Human Rights and the Danish section of the International, and Commission of Jurists (n 233).

[235] *Legal Consequences of the Construction of a Wall in the Occupied Palestinian Territory* (n 228) paras 109–111; *Application of the International Convention on the Elimination of All Forms of Racial Discrimination (Georgia v Russian Federation)* (n 230).

[236] McCorquodale and Simons (n 27); Seck (n 233); Henry (n 233); Expert meeting on the role of states in regulating and adjudicating the activities of corporations with respect to human rights, organized by the Special Representative of the UN Secretary-General on Business and Human Rights and the Danish section of the International, and Commission of Jurists (n 233).

[237] Claire Methven O'Brien, 'The Home State Duty to Regulate the Human Rights Impacts of TNCs Abroad: A Rebuttal' (2018) 3 BHRJ 47, 56–60.

[238] *Al-Skeini and Others v United Kingdom* (European Court of Human Rights, Grand Chamber, Application No 55721/07) [74].

[239] ibid.

The issue of whether States have an obligation to regulate the activities of business that operate outside their territory has been the subject of extensive discussion between 2006 and 2011, before the adoption of the UNGPs.[240] The conclusion of those discussions has been summarised in the commentary to UNGP 2, by John Ruggie in the following manner:

> At present States are not generally required under international law to regulate the extraterritorial activities of businesses domiciled in their territory and/or jurisdiction. Nor are they generally prohibited from doing so, provided there is a recognised jurisdictional basis. Within these parameters some human rights treaty bodies recommend that home States take steps to prevent abuse by business enterprises within their jurisdiction. There are strong policy reasons for home States to set out clearly the expectation that businesses respect human rights abroad, *especially where the State itself is involved in or supports those businesses. The reasons include ensuring predictability for business enterprises by involving coherent and consistent messages, and preserving the State's own reputation.*[241]

In this view, any action by a State in this area is thus prompted by matters pertaining to that State's internal policy or by concerns relating to reputation, rather than by an obligation to do so in the legal sense. In later reports, John Ruggie further analysed the role of extraterritorial jurisdiction and States' duty to protect human rights and declared it an 'unsettled' issue in international law. From this position, Ruggie pointed to the general difficulties surrounding this issue and purported to create a 'matrix' to better understand the extent of States' obligations in this area:

> [O]ne can imagine a matrix, with two rows and three columns. Its rows would be domestic measures with extraterritorial implications; and direct extraterritorial jurisdiction over actors or activities abroad. Its columns would be public policies for companies (such as CSR and public procurement policies, export credit agency criteria, or consular support); regulation

---

[240] John Ruggie, 'Corporate Responsibility under International Law and Issues in Extraterritorial Regulation: Summary of Legal Workshops (Report of the Special Representative of the Secretary-General on the Issue of Human Rights and Transnational Corporations and Other Business Enterprises)' (2007) A/HRC/4/35/Add. 2; Ruggie, 'Business and Human Rights: Further Steps toward the Operationalization of the "Protect, Respect and Remedy" Framework (Report of the Special Representative of the Secretary- General on the Issue of Human Rights and Transnational Corporations and Other Business Enterprises, John Ruggie' (n 128) 11–12.

[241] Ruggie, 'Guiding Principles on Business and Human Rights: Implementing the United Nations "Protect, Respect and Remedy" Framework (Report of the Special Representative of the Secretary-General on the Issue of Human Rights and Transnational Corporations and Other Business Enterprises)' (n 191) 7. (Emphasis added).

(though corporate law, for instance); and enforcement actions (adjudicating alleged breaches and enforcing judicial and executive decisions). Their combination yields six types of 'extraterritorial' form, each in turn offering a range of options. Not all are equally likely to trigger objections under all circumstances.[242]

'The legal-doctrinal virtues and pitfalls of this matrix' have been called into question and have been criticised for obscuring the distinction between the extraterritorial obligations of States by virtue of human rights law and the 'State's policy rationales to protect human rights against extraterritorial viola-tions'.[243] Under this view, Ruggie's focus on de jure authority to exercise extraterritorial jurisdiction is misfocused and instead 'what is decisive for extraterritorial human rights obligations is States asserting *de facto* control over the individual rights-holder'.[244] Many other academic commentators have reinforced this position and support the position that States do have an obligation to regulate the extraterritorial activities of all business incorporated in their territory.[245] On the other hand, other commentators still endorse the view that a State's jurisdiction is, in essence, territorial.[246] Given the import-ance of this issue, it is likely that this dynamic debate will continue, even though the commentators that do not generally agree that States have extra-territorial obligations have conceded that by virtue of their connection with the State that owns them, SOEs are in a different position and that States should generally have an obligation to regulate the extraterritorial activities of those entities. In this context, O'Brien notes:

---

[242] Ruggie, 'Business and Human Rights: Further Steps toward the Operationalization of the "Protect, Respect and Remedy" Framework (Report of the Special Representative of the Secretary-General on the Issue of Human Rights and Transnational Corporations and Other Business Enterprises, John Ruggie' (n 128) 11.

[243] Daniel Augenstein and David Kinley, 'When Human Rights "Responsibilities" Become "Duties": The Extra-Territorial Obligations of States That Bind Corporations' in Surya Deva and David Bilchitz (eds), *Human Rights Obligations of Business: Beyond the Corporate Responsibility to Respect* (Cambridge University Press 2013) 277–278.

[244] ibid 291.

[245] Maastricht Principles on Extraterritorial Obligations of States in the Area of Economic, Social and Cultural Rights 2013; Olivier De Schutter and others, 'Commentary to the Maastricht Principles on Extraterritorial Obligations of States in the Area of Economic, Social and Cultural Rights' (2012) 34 HRQ 1084; Olivier De Schutter, 'Towards a New Treaty on Business and Human Rights' (2016) 1 BHRJ 41; 'States' Obligations to Respect and Protect Human Rights Abroad Joint Statement on John Ruggie's Draft Guiding Principles (Statement by a Group of International Organisations and Eminent Scholars)' <https://www.fidh.org/en/>; Mark Gibney, Katarina Tomasevski and Jens Vedsted-Hansen, 'Transnational State Responsibility for Violations of Human Rights' (1999) 12 Harv. Hum. Rts. J. 267.

[246] Methven O'Brien (n 237).

Besides additional obstacles posed, for instance, by the 'corporate veil', the principles, rules and precedents of extraterritorial human rights jurisdiction do not justify a claim that the obligations of some home states arising under human rights treaties extend to the acts and impact of TNC in other states, with one possible, and potentially significant *caveat*, concerning certain scenarios where the TNC is a state-owned or controlled enterprise.[247]

The analysis will now turn to analyse *nexus based on control* and *nexus based on knowledge* in the context of extraterritoriality.

5.3.3.2 Nexus Based on Control

The issue of nexus based on control was clarified in General Comment No. 2 of the Torture Convention in the following manner:

[T]he concept of 'any territory under its jurisdiction', linked as it is with the principle of non-derogability, includes any territory or facilities and must be applied to protect any person, citizen or non-citizen without discrimination subject to the de jure or de facto control of a State party. The Committee emphasizes that the State's obligation to prevent torture also applies to all persons who act, de jure or de facto, in the name of, in conjunction with, or at the behest of the State party.[248]

Under General Comment No. 2, a nexus based on control can be found between 'persons' that are deemed to 'act in the name of' or 'in conjunction with' the State. Furthermore, General Comment No. 24, which concerns States' obligations under the ICCPR, seems to take an even broader view and reiterates that 'States parties' obligations under the Covenant did not stop at their territorial borders',[249] as does General Comment No. 31,[250] a view that was further supported by the Committee on Economic, Social and Cultural Rights in its 'Statement on the Obligations of State Parties Regarding the

---

[247] ibid 60.
[248] UN Committee against Torture (CAT), General Comment No. 2: Implementation of Article 2 by States Parties, 24 January 2008, CAT/C/GC/2 para 7. (Emphasis added).
[249] UN Committee on Economic, Social and Cultural Rights, General comment No. 24 (2017) on State obligations under the International Covenant on Economic, Social and Cultural Rights in the context of business activities, 10 August 2017, E/C.12/GC/24 para 27.
[250] UN Human Rights Committee (HRC), General comment no. 31, The nature of the general legal obligation imposed on States Parties to the Covenant, 26 May 2004, CCPR/C/21/Rev.1/ Add.13. ('States Parties are required by article 2, paragraph 1, to respect and to ensure the Covenant rights to all persons who may be within their territory and to all persons subject to their jurisdiction. This means that a State party must respect and ensure the rights laid down in the Covenant to anyone within the power or effective control of that State Party, even if not situated within the territory of the State Party.').

Corporate Sector and Economic Social and Cultural Rights'.[251] General Comment 24 reiterates that States 'should also encourage business actors whose conduct they are in a position to influence to ensure that they do not undermine the efforts of the States in which they operate to fully realize covenant rights'.[252] General Comment 16 of the UN Committee on the Rights of the Child concerning the State's obligations relating to the impact of business on children's rights also makes further reference to the role that SOEs can have on the fulfillment of children's rights and in this context calls on all States that have SOEs to 'undertake child rights due diligence and to publicly communicate their reports on the impact on children's rights, including regular reporting'.[253]

Principle 3 of the Maastricht Principles on Extraterritorial Obligations of States in the Area of Economic, Social and Cultural Rights (Maastricht Principles)[254] also explains that all States 'have obligations to respect and fulfill human rights, including civil, cultural, economic, political and social rights, both within their territories and extraterritorially'.[255] This does not mean,

---

[251] Committee on Economic, Social and Cultural Rights, 'Statement on the Obligations of States Parties Regarding the Corporate Sector and Economic, Social and Cultural Rights (UN Doc. E/C.12/2011/1)'.

[252] UN Committee on Economic, Social and Cultural Rights, General comment No. 24 (2017) on State obligations under the International Covenant on Economic, Social and Cultural Rights in the context of business activities, 10 August 2017, E/C.12/GC/24 paras 31, 37.

[253] UN Committee on the Rights of the Child (CRC), General comment No. 16 (2013) on State obligations regarding the impact of the business sector on children's rights, 17 April 2013, CRC/C/GC/16 para 64.

[254] Maastricht Principles on Extraterritorial Obligations of States in the Area of Economic, Social and Cultural Rights 3–5. The Maastricht Principles are not a binding instrument of international law, but many distinguished international law experts have been involved in their making, including former members of regional and international human rights bodies as well as former and current special rapporteurs of the United Nations Human Rights Council. As such, they can be considered as being a legitimate source of international law under Article 38 (1)(d) of the Statute of the International Court of Justice. The Principles 'complement and build on the Limburg Principles on the Implementation of the International Covenant on Economic, Social and Cultural Rights (1986) and on the Maastricht Guidelines on Violations of Economic, Social and Cultural Rights (1997))'.

[255] The basis for protection is found in Principle 25: 'States must adopt and enforce measures to protect economic, social and cultural rights through legal and other means, including diplomatic means, in each of the following circumstances: a) the harm or threat of harm originates or occurs on its territory; b) where the non-State actor has the nationality of the State concerned; c) as regards business enterprises, where the corporation, or its parent or controlling company, has its centre of activity, is registered or domiciled, or has its main place of business or substantial business activities, in the State concerned; d) where there is a reasonable link between the State concerned and the conduct it seeks to regulate, including where relevant aspects of a non-state actor's activities are carried out in that State's territory; e) where any conduct impairing economic, social and cultural rights constitutes a violation of a peremptory

however, that States are responsible 'for ensuring the human rights of every person in the world'.[256] The scope of the extraterritorial obligations of States are defined in Principle 8, which refers to acts and omissions of a State 'within or beyond its territory, that have effects on the enjoyment of human rights outside of that State's territory' (Principle 8(a)) as well as those obligations of cooperation that are of a global character and which stem mainly from the Charter of the United Nations (Principle 8(b)). In addition, Principle 9 states that

> a State has obligations to respect, protect, and fulfill economic, social and cultural rights in any of the following: a) situations over which it exercises authority or effective control, whether or not such control is exercised in accordance with international law; b) situations over which State acts or omissions bring foreseeable effects on the enjoyment of economic, social and cultural rights, whether within or outside its territory; c) situations in which the State, acting separately or jointly whether through its executive, legislative or judicial branches, is in a position to exercise decisive influence or to take measures to realize economic, social and cultural rights extraterritorially in accordance with international law.[257]

Consequently, under Principle 8, a State's extraterritorial obligations can arise on the basis of either the situation referred to in Principle 8(a) or 8(b), or both, which in effect means that States would have to ensure its SOEs do not violate human rights. Furthermore, the home State may also have an obligation to provide assistance to other States to strengthen their observance of human rights based on cooperation.[258]

Of particular importance are the provisions of Principle 9, reproduced above, since they define 'the situations which obligations corresponding to a State's undertaking to comply with human rights may arise although such situations may occur outside its national territory'.[259] The Commentary to the

---

norm of international law. Where such a violation also constitutes a crime under international law, States must exercise universal jurisdiction over those bearing responsibility or lawfully transfer them to an appropriate jurisdiction.' Thus, the active personality principle can be found in the situations contained in a), b) and c).

[256] De Schutter and others (n 245) 1090.

[257] Principle 9(c) imposes obligations of cooperation similar to those found in Principle 8(b).

[258] De Schutter and others (n 245) 1104. ('International cooperation must be understood broadly to include the development of international rules to establish an enabling environment for the realization of human rights and the provision of financial or technical assistance. It also includes an obligation to refrain from nullifying or impairing human rights in other countries and to ensure that non-State actors whose conduct the state is in a position to influence are prohibited from impairing the enjoyment of such rights.').

[259] ibid 1105.

Maastricht Principles makes it clear that human rights obligations are imposed on States in 'any situation over which they exercise effective control'. However, this provision also appears to have narrower application than the situations covered by Principle 9(b), because the factual situations envisaged by Principle 9(a) seem to be linked to the notions of effective control, governmental authority and arguably to the use of force,[260] which for the purposes of attribution would likely fall under Article 4 of the ILC Articles. Such situations are probably best represented by the facts of *Loizidou v Turkey*[261] and other cases discussed at the beginning of this section. This view appears supported by the Commentary to the Principles, which state that 'Principle 9(a) relates to situations where the concerned State has effective control over territory and persons or otherwise exercises State authority'.[262]

5.3.3.3 Nexus Based on Knowledge

Principle 9(b) of the Maastricht Principles is by far the widest provision. In light of the jurisprudence discussed in the context of a State's broader due diligence obligations under international law, it is not far-fetched to assume that a State either *is* or *should be aware* that the activities of its SOEs could impact and 'bring foreseeable effects' on the human rights of those with whom it enters into contact. A broad interpretation of Principle 9 could even allow for an argument that a State has an obligation to protect against the human rights violations of *all* corporate actors, regardless whether they are public or privately owned, by virtue of the link between the State and the corporate entity provided by the act of incorporation, which places a corporate actor within the jurisdiction of the State is not diminished in the case of SOEs. In fact, the opposite is true. Since, for the majority of SOEs whose activities have been internationalised, the State not only sets out the corporate strategy, but also often acts as the 'mind and will' of the SOEs in question, it may be difficult to envisage a situation where a State could posit that it was not aware of the actions and activities of its own SOEs. The same argument could be applicable in the case of SWFs and export credit agencies.[263] Given that, in most, if not all, cases the State sets the investment strategy of the fund in question (often through its Central Bank), it would be implausible to argue

---

[260] ibid 1107–1108.
[261] *Loizidou v Turkey* (n 232) paras 11–25. It should be recalled that in this case Turkish soldiers denied Ms Loizidou access to her house and land.
[262] De Schutter and others (n 245) 1106–1107.
[263] Augenstein and Kinley (n 243) 293.

that the State did not know which companies its SWFs invested in, so States must ensure that they do not indirectly violate human rights, for example by providing funding to projects that could do so.

This line of reasoning is supported by the Commentary to the Maastricht Principles:

> Principle 9(b) acknowledges that the obligations of a state under international human rights law may effectively be triggered when its responsible authorities *know or should have known* the conduct of the state will bring about substantial human rights effects in another territory. Because this element of *foreseeability* must be present, a state will not necessarily be held liable for all the consequences that result from its conduct where the proximity between that conduct and the consequences is remote.[264]

Foreseeability is covered by Principle 13[265] and – to a certain extent – by Principle 14 of the Maastricht Principles. The Commentary notes that under Principle 13 a State may be internationally responsible where human rights violations have occurred out of conduct that may be foreseeable:

> By introducing the condition of foreseeability, Principle 13 sets out a standard of liability that is distinct from strict liability, and constitutes a strong incentive for states *to assess the impact of their choices* on the enjoyment of economic, social and cultural rights abroad, because their international responsibility will be assessed on the basis of what their authorities knew or should have known. Foreseeability serves an important limiting function by ensuring that a state shall not be surprised with claims of responsibility for unforeseeable risks that are only remotely connected to its conduct.[266]

Foreseeability was also addressed in Article 23 to the ILC Articles which further clarifies that 'to have been "unforeseen" the event must have been neither foreseen nor of an easily foreseeable kind'.[267] To have an event that is of an 'easily foreseeable kind' would imply that some requirement for 'assessing whether at the time of conduct steps were taken to obtain the scientific

---

[264] De Schutter and others (n 245) 1109. (Emphasis added).

[265] Under Principle 13: 'States must desist from acts and omissions that create a real risk of nullifying or impairing the enjoyment of economic, social and cultural rights extraterritorially. The responsibility of States is engaged where such nullification or impairment is a foreseeable result of their conduct. Uncertainty about potential impacts does not constitute justification for such conduct.'

[266] De Schutter and others (n 245) 1113. (Emphasis added).

[267] International Law Commission, *Draft Articles on Responsibility of States for Internationally Wrongful Acts, with Commentaries* (n 33) 77.

knowledge necessary to undertake the determination of risk'.[268] Consequently, the focus on foreseeability shows that this concept has two dimensions.[269] According to Principle 13, a State would be responsible not only if it *knew* about the conduct in question, but also whether *it should have known*, but failed to do so, by not acting with due diligence.[270] Furthermore, Principle 11 states that 'State responsibility is engaged as a result of conduct attributable to a State, acting separately or jointly with other States or entities, that constitutes a breach of its international human rights obligations whether within its territory or extraterritorially', thus providing the necessary link between the Maastricht Principles and the rules of State responsibility. The Commentary notes,[271] that Principle 11[272] expresses the content of ILC Article 2, while Principle 12[273] mirrors the text of ILC Articles 4, 5 and 8. In particular, Principle 12(a) seeks to 'take account of increasingly common phenomenon of parastatal entities, which exercise elements of governmental authority in place of State organs, as well as situations where former State corporations have been privatised but retain certain public or regulatory functions'.[274]

The general conclusion that can be drawn in this section is that States can, but do not have, as a matter of international law, an obligation to regulate the extraterritorial activities of businesses that are incorporated in their territories, unless those business entities are State owned. The extraterritorial obligation of States to regulate the activities of their SOEs arises by virtue of the nexus between the State and the SOE in question. The nexus can be based on control, such as control over the day-to-day activities of the business in

---

[268] De Schutter and others (n 245) 1113–1114.

[269] ibid 1113.

[270] Maastricht Principles on Extraterritorial Obligations of States in the Area of Economic, Social and Cultural Rights. ('States must conduct prior assessment, with public participation, of the risks and potential extraterritorial impacts of their laws, policies and practices on the enjoyment of economic, social and cultural rights. The results of the assessment must be made public. The assessment must also be undertaken to inform the measures that States must adopt to prevent violations or ensure their cessation as well as to ensure effective remedies.').

[271] De Schutter and others (n 245) 1110–1111.

[272] Principle 11: 'There is an internationally wrongful act of a State when conduct consisting of an action or omission: (a) is attributable to the State under international law; and (b) constitutes a breach of an international obligation of the State.'

[273] Principle 12 states that State responsibility extends to '(a) acts and omissions of non-State actors acting on the instructions or under the direction or control of the State; and (b) acts and omissions of persons or entities which are not organs of the State, such as Corporations and other business enterprises, where they are empowered by the State to exercise elements of governmental authority, provided those persons or entities are acting in that capacity in the particular instance'.

[274] De Schutter and others (n 245) 1111. This paragraph is in fact quoted from the Commentaries to the ILC Articles on State Responsibility.

question, or on an element of knowledge, whereby there is a reasonable expectation that States either already know or should know about the activities of their SOEs.

5.4 INTERIM CONCLUSION

This chapter has examined the topic of State responsibility and SOEs by analysing the customary rules for attribution of conduct as found in Articles 4, 5 and 8 of the ILC Articles. Overall, what can be observed is that the high thresholds for attribution found in all the rules examined could make a large proportion of the conduct unattributable to the State. For instance, under Article 4, the high degree of dependence required to determine that an SOE is a State organ would make attribution under Article 4 an extremely unlikely situation, which could occur in only a handful of situations. The wide margin of discretion given to dispute settlement bodies in interpreting the concept of 'governmental authority' and the requirement for a domestic law to expressly empower an entity to exercise governmental authority would lead to a similar conclusion under Article 5. Attribution under Article 8, which could, at least initially, be read broadly, does not change the status quo much either. While the overall control test, significantly eases attribution, which could ultimately lead to a wide range of acts and omissions being attributable to the State, the rejection of this test by the ICJ and the express support for the effective control test makes attribution under Article 8 an onerous exercise. The further confirmation by the ICJ that the rules for attributing conduct do not vary with the nature of the wrongful act in question in the absence of a clearly expressed *lex specialis* further entrenches the application of the effective control test across different areas of international law. The jurisprudence of the ECHR further demonstrates that the ILC articles are fully applicable in the context of human rights as the relevant secondary rules on State responsibility. In particular, by reading the rich jurisprudence of the ECHR concerning SOEs, which although at times appears contextual and is often unreasoned, it cannot be concluded with any certainty that any special rules of attribution have been developed by the Court. As discussed in Section 5.1, a lack of clarity in the reasoning or a failure to extensively engage with the ILC Articles cannot be taken to mean that the general rules of attribution are no longer applicable. It can thus be concluded that human rights law has had a 'minimal impact on the general international law of state responsibility in regard to attribution to the state'.[275] Of course, this is not to say that new special rules of

---

[275] McCorquodale, 'The Impact of International Human Rights Law on State Responsibility' (n 127).

attribution cannot develop. They most certainly can if such possibility is clearly expressed, as it is envisaged in Article 55 of the ILC Articles. However, even in such cases, the adjudicative body in question should commence its inquiry by looking at the general rules of attribution as codified by the ILC Articles and any following departures, reflecting a given *lex specialis* be clearly reasoned and justified. Such an approach would ultimately promote consistency between existing or emerging specialised fields of international law and general international law. This does not mean, however, that the ILC Articles, as they currently stand, would always remain the 'last word'[276] on this subject.[277] Just as the nature of the State itself has been constantly evolving, so has the law of international responsibility, which is now equally applicable, for instance, to other subjects of international law,[278] so further development in this area is entirely possible.[279]

Section 5.2 has examined the concept of due diligence, which becomes relevant when certain acts and omissions cannot be attributed to the State, because, for example, they are not perpetrated by State organs, by actors that are exercising governmental authority or those that are not under the effective control of the State. It has been concluded that, in such circumstances, a State can nevertheless be held responsible for failure to act diligently, to take all the necessary measures available to prevent or punish the occurrence of a specific act. Specific State practice applicable in the context of SOEs demonstrates that it is States that ultimately determine how well SOEs are regulated. Consequently, even if, as a result of corporate structuring, it may not be possible to attribute the acts or omissions of an SOE back to the State, States may still have due diligence obligations, as a matter of international law – obligations which are applicable extraterritorially – to ensure that the entities that they own or control do not violate human rights. Overall, this demonstrates how international law can provide adequate answers to a lot of the challenges associated with States and their SOEs.

---

[276] Antônio AC Trindade, *International Law for Humankind: Towards a New Jus Gentium* (Brill Nijhoff 2010) 467–468. (The ILC 'are far from being the last word on the subject as they reckon on by themselves that in some respects the law on the subject is still in a stage of development, not ripe yet for codification'.).

[277] Philip Allott, 'State Responsibility and the Unmaking of International Law' (1988) 29 Harv. Int'l. L.J. 1, 2.

[278] Pellet (n 4) 6.

[279] General Assembly Resolution A/Res/74/180, 18 December 2019 para 9. (The UN General Assembly decided 'to include in the provisional agenda of its seventy-seventh session the item entitled "Responsibility of States for internationally wrongful acts" and to further examine, within the framework of a working group of the Sixth Committee and with a view to taking a decision, the question of a convention on responsibility of States for internationally wrongful acts or other appropriate action on the basis of the articles'.).

6

Concluding Remarks

SOEs have had a significant and long-lasting influence upon the development of international law and international law currently plays a key role in the shaping of SOEs as participants on the international plane. The current period of revival in State corporate ownership has brought with it a new set of challenges which go beyond some of the classic concerns associated with SOEs. The firmly entrenched duty of States to 'respect, protect and fulfill' human rights and the special link that exists between States and their SOEs supports a conclusion that State corporate ownership could have an important regulatory function in a human rights context. From this vantage point, international law has a key role to play in the shaping of SOEs as actors on the international plane and various types of instruments have been created to address the human rights challenges associated with State corporate ownership. In this complex and dynamic regulatory framework, the interplay between 'hard' and 'soft' instruments and between the various levels of regulation has a continuous influence on State practice, which could ultimately lead to the development of customary norms in this area.

International law can also offer new perspectives on SOEs as actors in the international arena, with the concept of legal personality being particularly relevant in this context. Driven largely by practical considerations, the evolution of the various conceptualisations of legal personality shows how international law has had to adapt and to find ways to address the emergence of participants that did not initially form part of the system. While belonging to the broader category of corporations, as participants in international law, SOEs have certain distinguishing characteristics that make them different from privately owned entities. The emergence of SOEs as participants in the international legal system shows the increased heterogeneity and complexity of the notion of participation on the international plane and that, in international law, one may encounter certain corporate entities such as SOEs which may have obligations to respect human rights, rather than a mere responsibility to do so.

Looked at from a bilateral perspective, the relationship between SOEs and international law not only reveals certain basic structures and core processes that underpin international law, but it also keeps us alerted to the reality that those structures and processes are not static, but subject to continuous change. There can be no better illustration of this continuous process of change than the fundamental shift from absolute to restrictive State immunity, a shift that was caused by the first wave of internationalisation of SOEs and the increase in their trading activities in the 1950s and 1960s. While the shift from absolute to restrictive immunity altered the very fabric of international law through a redefinition of the concept and content of sovereignty – immunity is preserved for acts *jure imperii* but not for acts *jure gestionis* – it also brought to light the inherent flexibility of international law. Largely informed by the developing judicial practice in domestic courts, the development of frameworks and concepts to assimilate various entities into the State, the various techniques used to differentiate between acts *jure gestionis* and acts *jure imperii*, the emergence of exceptions to immunity and the ability to pierce the corporate veil are features that also became part of international law.

While in some areas, international law has been receptive to changes in order to reflect the realities of economic life, the development of other interconnected areas is lagging behind. The expansion of human rights represents a development that poses new challenges to traditional doctrines of international law, such as State immunity, particularly in cases that have extraterritorial elements, as evidenced by the fact that currently there is no exception to State immunity for human rights violations, not even in cases when those violations involve norms *jus cogens*. Similar limitations can be said to exist in the law of State responsibility, particularly in the process of attribution, whereby the high thresholds applicable could make a large proportion of conduct by SOEs unattributable to the State, which could potentially lead to an accountability void. Nevertheless, solutions do exist for all these challenges and limitations. Since the law of State immunity is largely customary in nature, a human rights exception to immunity could develop in a way that would allow for a balance between the protection of the rights of individuals and the preservation of the privileges of sovereigns. The adoption of a lower threshold for the attribution of conduct, as expressed through the concept of 'overall control' is another solution which would allow for more flexibility in a given set of circumstances. The principle of due diligence can also provide adequate answers to a lot of the questions and challenges associated with States and their SOEs.

Inasmuch as the focus of this monograph has been on the human rights challenges associated with SOEs, it has also exposed some of the inner processes and the continuous evolution of international law. Over its course, international law has had to overcome many challenges – war atrocities, slavery, the threat of terrorism and many others[1] – and it will have to deal with many more challenges in the future – such as climate change, environmental degradation, cyberattacks and the aftermath of a worldwide pandemic – its role in dealing with some of the most urgent needs of the international community remains more important than ever.

* * *

---

[1] James Crawford, 'Chance, Order, Change: The Course of International Law, General Course on Public International Law' (Hague Academy of International Law 2014) 506. (International law 'is an expression of a "rage for order" which we may hope will meet the obvious and increasing need for coordination between the two hundred self-governing communities which are neighbours each to each in our one world. It has many weaknesses, faces many difficulties, is changing and needs to change further. But in the race for order, it is part of our common heritage, and a vital one.').

Bibliography

BOOKS

Anghie A, *Imperialism, Sovereignty, and the Making of International Law* (1st pbk. edn, Cambridge University Press 2007)

Alston P (ed), *Non-State Actors and Human Rights* (Oxford University Press 2005)

Aristotle, *Nicomachean Ethics* (Hackett 2014)

Arrowsmith S, Linarelli J and Wallace D, *Regulating Public Procurement – National and International Perspectives* (Kluwer Law International BV 2000)

Badia A, *Piercing the Veil of State Enterprises in International Arbitration* (Kluwer Law International 2014)

Baldwin R, Cave M and Lodge M, *Understanding Regulation: Theory, Strategy, and Practice* (Oxford University Press 2012)

Baslar K, *The Concept of the Common Heritage of Mankind in International Law* (Martinus Nijhoff Publishers 1998)

Bassan F, *The Law of Sovereign Wealth Funds* (Edward Elgar 2011)

Benvenisti E, *The Law of Global Governance* (Brill Nijhoff 2014)

Bernaz N, *Business and Human Rights: History, Law and Policy: Bridging the Accountability Gap* (Routledge 2017)

Bianchi A, *International Law Theories: An Inquiry into Different Ways of Thinking* (Oxford University Press 2016)

Bianchi A, (ed), *Non-State Actors and International Law* (Routledge 2017)

Blackstone W, *Commentaries on the Laws of England, Volume 2: A Facsimile of the First Edition of 1765–1769* (University of Chicago Press 1979)

Bomann-Larsen L and Wiggen O, *Responsibility in World Business: Managing Harmful Side-Effects of Corporate Activity* (United Nations University Press 2004)

Bremmer I, *The End of the Free Market: Who Wins the War between States and Corporations?* (Penguin 2010)

Butt P, *Butterworths Concise Australian Legal Dictionary* (LexisNexis Butterworths 2004)

Clapham A, *Human Rights in the Private Sphere* (Clarendon Press 1996)

Human Rights Obligations of Non-State Actors (Oxford University Press 2006)

Collier P, *The Bottom Billion: Why the Poorest Countries Are Failing and What Can Be Done about It* (Oxford University Press 2007)

Crawford J, *Brownlie's Principles of Public International Law* (Oxford University Press 2012)

 State Responsibility: The General Part (Cambridge University Press 2013)

 Chance, Order, Change: The Course of International Law (Hague Academy of International Law 2014)

 State Responsibility: The General Part (1st pbk. edn, Cambridge University Press 2014)

d'Aspremont J (ed), *Participants in the International Legal System: Multiple Perspectives on Non-State Actors in International Law* (Taylor & Francis 2011)

Dellapenna JW, *Suing Foreign Governments and Their Corporations* (2nd edn, Transnational Publishers 2003)

Deva S, *Regulating Corporate Human Rights Violations: Humanizing Business* (1st pbk. edn, Routledge 2014)

Deva S and Bilchitz D (eds), *Human Rights Obligations of Business: Beyond the Corporate Responsibility to Respect?* (Cambridge University Press 2013)

Donaldson T, *Corporations and Morality* (Prentice-Hall 1982)

Evans MD (ed), *International Law* (4th edn, Oxford University Press 2014)

Fox H and Webb P, *The Law of State Immunity* (3rd edn, Oxford University Press 2013)

Friedmann W, *The Changing Structure of International Law* (Columbia University Press, 1966)

Fuchs DA, *An Institutional Basis for Environmental Stewardship* (Springer Science & Business Media 2003)

Gary I and Karl TL, *Bottom of the Barrel: Africa's Oil Boom and the Poor* (Catholic Relief Services 2003)

Gianturco DE, *Export Credit Agencies: The Unsung Giants of International Trade and Finance* (Greenwood Publishing Group 2001)

Grewe WG, *The Epochs of International Law* (Walter de Gruyter 2013)

Hegel GWF, *Hegel: Elements of the Philosophy of Right* (Cambridge University Press 1991)

Hepburn S, *Australian Principles of Property Law* (Routledge 2013)

Herdegen M, *Principles of International Economic Law* (Oxford University Press 2013)

Higgins R, *Problems and Process: International Law and How We Use It* (Clarendon Press 1994)

 Problems and Process: International Law and How We Use It (Repr, Clarendon Press 2001)

Hobbes T, *Hobbes: Leviathan: Revised Student Edition* (Cambridge University Press 1996)

Hults DR, Thurber MC and Victor DG (eds), *Oil and Governance: State-Owned Enterprises and the World Energy Supply* (Cambridge University Press 2012)

Humphreys M and others, *Escaping the Resource Curse* (Columbia University Press 2007)

Johns F (ed), *International Legal Personality* (Ashgate 2010)

Karl TL, *The Paradox of Plenty: Oil Booms and Petro-States* (University of California Press 1997)

Kelly MJ, *Prosecuting Corporations for Genocide* (Oxford University Press 2016)

Kelsen H, *General Theory of Law and State* (The Lawbook Exchange, Ltd 2007)

Kolb R, *The International Law of State Responsibility: An Introduction* (Edward Elgar 2018)

Kulesza J, *Due Diligence in International Law* (Brill Nijhoff 2016)

Lauterpacht H, *International Law: Being the Collected Papers of Hersch Lauterpacht (Volume 2, Part I International Law in General)* (Elihu Lauterpacht ed, Cambridge University Press 1975)

Locke J, *Two Treatises of Government* (C and J Rivington 1824)

Lustig D, *Veiled Power: International Law and the Private Corporation, 1886–1981* (Oxford University Press 2020)

Marx K, *Economic and Philosophic Manuscripts of 1844* (Prometheus Books 1988) *Capital: A Critique of Political Economy* (Penguin UK 2004)

McBeth A, *International Economic Actors and Human Rights* (Routledge 2009)

McConnell L, *Extracting Accountability from Non-State Actors in International Law: Assessing the Scope for Direct Regulation* (Taylor & Francis 2016)

McCorquodale R, *International Law beyond the State: Essays on Sovereignty, Non-State Actors and Human Rights* (CMP 2011)

Milanovic M, *Extraterritorial Application of Human Rights Treaties: Law, Principles, and Policy* (Oxford University Press 2011)

Morrison R, *The Principles of Project Finance* (Routledge 2016)

Muchlinski PT, *Multinational Enterprises and the Law* (2nd edn, Oxford University Press 2007)

Musacchio A and Lazzarini SG, *Reinventing State Capitalism* (Harvard University Press 2014)

Nijman JE, *The Concept of International Legal Personality: An Inquiry into the History and Theory of International Law* (TMC Asser Press 2004)

Noortmann M, Reinisch A and Ryngaert C, *Non-State Actors in International Law* (Bloomsbury 2015)

Oppenheim L, *International Law: A Treatsie*, vol 1 (2nd edn, Longmans, Green and Co 1912)

Parker D, *The Official History of Privatisation Vol. I: The Formative Years 1970–1987* (1st edn, Routledge 2009)

Parlett K, *The Individual in the International Legal System: Continuity and Change in International Law* (Cambridge University Press 2011)

Pauwelyn J, Wessel RA and Wouters J (eds), *Informal International Lawmaking* (1st edn, Oxford University Press 2012)

Plato, *The Republic of Plato* (Basic Books 1991)

Pogge TW, *World Poverty and Human Rights* (Polity 2008)

Portmann R, *Legal Personality in International Law* (Cambridge University Press 2010)

Prosser T, *The Regulatory Enterprise: Government, Regulation, and Legitimacy* (Oxford University Press 2010)

Proudhon P-J, *What Is Property?: An Inquiry Into the Principle of Right and of Government* (BR Tucker 1876)

Roland G, *Privatization: Successes and Failures* (Columbia University Press 2013)

Sauvant KP, Sachs LE and Jongbloed WPFS (eds), *Sovereign Investment: Concerns and Policy Reactions* (Oxford University Press 2012)

Scelle G, *Précis de droit des gens: principes et systématique* (Librairie du Recueil Sirey (société anonyme) 1932)

Schreuer CH, *State Immunity: Some Recent Developments*, vol 8 (Grotius 1988)
Schultz T, *Transnational Legality: Stateless Law and International Arbitration* (Oxford University Press 2014)
Schutter OD, *International Human Rights Law: Cases, Materials, Commentary* (2nd edn, Cambridge University Press 2014)
Shaw MN, *International Law* (Cambridge University Press 2008)
  International Law (7th edn, Cambridge University Press 2014)
Sinclair HM, *The Principles of International Trade* (The Macmillan Company 1932)
Solomon J, *Corporate Governance and Accountability* (John Wiley & Sons 2007)
Stern PJ, *The Company-State: Corporate Sovereignty and the Early Modern Foundations of the British Empire in India* (Oxford University Press 2012)
Thirlway H, *The Sources of International Law* (Oxford University Press 2014)
Toninelli PM (ed), *The Rise and Fall of State-Owned Enterprise in the Western World* (Cambridge University Press 2000)
Tordo S, *National Oil Companies and Value Creation* (The World Bank 2011)
Trindade AAC, *International Law for Humankind: Towards a New Jus Gentium* (Brill Nijhoff 2010)
Xing L, *The Rise of China and the Capitalist World Order* (Ashgate 2013)
Yang X, *State Immunity in International Law* (Cambridge University Press 2012)
Zerk JA, *Multinationals and Corporate Social Responsibility: Limitations and Opportunities in International Law* (1st pbk. edn, Cambridge University Press 2011)

BOOK CHAPTERS

Aharoni Y, 'The Evolution of State-Owned Multinational Enterprise Theory' in Alvaro Cuervo-Cazurra (ed), *State-Owned Multinationals: Governments in Global Business* (Palgrave Macmillan 2018)
Alston P, 'The "Not-a-Cat" Syndrome: Can the International Human Rights Regime Accommodate Non-State Actors?' in Philip Alston (ed), *Non-State Actors and Human Rights* (Oxford University Press 2005)
Amatori F, 'Beyond State and Market: Italy's Futile Search for a Third Way' in Pier Angelo Toninelli (ed), *The Rise and Fall of State-Owned Enterprise in the Western World* (Cambridge University Press 2000)
Augenstein D and Kinley D, 'When Human Rights "Responsibilities" Become "Duties": The Extra-Territorial Obligations of States That Bind Corporations' in Surya Deva and David Bilchitz (eds), *Human Rights Obligations of Business: Beyond the Corporate Responsibility to Respect* (Cambridge University Press 2013)
Backer LC, 'Human Rights Responsibilities of State-Owned Enterprises' in Surya Deva and David Birchall (eds), *Research Handbook on Human Rights and Business* (Edward Elgar 2020)
Banifatemi Y, 'Jurisdictional Immunity of States – Commercial Transactions' in Nicolas Angelet and Luca Ferro (eds), *The Cambridge Handbook of Immunities and International Law* (Cambridge University Press 2019)
Barnes MM, 'International Investment Law and State-Owned Entities: Recurrent Key Issues and Future Directions' in Lisa E Sachs and others (eds), *2018 Yearbook of International Investment Law and Policy* (Oxford University Press 2019)

Bellini N, 'The Decline of State-Owned Enterprise and the New Foundations of the State–Industry Relationship' in Pier Angelo Toninelli (ed), *The Rise and Fall of State-Owned Enterprise in the Western World* (Cambridge University Press 2000)

Bianchi A, 'Reflexive Butterfly Catching: Insights from a Situated Catcher' in Joost Pauwelyn, Ramses A Wessel and Jan Wouters (eds), *Informal International Lawmaking* (Oxford University Press 2012)

Bilchitz D, 'A Chasm between "Is" and "Ought"? A Critique of the Normative Foundations of the SRSG's Framework and the Guiding Principles' in Surya Deva and David Bilchitz (eds), *Human Rights Obligations of Business: Beyond the Corporate Responsibility to Respect?* (Cambridge University Press 2013)

Bilchitz D and Deva S, 'The Human Rights Obligations of Business: A Critical Framework for the Future' in Surya Deva and David Bilchitz (eds) *Human Rights Obligations of Business: Beyond the Corporate Responsibility to Respect?* (Cambridge University Press 2013)

Boyle A, 'Soft Law in International Law-Making' in Malcolm D Evans (ed), *International Law* (4th edn, Oxford University Press 2014)

Brölmann CM and Nijman JE, 'Legal Personality as a Fundamental Concept for International Law' in Jean D'Aspremont and Sahib Singh (eds), *Concepts for International Law* (Edward Elgar 2019)

Brownsword R, 'What the World Needs Now: Techno-Regulation, Human Rights and Human Dignity' in Roger Brownsword (ed), *Global Governance and the Quest for Justice*, vol IV: Human Rights (Oxford University Press 2004)

Buhmann K, 'Navigating from "Train Wreck" to Being "Welcomed": Negotiation Strategies and Argumentative Patterns in the Development of the UN Framework' in Surya Deva and David Bilchitz (eds), *Human Rights Obligations of Business: Beyond the Corporate Responsibility to Respect* (Cambridge University Press 2013)

Carreras A, Tafunell X and Torres E, 'The Rise and Decline of Spanish State-Owned Firms' in Pier Angelo Toninelli (ed), *The Rise and Fall of State-Owned Enterprise in the Western World* (Cambridge University Press 2000)

Chadeau E, 'The Rise and Decline of State-Owned Industry in Twentieth-Century France' in Pier Angelo Toninelli (ed), *The Rise and Fall of State-Owned Enterprise in the Western World* (Cambridge University Press 2000)

Charlesworth H, 'A Regulatory Perspective on the International Human Rights System' in Peter Drahos (ed), *Regulatory Theory: Foundations and Applications* (ANU Press 2017)

Chetail V, 'The Legal Personality of Multinational Corporations, State Responsibility and Due Diligence: The Way Forward' in Denis Alland and others (eds), *Unity and Diversity of International Law: Essays in Honour of Professor Pierre-Marie Dupuy* (Brill 2014)

Chinkin C, 'Normative Development in the International Legal System' in Dinah Shelton (ed), *Commitment and Compliance: The Role of Non-binding Norms in the International Legal System* (Oxford University Press 2003)

Choudhury P and Khanna T, 'Toward Resource Independence – Why State-Owned Entities Become Multinationals: An Empirical Study of India's Public R&D Laboratories' in Alvaro Cuervo-Cazurra (ed), *State-Owned Multinationals: Governments in Global Business* (Palgrave Macmillan 2018)

Crawford J and Keene A, 'The Structure of State Responsibility under the European Convention on Human Rights' in Anne van Aaken and Iulia Motoc (eds), *The European Convention on Human Rights and General International Law* (Oxford University Press 2018)

Crawford J and Olleson S, 'The Character and Forms of International Responsibility' in Malcolm D Evans (ed), *International Law* (4th edn, Oxford University Press 2014)

Cuervo-Cazurra A, 'State-Owned Multinationals: An Introduction' in Alvaro Cuervo-Cazurra (ed), *State-Owned Multinationals: Governments in Global Business* (Palgrave Macmillan 2018)

Cui L and Jiang F, 'State Ownership Effect on Firms' FDI Ownership Decisions under Institutional Pressure: A Study of Chinese Outward-Investing Firms' in Alvaro Cuervo-Cazurra (ed), *State-Owned Multinationals: Governments in Global Business* (Palgrave Macmillan 2018)

d'Argent P and Lesaffre P, 'Immunities and Jus Cogens Violations' in Nicolas Angelet and Luca Ferro (eds), *The Cambridge Handbook of Immunities and International Law* (Cambridge University Press 2019)

d'Aspremont J, 'Bindingness' in Jean d'Aspremont and Sahib Singh (eds), *Concepts for International Law* (Edward Elgar 2019)

Damrosch LF, 'The Sources of Immunity Law: Between International and Domestic Law' in Tom Ruys and Nicolas Angelet (eds), *The Cambridge Handbook of Immunities and International Law* (Cambridge University Press 2019)

Davids M and Van Zanden JL, 'A Reluctant State and Its Enterprises State-Owned Enterprises in the Netherlands in the "Long" Twentieth Century' in Pier Angelo Toninelli (ed), *The Rise and Fall of State-Owned Enterprise in the Western World* (Cambridge University Press 2000)

Den Hertog J, 'General Theories of Regulation' in Boudewijn Bouckaert and Gerrit de Geest (eds.), *Encyclopedia of Law and Economics, Vol. III, The Regulation of Contracts* (Edward Elgar 2000)

Deva S, 'Treating Human Rights Lightly: A Critique of the Consensus Rhetoric and the Language Employed by the Guiding Principles' in Surya Deva and David Bilchitz (eds), *Human Rights Obligations of Business: Beyond the Corporate Responsibility to Respect* (Cambridge University Press 2013)

'From Business or Human Rights to Business and Human Rights: What Next?' in Surya Deva and David Birchall, *Research Handbook on Human Rights and Business* (Edward Elgar 2020)

Douglas Z, 'Other Specific Regimes of Responsibility: Investment Treaty Arbitration and ICSID' in James Crawford and others (eds), *The Law of International Responsibility* (Oxford University Press 2010)

El Sawah S, 'Jurisdictional Immunity of States and Non-Commercial Torts' in Tom Ruys and Nicolas Angelet (eds), *The Cambridge Handbook of Immunities and International Law* (Cambridge University Press 2019)

Evans M, 'State Responsibility and the European Convention on Human Rights: Role and Realm' in Malgosia Fitzmaurice and Dan Sarooshi (eds), *Issues of State Responsibility before International Judicial Institutions* (Hart 2004)

Fox H, 'The Restrictive Rule of State Immunity: The 1970s Enactment and Its Contemporary Status' in Tom Ruys and Nicolas Angelet (eds), *The Cambridge*

Handbook of Immunities and International Law (Cambridge University Press 2019)

Galambos L, 'State-Owned Enterprises in a Hostile Environment: The U.S. Experience' in Pier Angelo Toninelli (ed), *The Rise and Fall of State-Owned Enterprise in the Western World* (Cambridge University Press 2000)

Galambos L and Baumol W, 'Conclusion' in Pier Angelo Toninelli (ed), *The Rise and Fall of State-Owned Enterprise in the Western World* (Cambridge University Press 2000)

Goldmann M, 'Relative Normativity' in Jean d'Aspremont and Sahib Singh (eds), *Concepts for International Law* (Edward Elgar 2019)

Hua Li M, Cui L and Lu J, 'Varieties in State Capitalism: Outward FDI Strategies of Central and Local State-Owned Enterprises from Emerging Economy Countries' in Alvaro Cuervo-Cazurra (ed), *State-Owned Multinationals: Governments in Global Business* (Palgrave Macmillan 2018)

Ietto-Gillies G, 'The Role of Transnational Corporations in the Globalisation Process' in Jonathan Michie (ed), *The Handbook of Globalisation* (2nd edn, Edward Elgar 2011)

Page J, 'Towards an Understanding of Public Property' in Nicholas Hopkins (ed), *Modern Studies in Property Law* (Bloomsbury 2013)

Johns F, 'Theorizing the Corporation in International Law' in Anne Orford and Florian Hoffmann (eds), *The Oxford Handbook of the Theory of International Law* (Oxford University Press 2016)

Kammerhofer J, 'Hans Kelsen in Today's International Legal Scholarship' in Jörg Kammerhofer and Jean D'Aspremont (eds), *International Legal Positivism in a Post-Modern World* (Cambridge University Press 2014)

Kammerhofer J and D'Aspremont J, 'Introduction: The Future of International Legal Positivism' in Jörg Kammerhofer and Jean D'Aspremont (eds), *International Legal Positivism in a Post-Modern World* (Cambridge University Press 2014)

Krajewski M and Singer C, 'Should Judges Be Front-Runners? The ICJ, State Immunity and the Protection of Fundamental Human Rights' in A Bogdandy von and R Wolfrum (eds), *Max Planck Yearbook of United Nations Law*, vol 16 (Brill 2012)

Lauterpacht H, 'The Subjects of International Law' in Elihu Lauterpacht (ed), *International Law: Volume 1, The General Works: Being the Collected Papers of Hersch Lauterpacht* (Cambridge University Press 1970)

Marks S and Azizi F, 'Responsibility for Violations of Human Rights Obligations: International Mechanisms' in James Crawford and others (eds), *The Law of International Responsibility* (Oxford University Press 2010)

Martin-Ortega O and O'Brien CM, *Public Procurement and Human Rights* (Edward Elgar 2019)

Mazzolini R, 'European Government-Controlled Enterprises: Explaining International Strategic and Policy Decisions' in Alvaro Cuervo-Cazurra (ed), *State-Owned Multinationals: Governments in Global Business* (Palgrave Macmillan 2018)

McCorquodale R, 'The Impact of International Human Rights Law on State Responsibility' in Menno T Kamminga and M Scheinin (eds), *The Impact of Human Rights on General International Law* (Oxford University Press 2009)

'The Individual and the International Legal System' in Malcolm D Evans (ed), *International Law* (4th edn, Oxford University Press 2014)

'Sources and the Subjects of International Law: A Plurality of Law-Making Participants' in Samantha Besson and Jean d'Aspremont (eds), *The Oxford Handbook on the Sources of International Law* (1st edn, Oxford University Press 2017)

Meyer KE, Ding Y and Zhang H, 'Overcoming Distrust: How State-Owned Enterprises Adapt Their Foreign Entries to Institutional Pressures Abroad' in Alvaro Cuervo-Cazurra (ed), *State-Owned Multinationals: Governments in Global Business* (Palgrave Macmillan 2018)

Michalowski S, 'Due Diligence and Complicity: A Relationship in Need of Clarification' in Surya Deva and David Bilchitz (eds), *Human Rights Obligations of Business: Beyond the Corporate Responsibility to Respect?* (Cambridge University Press 2013)

Millward R and Toninelli PA, 'State Enterprise in Britain in the Twentieth Century' in Pier Angelo Toninelli (ed), *The Rise and Fall of State-Owned Enterprise in the Western World* (Cambridge University Press 2000)

Motoc I and Vasel JJ, 'The ECHR and Responsibility of the State: Moving Towards Judicial Integration' in Anne van Aaken and Iulia Motoc (eds), *The European Convention on Human Rights and General International Law* (Oxford University Press 2018)

Mulligan M, 'East India Company: Non-State Actor as Treaty-Maker' in James Summers and Alex Gough (eds), *Non-State Actors and International Obligations* (Brill Nijhoff 2018)

Musacchio A and Lazzarini SG, 'State-Owned Enterprises as Multinationals: Theory and Research Directions' in Alvaro Cuervo-Cazurra (ed), *State-Owned Multinationals: Governments in Global Business* (Palgrave Macmillan 2018)

Nolan J, 'The Corporate Responsibility to Respect Human Rights: Soft Law or Not Law?' in Surya Deva and David Bilchitz (eds), *Human Rights Obligations of Business: Beyond the Corporate Responsibility to Respect?* (Cambridge University Press 2013)

O'Brien CM and Martin-Ortega O, 'Human Rights and Public Procurement of Goods and Services' in Surya Deva and David Birchall (eds), *Research Handbook on Human Rights and Business* (Edward Elgar 2020)

Orakhelashvili A, 'Jurisdictional Immunities of States and General International Law: Explaining the Jus Gestionis v. Jus Imperii Divide' in Tom Ruys and Nicolas Angelet (eds), *The Cambridge Handbook of Immunities and International Law* (Cambridge University Press 2019)

Pauwelyn J, 'Is It International Law or Not, and Does It Even Matter?' in Joost Pauwelyn, Ramses A Wessel and Jan Wouters (eds), *Informal International Lawmaking* (Oxford University Press 2012)

Pellet A, 'The Definition of Responsibility in International Law' in James Crawford and others (eds), *The Law of International Responsibility* (Oxford University Press 2010)

Russo D, 'The Attribution to States of the Conduct of Public Enterprises in the Fields of Investment and Human Rights Law', *The Italian Yearbook of International Law 2019* (Brill Nijhoff 2020)

Ruys T, Angelet N and Ferro L, 'Introduction: International Immunities in a State of Flux?' in Nicolas Angelet and Luca Ferro (eds), *The Cambridge Handbook of Immunities and International Law* (Cambridge University Press 2019)

Shan W and Wang P, 'Divergent Views on State Immunity in the International Community' in Nicolas Angelet and Luca Ferro (eds), *The Cambridge Handbook of Immunities and International Law* (Cambridge University Press 2019)

Shapiro D and Globerman S, 'The International Activities and Impacts of State-Owned Enterprises' in Karl P Sauvant, Lisa E Sachs and Schmit Jongbloed PF Wouter (eds), *Sovereign Investment: Concerns and Policy Reactions* (Oxford University Press 2012)

Shelton D, 'Law, Non-Law and the Problem of "Soft-Law"' in Dinah Shelton (ed), *Commitment and Compliance: The Role of Non-binding Norms in the International Legal System* (Oxford University Press 2003)

Shue H, 'The Interdependence of Duties' in Alston Philip and Tomaševski Katarina (eds), *The Right to Food* (Martinus Nijhoff 1984)

Simma B and Pulkowski D, 'Leges Speciales and Self-Contained Regimes' in James Crawford and others (eds), *The Law of International Responsibility* (Oxford University Press 2010)

Stewart DP, 'Immunity and Terrorism' in Tom Ruys and Nicolas Angelet (eds), *The Cambridge Handbook of Immunities and International Law* (Cambridge University Press 2019)

Stiefel D, 'Fifty Years of State-Owned Industry in Austria, 1946–1996' in Pier Angelo Toninelli (ed), *The Rise and Fall of State-Owned Enterprise in the Western World* (Cambridge University Press 2000)

Stiglitz JE, 'On Liberty, the Right to Know, and Public Discourse: The Role of Transparency in Public Life' in Gibney Matthew J (ed), *Globalizing Rights: The Oxford Amnesty Lectures 1999* (Oxford University Press 2003)

'Making Natural Resources into a Blessing Rather Than a Curse' in S Tsalik and A Schiffrin (eds), *Covering Oil: A Reporter's Guide to Energy and Development* (New York Revenue Watch, Open Society Institute 2005)

Sullivan D, 'The Public/Private Distinction in International Human Rights Law' in Peters Julie and Wolper Andrea (eds), *Women's Rights, Human Rights: International Feminist Perspectives* (Routledge 1995)

Toninelli PA, 'Preface' in Pier Angelo Toninelli (ed), *The Rise and Fall of State-Owned Enterprise in the Western World* (Cambridge University Press 2000)

'The Rise and Fall of Public Enterprise: The Framework' in Pier Angelo Toninelli (ed), *The Rise and Fall of State-Owned Enterprise in the Western World* (Cambridge University Press 2000)

Vernon R, 'The International Aspects of State-Owned Enterprises' in Alvaro Cuervo-Cazurra (ed), *State-Owned Multinationals: Governments in Global Business* (Palgrave Macmillan 2018)

Webb P, 'A Moving Target: The Approach of the Strasbourg Court to Immunity' in Anne van Aaken and Iulia Motoc (eds), *The European Convention on Human Rights and General International Law* (Oxford University Press 2018)

Wegenroth U, 'The Rise and Fall of State-Owned Enterprise in Germany' in Pier Angelo Toninelli (ed), *The Rise and Fall of State-Owned Enterprise in the Western World* (Cambridge University Press 2000)

Wettstein F, 'Making Noise about Silent Complicity: The Moral Inconsistency of the "Protect, Respect and Remedy" Framework' in Surya Deva and David Bilchitz (eds) *Human Rights Obligations of Business beyond the Corporate Responsibility to Respect?* (Cambridge University Press 2013)

JOURNAL ARTICLES

Aidoo R and others, 'Footprints of the Dragon: China's Oil Diplomacy and Its Impacts on Sustainable Development Policy in Ecuador and Ghana' (2017) 8 Revue internationale de politique de développement <https://doi:10.4000/poldev.2408>

Allott P, 'State Responsibility and the Unmaking of International Law' (1988) 29 Harv. Int'l. L.J. 1

Alvarez JE, 'Are Corporations "Subjects" of International Law?' (2011) 9 Santa Clara J. Int'l L. 1

'The Relativity Apocalypse Is Nigh' (2020) 114 AJIL Unbound 77

Arnold DG, 'Transnational Corporations and the Duty to Respect Basic Human Rights' (2010) 20 Bus. Ethics Q. 371

Augustine ZP, 'Cyber Neutrality: A Textual Analysis of Traditional Jus in Bello Neutrality Rules through a Purpose-Based Lens' (2014) 71 AFL Rev. 69

Backer LC, 'Sovereign Investing in Times of Crisis: Global Regulation of Sovereign Wealth Funds, State-Owned Enterprises, and the Chinese Experience' (2010) 19 Transnat'l L. & Contemp. Probs. 3

'Sovereign Investing and Markets Based Transnational Rule of Law Building: The Norwegian Sovereign Wealth Fund in Global Markets' (2013) 29 Am. Univ. Int. Law Rev. 1

'The Human Rights Obligations of State-Owned Enterprises (SOEs): Emerging Conceptual Structures and Principles in National and International Law and Policy' (2017) 50 Vand. J. Transnat'l L. 827

Barelli M, 'The Role of Soft Law in the International Legal System: The Case of the United Nations Declaration on the Rights of Indigenous Peoples' (2009) 58 Int'l & Comp. L.Q. 957

Barnes MM, 'The United Nations Guiding Principles on Business and Human Rights, the State Duty to Protect Human Rights and the State-Business Nexus' (2018) 15 Brazilian J. Int. Law 42.

'State-Owned Entities as Key Actors in the Promotion and Implementation of the Agenda 2030 for Sustainable Development: Examples of Good Practices' (2019) Laws 1

Barnett GM, 'Combating Trade Secret Theft by Foreign State-Owned Entities: An International Law Approach' (2016) 5 J. Int. and Comp. Law 2

Barnidge RP Jr, 'The Due Diligence Principle under International Law' 8 ICLR 81

Baxter RR, 'International Law in "Her Infinite Variety"' (1980) 29 Int'l & Comp. L.Q. 549

Baylis E, 'The International Law Commission's Soft Law Influence' (2019) 13 Fla. Int'l U. L. Rev. 1007

Belsky AC, Merva M and Roht-Arriaza N, 'Implied Waiver under the FSIA: A Proposed Exception to Immunity for Violations of Peremptory Norms of International Law' (1989) 77 Cal. L. Rev. 365

Bianchi A, 'Immunity versus Human Rights: The Pinochet Case' (1999) 10 Eur. J. Int. Law 237

'Human Rights and the Magic of Jus Cogens' (2008) 19 Eur. J. Int. Law 491

'Gazing at the Crystal Ball (Again): State Immunity and Jus Cogens beyond Germany v Italy' (2013) 4 J. Int. Dispute Settl. 457

Blank Y and Rosen-Zvi I, 'The Persistence of the Public/Private Divide in Environmental Regulation' (2014) 15 Theor. Inq. Law 199

Blyschak P, 'State-Owned Enterprises and International Investment Treaties: When Are State-Owned Entities and Their Investments Protected (2011) 6 J. Int'l L. & Int'l Rel. 1

Bonnitcha J and McCorquodale R, 'The Concept of "Due Diligence" in the UN Guiding Principles on Business and Human Rights' (2017) 28 Eur. J. Int. Law 899

'The Concept of "Due Diligence" in the UN Guiding Principles on Business and Human Rights: A Rejoinder to John Gerard Ruggie and John F. Sherman, III' (2017) 28 Eur. J. Int. Law 929

Boon KE, 'Are Control Tests Fit for the Future: The Slippage Problem in Attribution Doctrines' (2014) 15 Melb. J. Int'l L. 330

Borlini L, 'When the Leviathan Goes to the Market: A Critical Evaluation of the Rules Governing State-Owned Enterprises in Trade Agreements' (2020) 33 Leiden J. Int. Law 313

Bruton GD and others, 'State-Owned Enterprises around the World as Hybrid Organizations' (2015) 29 Acad. Manag. Perspect. 92

Buhi J, 'Negocio de China: Building Upon the Santiago Principles to Form an Effective International Approach to Sovereign Wealth Fund Regulation' (2009) 39 Hong Kong L.J. 197

Caplan LM, 'State Immunity, Human Rights, and Jus Cogens: A Critique of the Normative Hierarchy Theory' (2003) 97 Am. J. Int. Law 741

Caron DD, 'The ILC Articles on State Responsibility: The Paradoxical Relationship between Form and Authority' (2002) 96 Am. J. Int. Law 857

Casini L, '"Down the Rabbit-Hole": The Projection of the Public/Private Distinction beyond the State' (2014) 12 Int. J. Const. Law 402

Caudill DS, 'Breaking Out of the Capitalist Paradigm: The Significance of Ideology in Determining the Sovereign Immunity of Soviet and Eastern-Bloc Commercial Entities' (1979) 2 Houst. J. Int. Law 425

Chaisse J, 'State Capitalism on the Ascent: Stress, Shock, and Adaptation of the International Law on Foreign Investment' (2018) 27 Minn. J. Int'l L. 339

Charlesworth H, 'The Public/Private Distinction and the Right to Development in International Law' (1988) 12 Aust. YBIL 190

Chick M, 'Review of The First Privatisation: The Politicians, the City, and the Denationalisation of Steel' (1989) 63 Bus. Hist. Rev. 986

Chinkin C, 'A Critique of the Public/Private Dimension' (1999) 10 Eur. J. Int. Law 387

'The Challenge of Soft Law: Development and Change in International Law' (1989) 38 Int'l & Comp. L.Q. 850

Chirwa DM, 'The Doctrine of State Responsibility as a Potential Means of Holding Private Actors Accountable for Human Rights' (2004) 5 Melb. J. Int'l L. 1

Christenson GA, 'Attributing Acts of Omission to the State' (1991) 12 Mich. J. Int'l L 60

Ciriacy-Wantrup SV and Bishop RC, 'Common Property as a Concept in Natural Resources Policy' (1975) 15 Nat. Resources J. 713

Cleveland SH, 'After Kiobel' (2014) 12 J. Int. Crim. Justice 551

Cragg W, 'Ethics, Enlightened Self-Interest, and the Corporate Responsibility to Respect Human Rights: A Critical Look at the Justificatory Foundations of the UN Framework' (2012) 22 Bus. Ethics Q. 9

Crawford J, 'International Law and Foreign Sovereigns: Distinguishing Immune Transactions' (1984) 54 Br. Yearb. Int. Law 75

'Revising the Draft Articles on State Responsibility' (1999) 10 Eur. J. Int. Law 435

Crow ME, 'Smokescreens and State Responsibility: Using Human Rights Strategies to Promote Global Tobacco Control' (2004) 29 Yale J. Int'l L. 209

Cuervo-Cazzura A, 'Governments as Owners: State-Owned Multinational Companies' (2014) 45 J. Int. Bus. Stud. 919

d'Aspremont J, 'Softness in International Law: A Self-Serving Quest for New Legal Materials' (2008) 19 Eur. J. Int. Law, 1075

De Schutter O, 'Commentary to the Maastricht Principles on Extraterritorial Obligations of States in the Area of Economic, Social and Cultural Rights' (2012) 34 HRQ 1084

'Towards a New Treaty on Business and Human Rights' (2016) 1 BHRJ 41

De Sena P and De Vittor F, 'State Immunity and Human Rights: The Italian Supreme Court Decision on the Ferrini Case' (2005) 16 Eur. J. Int. Law 89

Demsetz H, 'Toward a Theory of Property Rights' (1967) 57 Am. Econ. Rev. 347

Deva S, 'Global Compact: A Critique of the UN's Public-Private Partnership for Promoting Corporate Citizenship' (2006) 34 Syracuse J. Int'l L. & Com. 107

Dickinson LA, 'Government for Hire: Privatizing Foreign Affairs and the Problem of Accountability under International Law' (2005) 47 Wm. & Mary L. Rev. 135

Dixon AD, 'Enhancing the Transparency Dialogue in the Santiago Principles for Sovereign Wealth Funds' (2013) 37 Seattle UL Rev. 581

Du M, 'China's State Capitalism and World Trade Law' (2014) 63 Int. Comp. Law Q. 409

Dufresne R, 'Opacity of Oil: Oil Corporations, Internal Violence, and International Law, The' (2003) 36 NYUJ Int'l. L. & Pol. 331

Dupuy P, 'Reviewing the Difficulties of Codification: On Ago's Classification of Obligations of Means and Obligations of Result in Relation to State Responsibility' (1999) 10 Eur. J. Int. Law 371

Dupuy P-M, 'The International Law of State Responsibility: Revolution or Evolution?' (1989) 11 Mich. J. Int'l L.

'Soft Law and the International Law of the Environment' (1991) 12 Mich. J. Int'l L.

'Prosper Weil's Article: A Stimulating Warning' (2020) 114 AJIL Unbound 72

Epstein RA and Rose AM, 'The Regulation of Sovereign Wealth Funds: The Virtues of Going Slow' (2009) 76 U. Chi. L. Rev. 111

Feit M, 'Responsibility of the State under International Law for the Breach of Contract Committed by a State-Owned Entity' (2010) 28 Berkeley J. Int'l L. 142

'Attribution and the Umbrella Clause: Is There a Way out of the Deadlock' (2012) 21 Minn. J. Int'l L. 21

Finke J, 'Sovereign Immunity: Rule, Comity or Something Else?' (2010) 21 Eur. J. Int. Law 853

Forcese C, '"Militarized Commerce" in Sudan's Oilfields: Lessons for Canadian Foreign Policy' (2001) 8 Can. Foreign Policy J. 37

Fortineaux E, 'Fight against the Extractive Industries Transparency Initiative, The' (2013) 11 Loy. U. Chi. Int'l L. Rev. 65

Friedmann W, 'International Public Corporations' (1943) 6 Mod. L. Rev. 185

'The Legal Status and Organization of the Public Corporation' (1951) 16 Law & Contemp. Probs. 576

'Some Impacts of Social Organisation on International Law' (1956) 50(3) Am. J. Int. Law 475

'Changing Social Arrangements in State-Trading States and Their Effect on International Law' (1959) 24 Law & Contemp. Probs. 350

Federico G and Tena-Junguito A, 'A Tale of Two Globalizations: Gains from Trade and Openness 1800–2010' (2017) 153 Rev. World Econ. 601

Gaeta P, 'The Super-Normativity of International Criminal Law' (2020) 114 AJIL Unbound 82

Galai K, 'Companies of Past and Present: Lessons from the East Indian Company on the Use and Regulation of Private Forces Today' (2016) 4 Legal Issues J. 1

Gallo D, 'The Rise of Sovereign Wealth Funds (SWFs) and the Protection of Public Interest (s): The Need for a Greater External and Internal Action of the European Union' (2016) 27 Eur. Bus. Law Rev. 459

Gallus N, 'State Enterprises as Organs of the State and BIT Claims' (2006) 7 JWIT 761

Garcia Sanchez GJ, 'A Critical Approach to International Investment Law, the Hydrocarbons Industry, and Its Relation to Domestic Institutions' (2016) 57 Harv. Int'l L.J. 475

García-Salmones Rovira M, 'What Is Positivism Today?' (2020) 114 AJIL Unbound 87

Gathii J and Puig S, 'Introduction to the Symposium on Investor Responsibility: The Next Frontier in International Investment Law' (2019) 113 AJIL Unbound 1

Gavison R, 'Feminism and the Public/Private Distinction' (1992) 45 Stan. Law Rev. 1

Gerber P, Kyriakakis J and O'Byrne K, 'General Comment No. 16 on State Obligations Regarding the Impact of the Business Sector on Children's Rights: What Is Its Standing, Meaning and Effect' (2013) 14 Melb. J. Int'l L. 93

Gibney M, Tomasevski K and Vedsted-Hansen J, 'Transnational State Responsibility for Violations of Human Rights' (1999) 12 Harv. Hum. Rts. J. 267

Gillies A and Heuty A, 'Does Transparency Work: The Challenges of Measurement and Effectiveness in Resource-Rich Countries' (2011) 6 Yale J. Int'l Aff. 25

Gilson RJ and Milhaupt CJ, 'Sovereign Wealth Funds and Corporate Governance: A Minimalist Response to the New Mercantilism' (2007) 60 Stan. L. Rev. 1345

Goldmann M, 'A Matter of Perspective: Global Governance and the Distinction between Public and Private Authority (and Not Law)' (2016) 5 GlobCon 48

Guttman D and others, 'Environmental Governance in China: Interactions between the State and "Nonstate Actors"' (2018) 220 J. Environ. Manage. 126

Hackett C and Moffett L, 'Mapping the Public/Private-Law Divide: A Hybrid Approach to Corporate Accountability' (2016) 12 Int. J. Law Context. 312

Hart O, Shleifer A and Vishny RW, 'The Proper Scope of Government: Theory and an Application to Prisons' (1997) 112 Q. J. Econ. 1127

Hazard JN, 'State Trading in History and Theory' (1959) 24 Law & Contemp. Probs. 243

Heller MA, 'The Tragedy of the Anticommons: Property in the Transition from Marx to Markets' (1998) 111 Harv. L. Rev. 621

Henry WM Jr, 'Litigating Global Warming: Substantive Law in Search of a Forum' (2004) 16 Fordham Envtl. L. Rev. 371

Hessbruegge JA, 'The Historical Development of the Doctrines of Attribution and Due Diligence in International Law' (2003) 36 NYUJ Int'l. L. & Pol. 265

Hillgenberg H, 'A Fresh Look at Soft Law' (1999) 10 Eur. J. Int. Law 499

Holcombe K, 'JASTA Straw Man: How the Justice against Sponsors of Terrorism Act Undermines Our Security and Its Stated Purpose' (2017) 25 Am. U.J. Gender Soc. Pol'y & Law 359

Horwitz MJ, 'The History of the Public/Private Distinction' (1982) 130 U. Pa. L. Rev. 1423

Hu S., 'Clash of Identifications: State Enterprises in International Law' 19 UC Davis Bus. L.J. 171

Hyclak TJ and King AE, 'The Privatisation Experience in Eastern Europe' (1994) 17 World Econ. 529

Jachtenfuchs M and Krisch N, 'Subsidiarity in Global Governance' (2016) 79 Law & Contemp. Probs. 1

Jarvis RM, 'The Tate Letter: Some Words Regarding Its Authorship' (2015) 55 Am. J. Legal Hist. 465

Kaeb C and Scheffer D, 'The Paradox of Kiobel in Europe' (2013) 107 Am. J. Int. Law 852

Kelly M, 'Ending Corporate Impunity for Genocide: The Case against China's State-Owned Petroleum Company in Sudan' (2011) 90 Or. L. Rev. 413

Kennedy D, 'The Stages of the Decline of the Public/Private Distinction' (1981) 130 U. Pa. L. Rev. 1349

Klabbers J, 'The Redundancy of Soft Law' (1996) 65 Nord. J. Int. Law 167

Klare KE, 'The Public/Private Distinction in Labor Law' (1982) 130 U. Pa. L. Rev. 1358

KløCker Larsen R and Atler S, 'Applying the First Pillar of the UN Guiding Principles to Development Cooperation: The Performance of Swedish Agencies and State-Owned Enterprises' (2018) 3 BHRJ 131

Knop K, 'Introduction to the Symposium on Prosper Weil, "Towards Relative Normativity in International Law?"' (2020) 114 AJIL Unbound 67

Koskenniemi M, 'Global Governance and Public International Law' (2004) 37 Kritische Justiz 241

Kotter J and Lel U, 'Friends or Foes? Target Selection Decisions of Sovereign Wealth Funds and Their Consequences' (2011) 101 J. Financ. Econ. 360

Krajewski, M 'The State Duty to Protect against Human Rights Violations through Transnational Business Activities' (2018) 23 Deakin L. Rev. 13

Lauterpacht H, 'The Problem of Jurisdictional Immunities of Foreign States' (1951) 28 Brit. YB Int'l L. 220

Le Moli G, 'The Human Rights Committee, Environmental Protection and the Right to Life' (2020) 69 Int. Comp. Law Q. 735

Lee J, 'State Responsibility and Government-Affiliated Entities in International Economic Law: The Danger of Blurring the Chinese Wall between "State Organ" and "Non-State Organ" as Designed in the ILC Draft Articles' (2015) 49 J. World Trade 117

Lerrick A, 'Venezuela's Debt: Untying the PDVSA Knot' (2018) 13 Cap. Mark. Law J. 131

Li T and Belal A, 'Authoritarian State, Global Expansion and Corporate Social Responsibility Reporting: The Narrative of a Chinese State-Owned Enterprise' (2018) 42 Account. Forum 199

Lin L-W and Milhaupt CJ, 'We Are the (National) Champions: Understanding the Mechanisms of State Capitalism in China' (2013) 65 Stan. L. Rev. 697

Loncle J-M and Morel J-B, 'Emanations of States and ICSID Arbitration' (2008) Int'l Bus. L.J. 29

Macchi C, 'Right to Water and the Threat of Business: Corporate Accountability and the State's Duty to Protect' (2017) 35 Nord. J. Hum. Rights 186

Malekos Smith JZ, 'No State Is an Island in Cyberspace' (2016) 5 J.L. & Cyber Warfare 4

Marquis C and Qian C, 'Corporate Social Responsibility Reporting in China: Symbol or Substance?' (2014) 25 Organ. Sci. 127

Marquis C, Yin J and Yang D, 'State-Mediated Globalization Processes and the Adoption of Corporate Social Responsibility Reporting in China' (2017) 13 Manag. Organ. Rev. 167

Martin-Ortega O, 'Public Procurement as a Tool for the Protection and Promotion of Human Rights: A Study of Collaboration, Due Diligence and Leverage in the Electronics Industry' (2018) 3 BHRJ 75

Martin-Ortega O and O'Brien CM, 'Advancing Respect for Labour Rights Globally through Public Procurement' (2017) 5 Politics Gov. 69

Marx A, 'The Public-Private Distinction in Global Governance: How Relevant Is It in the Case of Voluntary Sustainability Standards?' (2017) 3 CJGG 1

Maupin JA, 'Public and Private in International Investment Law: An Integrated Systems Approach' (2013) 54 Va. J. Int'l L. 367

McCorquodale R, 'An Inclusive International Legal System' (2004) 17 Leiden J. Int. Law 477

'Beyond State Sovereignty: The International Legal System and Non-State Participants' (2006) Revista Colombiana de Derecho Internacional 103

'Waving Not Drowning: Kiobel Outside the United States' (2013) 107 Am. J. Int. Law 846

'Human Rights Due Diligence in Law and Practice: Good Practices and Challenges for Business Enterprises' (2017) 2 BHRJ 195

McCorquodale R and Simons P, 'Responsibility Beyond Borders: State Responsibility for Extraterritorial Violations by Corporations of International Human Rights Law' (2007) 70 Mod. L. Rev. 598

McGregor L, 'State Immunity and Human Rights: Is There a Future after Germany v. Italy?' (2013) 11 J. Int. Crim. Justice 125

McIntyre O, 'The Proceduralisation and Growing Maturity of International Water Law: Case concerning Pulp Mills on the River Uruguay (Argentina v Uruguay), International Court of Justice, 20 April 2010' (2010) 22 J. Environ. Law 475

Methven O'Brien C, 'The Home State Duty to Regulate the Human Rights Impacts of TNCs Abroad: A Rebuttal' (2018) 3 BHRJ 47

Milanovic M, 'Special Rules of Attribution of Conduct in International Law' (2020) 96 Int. Law Stud. 295

Milin Z, 'Mapping Recent Developments in Transparency of Extractive Industries' (2016) 1 BHRJ 321

Mizsei K, 'Privatisation in Eastern Europe: A Comparative Study of Poland and Hungary' (1992) 44 Sov. Stud. 283

Mnookin RH, 'Public/Private Dichotomy: Political Disagreement and Academic Repudiation' (1981) 130 U. Pa. L. Rev. 1429

Morris PS, 'Lex Internationalis: Kiobel, Empires, and the Color of Human Rights' (2015) 7 Geo. J.L. & Mod. Critical Race Persp. 71

Norton JJ, 'The Santiago Principles and the International Forum of Sovereign Wealth Funds: Evolving Components of the New Bretton Woods II Post-Global Financial Crisis Architecture and Another Example of Ad Hoc Global Administrative Networking and Related Soft Rulemaking' (2009) 29 Rev. Banking & Fin. L. 465

Nayyar D, 'Globalisation, History and Development: A Tale of Two Centuries' (2006) 30 Camb. J. Econ. 137

Odudu O, 'The Public/Private Distinction in EU Internal Market Law' (2003) 62 ECLR 62

Ofodile UE, 'Trade, Empires, and Subjects-China-Africa Trade: A New Fair-Trade Arrangement, or the Third Scramble for Africa' (2008) 41 Vand. J. Transnat'l L. 505

Olsen FE, 'The Family and the Market: A Study of Ideology and Legal Reform' (1983) Harv. L. Rev. 1497

Orakhelashvili A, 'Case Note on Jurisdictional Immunities of the State' (2012) 106 Am. J. Int. Law 609

Page J, 'Common Property and the Age of Aquarius' (2010) 19 Griffith L. Rev. 172

Payne T, 'Teaching Old Law New Tricks: Applying and Adapting State Responsibility to Cyber Operations' (2016) 20 Lewis & Clark L. Rev. 683

Pellet A, 'The Normative Dilemma: Will and Consent in International Law-Making' (1992) 12 AYBIL 22

Peng MW and others, 'Theories of the (State-Owned) Firm' (2016) 33 Asia Pac. J. Manag. 293

Perera SM, 'State Responsibility: Ascertaining the Liability of States in Foreign Investment Disputes' (2005) 6 JWIT 499

Perruso R, 'Development of the Doctrine of Res Communes in Medieval and Early Modern Europe, The' (2002) 70 Tijdschrift voor Rechtsgeschiedenis 69

Philip G, 'When Oil Prices Were Low: Petroleos de Venezuela (PdVSA) and Economic Policy-Making in Venezuela since 1989' (1999) 18 Bull. Lat. Am. Res. 361

Pisillo-Mazzeschi R, 'The Due Diligence Rule and the Nature of the International Responsibility of States' 35 Ger. Yearb. Int. Law 9

Posner EA and Sykes AO, 'An Economic Analysis of State and Individual Responsibility under International Law' (2007) 9 Am. L. & Econ. Rev. 72

Pugh GW, 'Historical Approach to the Doctrine of Sovereign Immunity' (1953) 13 La. L. Rev. 476

Qiu J, 'Quality of CSR Reporting in China: A Comparative Analysis between State- and Privately-Owned Real Estate Companies' (2017) 50 SIRE 38

Rajavuori M, 'How Should States Own? Heinisch v. Germany and the Emergence of Human Rights-Sensitive State Ownership Function' (2015) 26 Eur. J. Int. Law 727
'State Ownership and the United Nations Business and Human Rights Agenda: Three Instruments, Three Narratives' (2016) 23 Indiana J. Glob. Leg. Stud. 665
'Making International Legal Persons in Investment Treaty Arbitration: State-Owned Enterprises Along the Person/Thing Distinction' (2017) 18 Ger. Law J.
'Governing the Good State Shareholder: The Case of the OECD Guidelines on Corporate Governance of State-Owned Enterprises' (2018) 29 Eur. Bus. Law Rev. 103
Rasche A and others, 'Which Firms Leave Multi-Stakeholder Initiatives? An Analysis of Delistings from the United Nations Global Compact' (2020) Regul. and Gov. < https://doi.org/10.1111/rego.12322>
Ratner SR, 'Corporations and Human Rights: A Theory of Legal Responsibility' (2001) 111 Yale L.J. 443
'Introduction to the Symposium on Soft and Hard Law on Business and Human Rights' (2020) 114 AJIL Unbound 163
Raymond H, 'Sovereign Wealth Funds as Domestic Investors of Last Resort during Crises' (2010) 123 Int. Econ. 121
Romany C, 'Women as Aliens: A Feminist Critique of the Public/Private Distinction in International Human Rights Law' (1993) 6 Harv. Hum. Rts. J. 87
Rose P, 'Sovereigns as Shareholders' (2008) 87 N.C. L. Rev. 83
Ruggie JG and Sherman JF, 'The Concept of "Due Diligence" in the UN Guiding Principles on Business and Human Rights: A Reply to Jonathan Bonnitcha and Robert McCorquodale' (2017) 28 Eur. J. Int. Law 921
Schachter O, 'The Twilight Existence of Nonbinding International Agreements' (1977) 71 Am. J. Int. Law 296
Schicho L, 'Attribution and State Entities: Diverging Approaches in Investment Arbitration' (2011) 12 JWIT 283
Schmitt M and Vihul L, 'Proxy Wars in Cyberspace: The Evolving International Law of Attribution' (2014) 1 Fletcher Sec. Rev. 53
Schönsteiner J, 'Attribution of State Responsibility for Actions or Omissions of State-Owned Enterprises in Human Rights Matters' (2019) 40 U. Pa. J. Int'l L. 42
Seck SL, 'Home State Responsibility and Local Communities: The Case of Global Mining' (2014) 11 Yale Hum. Rts. & Dev. L.J. 10
Shackelford SJ, Russell S and Kuehn A, 'Unpacking the International Law on Cybersecurity Due Diligence: Lessons from the Public and Private Sectors' (2016) 17 Chi. J. Int'l L. 1
Shaffer GC and Pollack MA, 'Hard vs. Soft Law: Alternatives, Complements, and Antagonists in International Governance' (2010) 94 Minn. L. Rev. 706
Shamir H, 'The Public/Private Distinction Now: The Challenges of Privatization and of the Regulatory State' (2014) 15 Theor. Inq. Law 1
Simma B, 'Of Planets and the Universe: Self-Contained Regimes in International Law' (2006) 17 Eur. J. Int. Law 483
Sovacool BK and others, 'Energy Governance, Transnational Rules, and the Resource Curse: Exploring the Effectiveness of the Extractive Industries Transparency Initiative (EITI)' (2016) 83 World Dev. 179

Stebek EN, 'Conceptual Foundations of Property Rights: Rethinking De Facto Rural Open Access to Common-Pool Resources in Ethiopia' (2011) 5 Mizan L. Rev. 1

Stone CD, 'Corporate Vices and Corporate Virtues: Do Public/Private Distinctions Matter?' (1982) 130 U. Pa. L. Rev. 1441

Stoyanova V, 'Fault, Knowledge and Risk within the Framework of Positive Obligations under the European Convention on Human Rights' (2020) Leiden J. Int. Law 1

Takano A, 'Due Diligence Obligations and Transboundary Environmental Harm: Cybersecurity Applications' (2018) 7 Laws 36

Tasioulas J, 'Prosper Weil and the Mask of Classicism' (2020) 114 AJIL Unbound 92

Tejera V, 'The US Law Regime of Sovereign Immunity and the Sovereign Wealth Funds' (2016) 25 U. Miami Bus. L. Rev. 1

Thomas N, 'Regulating Sovereign Wealth Funds through Contract' (2013) 24 Duke J. Comp. & Int'l L. 459

Tsagourias N and Farrell M, 'Cyber Attribution: Technical and Legal Approaches and Challenges' (2020) 31 Eur. J. Int. Law 23

Tsikata DA, 'The International Public Corporation: A Concept More Relevant Than Ever?' (2017) 14 Int. Organ. L. Rev. 120

Van der Vyver JD, 'Ownership in Constitutional and International Law' (1985) Acta Juridica 119

Van Harten G, 'The Public–Private Distinction in the International Arbitration of Individual Claims against the State' (2007) 56 Int. Comp. Law Q. 371

Vázquez CM, 'Direct vs. Indirect Obligations of Corporations under International Law' 43 Colum. J. Transnat'l Law 928

Villapando S, 'Attribution of Conduct to the State: How the Rules of State Responsibility May Be Applied within the WTO Dispute Settlement System' (2002) J. Int. Econ. Law 393

Weil P, 'Towards Relative Normativity in International Law' (1983) 77 Am. J. Int. Law

Werhane PH, 'Corporate Moral Agency and the Responsibility to Respect Human Rights in the UN Guiding Principles: Do Corporations Have Moral Rights?' (2016) 1 BHRJ 5

Willis HE, 'Capitalism, The United States Constitution and the Supreme Court' (1934) XXII Ky. L.J. 343

Wong A, 'Sovereign Wealth Funds and the Problem of Asymmetric Information: The Santiago Principles and International Regulations' (2008) 34 Brook. J. Int'l L. 1081

Xili M, 'Advancing Direct Corporate Accountability in International Human Rights Law: The Role of State-Owned Enterprises' (2019) 14 Front. Law China 43

Xu D, Wang L and Liu J, 'Assessing the Social Performance of State-Owned Forest Farms in China: Integrating Forest Social Values and Corporate Social Responsibility Approaches' (2017) 32 Scand. J. For. Res. 338

Xun A, Hanrui B and Xiaoyang Z, 'A DEA Approach to Evaluate Economical and Social Roles of NOCs' (2011) 5 Energy Procedia 763

Yee S, 'The International Law of Co-Progressiveness as a Response to the Problems Associated with "Relative Normativity"' (2020) 114 AJIL Unbound 97

Yu X, 'State Legalism and the Public/Private Divide in Chinese Legal Development' (2014) 15 Theor. Inq. Law 27

Zhang M, 'From Public to Private: The Newly Enacted Chinese Property Law and the Protection of Property Rights in China' (2008) 5 Berkeley Bus. Law J. 317

Zhu J, 'The 2030 Agenda for Sustainable Development and China's Implementation' (2017) 15 CJPRE 142

REPORTS AND WORKING PAPERS

'Annual Report on the OECD Guidelines for Multinational Enterprises 2016' (OECD 2017)

Augenstein D, 'State Responsibilities to Regulate and Adjudicate Corporate Activities under the European Convention on Human Rights' (2011) Submission to the Special Representative of the United Nations Secretary-General (SRSG) on the Issue of Human Rights and Transnational Corporations and Other Business Enterprises

Bortolotti B and Fotak V, 'The Rise of Sovereign Wealth Funds: Definition, Organisation and Governance' [2014] BAFFI Center Research Paper Series No. 2014-163 26

Capobianco A and Christiansen H, 'Competitive Neutrality and State-Owned Enterprises' (2011) OECD Corporate Governance Working Papers 1

Christiansen H, 'Balancing Commercial and Non-Commercial Priorities of State-Owned Enterprises' (2013) OECD Corporate Governance Working Papers 6

Clapham A and Rubio MG, 'The Obligations of States with Regard to Non-State Actors in the Context of the Right to Health' (2002) Health and Human Rights Working Paper Series

De Schutter O, 'Human Rights Due Diligence: The Role of States'

'Diverse and Value-Creating Ownership' (2014) Meld. St. 27 (2013–2014) Report to the Storting (white paper) Recommendation of the Ministry of Trade, Industry and Fisheries of 20 June 2014, approved in the Council of State the same day. (The Solberg Government) <https://www.regjeringen.no/en/dokumenter/meld.-st.-27-2013-2014/id763968/>

'Draft Report with Recommendations to the Commission on Corporate Due Diligence and Corporate Accountability' (European Parliament, Committee on Legal Affairs 2020) 2020/2129(INL)

EITI International Secretariat, 'Chinese Companies Reporting in EITI Countries: Review of the Engagement of Chinese Firms in Countries Implementing the EITI' (2016)

Expert meeting on the role of states in regulating and adjudicating the activities of corporations with respect to human rights, organized by the Special Representative of the UN Secretary-General on Business and Human Rights and the Danish section of the International, and Commission of Jurists, 'The Role of States in Effectively Regulating and Adjudicating the Activities of Corporations with Respect to Human Rights'

Finnish Ministry of Employment and the Economy (46/2014), 'National Action Plan for the Implementation of the UN Guiding Principles on Business and Human Rights'

'First Report Submitted to the Council by the Preparatory Committee for the Codification' (Preparatory Committee for the Codification Conference (Conference for the Codification of International Law) 1930)

Fox H, 'Resolution on the Immunity from Jurisdiction of the State and of Persons Who Act on Behalf of the State in Case of International Crimes (Napoli Session)' (Institut de Droit International 2009)

French D and Stephens T, 'ILA Study Group on Due Diligence in International Law (First Report)' (International Law Association 2014)

'ILA Study Group on Due Diligence in International Law (Second Report)' (International Law Association 2016)

Government of Finland, 'Government Ownership Steering: Financial Annual Report 2015' (2015) <vnk.fi/government-ownership-steering>

Government of Sweden, Ministry of Enterprise and Innovation, 'The State's Ownership Policy and Guidelines for State-Owned Enterprises 2017' <https://www.government.se/reports/2017/06/the-states-ownership-policy-and-guidelines-for-state-owned-enterprises-2017/>

Heller PRP, Mahdavi P and Schreuder J, 'Reforming National Oil Companies: Nine Recommendations' Natural Resource Governance Institute, Research Paper (July 2014)

Human Rights Council, 'Towards Operationalizing the "Protect, Respect and Remedy" Framework; Report of the Special Representative of the Secretary-General on the Issue of Human Rights and Transnational Corporations and Other Business Enterprises' (2009) A/HRC/11/13

'Report of the Working Group on the Issue of Human Rights and Transnational Corporations and Other Business Enterprises' (2013) A/HRC/23/32/Add.2

'Report of the Working Group on the Issue of Human Rights and Transnational Corporations and Other Business Enterprises' (Human Rights Council, Seventeenth Session, Agenda Item 3 2016) A/HRC/32/45

'Implementing the OECD Guidelines for Multinational Enterprises: The National Contact Points from 2000 to 2015' (OECD 2016)

'Indigenous and Tribal Peoples' Rights over Their Ancestral Lands and Natural Resources: Norms and Jurisprudence of the Inter-American Human Rights System' (Inter-American Commission on Human Rights 2009) OEA/Ser.L/V/II. Doc. 56/09

Institute for Human Rights and Business, 'Protecting Rights by Purchasing Right: The Human Rights Provisions, Opportunities and Limitations under the 2014 EU Public Procurement Directives' (2015)

International Labour Organisation, 'Report III (Part 1B): General Survey concerning the Labour Clauses (Public Contracts) Convention 1949 (No. 84)' (International Labour Office 2008)

International Law Commission, 'Report of the International Law Commission on the Work of Its Twenty-Sixth Session, 6 May–26 July 1974, Official Records of the General Assembly, Twenty-Ninth Session, Supplement No. 10' (1974) A/9610/Rev.1

International Law Commission, 'Yearbook of the International Law Commission: Documents of the Twenty-Sixth Session: Reports of Special Rapporteurs, Other

Documents Submitted by Members of the Commission and Report of the Commission to the General Assembly' (1974) A/CN.4/SER.A/1974/Add.1 (Part 1)

International Law Commission, 'First Report on State Responsibility, by Mr. James Crawford, Special Rapporteur' (1998) DOCUMENT A/CN.4/490 and Add. 1–7*

International Law Commission, *Draft Articles on Responsibility of States for Internationally Wrongful Acts, with Commentaries* (Yearbook of the International Law Commission, Vol II, Part Two 2001)

International Law Commission, 'Draft Conclusions on Identification of Customary International Law, with Commentaries, 2018 (A/73/10)' (2018)

International Monetary Fund, Fiscal Monitor: Policies to Support People during the COVID-19 Pandemic (Washington, April 2020)

Krajewski M and others, 'Human Rights Due Diligence Legislation – Options for the EU' (European Union, Policy Department for External Relations 2020)

Lagoutte S, 'The State Duty to Protect against Business-Related Human Rights Abuses. Unpacking Pillar 1 and 3 of the UN Guiding Principles on Human Rights and Business' (Danish Institute for Human Rights 2014) 2014/1

'Leading by Example: The State, State-Owned Enterprises and Human Rights (Report of the Working Group on the Issue of Human Rights and Transnational Corporations and Other Business Enterprises)' (2016) A/HRC/32/45

'List of Issues and Questions in Relation to the Combined Eighth and Ninth Periodic Reports of Portugal' (Committee on the Elimination of Discrimination against Women 2015) CEDAW/C/PRT/Q/8–9

McCorquodale R, 'Survey of the Provision in the United Kingdom of Access to Remedies for Victims of Human Rights Harms Involving Business Enterprises' (British Institute of International and Comparative Law 2015)

Methven O'Brien C and Martin-Ortega O, 'The Role of the State as Buyer under UN Guiding Principle 6 (Submission to UN Working Group on Business and Human Rights Consultation on "The State as an Economic Actor: The Role of Economic Diplomacy Tools to Promote Business Respect of Human Rights")' [2018] University of Groningen Faculty of Law Research Paper Series No. 14/2018

Morrison J and St. Dennis H, 'State of Play: Human Rights in the Political Economy of States: Avenues for Application' (Institute for Human Rights and Business 2014) <https://www.ihrb.org/pdf/2014-03-18_State-of-Play_HR-Political-Economy-States.pdf>

Musacchio A and Lazzarini SG, 'Leviathan in Business: Varieties of State Capitalism and Their Implications for Economic Performance' [2012] Harvard Business School Working Paper, No. 12–108, June 2012

'OHCHR | State National Action Plans on Business and Human Rights' <https://www.ohchr.org/EN/Issues/Business/Pages/NationalActionPlans.aspx> accessed 10 August 2020

'OHCHR | Working Group Surveys on Implementation of the UN Guiding Principles on Business and Human Rights' <https://www.ohchr.org/EN/Issues/Business/Pages/ImplementationGP.aspx> accessed 18 August 2020

'Opportunities for All: Human Rights in Norway's Foreign Policy and Development Cooperation' (2014) Meld. St. 10 (2014–2015) Report to the Storting (white paper)

'Outcome of the Seventh Session of the Working Group on the Issue of Human Rights and Transnational Corporations and Other Business Enterprises (A/HRC/WG.12/7/1)'

'Remarks by SRSG John Ruggie "Engaging Export Credit Agencies in Respecting
    Human Rights" OECD Export Credit Group's "Common Approaches" Meeting'
'Report of the International Law Commission' (International Law Commission 1999)
    A/54/10
'Report of the Working Group on the Issue of Human Rights and Transnational
    Corporations and Other Business Enterprises (A/HRC/32/45)'
Ruggie JG, 'Promotion and Protection of Human Rights (Interim Report of the Special
    Representative of the Secretary-General on the Issue of Human Rights and
    Transnational Corporations and Other Business Enterprises)' (2006) E/CN.4/
    2006/97
'Corporate Responsibility under International Law and Issues in Extraterritorial
    Regulation: Summary of Legal Workshops (Report of the Special Representative
    of the Secretary-General on the Issue of Human Rights and Transnational
    Corporations and Other Business Enterprises)' (2007) A/HRC/4/35/Add.2
'State Responsibilities to Regulate and Adjudicate Corporate Activities under the
    United Nations Core Human Rights Treaties: An Overview of Treaty Body
    Commentaries (Report of the Special Representative of the Secretary-General
    on the Issue of Human Rights and Transnational Corporations and Other
    Business Enterprises)' (2007) A/HRC/4/35/Add.1
'State Responsibilities to Regulate and Adjudicate Corporate Activities under the
    United Nations' Core Human Rights Treaties (Report of the Special
    Representative of the Secretary-General on the Issue of Human Rights and
    Transnational Corporations and Other Business Enterprises)' (John F Kennedy
    School of Government 2007)
'Protect, Respect and Remedy: A Framework for Business and Human Rights
    (Report of the Special Representative of the Secretary-General on the Issue of
    Human Rights and Transnational Corporations and Other Business Enterprises,
    John Ruggie)' (2008) A/HRC/8/5
'Corporations and Human Rights: A Survey of the Scope and Patterns of Alleged
    Corporate-Related Human Rights Abuse (Report of the Special Representative of
    the Secretary-General on the Issue of Human Rights and Transnational
    Corporations and Other Business Enterprises)' (2008) A/HRC/8/5/Add.2
'Summary of Five Multi-Stakeholder Consultations (Report of the Special
    Representative of the Secretary-General on the Issue of Human Rights and
    Transnational Corporations and Other Business Enterprises)' (2008) A/HRC/8/5/
    Add.1
'State Obligations to Provide Access to Remedy for Human Rights Abuses by Third
    Parties, Including Business: An Overview of International and Regional
    Provisions, Commentary and Decisions (Report of the Special Representative of
    the Secretary-General on the Issue of Human Rights and Transnational
    Corporations and Other Business Enterprises, John Ruggie)' (2009) A/HRC/11/
    13/Add.1
'Business and Human Rights: Further Steps toward the Operationalization of the
    "Protect, Respect and Remedy" Framework (Report of the Special Representative
    of the Secretary-General on the Issue of Human Rights and Transnational
    Corporations and Other Business Enterprises, John Ruggie' (2010) A/HRC/14/27

'Guiding Principles on Business and Human Rights: Implementing the United Nations "Protect, Respect and Remedy" Framework (Report of the Special Representative of the Secretary-General on the Issue of Human Rights and Transnational Corporations and Other Business Enterprises)' (2011) A/HRC/17/31

'Guiding Principles on Business and Human Rights: Implementing the United Nations "Protect, Respect and Remedy" Framework (Report of the Special Representative of the Secretary-General on the Issue of Human Rights and Transnational Corporations and Other Business Enterprises, John Ruggie)' (Human Rights Council, Seventeenth Session, Agenda Item 3 2011) A/HRC/17/31

'Human Rights and Corporate Law: Trends and Observations from a Crossnational Study Conducted by the Special Representative (Report of the Special Representative of the Secretary-General on the Issue of Human Rights and Transnational Corporations and Other Business Enterprises, John Ruggie)' (2011) A/HRC/17/31/Add.2

Sachs JD and Warner AM, 'Natural Resource Abundance and Economic Growth' (National Bureau of Economic Research 1995)

Sartori N, 'The European Commission's Policy towards the Southern Gas Corridor: Between National Interests and Economic Fundamentals', IAI Working Papers 12/01 January 2012

Shahab Y, Ntim CG and Ullah F, 'The Brighter Side of Being Socially Responsible: CSR Ratings and Financial Distress among Chinese State and Non-State Owned Firms' (2018) Applied Economics Letters < https://doi: 10.1080/13504851.2018.1450480>

Sucharitkul S, 'Fifth Report on Jurisdictional Immunities of States and Their Property (UN Doc. A/CN.4/363 and Add.1*, 22 March and 11 April 1983)' (Yearbook of the International Law Commission 1983)

Szamosszegi A and Cole K, 'An Analysis of State-Owned Enterprises and State Capitalism in China' (US-China Economic and Security Review Commission 2011)

'The State's Direct Ownership of Companies: Sustainable Value Creation' The State's Direct Ownership of Companies Meld. St. 8 (2019–2020) Report to the Storting (white paper)

UNCTAD, 'World Investment Report 2007: Transnational Corporations, Extractive Industries and Development' (United Nations 2007)

UNCTAD, 'World Investment Report 2014: Investing in the SDGs: An Action Plan' (United Nations 2014)

UNCTAD, 'World Investment Report 2017: Investment and the Digital Economy' (United Nations 2017)

UNCTAD, 'World Investment Report 2017: Investment and the Digital Economy (Methodological Note)' (2017)

'UNCTAD's Reform Package for the International Investment Regime (2018 Edition)'

World Bank, Corporate Governance of State-Owned Enterprises: A Toolkit (2014)

INTERNATIONAL AND DOMESTIC STANDARDS AND GUIDELINES

China Chamber of Commerce of Metals, Minerals & Chemicals Importers & Exporters, 'CCMCMC Guidelines for Social Responsibility in Outbound Mining Investments' (2014)

EITI International Secretariat, 'The EITI Standard 2016' (EITI 2016)

EITI International Secretariat, 'EITI Standard 2019'

'FIFA's Human Rights Policy' (May 2017 Edition)

G20/OECD Principles of Corporate Governance 2015 (OECD 2015)

'Guidelines to the State-Owned Enterprises Directly under the Central Government' <http://en.sasac.gov.cn/2011/12/06/c_313.htm> accessed 18 August 2020

Guidelines on Corporate Social Responsibility and Sustainability for Central Public Sector Enterprises (India)

OECD, *Accountability and Transparency: A Guide for State Ownership* (OECD 2010)

OECD, *Guidelines for Multinational Enterprises, 2011 Edition* (OECD 2011)

OECD, Due Diligence Guidance for Responsible Supply Chains of Minerals from Conflict-Affected and High-Risk Areas (17 July 2012)

OECD, *Boards of Directors of State-Owned Enterprises: An Overview of National Practices* (OECD 2013)

OECD, *Due Diligence Guidance for Responsible Supply Chains of Minerals from Conflict-Affected and High-Risk Areas* (OECD 2013)

OECD, Competition Assessment Toolkit Volume III: Operational Manual (Version 3, 2015)

OECD, Due Diligence Guidance for Meaningful Stakeholder Engagement in the Extractive Sector (4 December 2015)

OECD, *OECD Guidelines on Corporate Governance of State-Owned Enterprises* (OECD 2015)

OECD, *Policy Framework for Investment, 2015 Edition* (OECD 2015)

OECD, State-Owned Enterprise Governance: A Stocktaking of Government Rationales for State Ownership (2015)

OECD, Common Approaches for Officially Supported Export Credits and Environmental and Social Due Diligence (TAD/ECG(2016)3) 2016

OECD, Competition Assessment Toolkit Volume I: Principles (Version 3, 2016)

OECD, Competition Assessment Toolkit Volume II: Guidance (Version 3, 2016)

Publications WB, *Corporate Governance of State-Owned Enterprises: A Toolkit* (World Bank 2014)

IFC Performance Standards on Environmental and Social Sustainability (2012)

ILO Tripartite Declaration of Principles concerning Multinational Enterprises and Social Policy 2017

Sovereign Wealth Funds Generally Accepted Principles and Practices 'Santiago Principles' 2008

World Bank Group Environmental, Health, and Safety Guidelines (30 April 2007)

UNITED NATIONS RESOLUTIONS, GENERAL COMMENTS, STATEMENTS AND GUIDELINES

Committee on Economic, Social and Cultural Rights, 'Statement on the Obligations of States Parties Regarding the Corporate Sector and Economic, Social and Cultural Rights (UN Doc. E/C.12/2011/1)'

'Consideration of Reports Submitted by States Parties under Article 12, Paragraph 1, of the Optional Protocol to the Convention on the Rights of the Child on the Sale of

Children, Child Prostitution and Child Pornography' (Committee on the Rights of the Child 2012) CRC/C/OPSC/SWE/CO/1

Guiding Principles on Business and Human Rights: Implementing the United Nations 'Protect, Respect and Remedy' Framework 2011

Basic Principles and Guidelines on the Right to a Remedy and Reparation for Victims of Gross Violations of International Human Rights Law and Serious Violations of International Humanitarian Law (A/RES/60/147)

General Assembly, Human Rights Council, Human Rights and Transnational Corporations and other Business Enterprises (A/HRC/RES/17/4)

General Assembly Resolution A/Res/74/180, 18 December 2019

General Recommendation No. 19 (UN Doc. A/47/38, 1992)

Guide to Enactment of the UNCITRAL Model Law on Public Procurement 2014

Human Rights Commission, Human Rights and Transnational Corporations and Other Business Enterprises SRSG mandate 2005 (E/CN4/RES/2005/69)

Human Rights Council, Resolution 17/4 Human Rights and Transnational Corporations and Other Business Enterprises 2011 (A/HRC/RES/17/4)

Towards Global Partnerships: A Principle-Based Approach to Enhanced Cooperation between the United Nations and All Relevant Partners (A/RES/73/254) 2019

UN Committee against Torture (CAT), General Comment No. 2: Implementation of Article 2 by States Parties, 24 January 2008, CAT/C/GC/2

UN Committee on Economic, Social and Cultural Rights (CESCR), General Comment No. 3: The Nature of States Parties' Obligations (Art. 2, Para. 1, of the Covenant), 14 December 1990, E/1991/23

UN Committee on Economic, Social and Cultural Rights (CESCR), General Comment No. 14: The Right to the Highest Attainable Standard of Health (Art. 12 of the Covenant), 11 August 2000, E/C.12/2000/4 2000

UN Committee on Economic, Social and Cultural Rights (CESCR), General comment No. 24 (2017) on State obligations under the International Covenant on Economic, Social and Cultural Rights in the context of business activities, 10 August 2017, E/C.12/GC/24

UN Committee on the Rights of the Child (CRC), General comment No. 16 (2013) on State obligations regarding the impact of the business sector on children's rights, 17 April 2013, CRC/C/GC/16

UN Human Rights Committee (HRC), General comment no. 31, The nature of the general legal obligation imposed on States Parties to the Covenant, 26 May 2004, CCPR/C/21/Rev.1/Add.13

UN Human Rights Committee (HRC), General comment no. 36, Article 6 (Right to Life), 3 September 2019, CCPR/C/GC/35

UN Working Group on Business and Human Rights, 'Guidance on National Action Plans on Business and Human Rights' (United Nations 2016)

DRAFT CONVENTIONS AND CODIFICATION PROJECTS

Articles on Responsibility of States for Internationally Wrongful Acts (November 2001, Supplement No. 10 (U.N. Doc. A/56/83 (2001)

Draft Articles on Jurisdictional Immunities of States and Their Property, with Commentaries (1991) Yearbook of the International Law Commission, 1991, vol. II, part 2. (A/46/10)

Draft Articles on Prevention of Transboundary Harm from Hazardous Activities, with commentaries 2001

Legally Binding Instrument to Regulate, in International Human Rights Law, the Activities of Transnational Corporations and Other Business Enterprises (Zero Draft July 16, 2018)

Maastricht Principles on Extraterritorial Obligations of States in the Area of Economic, Social and Cultural Rights 2013

Second Revised Draft, Legally Binding Instrument to Regulate, in International Human Rights Law, the Activities of Transnational Corporations and Other Business Enterprises (August 6 2020)

UNCITRAL Model Law on Public Procurement (2011)

THESES

Castro JMA, 'Human Rights and the Critiques of the Public-Private Distinction' (Vrije Universiteit Amsterdam, Faculty of Law 2010)

Tejera V, 'The Interaction of the Jurisdictional Immunities of the State and the Sovereign Wealth Funds: The Case of the US FSIA Vis-à-Vis the 2004 UN Convention' (Graduate Institute of International and Development Studies 2017)

WEBSITES

'About Us | International Forum of Sovereign Wealth Funds' <https://www.ifswf.org/about-us> accessed 10 August 2020

'Case Database – OECD Watch Case Database' <https://complaints.oecdwatch.org/cases> accessed 11 August 2020

'Chile's Response to the Survey on the Implementation of the Guiding Principles on Business and Human Rights: The Role of States as Economic Actors' <https://www.ohchr.org/EN/Issues/Business/Pages/2015Survey.aspx>

'Clarifying Kiobel's "Touch and Concern" Test' <https://harvardlawreview.org/2017/05/clarifying-kiobels-touch-and-concern-test/> accessed 12 August 2020

'Colombia's Response to the Survey on the Implementation of the Guiding Principles on Business and Human Rights: The Role of States as Economic Actors' <https://www.ohchr.org/EN/Issues/Business/Pages/2015Survey.aspx>

'Countries' (Extractive Industries Transparency Initiative) <https://eiti.org/countries> accessed 12 August 2020

'Cuba's Response to the Survey on the Implementation of the Guiding Principles on Business and Human Rights: The Role of States as Economic Actors' <https://www.ohchr.org/EN/Issues/Business/Pages/2015Survey.aspx>

'Cyprus' Response to the Survey on the Implementation of the Guiding Principles on Business and Human Rights: The Role of States as Economic Actors' <https://www.ohchr.org/EN/Issues/Business/Pages/2015Survey.aspx>

'Denmark's Response to the Survey on the Implementation of the Guiding Principles on Business and Human Rights: The Role of States as Economic Actors' <https://www.ohchr.org/EN/Issues/Business/Pages/2015Survey.aspx>

'Environmental and Social Policies' (World Bank) <http://www.worldbank.org/en/projects-operations/environmental-and-social-policies> accessed 10 July 2020

Fan G and Hope NC, 'Chapter 16: The Role of State-Owned Enterprises in the Chinese Economy' [2013] China US Focus <www.chinausfocus.com> accessed 12 December 2020

'Foreign Government Investors [GN23] | Foreign Investment Review Board' <https://firb.gov.au/resources/guidance/gn23> accessed 26 July 2020

'France's Response to the Survey on the Implementation of the Guiding Principles on Business and Human Rights: The Role of States as Economic Actors' <https://www.ohchr.org/EN/Issues/Business/Pages/2015Survey.aspx>

'Georgia's Response to the Survey on the Implementation of the Guiding Principles on Business and Human Rights: The Role of States as Economic Actors' <https://www.ohchr.org/EN/Issues/Business/Pages/2015Survey.aspx>

'Ghana's Response to the Survey on the Implementation of the Guiding Principles on Business and Human Rights: The Role of States as Economic Actors' <https://www.ohchr.org/EN/Issues/Business/Pages/2015Survey.aspx>

'History of the EITI' (Extractive Industries Transparency Initiative) <https://eiti.org/history> accessed 12 August 2020

'Homepage | UN Global Compact' <https://www.unglobalcompact.org/> accessed 12 August 2020

'Human Rights and Business Dilemmas Forum – Dilemmas' <https://hrbdf.org/dilemmas/working-soe/> accessed 27 July 2020

'ILO Revises Its Landmark Declaration on Multinational Enterprises' (17 March 2017) <http://www.ilo.org/global/about-the-ilo/newsroom/news/WCMS_547615/lang–en/index.htm> accessed 12 August 2020

IMFBlog, 'State-Owned Enterprises in the Time of COVID-19' (IMF Blog) <https://blogs.imf.org/2020/05/07/state-owned-enterprises-in-the-time-of-covid-19/> accessed 9 December 2020

'Italy's Response to the Survey on the Implementation of the Guiding Principles on Business and Human Rights: The Role of States as Economic Actors' <https://www.ohchr.org/EN/Issues/Business/Pages/2015Survey.aspx>

Kenya's Response to the Survey on the Implementation of the Guiding Principles on Business and Human Rights: The Role of States as Economic Actors' <https://www.ohchr.org/EN/Issues/Business/Pages/2015Survey.aspx>

Ministry of Enterprise and Innovation: Sweden, 'Response to Working Group Survey on Implementation of the Guiding Principles – Business Enterprises Owned or Controlled by the State' (2016) <https://www.ohchr.org/EN/Issues/Business/Pages/2015Survey.aspx>

'MOFCOM and MEP Jointly Issued Guidance on Environmental Protection in Foreign Investment and Cooperation' <http://english.mofcom.gov.cn/article/newsrelease/significantnews/201303/20130300043146.shtml> accessed 18 August 2020

'National Action Plans on Business and Human Rights' (National Action Plans on Business and Human Rights) <https://globalnaps.org/> accessed 10 August 2020

'National Contact Points – Organisation for Economic Co-Operation and Development' <http://mneguidelines.oecd.org/ncps/> accessed 11 August 2020

'National Human Rights Action Plan of China (2016–2020)' <http://english.gov.cn/archive/publications/2016/09/29/content_281475454482622.htm> accessed 18 August 2020

'Netherland's Response to the Survey on the Implementation of the Guiding Principles on Business and Human Rights: The Role of States as Economic Actors' <https://www.ohchr.org/EN/Issues/Business/Pages/2015Survey.aspx>

'Norway's Response to the Survey on the Implementation of the Guiding Principles on Business and Human Rights: The Role of States as Economic Actors' <https://www.ohchr.org/EN/Issues/Business/Pages/2015Survey.aspx>

Norges Bank Investment Management, 'Human Rights Expectations towards Companies' <https://www.nbim.no/contentassets/3258fe10181544cc8e02566c7237fa5f/human-rights-expectations-document2.pdf> 29 December 2020

Norwegian Government, 'Response to Working Group Survey on Implementation of the Guiding Principles – Business Enterprises Owned or Controlled by the State' (2016) <https://www.ohchr.org/EN/Issues/Business/Pages/2015Survey.aspx>

Norwegian Ministry of Foreign Affairs, 'Business and Human Rights National Action Plan for the Implementation of the UN Guiding Principles' <https://www.regjeringen.no/en/dokumenter/business_hr/id2457944/>

'Notice of the CBRC on Issuing the Green Credit Guidelines' <http://www.cbrc.gov.cn/EngdocView.do?docID=3CE646AB629B46B9B533B1D8D9FF8C4A> accessed 18 August 2020

'Observation and Exclusion of Companies' (*Norges Bank Investment Management*) <https://www.nbim.no/en/the-fund/responsible-investment/exclusion-of-companies/> accessed 13 December 2020

Office of the United Nations Commissioner for Human Rights, 'Status of Ratification of the 18 International Human Rights Treaties' <http://indicators.ohchr.org/> accessed 10 December 2020

'Policy Documents | Foreign Investment Review Board' <https://firb.gov.au/guidance-resources/policy-documents> accessed 26 July 2020

'Publish What You Pay: History' <http://www.publishwhatyoupay.org/about/history/> accessed 12 August 2020

'Russia's Response to the Survey on the Implementation of the Guiding Principles on Business and Human Rights: The Role of States as Economic Actors' <https://www.ohchr.org/EN/Issues/Business/Pages/2015Survey.aspx>

'SASAC' <http://en.sasac.gov.cn/index.html> accessed 18 August 2020

'SASAC About SASAC – SASAC Main Functions – SASAC' <http://en.sasac.gov.cn/n1408028/n1408521/index.html> accessed 4 February 2019

'Secretary-General Proposes Global Compact on Human Rights, Labour, Environment, in Address to World Economic Forum in Davos | Meetings Coverage and Press Releases' <https://www.un.org/press/en/1999/19990201.sgsm6881.html> accessed 12 August 2020

'States' Obligations to Respect and Protect Human Rights Abroad Joint Statement on John Ruggie's Draft Guiding Principles (Statement by a Group of International Organisations and Eminent Scholars)' <https://www.fidh.org/en/>

'Status: UNCITRAL Model Law on Public Procurement (2011) | United Nations Commission On International Trade Law' <https://uncitral.un.org/en/texts/procurement/modellaw/public_procurement/status> accessed 16 August 2020

'Sustainability – GIEK' <https://www.giek.no/sustainability/> accessed 31 August 2020

'Sweden's Response to the Survey on the Implementation of the Guiding Principles on Business and Human Rights: The Role of States as Economic Actors' <https://www.ohchr.org/EN/Issues/Business/Pages/2015Survey.aspx>

'Switzerland's Response to the Survey on the Implementation of the Guiding Principles on Business and Human Rights: The Role of States as Economic Actors' <https://www.ohchr.org/EN/Issues/Business/Pages/2015Survey.aspx>

'The COVID-19 Crisis and State Ownership in the Economy: Issues and Policy Considerations' (OECD) <https://www.oecd.org/coronavirus/policy-responses/the-covid-19-crisis-and-state-ownership-in-the-economy-issues-and-policy-considerations-ce417c46/> accessed 10 December 2020

'The EITI Principles' (Extractive Industries Transparency Initiative, 27 January 2017) <https://eiti.org/document/eiti-principles> accessed 12 August 2020

'The Kyrgyz Republic's Response to the Survey on the Implementation of the Guiding Principles on Business and Human Rights: The Role of States as Economic Actors' <https://www.ohchr.org/EN/Issues/Business/Pages/2015Survey.aspx>

'The Ten Principles | UN Global Compact' <https://www.unglobalcompact.org/what-is-gc/mission/principles> accessed 12 August 2020

'Top 91 Largest Sovereign Wealth Fund Rankings by Total Assets – SWFI' <https://www.swfinstitute.org/fund-rankings/sovereign-wealth-fund> accessed 26 July 2020

'UK's Response to the Survey on the Implementation of the Guiding Principles on Business and Human Rights: The Role of States as Economic Actors' <https://www.ohchr.org/EN/Issues/Business/Pages/2015Survey.aspx>

'UN Global Compact Policy on Communicating Progress' <https://www.unglobalcompact.org/participation/report/cop>

'USA's Response to the Survey on the Implementation of the Guiding Principles on Business and Human Rights: The Role of States as Economic Actors' <https://www.ohchr.org/EN/Issues/Business/Pages/2015Survey.aspx>

'What We Do' <http://en.sasac.gov.cn/2018/07/17/c_7.htm> accessed 18 August 2020

'What's the Commitment? | UN Global Compact' <https://www.unglobalcompact.org/participation/join/commitment> accessed 26 August 2020

'Who We Are' (*Extractive Industries Transparency Initiative*) <https://eiti.org/who-we-are> accessed 12 August 2020

Index

·

Printed by Printforce, the Netherlands